WILLIAM SHAKESPE[...] [...]n-Avon in April, 1564, and [...]ed on April 23. The facts of [...], known from surviving documents, are sparse. He was one of eight children born to John Shakespeare, a merchant of some standing in his community. William probably went to the King's New School in Stratford, but he had no university education. In November 1582, at the age of eighteen, he married Anne Hathaway, eight years his senior, who was pregnant with their first child, Susanna. She was born on May 26, 1583. Twins, a boy, Hamnet (who would die at age eleven), and a girl, Judith, were born in 1585. By 1592 Shakespeare had gone to London, working as an actor and already known as a playwright. A rival dramatist, Robert Greene, referred to him as "an upstart crow, beautified with our feathers." Shakespeare became a principal shareholder and playwright of the successful acting troupe the Lord Chamberlain's men (later, under James I, called the King's men). In 1599 the Lord Chamberlain's men built and occupied the Globe Theatre in Southwark near the Thames River. Here many of Shakespeare's plays were performed by the most famous actors of his time, including Richard Burbage, Will Kempe, and Robert Armin. In addition to his 37 plays, Shakespeare had a hand in others, including *Sir Thomas More* and *The Two Noble Kinsmen*, and he wrote poems, including *Venus and Adonis* and *The Rape of Lucrece*. His 154 sonnets were published, probably without his authorization, in 1609. In 1611 or 1612 he gave up his lodgings in London and devoted more and more of his time to retirement in Stratford, though he continued writing such plays as *The Tempest* and *Henry VIII* until about 1613. He died on April 23, 1616, and was buried in Holy Trinity Church, Stratford. No collected edition of his plays was published during his lifetime, but in 1623 two members of his acting company, John Heminges and Henry Condell, published the great collection now called the First Folio.

Bantam Shakespeare
The Complete Works—29 Volumes
Edited by David Bevington
With forewords by Joseph Papp on the plays

The Poems: Venus and Adonis, The Rape of Lucrece, The
Phoenix and Turtle, A Lover's Complaint,
the Sonnets

Antony and Cleopatra	*The Merchant of Venice*
As You Like It	*A Midsummer Night's Dream*
The Comedy of Errors	*Much Ado about Nothing*
Hamlet	*Othello*
Henry IV, Part One	*Richard II*
Henry IV, Part Two	*Richard III*
Henry V	*Romeo and Juliet*
Julius Caesar	*The Taming of the Shrew*
King Lear	*The Tempest*
Macbeth	*Twelfth Night*

Together in one volume:

Henry VI, Parts One, Two, and Three
King John and Henry VIII
Measure for Measure, All's Well that Ends Well, and
Troilus and Cressida
Three Early Comedies: Love's Labor's Lost, The Two
Gentlemen of Verona, The Merry
Wives of Windsor
Three Classical Tragedies: Titus Andronicus, Timon
of Athens, Coriolanus
The Late Romances: Pericles, Cymbeline, The Winter's
Tale, The Tempest

Two collections:

Four Comedies: The Taming of the Shrew, A Midsummer
Night's Dream, The Merchant of Venice,
Twelfth Night
Four Tragedies: Hamlet, Othello, King Lear, Macbeth

SIC·A BANTAM CLASSIC·A BANTAM CLASSIC·A BANTAM CLASSIC·A BANTAM CLASSIC·A BANTAM

William Shakespeare

THREE CLASSICAL TRAGEDIES

Titus Andronicus
Timon of Athens
Coriolanus

Edited by
David Bevington

David Scott Kastan,
James Hammersmith,
and Robert Kean Turner,
Associate Editors

With a Foreword by
Joseph Papp

BANTAM BOOKS
TORONTO / NEW YORK / LONDON / SYDNEY / AUCKLAND

THREE CLASSICAL TRAGEDIES
*A Bantam Book / published by arrangement
with Scott, Foresman and Company*

PRINTING HISTORY
*Scott, Foresman edition published / January 1980
Bantam edition, with newly edited text and substantially revised, edited,
and amplified notes, introductions, and other
materials, published / February 1988
Valuable advice on staging matters has been provided by Richard Hosley.
Collations checked by Eric Rasmussen.
Additional editorial assistance by Claire McEachern.*

*All rights reserved.
Copyright © 1980, 1973, 1961, 1950 by Scott, Foresman and Company.
Volume introduction copyright © 1988 by David Bevington.
Foreword copyright © 1988 by New York Shakespeare Festival.
Cover art copyright © 1988 by Mark English.
This edition copyright © 1988 by Bantam Books.
Revisions and annotations to Shakespeare text and its footnotes and
textual notes, Shakespeare's Sources essays and notes
for the sources, and individual play introductions
copyright © 1988 by David Bevington.
The Playhouse text copyright © 1988 by David Bevington.
Performance histories copyright © 1988 by
David Bevington and David Scott Kastan.
Annotated bibliographies copyright © 1988 by
David Scott Kastan and James Shapiro.
Memorable Lines copyright © 1988 by Bantam Books.
No part of this book may be reproduced or transmitted
in any form or by any means, electronic or mechanical,
including photocopying, recording, or by any information
storage and retrieval system, without permission
in writing from the publisher.
For information address: Bantam Books.*

Library of Congress Cataloging-in-Publication Data

Shakespeare, William, 1564–1616.
   Three classical tragedies.

   (A Bantam classic)
   "Bantam edition, with newly edited text and substantially
revised, edited, and amplified notes, introductions,
and other materials"—T.p. verso.
   Includes bibliographies.
   Contents: Titus Andronicus—Timon of Athens—
Coriolanus.
   I. Bevington, David M. II. Title. III. Title:
3 classical tragedies.
[PR3763.B48 1988b]   822.3'3   87–19541
ISBN 0-553-21284-2 (pbk.)

Published simultaneously in the United States and Canada

*Bantam Books are published by Bantam Books, a division of Bantam
Doubleday Dell Publishing Group, Inc. Its trademark, consisting of the
words "Bantam Books" and the portrayal of a rooster, is Registered in
U.S. Patent and Trademark Office and in other countries. Marca Regis-
trada. Bantam Books, 666 Fifth Avenue, New York, New York 10103.*

PRINTED IN THE UNITED STATES OF AMERICA

O   0 9 8 7 6 5 4 3 2 1

Contents

Foreword

It's hard to imagine, but Shakespeare wrote all of his plays with a quill pen, a goose feather whose hard end had to be sharpened frequently. How many times did he scrape the dull end to a point with his knife, dip it into the inkwell, and bring up, dripping wet, those wonderful words and ideas that are known all over the world?

In the age of word processors, typewriters, and ballpoint pens, we have almost forgotten the meaning of the word "blot." Yet when I went to school, in the 1930s, my classmates and I knew all too well what an inkblot from the metal-tipped pens we used would do to a nice clean page of a test paper, and we groaned whenever a splotch fell across the sheet. Most of us finished the school day with ink-stained fingers; those who were less careful also went home with ink-stained shirts, which were almost impossible to get clean.

When I think about how long it took me to write the simplest composition with a metal-tipped pen and ink, I can only marvel at how many plays Shakespeare scratched out with his goose-feather quill pen, year after year. Imagine him walking down one of the narrow cobblestoned streets of London, or perhaps drinking a pint of beer in his local alehouse. Suddenly his mind catches fire with an idea, or a sentence, or a previously elusive phrase. He is burning with impatience to write it down—but because he doesn't have a ballpoint pen or even a pencil in his pocket, he has to keep the idea in his head until he can get to his quill and parchment.

He rushes back to his lodgings on Silver Street, ignoring the vendors hawking brooms, the coaches clattering by, the piteous wails of beggars and prisoners. Bounding up the stairs, he snatches his quill and starts to write furiously, not even bothering to light a candle against the dusk. "To be, or not to be," he scrawls, "that is the—." But the quill point has gone dull, the letters have fattened out illegibly, and in the middle of writing one of the most famous passages in the history of dramatic literature, Shakespeare has to stop to sharpen his pen.

Taking a deep breath, he lights a candle now that it's dark, sits down, and begins again. By the time the candle has burned out and the noisy apprentices of his French Huguenot landlord have quieted down, Shakespeare has finished Act 3 of *Hamlet* with scarcely a blot.

Early the next morning, he hurries through the fog of a London summer morning to the rooms of his colleague Richard Burbage, the actor for whom the role of Hamlet is being written. He finds Burbage asleep and snoring loudly, sprawled across his straw mattress. Not only had the actor performed in *Henry V* the previous afternoon, but he had then gone out carousing all night with some friends who had come to the performance.

Shakespeare shakes his friend awake, until, bleary-eyed, Burbage sits up in his bed. "Dammit, Will," he grumbles, "can't you let an honest man sleep?" But the playwright, his eyes shining and the words tumbling out of his mouth, says, "Shut up and listen—tell me what you think of *this*!"

He begins to read to the still half-asleep Burbage, pacing around the room as he speaks. ". . . Whether 'tis nobler in the mind to suffer the slings and arrows of outrageous fortune—"

Burbage interrupts, suddenly wide awake, "That's excellent, very good, 'the slings and arrows of outrageous fortune,' yes, I think it will work quite well. . . ." He takes the parchment from Shakespeare and murmurs the lines to himself, slowly at first but with growing excitement.

The sun is just coming up, and the words of one of Shakespeare's most famous soliloquies are being uttered for the first time by the first actor ever to bring Hamlet to life. It must have been an exhilarating moment.

Shakespeare wrote most of his plays to be performed live by the actor Richard Burbage and the rest of the Lord Chamberlain's men (later the King's men). Today, however, our first encounter with the plays is usually in the form of the printed word. And there is no question that reading Shakespeare for the first time isn't easy. His plays aren't comic books or magazines or the dime-store detective novels I read when I was young. A lot of his sentences are complex. Many of his words are no longer used in our everyday

speech. His profound thoughts are often condensed into poetry, which is not as straightforward as prose.

Yet when you hear the words spoken aloud, a lot of the
language may strike you as unexpectedly modern. For
Shakespeare's plays, like any dramatic work, weren't really
meant to be read; they were meant to be spoken, seen, and
performed. It's amazing how lines that are so troublesome
in print can flow so naturally and easily when spoken.

I think it was precisely this music that first fascinated
me. When I was growing up, Shakespeare was a stranger to
me. I had no particular interest in him, for I was from a
different cultural tradition. It never occurred to me that his
plays might be more than just something to "get through"
in school, like science or math or the physical education
requirement we had to fulfill. My passions then were
movies, radio, and vaudeville—certainly not Elizabethan
drama.

I was, however, fascinated by words and language. Because I grew up in a home where Yiddish was spoken, and
English was only a second language, I was acutely sensitive
to the musical sounds of different languages and had an ear
for lilt and cadence and rhythm in the spoken word. And so
I loved reciting poems and speeches even as a very young
child. In first grade I learned lots of short nature verses—
"Who has seen the wind?," one of them began. My first
foray into drama was playing the role of Scrooge in Charles
Dickens's *A Christmas Carol* when I was eight years old. I
liked summoning all the scorn and coldness I possessed
and putting them into the words, "Bah, humbug!"

From there I moved on to longer and more famous poems
and other works by writers of the 1930s. Then, in junior
high school, I made my first acquaintance with Shakespeare through his play *Julius Caesar*. Our teacher, Miss
McKay, assigned the class a passage to memorize from the
opening scene of the play, the one that begins "Wherefore
rejoice? What conquest brings he home?" The passage
seemed so wonderfully theatrical and alive to me, and the
experience of memorizing and reciting it was so much fun,
that I went on to memorize another speech from the play on
my own.

I chose Mark Antony's address to the crowd in Act 3,

scene 2, which struck me then as incredibly high drama. Even today, when I speak the words, I feel the same thrill I did that first time. There is the strong and athletic Antony descending from the raised pulpit where he has been speaking, right into the midst of a crowded Roman square. Holding the torn and bloody cloak of the murdered Julius Caesar in his hand, he begins to speak to the people of Rome:

> If you have tears, prepare to shed them now.
> You all do know this mantle. I remember
> The first time ever Caesar put it on;
> 'Twas on a summer's evening in his tent,
> That day he overcame the Nervii.
> Look, in this place ran Cassius' dagger through.
> See what a rent the envious Casca made.
> Through this the well-belovèd Brutus stabbed,
> And as he plucked his cursèd steel away,
> Mark how the blood of Caesar followed it,
> As rushing out of doors to be resolved
> If Brutus so unkindly knocked or no;
> For Brutus, as you know, was Caesar's angel.
> Judge, O you gods, how dearly Caesar loved him!
> This was the most unkindest cut of all . . .

I'm not sure now that I even knew Shakespeare had written a lot of other plays, or that he was considered "timeless," "universal," or "classic"—but I knew a good speech when I heard one, and I found the splendid rhythms of Antony's rhetoric as exciting as anything I'd ever come across.

Fifty years later, I still feel that way. Hearing good actors speak Shakespeare gracefully and naturally is a wonderful experience, unlike any other I know. There's a satisfying fullness to the spoken word that the printed page just can't convey. This is why seeing the plays of Shakespeare performed live in a theater is the best way to appreciate them. If you can't do that, listening to sound recordings or watching film versions of the plays is the next best thing.

But if you do start with the printed word, use the play as a script. Be an actor yourself and say the lines out loud. Don't worry too much at first about words you don't immediately understand. Look them up in the footnotes or a dictionary, but don't spend too much time on this. It is more profitable (and fun) to get the sense of a passage and sing it out. Speak naturally, almost as if you were talking to a friend, but be sure to enunciate the words properly. You'll be surprised at how much you understand simply by speaking the speech "trippingly on the tongue," as Hamlet advises the Players.

You might start, as I once did, with a speech from *Julius Caesar*, in which the tribune (city official) Marullus scolds the commoners for transferring their loyalties so quickly from the defeated and murdered general Pompey to the newly victorious Julius Caesar:

> Wherefore rejoice? What conquest brings he home?
> What tributaries follow him to Rome
> To grace in captive bonds his chariot wheels?
> You blocks, you stones, you worse than senseless things!
> O you hard hearts, you cruel men of Rome,
> Knew you not Pompey? Many a time and oft
> Have you climbed up to walls and battlements,
> To towers and windows, yea, to chimney tops,
> Your infants in your arms, and there have sat
> The livelong day, with patient expectation,
> To see great Pompey pass the streets of Rome.

With the exception of one or two words like "wherefore" (which means "why," not "where"), "tributaries" (which means "captives"), and "patient expectation" (which means patient waiting), the meaning and emotions of this speech can be easily understood.

From here you can go on to dialogues or other more challenging scenes. Although you may stumble over unaccustomed phrases or unfamiliar words at first, and even fall flat when you're crossing some particularly rocky passages, pick yourself up and stay with it. Remember that it takes time to feel at home with anything new. Soon you'll come to recognize Shakespeare's unique sense of humor and way of saying things as easily as you recognize a friend's laughter.

And then it will just be a matter of choosing which one of Shakespeare's plays you want to tackle next. As a true fan of his, you'll find that you're constantly learning from his plays. It's a journey of discovery that you can continue for the rest of your life. For no matter how many times you read or see a particular play, there will always be something new there that you won't have noticed before.

Why do so many thousands of people get hooked on Shakespeare and develop a habit that lasts a lifetime? What can he really say to us today, in a world filled with inventions and problems he never could have imagined? And how do you get past his special language and difficult sentence structure to understand him?

The best way to answer these questions is to go see a live production. You might not know much about Shakespeare, or much about the theater, but when you watch actors performing one of his plays on the stage, it will soon become clear to you why people get so excited about a playwright who lived hundreds of years ago.

For the story—what's happening in the play—is the most accessible part of Shakespeare. In *A Midsummer Night's Dream*, for example, you can immediately understand the situation: a girl is chasing a guy who's chasing a girl who's chasing another guy. No wonder *A Midsummer Night's Dream* is one of the most popular of Shakespeare's plays: it's about one of the world's most popular pastimes—falling in love.

But the course of true love never did run smooth, as the young suitor Lysander says. Often in Shakespeare's comedies the girl whom the guy loves doesn't love him back, or she loves him but he loves someone else. In *The Two Gentlemen of Verona*, Julia loves Proteus, Proteus loves Sylvia, and Sylvia loves Valentine, who is Proteus's best friend. In the end, of course, true love prevails, but not without lots of complications along the way.

For in all of his plays—comedies, histories, and tragedies—Shakespeare is showing you human nature. His characters act and react in the most extraordinary ways—and sometimes in the most incomprehensible ways. People are always trying to find motivations for what a character does. They ask, "Why does Iago want to destroy Othello?"

The answer, to me, is very simple—because that's the way Iago is. That's just his nature. Shakespeare doesn't explain his characters; he sets them in motion—and away they go. He doesn't worry about whether they're likable or not. He's interested in interesting people, and his most fascinating characters are those who are unpredictable. If you lean back in your chair early on in one of his plays, thinking you've figured out what Iago or Shylock (in *The Merchant of Venice*) is up to, don't be too sure—because that great judge of human nature, Shakespeare, will surprise you every time.

He is just as wily in the way he structures a play. In *Macbeth*, a comic scene is suddenly introduced just after the bloodiest and most treacherous slaughter imaginable, of a guest and king by his host and subject, when in comes a drunk porter who has to go to the bathroom. Shakespeare is tickling your emotions by bringing a stand-up comic on-stage right on the heels of a savage murder.

It has taken me thirty years to understand even some of these things, and so I'm not suggesting that Shakespeare is immediately understandable. I've gotten to know him not through theory but through practice, the practice of the *living* Shakespeare—the playwright of the theater.

Of course the plays are a great achievement of dramatic literature, and they should be studied and analyzed in schools and universities. But you must always remember, when reading all the words *about* the playwright and his plays, that *Shakespeare's* words came first and that in the end there is nothing greater than a single actor on the stage speaking the lines of Shakespeare.

Everything important that I know about Shakespeare comes from the practical business of producing and directing his plays in the theater. The task of classifying, criticizing, and editing Shakespeare's printed works I happily leave to others. For me, his plays really do live on the stage, not on the page. That is what he wrote them for and that is how they are best appreciated.

Although Shakespeare lived and wrote hundreds of years ago, his name rolls off my tongue as if he were my brother. As a producer and director, I feel that there is a professional relationship between us that spans the centuries. As a human being, I feel that Shakespeare has enriched my understanding of life immeasurably. I hope you'll let him do the same for you.

❖

Titus Andronicus is a revenge tragedy, extremely gory and violent. Titus himself, a beleaguered old man, reminds me of King Lear: he is subjected to unspeakable horrors, one after another, until he loses his sanity. But unlike Lear, Titus does get his revenge, and it is as gruesome and grotesque as the initial crime of the rape and mutilation of his daughter, Lavinia. Though the violence and gore in this play are overpowering, there's something audiences find gratifying in the story of one man's revenge against the people who have injured him. It's an old theme, even a primitive one, but we also see it in modern films where Rambo-esque acts of violence are carried out in the name of rightful revenge.

I think one of the most interesting characters in the play is the black man, Aaron the Moor, who is Tamora's lover. Though he's unquestionably diabolical, he's also treated with a great deal of understanding. Shakespeare put a tremendous spirit into him. For example, I love the moment in Act 4, scene 2, when Aaron stands up with his (and Tamora's) newly born son and says, "He dies upon my scimitar's sharp point / That touches this my firstborn son and heir!" There's something paternal and protective about his fierce defense of his baby boy that balances his evildoing elsewhere.

Titus Andronicus is a painful play to experience in the theater, because it's hard to watch violence being piled on violence and to see Titus beset by sorrow, grief, and finally the madness of revenge. But I've actually produced the play twice, once in the church on Manhattan's Lower East Side where I started, and later in Central Park. The production in the church had Roscoe Lee Browne as Aaron the Moor, Colleen Dewhurst as Tamora, Queen of the Goths, and a host of other actors. It was quite an event.

What's difficult about putting this play on the stage is that its pure goriness can become comic. The sight of Lavinia walking around with two stumps for hands and her tongue cut out, and Titus with his stump of a hand, and the baking of the human pies at the end, can make the audience laugh because it all seems so "gross." There isn't really enough psychological underpinning to the play to prevent the laughter, which can make it a challenge to perform.

❖

Timon of Athens is a dark and cynical play, not often performed on the stage today. It has an affinity with *Troilus and Cressida* because it's about corruption and bitterness, and possibly with *King Lear* because it concerns ingratitude. In a way, Timon could be seen as a preliminary sketch of Lear, someone driven by the madness of sorrow back to his most basic earthbound self. He goes from being a man who has everything—wealth, prestige, friends, and flatterers—to a man who digs in the earth and utters stunningly savage curses against humanity: "O blessèd breeding sun, draw from the earth / Rotten humidity; below thy sister's orb / Infect the air!" There's a primitive quality to Timon's retreat to the cave, his digging, and his guttural cursing that works powerfully in the theater.

❖

Coriolanus, like Timon and like Titus, is relentlessly and irrevocably committed to a certain way of life—in his case, the life of a Roman aristocrat trained to be a fighting machine. No matter how high the stakes, he simply can't change who he is; as he himself asks his mother, "Would you have me / False to my nature? Rather say I play / The man I am." He reminds me of the honor-bound Hotspur in the *Henry IV* plays: when compromises become necessary, neither Coriolanus nor Hotspur can make them.

I find the relationships between Coriolanus and the other characters in the play quite interesting. There's no question that he is a mother's boy. It's even suggested (as it was in Shakespeare's source, Plutarch) that Coriolanus has performed his deeds of strength and valor to please his mother, Volumnia. Certainly she influences his relationship with his wife, Virgilia, who is an almost nonexistent presence in the play.

But the relationship I find most complex and fascinating is the consuming rivalry and attraction between Coriolanus and Aufidius. It's obvious that Aufidius has felt just a little inferior to the Roman general, having lost to him in their previous encounters. There's something very physical, almost sexual, in their relationship, not unlike what you see in contact sports sometimes. There's a certain kind of physical affinity that these two men share which I find intriguing.

The feelings Coriolanus has for the common people who support and then banish him are unequivocal: he despises them from the start. He makes no secret of his contempt for the mob, calling them "You common cry of curs, whose breath I hate / As reek o' the rotten fens, whose loves I prize / As the dead carcasses of unburied men / That do corrupt my air." He resents their ingratitude for his services to them and claims that while he was fighting to defend their lives, they were running away like cowards or looting like thieves and petty criminals. What right, asks Coriolanus, do they have to challenge his leadership?

Here Shakespeare shows a less than honorable side of the common people. He knew that they could be sensible, ordinary, lovable characters, like the Fishermen in *Pericles*, but he knew too that they could turn into monsters—becoming, in the words of Coriolanus, "The beast / With many heads [that] butts me away."

Like *Timon of Athens*, *Coriolanus* is about ingratitude, disillusionment, and the inevitable destruction of someone embarked on an inherently catastrophic course of action. It's a fascinating play, but not very popular. I think this is because Coriolanus represents something we don't like to see in a democratic society, a certain elitism or aristocratic arrogance that doesn't play well with a contemporary audience.

But Shakespeare doesn't pull any punches here and doesn't try to make good out of bad. He shows Coriolanus in all his ingrained pride and egotism, asking us, not to like him, but just to accept that this is the way he is. And yet at the same time we feel sorry for him, a war hero who is kicked out of his own city by the people he's fought for simply because he won't bow to their demands. At times, Coriolanus even strikes us as a noble figure, determined to preserve his dignity and integrity at all costs.

JOSEPH PAPP

JOSEPH PAPP GRATEFULLY ACKNOWLEDGES THE HELP OF ELIZABETH KIRKLAND IN PREPARING THIS FOREWORD.

Three Classical Tragedies

While Shakespeare was at work in the years 1599 to 1607 on the so-called great tragedies—*Hamlet, Othello, King Lear,* and *Macbeth*—he also devoted his energies during this extraordinary period to the writing of tragedies based on history or legends of classical Rome and Greece. *Julius Caesar* was first performed in 1599; *Troilus and Cressida,* part history play, part tragedy, part dark comedy, was written and perhaps performed in about 1601–1602. *Timon of Athens, Antony and Cleopatra,* and *Coriolanus* followed in 1605 to 1608. Some years before, in about 1590–1591, Shakespeare had turned to legendary Roman history for *Titus Andronicus* also. Together, these six plays constitute Shakespeare's exploration of the only ancient civilization that was well known to the English Renaissance, one to which England felt uniquely indebted for its own rebirth of culture. The present volume does not include all six plays (*Julius Caesar, Troilus and Cressida,* and *Antony and Cleopatra* are available in other volumes) but brings together three of them to illustrate Shakespeare's achievement in this genre.

The Roman and Greek tragedies are distinctive. Whereas *Hamlet, Othello, King Lear,* and *Macbeth* look at crime in terms of good and evil—focusing on the villainous temptations and deceptions of Iago, Edmund, and the witches, and on the fatal human weakness of Claudius, Othello, and Macbeth—the Roman and Greek plays are primarily concerned with political struggle. In a pagan world lacking the Christian perspective on good and evil, although plentifully endowed with ancient classical ideas of virtuous conduct, these tragedies do not often present their characters as morally reprehensible or filled with grace. Apart from Aaron, Tamora and her son, and Saturninus in *Titus,* there are no villains in the Roman and Greek tragedies. We see Cassius tempt Brutus in *Julius Caesar,* but it is to a political cause in which Cassius believes. Octavius Caesar in *Antony and Cleopatra* is unattractive in some ways—calculating, inflexible, remorseless—but he is also efficient and uncorrupt, and we cannot be sure that his final triumph is a bad thing.

The issues in these tragedies frequently cannot be conveyed in terms of right and wrong. Are we to view Julius Caesar or his political enemies as possessed of a superior claim to truth? Does Rome need the single rule that Caesar offers, or should it cling to its senatorial and republican traditions? Is Antony to be admired or deplored, or both, for deserting Roman duty in favor of his Egyptian bacchanals? Do we hope for a Grecian or Trojan victory in the wars of *Troilus and Cressida*, and is either of the lovers more to blame than the other for the collapse of their love affair? These questions, not easily resolved, form the substance of a pagan world where Christian precepts and English monarchical traditions of government do not apply.

Of the three plays in this volume, *Titus Andronicus* is the least typically Roman or classical. Shakespeare wrote it, after all, some ten years before he turned to a more systematic study of ancient civilization, and in this case he chose a story that bears little relation to actual history. Its characters tend to be one-dimensional, either villainous or virtuous, though the title figure is a man whose mistakes precipitate a tragic action from which he must then suffer. We are invited to deplore the crimes committed against Lavinia and to applaud the punishment meted out to her persecutors. Titus' sufferings and outcries are somewhat like those of King Lear, and the outrages committed against him and his family are as heinous as the blinding of Gloucester. Even here, however, the Roman setting lends itself to an artistic vision that is more ironic and dispiriting than charged with moral fervor. The political struggles between Bassianus and Saturninus do not seem to offer a clear choice, even if in moral terms Saturninus proves to be the more reprehensible. Shakespeare's source for this play was obviously derived from Senecan drama of revenge, and accordingly, the play's ethic embraces savagery in a way that Shakespeare's non-Roman tragedies do not. Titus as the avenger punishes the villains, but he becomes so dehumanized that our experience of the play is apt to be ironic and disengaged.

Timon of Athens and *Coriolanus* offer similarly dispiriting views of human nature as it operates in political and ethical conflict. *Timon*, written perhaps at about the time of *King Lear*, shares with that play a devastating vision of human corruption and divine indifference. Timon rails against the world in a passionate indictment that seems as all-encompassing as Lear's futile prayers for heavenly assistance. Yet this play too does not engage its dilemmas in terms of good and evil. It has no villains, only craven flatterers and fair-weather friends. Those who turn their backs on Timon do so out of a self-protective interest that is distressingly, almost comically, human. Bitter laughter seems more appropriate than tears, in good part because Timon is so unsympathetic a protagonist. His misanthropy is a kind of narcissism, a solipsistic anger at others in place of self-examination and self-reproach, a longing for autonomy that merely denies what is maternal and tender in human nature rather than affirming any inner strength in Timon himself. His wrath at women, far in excess of any betrayal he has experienced from them during the play, seems rooted in a self-hatred and disillusionment occasioned more by his bitterness against his own human nature than by the world's indifference to his suffering. Politically, *Timon* ends in a draw; Alcibiades' successful reinstatement in Athens brings the play to a close and serves as an instructive contrast to Timon's failure, but it hardly expresses a restoration of order.

Coriolanus, of the three plays in this volume, perhaps best sums up Shakespeare's achievement in the writing of Roman and Greek tragedy. The conflict between patricians and plebeians that it portrays is serious and emotionally powerful, and yet neither side has a clear moral or political advantage over the other. Coriolanus' dislike of the tribunes' self-serving maneuvers is understandable, even laudable, but his own inflexible arrogance has helped to create the problem that his political opponents seek to redress. Rome's survival finally depends on the intentional destruction of her greatest war hero. The tragic irony of this dilemma is so complete that Coriolanus' own mother, wife, and child, on whose behalf he once served Rome as a proud warrior, must come to him with pleas of mercy for their city. The mother for whom this hero reluctantly entered politics must now witness how that political ambition destroys her son. His mother city and his flesh-and-blood mother, having bred Coriolanus and having used him, now cast him off. The misanthropy and self-reliance of this hero, as with Timon, seem to go beyond being a response to the immediate facts of the story to suggest a kind of inner hatred of his mother or all mothers that would so reject him. Coriolanus tries to escape this dependency by embracing a self-created identity in which he can be beholden to no one, but discovers that the attempt is doomed. His deluded effort drives him into the camp of Aufidius, his brother-soldier and alter ego and rival, where Coriolanus is betrayed once more. The world of Rome and Greece is, for Shakespeare, an arena devoid of Christian moral imperatives in which he can candidly discover what humankind will make of itself, politically and spiritually, when left to its own devices.

The Playhouse

UTRECHT UNIVERSITY LIBRARY

This early copy of a drawing by Johannes de Witt of the Swan Theatre in London (c. 1596), made by his friend Arend van Buchell, is the only surviving contemporary sketch of the interior of a public theater in the 1590s.

From other contemporary evidence, including the stage directions and dialogue of Elizabethan plays, we can surmise that the various public theaters where Shakespeare's plays were produced (the Theatre, the Curtain, the Globe) resembled the Swan in many important particulars, though there must have been some variations as well. The public playhouses were essentially round, or polygonal, and open to the sky, forming an acting arena approximately 70 feet in diameter; they did not have a large curtain with which to open and close a scene, such as we see today in opera and some traditional theater. A platform measuring approximately 43 feet across and 27 feet deep, referred to in the de Witt drawing as the *proscaenium*, projected into the yard, *planities sive arena*. The roof, *tectum*, above the stage and supported by two pillars, could contain machinery for ascents and descents, as were required in several of Shakespeare's late plays. Above this roof was a hut, shown in the drawing with a flag flying atop it and a trumpeter at its door announcing the performance of a play. The underside of the stage roof, called the heavens, was usually richly decorated with symbolic figures of the sun, the moon, and the constellations. The platform stage stood at a height of 5½ feet or so above the yard, providing room under the stage for underworldly effects. A trapdoor, which is not visible in this drawing, gave access to the space below.

The structure at the back of the platform (labeled *mimorum aedes*), known as the tiring-house because it was the actors' attiring (dressing) space, featured at least two doors, as shown here. Some theaters seem to have also had a discovery space, or curtained recessed alcove, perhaps between the two doors—in which Falstaff could have hidden from the sheriff (*1 Henry IV*, 2.4) or Polonius could have eavesdropped on Hamlet and his mother (*Hamlet*, 3.4). This discovery space probably gave the actors a means of access to and from the tiring-house. Curtains may also have been hung in front of the stage doors on occasion. The de Witt drawing shows a gallery above the doors that extends across the back and evidently contains spectators. On occasions when action "above" demanded the use of this space, as when Juliet appears at her "window" (*Romeo and Juliet*, 2.2 and 3.5), the gallery seems to have been used by the actors, but large scenes there were impractical.

The three-tiered auditorium is perhaps best described by Thomas Platter, a visitor to London in 1599 who saw on that occasion Shakespeare's *Julius Caesar* performed at the Globe:

> The playhouses are so constructed that they play on a raised platform, so that everyone has a good view. There are different galleries and places [*orchestra, sedilia, porticus*], however, where the seating is better and more comfortable and therefore more expensive. For whoever cares to stand below only pays one English penny, but if he wishes to sit, he enters by another door [*ingressus*] and pays another penny, while if he desires to sit in the most comfortable seats, which are cushioned, where he not only sees everything well but can also be seen, then he pays yet another English penny at another door. And during the performance food and drink are carried round the audience, so that for what one cares to pay one may also have refreshment.

Scenery was not used, though the theater building itself was handsome enough to invoke a feeling of order and hierarchy that lent itself to the splendor and pageantry onstage. Portable properties, such as thrones, stools, tables, and beds, could be carried or thrust on as needed. In the scene pictured here by de Witt, a lady on a bench, attended perhaps by her waiting-gentlewoman, receives the address of a male figure. If Shakespeare had written *Twelfth Night* by 1596 for performance at the Swan, we could imagine Malvolio appearing like this as he bows before the Countess Olivia and her gentlewoman, Maria.

TITUS
ANDRONICUS

Introduction

Titus Andronicus has drawn some unusually harsh criticism. Ben Jonson singled it out, in his Induction to *Bartholomew Fair* (1614), as a play loved by ignorant audiences for its bombastic rhetoric. T. S. Eliot called it "one of the stupidest and most uninspired plays ever written." Others have argued that it was not Shakespeare's at all, or that it was his perfunctory revision of an old play by Christopher Marlowe, Thomas Kyd, Robert Greene, or George Peele, or an early experimental work, or even a burlesque of the revenge play then in vogue. Early it surely was; it appeared in quarto in 1594 as played by Derby's, Pembroke's, and Sussex's men, and could well have been written in 1590 or even before. The allusion in theater owner and manager Philip Henslowe's *Diary* for January 24, 1594, to a new production by Sussex's men of "Titus & Ondronicus" could refer to a new play or one newly revised or newly acquired by the company. Shakespeare's *Titus Andronicus* was widely separated in time from the great tragedies; *Romeo and Juliet* is the only other tragedy (excluding the English history plays) of the decade preceding 1599, and it probably followed *Titus Andronicus* by five years or so. Unquestionably *Titus Andronicus* does fall short of the expectations we normally bring to Shakespearean tragedy. Such a judgment compares the play, however, with the greatest dramas of the English language. Probably its most serious critical liability is that it continually reminds us of the later Roman plays and of *Hamlet* and *King Lear*. By any other dramatist the play would not seem so imperfect as it seems when assigned to Shakespeare. *Titus Andronicus* was an early success onstage, and has shown its timeless theatrical appeal in a brilliant production at Stratford-upon-Avon starring Sir Laurence Olivier in 1955.

Titus Andronicus is studded with bookish references to classical authors—another likely indication of early date. No other tragedy, perhaps no other Shakespearean play, reveals such direct evidence of youthful learning. Some of its many untranslated Latin phrases are schoolboys' favorites, such as the *"Integer vitae"* of Horace that is immediately

recognized by Chiron. "I read it in the grammar long ago,"
he says (4.2.23). Classical allusions compare the chief characters of the play with Aeneas and Dido, Queen of Carthage;
Hector, King Priam, and Queen Hecuba of Troy; Ajax and
Odysseus among the Greeks; Hercules, Prometheus,
Orpheus, Coriolanus, Semiramis (the siren Queen of Assyria), Pyramus, Cornelia (the mother of the Gracchi), Actaeon, and others. Yet these learned references are far from
being a mere display of youthful learning; through a controlled and self-conscious artistry they enable us to explore
a tragic world whose moral dimensions are defined in
terms of classical literary models. Especially significant
are the references to victims of rape and vengeance: Vir-
ginia the Roman, killed by her father Virginius to save her
from rape; the chaste Lucrece, ravished by Tarquin; Philomel, raped and deprived of her tongue by Tereus, whose
name she then reveals by weaving the information into a
tapestry; and Procne, her sister and the wife of Tereus, who
avenges Philomel by serving Tereus' son Itys to him in a
meal.

Ovid's *Metamorphoses* gave Shakespeare his source for
many of the legends, especially that of Tereus, Philomel,
and Procne. Seneca's *Thyestes* offered him in dramatic
form a similar tale of vengeance, in which two sons are
slain and served to their parent in a grisly banquet. Shakespeare appears to have used a chapbook called *The History
of Titus Andronicus;* the only extant printed copy is from
the eighteenth century, but it may give a reliable version of
the original. Some scholars believe that one or even two
plays about Titus may have existed prior to Shakespeare's
and that we can deduce their contributions to his work by
examining two later continental plays derived from them:
Tragoedia von Tito Andronico (German, 1620) and *Aran en
Titus* (Dutch, 1641). Possibly one of these earlier plays was
the "Tittus & Vespacia" entered in Henslowe's *Diary* for
April 11, 1592, as acted by Lord Strange's men. Even if
Shakespeare used such prose and dramatic sources, however, he also knew well the Ovidian and Senecan originals
that had inspired them. Elizabethan revenge tragedy, containing some Senecan influences (though those Senecan
elements should not be overstressed), was a strongly

formative influence, especially Kyd's *The Spanish Tragedy* (c. 1587). The phenomenal recent stage successes of Marlowe had left their mark: Titus' killing of his son Mutius recalls *Tamburlaine, Part II*, and Aaron's Vice-like boasting of wanton villainy recalls *The Jew of Malta*. Shakespeare's reading in Virgil is evident not only in repeated references to the tragic love story of Dido and Aeneas but in his choice of the name Lavinia (*Aeneid*, Book 7 ff.).

As this sizable list of influences suggests, Shakespeare's first tragedy remains close to its models. Although the play anticipates several motifs in the later tragedies—the ingratitude of Rome toward its honored general as in *Coriolanus*, Roman political factionalism as in *Julius Caesar*, infirm old age confronted by human bestiality as in *King Lear*—*Titus Andronicus* is the kind of revenge play one might expect of a gifted young playwright in the early 1590s. The successful models for tragic writing in those years were Kyd and Marlowe; Greene, Peele, and others paid these two the flattery of imitation. So to an extent did Shakespeare. We can best understand *Titus Andronicus* if we view it as a revenge play in the sensational vein of Shakespeare's immediate predecessors, with generous additions of Ovidian pathos. We should not look in *Titus Andronicus* for that humane and compassionate wisdom we expect in mature Shakespearean tragedy; as a revenge play, *Titus Andronicus* focuses on violence and horror, and its mood is one of revulsion. The style too requires some adjustment in our expectations. Owing much to Kyd, Marlowe, and Ovid, it is replete with rhetorical figures and classical allusions in the manner of Shakespeare's Ovidian poems from the early 1590s, *Venus and Adonis* and *The Rape of Lucrece*. Even if its "early" features are manifest, the style works to good dramatic effect in highly wrought scenes, as when Titus pleads for justice to the unresponsive senators (3.1.1–47), or lays a trap for Tamora and her sons under the guise of his supposed madness (5.2). The seeming incongruity of violent action and elaborately refined metaphor, as in Titus' florid lament for Lavinia's mutilation (3.1.65 ff.), is not, as Eugene Waith has shown (*Shakespeare Survey* 10 [1957], 39–49), without its purpose, for it evokes pathos on behalf of gruesome suffering in a deliberately Ovidian manner, abstracting and generalizing human torment. As in Ovid, the interest is not in moralizing lessons but in the "transforming power of intense states of emotion."

Violence is an enduring feature of *Titus Andronicus,* and its function must be understood if the play is not to be dismissed as merely hyperbolical in its bloodshed. We are constantly aware of ritual human sacrifice, murder, and maiming, as in Titus' sentencing of Tamora's son Alarbus and his slaying of his own son Mutius, the massacre by Tamora's sons of Bassianus and their ravishing of Lavinia, the subsequent execution of two of Titus' sons wrongfully accused of Bassianus' murder, the cutting off of Titus' hand, the feeding to Tamora of her sons' bodies ground into a fine paste, and still more. Savage mutilation is characteristic of many of these atrocities, especially in the lopping off of hands and tongue. The play's climax is, in the manner of revenge tragedy, a spectacle of blood, with the deaths in rapid succession of Lavinia, Tamora, Titus, and Saturninus. These multiple slaughters cause revulsion in some viewers, such as T. S. Eliot, but to others the violence reveals a pattern and offers its own ethical stance on vengeance. Although we do not sense in this early play the same controlled perspective on human evil as in *Hamlet,* for example, we see that Shakespeare is intensely aware of the conflict between order and disorder. In the final scenes, Aaron the Moor is caught and sentenced to execution, Tamora and Saturninus are slain, Titus' brother Marcus appeals to Roman justice for vindication on the grounds that his family had no alternative, and Titus' last remaining son Lucius vows as the new emperor to "heal Rome's harms and wipe away her woe" (5.3.148). Even if this resolution does not fully satisfy the ethical dilemmas with which the play began, it reveals Shakespeare's disinclination to allow the fulfillment of private vengeance to be the play's ultimate concern. Shakespeare is interested throughout in the ethical problems generated by revenge, and the play's relentless horror may be a commentary on the self-defeating nature of a revenge code.

The first part of *Titus Andronicus* functions to give the avenger a motive for his bloody course of action. Ironically, Titus is himself responsible for setting in motion the events that will overwhelm him. His family, the Andronici, are the first to practice vengeance, a fact that diminishes the sympathy they might later have been able to enjoy as victims and exiles. In fact it is Lucius, ultimately to become the restorer of political stability, who first demands the ritual slaying of a captive Goth, Tamora's son Alarbus, to appease the spirits of the Andronici slain in battle. Such a demand is understandable in terms of family honor, but it is also vengeful and pagan. Despite the Romans' claim to be superior to the barbarians they fight (see 1.1.379, for example), their acts too often do not justify that claim to moral superiority. This irony is complete when the Gothic Queen Tamora and her sons plead for godlike mercy. As Tamora's son Chiron bitterly observes, "Was never Scythia half so barbarous" (1.1.131).

Equally violent and unnatural is Titus' slaying of his own son Mutius for assisting in the abduction of Titus' daughter, Lavinia. This tragic error stems, like the first, from Titus' narrow sense of family honor. Titus has unwisely refused the imperial crown, bestowing it instead on the treacherous Saturninus, and has promised Lavinia as bride to the new emperor despite her prior betrothal to Saturninus' virtuous rival and brother, Bassianus. When Titus' sons and Bassianus are driven to the expedient of abducting the lady, Titus cannot endure the shame of his violated promise and so kills Mutius in the ensuing melee. Yet for this sacrifice on behalf of the Emperor, Titus receives only ingratitude and hostility. Moreover, he has taught Tamora and her sons to seek vengeance.

Once the Andronici become the victims of Tamora and her supporters, they gain in sympathy. They suffer unspeakable atrocities. Hunted down by jeering sadists who amuse themselves through rape and mutilation, the Andronici band together in mutual tribulation and selflessly attempt to ease one another's agony. They discover Rome to be a "wilderness of tigers" (3.1.54) in which the law blindly condemns Titus' innocent sons for the murder of Bassianus. Still, Titus has committed the first barbarism and turns increasingly to barbarism in his desire for vengeance. Because the Andronici are too much like their enemies, the prevailing mood as in most revenge plays is more ironic than tragic. There is no strong sense (despite the capture of Aaron) that moral order is restored along with political or-

der. The Andronici are vindicated, and they have gained
some wisdom through suffering, but they are still the
avengers who gave the first offense.

Titus Andronicus displays many conventions of the revenge play found earlier in *The Spanish Tragedy*. The
avenger, Titus, is a man of high position conscientiously
serving the state, like Kyd's Hieronimo, who discovers that
the state itself is too corrupt to give him justice in his family wrong. The evildoers are members of the Emperor's
family, protected by their royal connection. Private and
public interests clash, and public welfare is the loser. The
avenger has difficulty proving the identity of the villains,
but finds an ingenious way at last (through Lavinia's writing in the sand). Once he becomes the avenger, like
Hieronimo, Titus grows as remorseless and canny as his enemies. He becomes a menace to public order, uttering enig-
matic threats and blazoning forth the injustices of the state.
Verging on true madness, he also employs madness as a
cloak for his Machiavellian intrigues. His plotting succeeds
in duping Queen Tamora into allowing him to arrange his
gruesome banquet. The drama ends, like *The Spanish Tragedy*, in a kind of play-within-the-play, as Tamora's two sons
take the roles of Rape and Murder, Tamora Revenge, and
Titus the cook. Playacting turns deadly earnest with a rapid
succession of slaughters. Titus and Lavinia, like Hieronimo
and Bel-Imperia, do not outlive their act of vengeance.

This conventional pattern embraces revenge as self-
justifying. As in *The Spanish Tragedy*, where the choric Revenge controls the action for his own sinister purposes and
welcomes the suffering of innocents or the collapse of gov-
ernments as grist for his mill, *Titus Andronicus* portrays a
world in which the avenger can act seemingly only through
violence. Even Lavinia and Titus' young grandson endorse
plotting and murder. Titus practices cunning toward his
enemies, vowing to "o'erreach them in their own devices"
(5.2.143). Our attention is increasingly drawn to the artistry
of the "devices" on both sides. The machinations of Aaron
and Tamora demand ingenuity in return. An eye must pay
for an eye; the punishment must fit the crime. To be sure,
Titus and his family do struggle to understand the moral
nature of their universe. "If any power pities wretched
tears, / To that I call," prays Titus, lifting his mangled hand

toward heaven and imploring divine assistance (3.1.208–209). Repeatedly the Andronici ask if a divine justice exists, if it cares about savagery among humans, and if that justice will assist the defenseless. "O heavens," asks Marcus, "can you hear a good man groan / And not relent, or not compassion him?" (4.1.125–126). Why should such terrible evils afflict the human race "Unless the gods delight in tragedies?" (l. 62). Marcus seeks the identities of his niece's ravishers, hoping that Lavinia will be able to "display at last / What God will have discovered for revenge" (ll. 75–76). Is revenge to be God's or humanity's? In part at least, Marcus sees himself and his family as agents of divine justice, like Hamlet, though Titus' own errors will also require his own destruction. Yet even these questionings about the cosmos are a part of the revenge tradition, for Hieronimo in *The Spanish Tragedy* implores the gods in similar terms. Titus, for all his pleas to the heavens, is ultimately the avenger in a revenge play. He does not, like Hamlet, submit himself to what he takes to be the will of providence and wait for whatever opportunity heaven will provide. Titus swears an oath of revenge and proceeds with the most gruesome acts imaginable. In his death there is no talk of reconciliation between divine and human will. As the moment of climax approaches, revenge is seen to be a force from hell, from the "infernal kingdom," while true justice is employed "with Jove in heaven" (5.2.30; 4.3.40). Titus is a protagonist suited to a play in which revenge proceeds by its own pitiless rules, in which brutality is the dominant fact of life, and in which violence is the only apparent means of redress. Divine ideas of justice mock humanity's blind attempts at self-governance without offering reassurance and direction.

As a tragedy of evil, then, *Titus Andronicus* illuminates the nature of that evil more than it attempts to transcend evil through human nobility, as in the later tragedies. This distinctive quality is made especially manifest by the play's outward resemblance to *King Lear*. Titus is old, infirm of judgment, and victimized by his own decision to relinquish power to a person whose villainy he does not comprehend. He is, as Lear says of himself, certainly more sinned against than sinning. Titus approaches madness and generalizes in his grief about the omnipresence of murder and ingratitude in nature (3.2.52–78). His reflections on human injustice suggest the inversion of appearance and reality ("Grief has so wrought on him / He takes false shadows for true substances," (ll. 79–80), a motif of illusion that reappears in the allegorical play-within-the-play. Queen Tamora reveals an innate viciousness and sexual depravity like that of Goneril and Regan. Aaron the Moor, perhaps the first of Shakespeare's gloating Vice-like villains, resembles Edmund in *King Lear* as well as Richard III, Don John (in *Much Ado about Nothing*), and Iago (in *Othello*). *Titus Andronicus* shows us, in embryonic form and close to their sources, many of Shakespeare's later tragic themes and methods.

Aaron the Moor is the most vital character in this early play. Like the Vice of the morality play or like Marlowe's stage Machiavel, Aaron takes delight in pure evil and displays his cunning for the admiration of the audience. Evil to him is "sport," "wit," "stratagem," and above all "policy" (5.1.96; 2.3.1; 2.1.104). His malice encompasses all humanity, and proceeds from no motive other than the sinister pleasure he takes in devising plots. When he is finally captured, Aaron boasts triumphantly of the extent and variety of his cruel accomplishments:

> Even now I curse the day—and yet, I think,
> Few come within the compass of my curse—
> Wherein I did not some notorious ill,
> As kill a man, or else devise his death,
> Ravish a maid, or plot the way to do it,
> Accuse some innocent and forswear myself,
> Set deadly enmity between two friends,
> Make poor men's cattle break their necks,
> Set fire on barns and haystacks in the night
> And bid the owners quench them with their tears.
> Oft have I digged up dead men from their graves
> And set them upright at their dear friends' door,
> Even when their sorrows almost was forgot.
>   (5.1.125–137)

Through its depiction of evil as both comic and diabolical, this portrait gives us a vivid insight into the origins of one type of Shakespearean villain.

The seemingly attractive side to Aaron, his fiercely protective instincts toward his bastard son born of Tamora, is part of the central evil of this play: pride of family turning to violent revenge. His black complexion, and that of his son, is equated with barbarism, pagan atheism (Aaron scoffs at those who believe in God), and diabolism. Through him, and through Tamora and her kindred, naked evil is rendered with a terrifying brilliance. As a revenge play *Titus Andronicus* is theatrically effective. To be appreciated properly, it should be seen or read in these terms rather than with the expectations we bring to *King Lear*. Shakespeare here presents barbarism and civilization as polar opposites, but he refuses to equate Rome with civilization and he allows Titus at last no escape from the barbarism that he himself sets in motion. No tragic self-awareness grows out of Titus' humiliation, as it does in *King Lear*, no regret other than for having relinquished power to Saturninus. Instead of tragic self-awareness we are left with an overpowering impression of humanity's potential for brutality. This vision is unameliorated. The constant reminder of a better world of justice and compassion merely serves to heighten the play's ironic and futile sense of wasted goodness.

Titus Andronicus
in Performance

Titus Andronicus was popular enough in Shakespeare's day to have elicited a sour comment from Ben Jonson, who was appalled at the success of what he took to be a bloody and sensational piece of dramatic fluff. "He that will swear *Jeronimo* or *Andronicus* are the best plays yet," wrote Jonson in his Induction to *Bartholomew Fair* in 1614, "shall pass unexcepted at here as a man whose judgment shows it is constant, and hath stood still these five-and-twenty or thirty years." Evidently *Titus Andronicus* had become, like Thomas Kyd's *The Spanish Tragedy* (i.e., *Jeronimo*), a byword for the kind of old-fashioned violent action and hyperbole that Jonson wished more than anything to avoid.

Other evidence indicates that Shakespeare's play did well in the late sixteenth and early seventeenth centuries. Theater-owner Philip Henslowe recorded a performance on January 23, 1594, by the Earl of Sussex's men acting probably at the Rose Theatre and other performances later that year by the Lord Admiral's and Lord Chamberlain's men in combination at the Newington Butts theater. A private performance took place in January 1596 at the manor of Sir John Harington of Exton. Quarto editions of the play appeared in 1594, 1600, and 1611, all of them suggesting recent performance by the Earl of Pembroke's and Sussex's men, the Lord Chamberlain's men, or the King's men. The evidence of performance by combined troupes is testimony to the play's very large casting requirements: even with the doubling of roles that must have occurred, as many as twenty-seven actors are required, especially for the crowded first scene.

Titus Andronicus seems to have been "acted now and then" after 1660 by His Majesty's players, according to the testimony of the prompter John Downes. Such an old warhorse as *Titus* could not, however, hope to escape the adapter's hands, and the play appeared in 1678 as *Titus Andronicus, or The Rape of Lavinia,* altered by Edward Ravenscroft and acted at the Theatre Royal, Drury Lane.

The play was revived sometime around 1686 and gradually became a staple of the theater's repertory. In the early eighteenth century James Quin took the part of Aaron which he played regularly until 1724, and, with some added lines and stage business, made it the star role of the play. As Ravenscroft recasts the story, Aaron is a dominating figure even in the very first scene. (Shakespeare brings him onstage, so that his baleful presence is felt from the start, but gives him no lines.) Aaron's last major scene (5.1), in which he defies his Goth captors and boasts of his villainies, is transferred to the conclusion of the cannibalistic banquet as a fitting climax to that gory display. Aaron is revealed rear stage, by the drawing of a curtain, on the rack and refusing at first to talk, having been brought to justice by an avenging Goth whose wife nursed Aaron's child and has been murdered for her pains. The drawing of a curtain similarly reveals the bodies of Demetrius and Chiron "in chains, in bloody linen"; their dismembered heads and hands, hanging up against the wall, answer in a grimly suitable gesture of reciprocity the fate suffered by Andronicus and Lavinia. Before Tamora is slain in the play's bloody catastrophe, she stabs the black child sired by Aaron. The death of Aaron by fire occupies the final moments of an adaptation clearly designed to highlight his monstrosity. (It was also intended to illustrate, by topical analogy, the dangers of treachery and perjury that had recently come to light in the Popish Plot of 1678.)

A play with so much onstage violence was certain to encounter resistance from audiences in the later eighteenth and the nineteenth centuries, and *Titus Andronicus* was seldom seen in any guise during this time. N. H. Bannister staged it at Philadelphia's Walnut Street Theatre in 1839, though taking care to assure his audience that "every expression calculated to offend the ear has been studiously avoided." In the judgment of the critic for the *Sunday Dispatch*, Bannister succeeded in turning *Titus* "into a beautiful play." In 1849, the American black actor Ira Aldridge, who had been successfully acting in England for almost twenty-five years, added Aaron to his repertory of Moorish and black roles that included Othello and Zanga the Moor in Edward Young's *The Revenge*—a part also taken earlier by Quin. In a version of the play that he prepared along with

C. A. Somerset, Aldridge provided English audiences with their one opportunity in the entire nineteenth century to see *Titus Andronicus*. Aldridge's adaptation, like Ravenscroft's, was notable for the added prominence it bestowed on Aaron. Aldridge went well beyond Ravenscroft in an attempt to make the play palatable to his spectators, elevating Aaron into a noble figure and defender of his child (who is stolen from him), removing the rape and mutilation of Lavinia, presenting Tamora as chaste and her sons as dutiful, and allowing only Saturninus to remain a villainous figure. Reviewers were impressed with Aldridge's performance and his adaptation (one reviewer was amazed that he provided "a play not only presentable but actually attractive"), while Shakespeare's original play was dismissed as not fit to be seen onstage. After 1860, when Aldridge acted *Titus* for a final time in Glasgow, the play disappeared from the nineteenth-century stage.

When Robert Atkins produced *Titus Andronicus* at the Old Vic in 1923, then, it had not been seen even in adaptation for over sixty years and not at all in Shakespeare's original form since the 1660s. This courageous revival, by a disciple of the visionary theatrical reformer William Poel, filled its apron stage (devoid of the realistic scenery that had dominated nineteenth-century productions) with spectacle and pageantry. Atkins's stage, by approximating the conditions of the Elizabethan theater, encouraged a rediscovery of the visual effects to which Shakespeare's script pays particular attention: the triumphal procession and jockeying for political advantage in the opening scene, the pit dug for the Andronici in Act 2, scene 3, the mutilations, the grisly banquet.

Twentieth-century spectators have been more ready than their predecessors to confront theatrical images of physical horror, though those images obviously require something more than the mere exploitation of grotesquerie and sensationalism. A production in 1953 by the Marlowe Society in Cambridge, England, emphasized the play's violence, and yet, as the reviewer for *The Times* noted, the production also "found amidst the brutalities more than one note of beauty and pathos." Peter Brook's striking production at Stratford-upon-Avon in 1955, with Laurence Olivier as Titus, Anthony Quayle as Aaron, and Vivien Leigh as Lavinia, explored the theatrical language of violence in a way that rendered it both formally abstract and deeply moving. Brook, taking the view that *Titus Andronicus* is unavoidably "about the most modern of emotions—about violence, hatred, cruelty, pain"—encased the severed hands in baskets and presented the mutilated Lavinia with her arms wrapped in gauze and with scarlet streamers flowing from her mouth and wrists. The scenery, costuming, and music contributed to an effect at once stylized and ominous. Brook cut and rearranged the text to heighten the visual statement.

Joseph Papp has introduced large audiences to *Titus Andronicus* at the New York Shakespeare Festival, first in 1956 at the Emmanuel Presbyterian Church (with Colleen Dewhurst as Tamora and Roscoe Lee Browne as Aaron under Frederick Rolf's direction), and then with great success eleven years later in a production directed by Gerald Freedman at the Delacorte Theater in Central Park. Freedman, like Peter Brook, chose to represent the blood and gore—which any audience must recognize as theatrically contrived—by means of visual impressions and nonliteral staging. The actors were attired in half-masks and long, priestlike robes. In the banquet scene, the victims of the climactic slaughter were enveloped in red cloth that unwound to reveal black shrouds beneath. Musicians appeared onstage among the play's characters, part of an emphasis throughout on breaking theatrical illusion in favor of ritual and symbolic motifs. The costumes, rather than being realistically antique, suggested something nonspecific in time, part of what Freedman called "our inherited primitive consciousness."

Attempts to heighten rather than formalize the play's violence are perhaps unavoidable in a modern theater so readily fascinated with cruelty. Kenneth Tynan and Peter Myers produced a thirty-minute version as part of a program of one-act plays at the Irving Theatre in London in 1951, removing Aaron entirely but still focusing on the carnage. A production by Douglas Seale at the Center Stage in Baltimore, in 1967, invoked the terrors of Mussolini and the fascists to make its point about holocaust. Christopher Martin's 1972 production at the CSC Repertory in New York left out much of the play except the mutilations. The

BBC television version in 1985, directed by Jane Howell, focused the violence through the eyes of Titus' grandson, young Lucius. Wearing steel-rimmed spectacles, Lucius is seen repeatedly in close-up reacting to the brutality of the world around him. Another way of dealing with the violence has been to shorten the play radically and pair it with something quite different in a double bill, as in the Tynan-Myers version of 1951, the Old Vic's production of 1957 (which shared the spotlight with a reduced *The Comedy of Errors*), and John Barton's version at Stratford-upon-Avon in 1981 (paired with *The Two Gentlemen of Verona*). This pairing device suggests a desire to juxtapose and thus neutralize (or perhaps, more grimly, associate) the play's shocking violence with something strikingly opposite to it.

At its best, however, as in the productions of Brook and Freedman, in director Brian Bedford's restrained and intelligent emphasis on the rituals that seek to control the play's appalling savagery (Stratford, Canada, 1978), in the Bristol New Vic's 1978 version directed by Adrian Noble that created the effect of watching the horrifying action in a bear pit, or even in Barton's truncated text, modern theater has shown a way to see the violence of *Titus Andronicus* in artistic perspective, through the medium of theatrical self-awareness. To the extent that Shakespeare's play deals with the inadequacy of both verbal and visual language to express the tragic condition of humanity, the vivid stage images of this play offer a moving commentary on art's ability—or inability—to communicate meaning. Few plays of Shakespeare offer as detailed stage directions as *Titus Andronicus*, calling for the use of the whole Elizabethan theater—senators entering aloft, elaborate processions, the laying of Alarbus' coffin into the tomb (probably the trapdoor), the sights and sounds of hunting, a fatal pit (the trapdoor again), Lucius' son with his Ovid, Lavinia guiding her staff with her mouth and her stumps to write in the sand, Aaron on a ladder, Titus above at his study door, two banquets, and of course the mutilations. The modern theater has made some rich discoveries of a visual language in this play that show it to be worthy, however early and imperfect, of Shakespeare's genius.

TITUS ANDRONICUS

[*Dramatis Personae*

SATURNINUS, *son of the late Emperor of Rome, and afterward*
   declared Emperor
BASSIANUS, *his brother*

TITUS ANDRONICUS, *a noble Roman, general against the Goths*
LUCIUS,
QUINTUS,
MARTIUS, } *his sons*
MUTIUS,
LAVINIA, *his daughter*
YOUNG LUCIUS, *a boy, Lucius' son*
MARCUS ANDRONICUS, *tribune of the people, and Titus' brother*
PUBLIUS, *Marcus' son*
SEMPRONIUS,
CAIUS, } *Titus' kinsmen*
VALENTINE,

TAMORA, *Queen of the Goths, afterward Empress of Rome*
ALARBUS,
DEMETRIUS, } *her sons*
CHIRON,
AARON, *a Moor, her lover*
NURSE

A Roman CAPTAIN
MESSENGER *to Titus*
CLOWN
AEMILIUS, *a noble Roman*
GOTHS
A Roman LORD
A ROMAN

Senators, Tribunes, Judges, Goths, Soldiers, Attendants, a Child
   of Aaron and Tamora

SCENE: *Rome, and the country near it*]

1.1   [*Flourish.*] *Enter the tribunes and senators aloft; and then enter [below] Saturninus and his followers at one door, and Bassianus and his followers [at the other,] with drums and trumpets.*

SATURNINUS
Noble patricians, patrons of my right,
Defend the justice of my cause with arms;
And, countrymen, my loving followers,
Plead my successive title with your swords.   4
I am his firstborn son that was the last
That ware the imperial diadem of Rome.   6
Then let my father's honors live in me,
Nor wrong mine age with this indignity.   8

BASSIANUS
Romans, friends, followers, favorers of my right,
If ever Bassianus, Caesar's son,
Were gracious in the eyes of royal Rome,   11
Keep then this passage to the Capitol,   12
And suffer not dishonor to approach
The imperial seat, to virtue consecrate,   14
To justice, continence, and nobility;   15
But let desert in pure election shine,   16
And, Romans, fight for freedom in your choice.

   [*Enter*] *Marcus Andronicus,* [*aloft,*] *with the crown.*

1.1. **Location: Rome. Before the Capitol. The tomb of the Andronici is
provided onstage, possibly as a large property backstage or at a trap
door.**
s.d. aloft i.e., probably in the gallery, rearstage above the tiring-house,
looking down on the main stage.   **followers** (including soldiers; see
Exeunt soldiers at ll. 55 s.d. and 59 s.d.).   **drums** drummers.   **trumpets**
trumpeters   **4 successive title** title to the succession   **6 ware** wore
8 age seniority   **11 Were gracious** found favor and acceptance   **12 Keep**
guard, defend   **14 consecrate** consecrated   **15 continence** restraint
16 pure election free choice, i.e., of the Roman citizens. (Bassianus
urges the Romans to let merit, or *desert*, prevail, rather than inherited
right.)

MARCUS
  Princes, that strive by factions and by friends
  Ambitiously for rule and empery,   19
  Know that the people of Rome, for whom we stand
  A special party, have by common voice   21
  In election for the Roman empery
  Chosen Andronicus, surnamèd Pius   23
  For many good and great deserts to Rome.
  A nobler man, a braver warrior,
  Lives not this day within the city walls.
  He by the Senate is accited home   27
  From weary wars against the barbarous Goths,
  That with his sons, a terror to our foes,   29
  Hath yoked a nation strong, trained up in arms.   30
  Ten years are spent since first he undertook
  This cause of Rome, and chastisèd with arms
  Our enemies' pride. Five times he hath returned
  Bleeding to Rome, bearing his valiant sons
  In coffins from the field.   35
  And now at last, laden with honor's spoils,
  Returns the good Andronicus to Rome,
  Renownèd Titus, flourishing in arms.
  Let us entreat, by honor of his name   39
  Whom worthily you would have now succeed,   40
  And in the Capitol and Senate's right,
  Whom you pretend to honor and adore,   42
  That you withdraw you and abate your strength,
  Dismiss your followers, and, as suitors should,
  Plead your deserts in peace and humbleness.

19 empery rule (as emperor)   **21 A special party** i.e., a representative
group specially chosen. (As a tribune, Marcus Andronicus has been
elected by the *people of Rome*, l. 20, the plebeians, to represent their
rights.)   **23 Chosen** i.e, nominated.   **Pius** dutiful, patriotic   **27 accited**
summoned   **29 That** who, i.e., Titus   **30 yoked** subdued   **35 field**
(The first quarto follows with three and one-half lines deleted from the
second and third quartos and the Folio because they are inconsistent
with ll. 96–147 below and probably represent a canceled first draft that
the printer of the first quarto mistakenly included: "and at this day / To
the monument of the Andronici, / Done sacrifice of expiation, / And
slain the noblest prisoner of the Goths.")   **39–40 by . . . succeed** i.e., by
the honorable name of him you choose as worthy candidate   **42 pretend**
assert, profess

SATURNINUS
  How fair the tribune speaks to calm my thoughts!   46
BASSIANUS
  Marcus Andronicus, so I do affy   47
  In thy uprightness and integrity,
  And so I love and honor thee and thine,
  Thy noble brother Titus and his sons,
  And her to whom my thoughts are humbled all,   51
  Gracious Lavinia, Rome's rich ornament,
  That I will here dismiss my loving friends,
  And to my fortunes and the people's favor
  Commit my cause in balance to be weighed.
                    Exeunt soldiers [of Bassianus].
SATURNINUS
  Friends, that have been thus forward in my right,
  I thank you all and here dismiss you all,
  And to the love and favor of my country
  Commit myself, my person, and the cause.
                [Exeunt the soldiers of Saturninus.]
  Rome, be as just and gracious unto me
  As I am confident and kind to thee.   61
  Open the gates and let me in.
BASSIANUS
  Tribunes, and me, a poor competitor.   63
            [Flourish.] They [Saturninus and Bassianus]
                go up into the Senate House.

    Enter a Captain.

CAPTAIN
  Romans, make way! The good Andronicus,
  Patron of virtue, Rome's best champion,
  Successful in the battles that he fights,
  With honor and with fortune is returned

---

46 fair courteously, gently   **47 affy** trust   **51 all** entirely   **61 confident**
without suspicion   **63 poor competitor** rival of lower rank. (Bassianus
is younger brother and thus not in the direct line of inheritance.)
s.d. go up (The *gates* mentioned in l. 62 are presumably a door in the
facade of the tiring-house, rearstage, below the gallery. Saturninus and
Bassianus presumably exit through this door and ascend inside the
tiring-house to the gallery or Senate House, where they reappear with
the tribunes and senators.)

From where he circumscribèd with his sword   68
And brought to yoke the enemies of Rome.   69

Sound drums and trumpets, and then enter two
of Titus' sons, [Martius and Mutius]; and then
two men bearing a coffin covered with black;
then two other sons [Lucius and Quintus]; then
Titus Andronicus; and then Tamora, the Queen of
Goths, and her three sons [Alarbus,] Chiron, and
Demetrius, with Aaron the Moor, and others as
many as can be. Then set down the coffin, and
Titus speaks.

TITUS
Hail, Rome, victorious in thy mourning weeds!   70
Lo, as the bark that hath discharged his freight   71
Returns with precious lading to the bay
From whence at first she weighed her anchorage,   73
Cometh Andronicus, bound with laurel boughs,
To re-salute his country with his tears,
Tears of true joy for his return to Rome.
Thou great defender of this Capitol,   77
Stand gracious to the rites that we intend!
Romans, of five-and-twenty valiant sons,
Half of the number that King Priam had,   80
Behold the poor remains, alive and dead.
These that survive let Rome reward with love;
These that I bring unto their latest home,   83
With burial amongst their ancestors.   84
Here Goths have given me leave to sheathe my sword.   85
Titus, unkind and careless of thine own,   86
Why suffer'st thou thy sons, unburied yet,

---

68 circumscribèd restrained   **69 s.d. Titus Andronicus** (Titus may enter
drawn in a chariot; he refers to his chariot in l. 250.)   **70 weeds** garments   **71 bark** sailing vessel.   **his** its   **73 anchorage** i.e., anchor
77 Thou i.e., Jupiter Capitolinus   **80 King Priam** King of Troy at the
time of its fall; he had fifty sons   **83 latest** final   **84 With** i.e., let Rome
reward with   **85 Here . . . sword** i.e., the defeated Goths have been so
good as to let me put up my weapons. (Said ironically; the Goths had no
choice.)   **86 unkind** deficient in natural feeling

To hover on the dreadful shore of Styx?   88
Make way to lay them by their brethren.
                              They open the tomb.
There greet in silence, as the dead are wont,
And sleep in peace, slain in your country's wars!
O sacred receptacle of my joys,
Sweet cell of virtue and nobility,
How many sons hast thou of mine in store,
That thou wilt never render to me more!

LUCIUS
Give us the proudest prisoner of the Goths,
That we may hew his limbs, and on a pile
Ad manes fratrum sacrifice his flesh   98
Before this earthy prison of their bones,
That so the shadows be not unappeased,   100
Nor we disturbed with prodigies on earth.   101

TITUS
I give him you, the noblest that survives,
The eldest son of this distressèd queen.

TAMORA [*Kneeling*]
Stay, Roman brethren! Gracious conqueror,   104
Victorious Titus, rue the tears I shed,
A mother's tears in passion for her son;   106
And if thy sons were ever dear to thee,
O, think my son to be as dear to me!
Sufficeth not that we are brought to Rome   109
To beautify thy triumphs, and return   110
Captive to thee and to thy Roman yoke,
But must my sons be slaughtered in the streets
For valiant doings in their country's cause?
O, if to fight for king and commonweal   114
Were piety in thine, it is in these.
Andronicus, stain not thy tomb with blood!   116

---

88 Styx river surrounding Hades across which souls might not cross
until they had received proper burial   **98 Ad manes fratrum** to the
departed spirits of (our) brothers   **100 shadows** shades, ghosts   **101 prodigies** omens, portents of ill   **104 s.d. Kneeling** (In a drawing of Act 1 of
Titus, done in about 1595 by Henry Peacham, Tamora's sons are also
shown kneeling.)   **106 passion** grief   **109 Sufficeth not** doesn't it suffice
110 return i.e., accompany your return   **114 commonweal** commonwealth   **116 tomb** family tomb

Wilt thou draw near the nature of the gods?
Draw near them then in being merciful.
Sweet mercy is nobility's true badge.
Thrice noble Titus, spare my firstborn son.

TITUS [*Raising her*]
Patient yourself, madam, and pardon me.   121
These are their brethren, whom your Goths beheld   122
Alive and dead, and for their brethren slain
Religiously they ask a sacrifice.
To this your son is marked, and die he must
T' appease their groaning shadows that are gone.

LUCIUS
Away with him! And make a fire straight,   127
And with our swords, upon a pile of wood,
Let's hew his limbs till they be clean consumed.   129
                    Exeunt Titus' sons with Alarbus.

TAMORA
O cruel, irreligious piety!

CHIRON
Was never Scythia half so barbarous.   131

DEMETRIUS
Oppose not Scythia to ambitious Rome.   132
Alarbus goes to rest, and we survive
To tremble under Titus' threatening look.
Then, madam, stand resolved, but hope withal   135
The selfsame gods that armed the Queen of Troy   136
With opportunity of sharp revenge
Upon the Thracian tyrant in his tent
May favor Tamora, the Queen of Goths—
When Goths were Goths and Tamora was queen—
To quit the bloody wrongs upon her foes.   141

    *Enter the sons of Andronicus again [with their
    swords bloody].*

---

121 Patient calm **122 their brethren** i.e., the brothers of those who
have been slain **127 straight** at once **129 clean** wholly **131 Scythia**
a region north of the Black Sea; its people were notorious for their
savagery **132 Oppose** compare **135 withal** besides **136 Queen of
Troy** Hecuba, wife of Priam, who after the fall of Troy was carried to
Greece as a slave; there she found occasion to avenge the death of her
son Polydorus by killing the two sons of the murderer, Polymnestor,
King of Thrace **141 quit** requite

LUCIUS

See, lord and father, how we have performed
Our Roman rites. Alarbus' limbs are lopped,
And entrails feed the sacrificing fire,
Whose smoke, like incense, doth perfume the sky.
Remaineth naught but to inter our brethren
And with loud 'larums welcome them to Rome.   147

TITUS

Let it be so, and let Andronicus
Make this his latest farewell to their souls.   149

       Sound trumpets, and lay the coffin in the tomb.

In peace and honor rest you here, my sons;
Rome's readiest champions, repose you here in rest,
Secure from worldly chances and mishaps!
Here lurks no treason, here no envy swells,
Here grow no damnèd drugs; here are no storms,   154
No noise, but silence and eternal sleep.
In peace and honor rest you here, my sons!

    Enter Lavinia.

LAVINIA

In peace and honor live Lord Titus long;
My noble lord and father, live in fame!
Lo, at this tomb my tributary tears   159
I render for my brethren's obsequies,   160
And at thy feet I kneel, with tears of joy   *[Kneeling]*
Shed on this earth for thy return to Rome.
O, bless me here with thy victorious hand,
Whose fortunes Rome's best citizens applaud!

TITUS

Kind Rome, that hast thus lovingly reserved
The cordial of mine age to glad my heart!   166
Lavinia, live; outlive thy father's days

---

147 'larums trumpet calls   **149 s.d. the coffin** (Although there is presumably more than one dead son, the staging may have relied on one coffin for economy.)   **154 drugs** poisonous plants   **159 tributary** paid in tribute   **160 obsequies** acts performed in honor of the dead **166 cordial** restorative; or comfort, pleasure

And fame's eternal date, for virtue's praise!   168

[She rises.]
[Marcus Andronicus speaks from above
where he is accompanied by Saturninus,
Bassianus, other tribunes, etc.]

MARCUS
Long live Lord Titus, my belovèd brother,
Gracious triumpher in the eyes of Rome!

TITUS
Thanks, gentle tribune, noble brother Marcus.

MARCUS
And welcome, nephews, from successful wars,
You that survive, and you that sleep in fame!
Fair lords, your fortunes are alike in all,   174
That in your country's service drew your swords;
But safer triumph is this funeral pomp
That hath aspired to Solon's happiness,   177
And triumphs over chance in honor's bed.   178
Titus Andronicus, the people of Rome,
Whose friend in justice thou hast ever been,
Send thee by me, their tribune and their trust,
This palliament of white and spotless hue,   182
And name thee in election for the empire   183
With these our late-deceasèd emperor's sons.
Be *candidatus* then, and put it on,   185
And help to set a head on headless Rome.

[A white cloak is brought to Titus.]

TITUS
A better head her glorious body fits
Than his that shakes for age and feebleness.
What should I don this robe and trouble you?   189
Be chosen with proclamations today,

---

168 date duration   **174 your . . . all** i.e., you who are alive and you
who are dead share a similar fame and good fortune in your victory
177 aspired risen.   **Solon's happiness** i.e., the happiness defined by
Solon (a Greek sage and lawgiver): that no man may be called happy
until after his death   **178 chance** the vicissitude of existence.   **honor's
bed** an honorable grave   **182 palliament** gown or cloak   **183 in election**
i.e., as a candidate   **185 candidatus** (Literally, one clad in white; a candidate.)   **189 What** why

Tomorrow yield up rule, resign my life,
And set abroad new business for you all?   192
Rome, I have been thy soldier forty years,
And led my country's strength successfully,
And buried one-and-twenty valiant sons,
Knighted in field, slain manfully in arms,
In right and service of their noble country.   197
Give me a staff of honor for mine age,
But not a scepter to control the world.
Upright he held it, lords, that held it last.

MARCUS
Titus, thou shalt obtain and ask the empery.   201

SATURNINUS
Proud and ambitious tribune, canst thou tell?   202

TITUS   Patience, Prince Saturninus.

SATURNINUS   Romans, do me right.
Patricians, draw your swords, and sheathe them not
Till Saturninus be Rome's emperor.
Andronicus, would thou were shipped to hell
Rather than rob me of the people's hearts!

LUCIUS
Proud Saturnine, interrupter of the good
That noble-minded Titus means to thee!

TITUS
Content thee, Prince. I will restore to thee
The people's hearts, and wean them from themselves.   212

BASSIANUS
Andronicus, I do not flatter thee,
But honor thee, and will do till I die.
My faction if thou strengthen with thy friends,
I will most thankful be; and thanks to men
Of noble minds is honorable meed.   217

TITUS
People of Rome, and people's tribunes here,
I ask your voices and your suffrages.   219
Will ye bestow them friendly on Andronicus?

---

192 abroad i.e., on foot   **197 In . . . of** serving the just cause of
201 obtain and ask i.e., obtain simply by asking   **202 canst thou tell**
i.e., that's what you think   **212 from themselves** i.e., from their present
intention   **217 meed** reward   **219 voices** votes.   **suffrages** votes

TRIBUNES
    To gratify the good Andronicus
    And gratulate his safe return to Rome,   222
    The people will accept whom he admits.
TITUS
    Tribunes, I thank you, and this suit I make:
    That you create our emperor's eldest son,   225
    Lord Saturnine, whose virtues will, I hope,
    Reflect on Rome as Titan's rays on earth,   227
    And ripen justice in this commonweal.
    Then, if you will elect by my advice,
    Crown him and say, "Long live our emperor!"
MARCUS
    With voices and applause of every sort,
    Patricians and plebeians, we create
    Lord Saturninus Rome's great emperor,
    And say, "Long live our Emperor Saturnine!"
                    [*Saturninus is crowned. A long
                    flourish till they come down.*]
SATURNINUS
    Titus Andronicus, for thy favors done
    To us in our election this day,
    I give thee thanks in part of thy deserts,   237
    And will with deeds requite thy gentleness.   238
    And, for an onset, Titus, to advance   239
    Thy name and honorable family,
    Lavinia will I make my empress,
    Rome's royal mistress, mistress of my heart,
    And in the sacred Pantheon her espouse.   243
    Tell me, Andronicus, doth this motion please thee?   244
TITUS
    It doth, my worthy lord, and in this match
    I hold me highly honored of Your Grace.   246
    And here in sight of Rome to Saturnine,
    King and commander of our commonweal,
    The wide world's emperor, do I consecrate
    My sword, my chariot, and my prisoners,

---

222 **gratulate** salute, rejoice in   225 **create** i.e., elect   227 **Titan's**
(Helios, the sun god, was a descendant of the Titans.)   237 **in** as
238 **gentleness** nobleness   239 **onset** beginning   243 **Pantheon** Roman
temple dedicated to all the gods   244 **motion** proposal   246 **of** by

Presents well worthy Rome's imperious lord.   251
Receive them, then, the tribute that I owe,
Mine honor's ensigns humbled at thy feet.   253
                    [*A tribute is laid at Saturninus' feet.*]

SATURNINUS
Thanks, noble Titus, father of my life!
How proud I am of thee and of thy gifts
Rome shall record, and when I do forget
The least of these unspeakable deserts,   257
Romans, forget your fealty to me.

TITUS [*To Tamora*]
Now, madam, are you prisoner to an emperor,
To him that for your honor and your state
Will use you nobly and your followers.

SATURNINUS [*Aside*]
A goodly lady, trust me, of the hue
That I would choose, were I to choose anew.—
Clear up, fair Queen, that cloudy countenance.
Though chance of war hath wrought this change
    of cheer,   265
Thou com'st not to be made a scorn in Rome.
Princely shall be thy usage every way.
Rest on my word, and let not discontent   268
Daunt all your hopes. Madam, he comforts you
Can make you greater than the Queen of Goths.   270
Lavinia, you are not displeased with this?

LAVINIA
Not I, my lord, sith true nobility   272
Warrants these words in princely courtesy.   273

SATURNINUS
Thanks, sweet Lavinia. Romans, let us go.
Ransomless here we set our prisoners free.
Proclaim our honors, lords, with trump and drum.
                    [*Flourish. Saturninus starts
                            to leave, attended.*]

BASSIANUS [*Seizing Lavinia*]
Lord Titus, by your leave, this maid is mine.

251 **imperious** imperial   253 **ensigns** tokens   257 **unspeakable** inex-
pressible   265 **cheer** countenance   268 **Rest** rely   270 **Can** who can
272 **sith** since   273 **Warrants** justifies

TITUS
How, sir? Are you in earnest then, my lord?
BASSIANUS
Ay, noble Titus, and resolved withal
To do myself this reason and this right.
MARCUS
Suum cuique is our Roman justice.   281
This prince in justice seizeth but his own.
LUCIUS
And that he will and shall, if Lucius live.
TITUS
Traitors, avaunt! Where is the Emperor's guard?   284
Treason, my lord! Lavinia is surprised!   285
SATURNINUS
Surprised? By whom?
BASSIANUS   By him that justly may
Bear his betrothed from all the world away.
MUTIUS
Brothers, help to convey her hence away,
And with my sword I'll keep this door safe.
          [*Exeunt Bassianus, Marcus, Lucius, Quintus,
                    and Martius, with Lavinia.*]
TITUS [*To Saturninus*]
Follow, my lord, and I'll soon bring her back.
MUTIUS [*Guarding the door*]
My lord, you pass not here.
TITUS   What, villain boy?
Barr'st me my way in Rome?   [*He stabs Mutius.*]
MUTIUS   Help, Lucius, help!   292
                              [*He dies.*]
          [*During the fray, exeunt Saturninus, Tamora,
                    Demetrius, Chiron, and Aaron.*]

          [*Enter Lucius.*]

---

281 Suum cuique to each his own   **284–285 Traitors . . . surprised** (Evidently Saturninus, starting to leave, has not quite realized what has happened, and his guard, accompanying him, has been caught napping.) **avaunt** begone.   **surprised** taken   **292 s.d. During . . . Aaron** (Evidently Saturninus, realizing he has been dishonored by the seizure of Lavinia and having decided in any case that he prefers Tamora, ll. 262–263, decides to make her his forthwith.)

LUCIUS [*To Titus*]
  My lord, you are unjust; and more than so,
  In wrongful quarrel you have slain your son.
TITUS
  Nor thou, nor he, are any sons of mine.   295
  My sons would never so dishonor me.
  Traitor, restore Lavinia to the Emperor.
LUCIUS
  Dead, if you will, but not to be his wife,
  That is another's lawful promised love.   [*Exit.*] 299

    Enter aloft the Emperor [Saturninus] with
    Tamora and her two sons and Aaron the Moor.

SATURNINUS
  No, Titus, no. The Emperor needs her not,
  Nor her, nor thee, nor any of thy stock.
  I'll trust by leisure him that mocks me once;   302
  Thee never, nor thy traitorous haughty sons,
  Confederates all thus to dishonor me.
  Was none in Rome to make a stale   305
  But Saturnine? Full well, Andronicus,
  Agree these deeds with that proud brag of thine
  That saidst I begged the empire at thy hands.
TITUS
  O monstrous! What reproachful words are these?
SATURNINUS
  But go thy ways; go, give that changing piece   310
  To him that flourished for her with his sword.   311
  A valiant son-in-law thou shalt enjoy,
  One fit to bandy with thy lawless sons,   313
  To ruffle in the commonwealth of Rome.   314
TITUS
  These words are razors to my wounded heart.

---

295 Nor neither. (Also in l. 301.)   **299 s.d. Exit** (Lucius may take Mutius'
body with him and return with it at l. 341, but the presence of the dead
body onstage from l. 299 to 341 would not be an inappropriate horror.)
302 by leisure with caution, barely   **305 Was . . . stale** was there no one
in Rome to be made a laughingstock   **310 changing piece** fickle wench
311 flourished . . . sword brandished his sword to obtain her
313 bandy brawl   **314 ruffle** swagger

SATURNINUS

　　And therefore, lovely Tamora, Queen of Goths,
　　That like the stately Phoebe 'mongst her nymphs   317
　　Dost overshine the gallant'st dames of Rome,
　　If thou be pleased with this my sudden choice,
　　Behold, I choose thee, Tamora, for my bride,
　　And will create thee Empress of Rome.
　　Speak, Queen of Goths, dost thou applaud my choice?
　　And here I swear by all the Roman gods,
　　Sith priest and holy water are so near,
　　And tapers burn so bright, and everything
　　In readiness for Hymenaeus stand,   326
　　I will not re-salute the streets of Rome,
　　Or climb my palace, till from forth this place
　　I lead espoused my bride along with me.

TAMORA

　　And here in sight of heaven to Rome I swear,
　　If Saturnine advance the Queen of Goths,
　　She will a handmaid be to his desires,
　　A loving nurse, a mother to his youth.

SATURNINUS

　　Ascend, fair Queen, Pantheon. Lords, accompany
　　Your noble emperor and his lovely bride,
　　Sent by the heavens for Prince Saturnine,
　　Whose wisdom hath her fortune conquerèd.   337
　　There shall we consummate our spousal rites.   338
　　　　　　　　　　　　　　Exeunt omnes [except Titus].

TITUS

　　I am not bid to wait upon this bride.   339
　　Titus, when wert thou wont to walk alone,
　　Dishonored thus, and challengèd of wrongs?   341

　　　　*Enter Marcus and Titus' sons [Lucius, Quintus,
　　　　and Martius].*

MARCUS

　　O Titus, see, O, see what thou hast done!
　　In a bad quarrel slain a virtuous son.

---

317 Phoebe (One of the names of the moon goddess.)　**326 Hymenaeus**
god of marriage　**337 Whose . . . conquerèd** i.e., whose wise choice to
be my queen has overcome her ill fortune of being conquered in battle
338 s.d. omnes all　**339 bid** invited　**341 challengèd** accused

TITUS
No, foolish tribune, no; no son of mine,
Nor thou, nor these, confederates in the deed
That hath dishonored all our family.
Unworthy brother, and unworthy sons!

LUCIUS
But let us give him burial as becomes,   348
Give Mutius burial with our brethren.

TITUS
Traitors, away! He rests not in this tomb.
This monument five hundred years hath stood,
Which I have sumptuously re-edified.   352
Here none but soldiers and Rome's servitors   353
Repose in fame, none basely slain in brawls.
Bury him where you can. He comes not here.

MARCUS
My lord, this is impiety in you.
My nephew Mutius' deeds do plead for him;
He must be buried with his brethren.

MARTIUS
And shall.

QUINTUS   Or him we will accompany.

TITUS
"And shall"? What villain was it spake that word?

MARTIUS
He that would vouch it in any place but here.   361

TITUS
What, would you bury him in my despite?   362

MARCUS
No, noble Titus, but entreat of thee
To pardon Mutius and to bury him.

TITUS
Marcus, even thou hast struck upon my crest,
And, with these boys, mine honor thou hast wounded.
My foes I do repute you every one.   367
So trouble me no more, but get you gone.

348 becomes is fitting   **352 re-edified** rebuilt   **353 servitors** armed
defenders   **361 vouch** maintain.   **any place but here** i.e., anywhere but
in this sacred place   **362 in my despite** in despite of me   **367 repute**
think of

QUINTUS
    He is not with himself. Let us withdraw.   369
MARTIUS
    Not I, till Mutius' bones be burièd.
                    The brother [Marcus] and the sons kneel.
MARCUS
    Brother, for in that name doth nature plead—
MARTIUS
    Father, and in that name doth nature speak—
TITUS
    Speak thou no more, if all the rest will speed.   373
MARCUS
    Renownèd Titus, more than half my soul—
LUCIUS
    Dear Father, soul and substance of us all—
MARCUS
    Suffer thy brother Marcus to inter   376
    His noble nephew here in virtue's nest,
    That died in honor and Lavinia's cause.
    Thou art a Roman; be not barbarous.
    The Greeks upon advice did bury Ajax,   380
    That slew himself, and wise Laertes' son
    Did graciously plead for his funerals.
    Let not young Mutius, then, that was thy joy,
    Be barred his entrance here.
TITUS   Rise, Marcus, rise.
                                              [They rise.]
    The dismal'st day is this that e'er I saw,
    To be dishonored by my sons in Rome!
    Well, bury him, and bury me the next.
                    They put him [Mutius] in the tomb.
LUCIUS
    There lie thy bones, sweet Mutius, with thy friends,

---

369 not with himself i.e., distracted   **373 if . . . speed** if all is to succeed; or, possibly, if you remaining sons do not wish to be slain like
Mutius   **376 Suffer** permit   **380 advice** deliberation.   **Ajax** Greek hero
of the Trojan War who went mad because the armor of Achilles was
awarded to Odysseus, slew a flock of sheep deludedly thinking them
Greeks, and later committed suicide in shame; he was refused burial
until *Laertes' son*, l. 381, Odysseus, successfully pleaded for his funeral rites

Till we with trophies do adorn thy tomb.   389
                              They all kneel.

ALL
    No man shed tears for noble Mutius;
    He lives in fame that died in virtue's cause.   391
              [*They rise.*] *Exeunt all but Marcus and Titus.*

MARCUS
    My lord, to step out of these dreary dumps,   392
    How comes it that the subtle Queen of Goths
    Is of a sudden thus advanced in Rome?

TITUS
    I know not, Marcus, but I know it is—
    Whether by device or no, the heavens can tell.   396
    Is she not then beholding to the man   397
    That brought her for this high good turn so far?

MARCUS
    Yes, and will nobly him remunerate.   399

        [*Flourish.*] *Enter the Emperor* [*Saturninus*],
        Tamora, and her two sons, with [*Aaron*] *the Moor,
        at one door. Enter at the other door Bassianus
        and Lavinia, with others,* [*Lucius, Martius, and
        Quintus*].

SATURNINUS
    So, Bassianus, you have played your prize.   400
    God give you joy, sir, of your gallant bride!

BASSIANUS
    And you of yours, my lord! I say no more,
    Nor wish no less; and so I take my leave.

SATURNINUS
    Traitor, if Rome have law or we have power,   404
    Thou and thy faction shall repent this rape.   405

---

389 trophies memorials   **s.d. They all kneel** (Some editors think it
unlikely that Titus joins his sons in kneeling or in saying ll. 390–391,
but Titus has relented and is not without feeling for the son he has
slain.)   **391 s.d. Exeunt** (Perhaps the sons go off in order to accompany
Bassianus' entry at 399, or they may simply stand aside.)   **392 dumps**
melancholy   **396 device** scheming   **397 beholding** beholden   **399 Yes
. . . remunerate** (Said sarcastically; Tamora will show her gratitude in
physical ways.)   **400 played your prize** played and won your bout (as in
fencing)   **404 we** I. (The royal plural; also at ll. 410–411, etc.)   **405 rape**
forcible seizure

BASSIANUS
   "Rape" call you it, my lord, to seize my own,
   My true-betrothèd love and now my wife?
   But let the laws of Rome determine all;
   Meanwhile am I possessed of that is mine.   409
SATURNINUS
   'Tis good, sir. You are very short with us,
   But if we live we'll be as sharp with you.
BASSIANUS
   My lord, what I have done, as best I may
   Answer I must, and shall do with my life.
   Only thus much I give Your Grace to know:
   By all the duties that I owe to Rome,
   This noble gentleman, Lord Titus here,
   Is in opinion and in honor wronged,   417
   That, in the rescue of Lavinia,
   With his own hand did slay his youngest son
   In zeal to you, and highly moved to wrath
   To be controlled in that he frankly gave.   421
   Receive him, then, to favor, Saturnine,
   That hath expressed himself in all his deeds
   A father and a friend to thee and Rome.
TITUS
   Prince Bassianus, leave to plead my deeds.   425
   'Tis thou, and those, that have dishonored me.   426
   Rome and the righteous heavens be my judge
   How I have loved and honored Saturnine! [*He kneels.*]
TAMORA [*To Saturninus*]
   My worthy lord, if ever Tamora
   Were gracious in those princely eyes of thine,
   Then hear me speak indifferently for all;   431
   And at my suit, sweet, pardon what is past.
SATURNINUS
   What, madam? Be dishonored openly,
   And basely put it up without revenge?   434
TAMORA
   Not so, my lord. The gods of Rome forfend   435

---

409 that that which   **417 opinion** reputation   **421 controlled** opposed,
restrained.   **in . . . gave** i.e., in his free bestowal of Lavinia on Saturninus   **425 leave to plead** cease pleading   **426 those** those sons of mine
431 indifferently impartially   **434 put it up** put up with it   **435 forfend** forbid

I should be author to dishonor you!   436
But on mine honor dare I undertake   437
For good Lord Titus' innocence in all,
Whose fury not dissembled speaks his griefs.   439
Then at my suit look graciously on him;
Lose not so noble a friend on vain suppose,   441
Nor with sour looks afflict his gentle heart.
[*Aside to Saturninus.*] My lord, be ruled by me. Be won
   at last;
Dissemble all your griefs and discontents.
You are but newly planted in your throne;
Lest then the people, and patricians too,
Upon a just survey take Titus' part
And so supplant you for ingratitude,
Which Rome reputes to be a heinous sin,
Yield at entreats; and then let me alone.   450
I'll find a day to massacre them all
And raze their faction and their family,
The cruel father and his traitorous sons
To whom I suèd for my dear son's life,
And make them know what 'tis to let a queen
Kneel in the streets and beg for grace in vain.—
[*Aloud.*] Come, come, sweet Emperor. Come,
   Andronicus.
Take up this good old man, and cheer the heart   458
That dies in tempest of thy angry frown.

SATURNINUS
Rise, Titus, rise. My empress hath prevailed.

TITUS [*Rising*]
I thank Your Majesty, and her, my lord.
These words, these looks, infuse new life in me.

TAMORA
Titus, I am incorporate in Rome,   463
A Roman now adopted happily,   464
And must advise the Emperor for his good.
This day all quarrels die, Andronicus.

---

436 author agent   **437 undertake** assert, vouch   **439 Whose . . . griefs**
whose unconcealed anger gives testimonial to his grievances   **441 vain**
suppose idle supposition   **450 at entreats** to entreaty.   **let me alone**
leave it to me   **458 Take up** raise from kneeling   **463 am incorporate**
in have been admitted to the fellowship of   **464 happily** fortunately

And let it be mine honor, good my lord,
That I have reconciled your friends and you.
For you, Prince Bassianus, I have passed
My word and promise to the Emperor
That you will be more mild and tractable.
And fear not, lords, and you, Lavinia;
By my advice, all humbled on your knees,
You shall ask pardon of His Majesty.   474
      [*Lucius, Martius, Quintus, and Lavinia kneel.*]

LUCIUS
We do, and vow to heaven and to His Highness
That what we did was mildly as we might,
Tend'ring our sister's honor and our own.   477

MARCUS [*Kneeling*]
That, on mine honor, here do I protest.

SATURNINUS [*Turning away*]
Away, and talk not! Trouble us no more.

TAMORA
Nay, nay, sweet Emperor, we must all be friends.
The tribune and his nephews kneel for grace;
I will not be denied. Sweet heart, look back.

SATURNINUS
Marcus, for thy sake and thy brother's here,
And at my lovely Tamora's entreats,
I do remit these young men's heinous faults.
Stand up.   [*The Andronici rise.*]
Lavinia, though you left me like a churl,
I found a friend, and sure as death I swore
I would not part a bachelor from the priest.   489
Come. If the Emperor's court can feast two brides,
You are my guest, Lavinia, and your friends.
This day shall be a love-day, Tamora.   492

TITUS
Tomorrow, an it please Your Majesty   493
To hunt the panther and the hart with me,
With horn and hound we'll give Your Grace *bonjour*.   495

---

474 s.d. Lucius . . . kneel (Perhaps Bassianus kneels also, though his pardon seems to have been assured at l. 469.) **477 Tend'ring** having regard for **489 part** depart **492 love-day** day appointed to settle disputes **493 an** if **495 bonjour** good morning

SATURNINUS
  Be it so, Titus, and gramercy too.   496

                   Exeunt. Sound trumpets. Manet
                        [Aaron the] Moor.

496 gramercy great thanks   **s.d. Manet** he remains onstage. (The Folio has Aaron exit with the rest and re-enter. The tomb of Act 1 is possibly concealed by a curtain backstage.)

2.1

AARON

Now climbeth Tamora Olympus' top,   1
Safe out of fortune's shot, and sits aloft,
Secure of thunder's crack or lightning flash,   3
Advanced above pale envy's threatening reach.   4
As when the golden sun salutes the morn
And, having gilt the ocean with his beams,
Gallops the zodiac in his glistering coach   7
And overlooks the highest-peering hills,   8
So Tamora.
Upon her wit doth earthly honor wait,   10
And virtue stoops and trembles at her frown.
Then, Aaron, arm thy heart and fit thy thoughts
To mount aloft with thy imperial mistress,
And mount her pitch whom thou in triumph long   14
Hast prisoner held, fettered in amorous chains
And faster bound to Aaron's charming eyes   16
Than is Prometheus tied to Caucasus.   17
Away with slavish weeds and servile thoughts!   18
I will be bright, and shine in pearl and gold,
To wait upon this new-made empress.
To wait, said I? To wanton with this queen,
This goddess, this Semiramis, this nymph,   22
This siren that will charm Rome's Saturnine
And see his shipwreck and his commonweal's.
Holla! What storm is this?   25

Enter Chiron and Demetrius, braving.

2.1. Location: Scene continues. Aaron remains onstage.
1 Olympus home of the Greek gods   **3 of** from   **4 envy's** hate's, malice's   **7 Gallops** i.e., gallops through   **8 overlooks** looks down on from
on high   **10 wit** wisdom, intelligence.   **wait** attend   **14 pitch** height
to which a falcon soars before descending on its prey. (The image of
mounting has sexual connotations also.)   **16 charming** exerting a magic
spell   **17 Prometheus** Titan who stole fire from the chariot of the sun
and gave it to man; as punishment, Zeus fastened him to a mountain
in the Caucasus and sent a vulture to feast on his liver   **18 weeds**
garments   **22 Semiramis** mythical Queen of Assyria, famous for her
cruelty and lust   **25 s.d. braving** defying (each other)

DEMETRIUS

Chiron, thy years wants wit, thy wits wants edge   26
And manners, to intrude where I am graced,   27
And may, for aught thou knowest, affected be.   28

CHIRON

Demetrius, thou dost overween in all,   29
And so in this, to bear me down with braves.   30
'Tis not the difference of a year or two
Makes me less gracious or thee more fortunate;
I am as able and as fit as thou
To serve, and to deserve my mistress' grace,
And that my sword upon thee shall approve,   35
And plead my passions for Lavinia's love.

AARON [*Aside*]

Clubs, clubs! These lovers will not keep the peace.   37

DEMETRIUS

Why, boy, although our mother, unadvised,   38
Gave you a dancing-rapier by your side,   39
Are you so desperate grown to threat your friends?   40
Go to! Have your lath glued within your sheath   41
Till you know better how to handle it.

CHIRON

Meanwhile, sir, with the little skill I have,
Full well shalt thou perceive how much I dare.

DEMETRIUS

Ay, boy, grow ye so brave?   *They draw.*

AARON [*Coming forward*]   Why, how now, lords?
So near the Emperor's palace dare ye draw   46
And maintain such a quarrel openly?
Full well I wot the ground of all this grudge.   48
I would not for a million of gold
The cause were known to them it most concerns,

---

26 wants lack.   **edge** sharpness, incisiveness   **27 graced** honored,
favored   **28 affected** loved   **29 overween** arrogantly presume
30 braves threats   **35 approve** prove   **37 Clubs, clubs** (A cry summoning the apprentices of London to join in or suppress a riot or rebellion.)
38 unadvised ill-advisedly   **39 a dancing-rapier** an ornamental weapon
worn in dancing   **40 to** as to   **41 Go to** (An expression of impatience.)
lath counterfeit stage weapon of wood   **46 So . . . palace** (It was usually
against the law to draw a sword in the presence of the King or near his
royal residence. See also l. 64.)   **48 wot** know

Nor would your noble mother for much more
Be so dishonored in the court of Rome.
For shame, put up.
DEMETRIUS   Not I, till I have sheathed   53
My rapier in his bosom, and withal   54
Thrust those reproachful speeches down his throat
That he hath breathed in my dishonor here.

CHIRON
For that I am prepared and full resolved,
Foul-spoken coward, that thunderest with thy tongue
And with thy weapon nothing dar'st perform!

AARON   Away, I say!
Now, by the gods that warlike Goths adore,
This petty brabble will undo us all.   62
Why, lords, and think you not how dangerous
It is to jet upon a prince's right?   64
What, is Lavinia then become so loose,
Or Bassianus so degenerate,
That for her love such quarrels may be broached   67
Without controlment, justice, or revenge?   68
Young lords, beware! And should the Empress know
This discord's ground, the music would not please.   70

CHIRON
I care not, I, knew she and all the world.   71
I love Lavinia more than all the world.

DEMETRIUS
Youngling, learn thou to make some meaner choice.   73
Lavinia is thine elder brother's hope.

AARON
Why, are ye mad? Or know ye not in Rome
How furious and impatient they be,
And cannot brook competitors in love?   77
I tell you, lords, you do but plot your deaths
By this device.

---

53 put up sheathe your swords   **54 withal** besides   **62 brabble** quarrel, brawl   **64 jet** encroach   **67 broached** begun, set flowing   **68 controlment** restraint   **70 ground** basis (with a pun on the musical meaning "bass upon which a melody is constructed")   **71 knew she** if she knew   **73 meaner** of lower degree   **77 brook** endure

CHIRON   Aaron, a thousand deaths
  Would I propose to achieve her whom I love.   80

AARON
  To achieve her? How?

DEMETRIUS   Why makes thou it so strange?   81
  She is a woman, therefore may be wooed;
  She is a woman, therefore may be won;
  She is Lavinia, therefore must be loved.
  What, man, more water glideth by the mill
  Than wots the miller of, and easy it is   86
  Of a cut loaf to steal a shive, we know.   87
  Though Bassianus be the Emperor's brother,
  Better than he have worn Vulcan's badge.   89

AARON [*Aside*]
  Ay, and as good as Saturninus may.

DEMETRIUS
  Then why should he despair that knows to court it   91
  With words, fair looks, and liberality?
  What, hast not thou full often struck a doe
  And borne her cleanly by the keeper's nose?   94

AARON
  Why, then, it seems some certain snatch or so   95
  Would serve your turns.

CHIRON   Ay, so the turn were served.   96

DEMETRIUS
  Aaron, thou hast hit it.

AARON   Would you had hit it too!   97
  Then should not we be tired with this ado.
  Why, hark ye, hark ye, and are you such fools
  To square for this? Would it offend you then   100
  That both should speed?   101

---

80 propose be ready to meet   **81 Why . . . strange** why do you act so
surprised   **86 wots** knows   **87 shive** slice   **89 Vulcan's badge** i.e.,
cuckold's horns, alluding to the public shame to which he was exposed
by his wife Venus' affair with Mars   **91 knows** knows how.   **court it**
play the wooer   **94 cleanly by** clean past, without being observed
95 snatch sudden or quick catch (with a probable bawdy pun)   **96 serve
your turns** answer your purposes (with sexual suggestion that is
underscored in Chiron's reply)   **97 hit it . . . hit it** hit the nail on the
head . . . scored sexually   **100 square** quarrel   **101 speed** succeed

CHIRON
  Faith, not me.
DEMETRIUS   Nor me, so I were one.   102
AARON
  For shame, be friends, and join for that you jar.   103
  'Tis policy and stratagem must do   104
  That you affect, and so must you resolve   105
  That what you cannot as you would achieve,   106
  You must perforce accomplish as you may.   107
  Take this of me: Lucrece was not more chaste   108
  Than this Lavinia, Bassianus' love.
  A speedier course than lingering languishment   110
  Must we pursue, and I have found the path.
  My lords, a solemn hunting is in hand;   112
  There will the lovely Roman ladies troop.
  The forest walks are wide and spacious,
  And many unfrequented plots there are,   115
  Fitted by kind for rape and villainy.   116
  Single you thither then this dainty doe,   117
  And strike her home by force, if not by words.   118
  This way, or not at all, stand you in hope.
  Come, come, our empress, with her sacred wit   120
  To villainy and vengeance consecrate,   121
  Will we acquaint withal what we intend;   122
  And she shall file our engines with advice,   123
  That will not suffer you to square yourselves,   124
  But to your wishes' height advance you both.
  The Emperor's court is like the house of Fame,   126
  The palace full of tongues, of eyes, and ears;

102 so so long as   **103 join . . . jar** conspire to obtain what you're
quarreling over   **104 policy** contrivance, craft   **105 That** that which.
affect desire   **106–107 That . . . may** that if you can't do this in the way
you'd prefer, you must necessarily accomplish it as best you can, by
whatever means   **108 Lucrece** a chaste Roman lady ravished by Tarquin, as told in Shakespeare's poem *The Rape of Lucrece*   **110 languishment** love distress   **112 solemn** ceremonial   **115 plots** i.e., plots of
ground   **116 by kind** by nature   **117 Single** single out (as in hunting)
118 home effectually, thoroughly, to the desired place (with sexual
suggestion)   **120 sacred** i.e., consecrated (to villainy)   **121 consecrate**
dedicated   **122 withal** with   **123 file our engines** sharpen our devices
124 square yourselves quarrel with one another   **126 house of Fame**
residence of rumor. (Described in Ovid and in Chaucer's *Hous of Fame*;
see also Virgil, *Aeneid*, 4.179–190.)

The woods are ruthless, dreadful, deaf, and dull.
There speak and strike, brave boys, and take your turns;
There serve your lust, shadowed from heaven's eye,
And revel in Lavinia's treasury.

CHIRON

Thy counsel, lad, smells of no cowardice.

DEMETRIUS

Sit fas aut nefas, till I find the stream   133
To cool this heat, a charm to calm these fits,
Per Stygia, per manes vehor.   *Exeunt.* 135

✤

2.2   *Enter Titus Andronicus and his three sons [and*
         Marcus], making a noise with hounds and
         horns.

TITUS

The hunt is up, the morn is bright and gray,   1
The fields are fragrant, and the woods are green.
Uncouple here, and let us make a bay,   3
And wake the Emperor and his lovely bride,
And rouse the Prince, and ring a hunter's peal,   5
That all the court may echo with the noise.
Sons, let it be your charge, as it is ours,
To attend the Emperor's person carefully.
I have been troubled in my sleep this night,
But dawning day new comfort hath inspired.   10

    Here a cry of hounds, and wind horns in a peal.
    Then enter Saturninus, Tamora, Bassianus,
    Lavinia, Chiron, Demetrius, and their attendants.

Many good morrows to Your Majesty!

---

133 Sit fas aut nefas be it right or wrong   **135 Per . . . vehor** I am
carried through the Stygian regions, through the realm of the shades.
(Adapted from Seneca's *Hippolytus*.)

2.2. Location: The grounds of the Emperor's palace.
1 gray cold, sunless light of early morning   **3 Uncouple** unleash the
hounds.   **make a bay** keep up a deep, prolonged barking   **5 ring a**
hunter's peal blow a peal on the hunting horns (to set the dogs going)
10 s.d. cry deep barking.   **wind** blow

Madam, to you as many and as good.
I promisèd Your Grace a hunter's peal.

SATURNINUS
And you have rung it lustily, my lords—   14
Somewhat too early for new-married ladies.

BASSIANUS
Lavinia, how say you?

LAVINIA   I say no;
I have been broad awake two hours and more.

SATURNINUS
Come on, then, horse and chariots let us have,
And to our sport. [*To Tamora.*] Madam, now shall ye see
Our Roman hunting.

MARCUS   I have dogs, my lord,
Will rouse the proudest panther in the chase   21
And climb the highest promontory top.

TITUS
And I have horse will follow where the game   23
Makes way and run like swallows o'er the plain.   24

DEMETRIUS [*To Chiron*]
Chiron, we hunt not, we, with horse nor hound,
But hope to pluck a dainty doe to ground.   *Exeunt.*

❖

2.3   *Enter Aaron alone [with a bag of gold].*

AARON
He that had wit would think that I had none,
To bury so much gold under a tree
And never after to inherit it.   3
Let him that thinks of me so abjectly
Know that this gold must coin a stratagem   5
Which, cunningly effected, will beget

14 lustily heartily   **21 Will** that will.   **chase** hunting ground   **23 horse
will** horses that will   **24 run** (The first quarto's *runs* is possible, in
parallel to *Makes*, but the verb probably applies to the *horse* rather
than to the *game*.)

**2.3. Location: A forest near Rome. A pit is provided in the stage, pre-
sumably at a trap door, and near it some representation of an elder
tree.**
3 inherit possess   **5 coin** fabricate (with a pun on the literal meaning)

A very excellent piece of villainy.
And so repose, sweet gold, for their unrest   8
That have their alms out of the Empress' chest.   9

                                    [*He hides the gold.*]

   Enter Tamora alone to the Moor.

TAMORA

My lovely Aaron, wherefore look'st thou sad,
When everything doth make a gleeful boast?   11
The birds chant melody on every bush,
The snake lies rollèd in the cheerful sun,   13
The green leaves quiver with the cooling wind
And make a checkered shadow on the ground.
Under their sweet shade, Aaron, let us sit,
And whilst the babbling echo mocks the hounds,
Replying shrilly to the well-tuned horns
As if a double hunt were heard at once,
Let us sit down and mark their yellowing noise;   20
And after conflict such as was supposed
The wandering prince and Dido once enjoyed,   22
When with a happy storm they were surprised   23
And curtained with a counsel-keeping cave,   24
We may, each wreathèd in the other's arms,
Our pastimes done, possess a golden slumber,
Whiles hounds and horns and sweet melodious birds
Be unto us as is a nurse's song
Of lullaby to bring her babe asleep.

AARON

Madam, though Venus govern your desires,
Saturn is dominator over mine.   31
What signifies my deadly-standing eye,   32
My silence, and my cloudy melancholy,   33
My fleece of woolly hair that now uncurls
Even as an adder when she doth unroll

8–9 for . . . chest i.e., to discomfit those who will find this gold taken
from Tamora's treasure chest **11 boast** display **13 rollèd** coiled
20 yellowing baying **22 prince** i.e., Aeneas, who, taking shelter from
a storm with Dido in a cave during a hunt, made love to her **23 happy**
fortunate **24 curtained with** concealed by. **counsel-keeping** secret-
keeping **31 Saturn . . . mine** i.e., Saturn, as the dominant planet in
my horoscope, governs my temperament and makes it cold and sullen
(unlike Venus' effect, which is amorous) **32 deadly-standing** fixed with
a death-dealing stare **33 cloudy** gloomy

To do some fatal execution?
No, madam, these are no venereal signs.   37
Vengeance is in my heart, death in my hand,
Blood and revenge are hammering in my head.
Hark, Tamora, the empress of my soul,
Which never hopes more heaven than rests in thee,
This is the day of doom for Bassianus:
His Philomel must lose her tongue today,   43
Thy sons make pillage of her chastity
And wash their hands in Bassianus' blood.
Seest thou this letter? Take it up, I pray thee,   46
                                    [*Giving her a letter*]
And give the King this fatal-plotted scroll.
Now question me no more; we are espied.
Here comes a parcel of our hopeful booty,   49
Which dreads not yet their lives' destruction.

    Enter Bassianus and Lavinia.

TAMORA
Ah, my sweet Moor, sweeter to me than life!
AARON
No more, great Empress. Bassianus comes.
Be cross with him, and I'll go fetch thy sons   53
To back thy quarrels, whatsoe'er they be.   [*Exit.*]
BASSIANUS
Who have we here? Rome's royal empress,
Unfurnished of her well-beseeming troop?   56
Or is it Dian, habited like her,   57
Who hath abandonèd her holy groves
To see the general hunting in this forest?
TAMORA
Saucy controller of my private steps!   60
Had I the power that some say Dian had,

---

37 venereal erotic, Venus-like   **43 Philomel** (An allusion to the story in
Ovid's *Metamorphoses* of Philomela, raped by her brother-in-law, Tereus;
cf. 2.4.26 below. He cut out her tongue so that she could not disclose his
villainy. She succeeded in weaving the account of her misfortune in a
tapestry.)   **46 Take it up** take it   **49 parcel** part.   **hopeful** hoped-for
53 Be cross pick a quarrel   **56 Unfurnished . . . troop** unprovided with a
suitable escort   **57 Dian** Diana, huntress and goddess of chastity. (Here
used sarcastically.)   **habited** dressed   **60 Saucy controller** impudent
critic, censurer

Thy temples should be planted presently 62
With horns, as was Actaeon's, and the hounds 63
Should drive upon thy new-transformèd limbs, 64
Unmannerly intruder as thou art!

LAVINIA
Under your patience, gentle Empress, 66
'Tis thought you have a goodly gift in horning, 67
And to be doubted that your Moor and you 68
Are singled forth to try experiments.
Jove shield your husband from his hounds today!
'Tis pity they should take him for a stag.

BASSIANUS
Believe me, Queen, your swarthy Cimmerian 72
Doth make your honor of his body's hue,
Spotted, detested, and abominable. 74
Why are you sequestered from all your train,
Dismounted from your snow-white goodly steed,
And wandered hither to an obscure plot,
Accompanied but with a barbarous Moor,
If foul desire had not conducted you?

LAVINIA
And, being intercepted in your sport,
Great reason that my noble lord be rated 81
For sauciness. [To Bassianus.] I pray you, let us hence,
And let her joy her raven-colored love; 83
This valley fits the purpose passing well. 84

BASSIANUS
The King my brother shall have notice of this.

LAVINIA
Ay, for these slips have made him noted long. 86
Good king, to be so mightily abused! 87

TAMORA
Why have I patience to endure all this?

62 presently immediately   **63 Actaeon's** (An allusion to the story of Actaeon, who was transformed into a stag by Diana and killed by his own hounds as punishment for having watched her and her nymphs at their bath.)   **64 drive** rush   **66 Under your patience** i.e., if you will allow my saying so   **67 horning** cuckolding   **68 doubted** suspected, feared   **72 Cimmerian** i.e., of black complexion. (The Cimmerii in the *Odyssey* live in perpetual darkness.)   **74 Spotted** smirched   **81 rated** berated, chidden   **83 joy** enjoy   **84 passing** surpassingly   **86 slips** offenses.   **noted** notorious, stigmatized   **87 abused** deceived

Enter Chiron and Demetrius.

DEMETRIUS
    How now, dear sovereign and our gracious mother,
    Why doth Your Highness look so pale and wan?

TAMORA
    Have I not reason, think you, to look pale?
    These two have 'ticed me hither to this place.   92
    A barren detested vale you see it is;
    The trees, though summer, yet forlorn and lean,
    Overcome with moss and baleful mistletoe;   95
    Here never shines the sun; here nothing breeds,
    Unless the nightly owl or fatal raven.   97
    And when they showed me this abhorrèd pit,
    They told me here at dead time of the night
    A thousand fiends, a thousand hissing snakes,
    Ten thousand swelling toads, as many urchins,   101
    Would make such fearful and confusèd cries
    As any mortal body hearing it
    Should straight fall mad or else die suddenly.
    No sooner had they told this hellish tale
    But straight they told me they would bind me here
    Unto the body of a dismal yew
    And leave me to this miserable death.
    And then they called me foul adulteress,
    Lascivious Goth, and all the bitterest terms   110
    That ever ear did hear to such effect;
    And had you not by wondrous fortune come,
    This vengeance on me had they executed.
    Revenge it, as you love your mother's life,
    Or be ye not henceforth called my children.

DEMETRIUS
    This is a witness that I am thy son.
                              Stab him [*Bassianus*].

CHIRON
    And this for me, struck home to show my strength.
                    [*He also stabs Bassianus, who dies.*]

---

92 'ticed enticed   **95 Overcome** overgrown   **97 fatal** ominous
101 urchins hedgehogs   **110 Goth** (A quibble; pronounced somewhat
like *goat*, symbolic of lechery.)

LAVINIA

  Ay, come, Semiramis, nay, barbarous Tamora,   118

  For no name fits thy nature but thy own!

TAMORA

  Give me the poniard. You shall know, my boys,

  Your mother's hand shall right your mother's wrong.

DEMETRIUS

  Stay, madam, here is more belongs to her.   122

  First thresh the corn, then after burn the straw.   123

  This minion stood upon her chastity,   124

  Upon her nuptial vow, her loyalty,

  And with that painted hope braves your mightiness;   126

  And shall she carry this unto her grave?

CHIRON

  An if she do, I would I were an eunuch.   128

  Drag hence her husband to some secret hole

  And make his dead trunk pillow to our lust.

TAMORA

  But when ye have the honey ye desire,

  Let not this wasp outlive, us both to sting.   132

CHIRON

  I warrant you, madam, we will make that sure.—

  Come, mistress, now perforce we will enjoy

  That nice-preservèd honesty of yours.   135

LAVINIA

  O Tamora! Thou bearest a woman's face—

TAMORA

  I will not hear her speak. Away with her!

LAVINIA

  Sweet lords, entreat her hear me but a word.

DEMETRIUS [*To Tamora*]

  Listen, fair madam. Let it be your glory

  To see her tears, but be your heart to them

  As unrelenting flint to drops of rain.

LAVINIA

  When did the tiger's young ones teach the dam?

118 Semiramis (See note to 2.1.22.)   **122 belongs to her** that is to be
her portion   **123 corn** grain   **124 minion** hussy, wench.   **stood upon**
preened herself upon   **126 painted** specious, unreal   **128 An if** if
132 outlive survive.   **sting** i.e., do harm to (us)   **135 nice** fastidiously.
honesty chastity

O, do not learn her wrath; she taught it thee!   143
The milk thou suck'st from her did turn to marble;   144
Even at thy teat thou hadst thy tyranny.   145
Yet every mother breeds not sons alike;
[*To Chiron.*] Do thou entreat her show a woman's pity.

CHIRON
What, wouldst thou have me prove myself a bastard?

LAVINIA
'Tis true, the raven doth not hatch a lark.
Yet have I heard—O, could I find it now!—   150
The lion, moved with pity, did endure
To have his princely paws pared all away.   152
Some say that ravens foster forlorn children   153
The whilst their own birds famish in their nests;   154
O, be to me, though thy hard heart say no,
Nothing so kind, but something pitiful!   156

TAMORA
I know not what it means. Away with her!   157

LAVINIA
O, let me teach thee! For my father's sake,
That gave thee life when well he might have slain thee,
Be not obdurate; open thy deaf ears.

TAMORA
Hadst thou in person ne'er offended me,
Even for his sake am I pitiless.
Remember, boys, I poured forth tears in vain
To save your brother from the sacrifice,
But fierce Andronicus would not relent.
Therefore away with her, and use her as you will—
The worse to her, the better loved of me.

LAVINIA
O Tamora, be called a gentle queen,
And with thine own hands kill me in this place!
For 'tis not life that I have begged so long;
Poor I was slain when Bassianus died.
                              [*She clutches Tamora imploringly.*]

---

143 learn teach   **144 thou suck'st** that you sucked   **145 hadst thy
tyranny** gained your cruelty   **150 find it** find it true   **152 paws** claws
153 forlorn abandoned (by other birds)   **154 birds** chicks   **156 Nothing
. . . pitiful** i.e., not so kind as the raven, but still showing some pity
157 it i.e., pity

TAMORA

　What begg'st thou, then? Fond woman, let me go.　172

LAVINIA

　'Tis present death I beg, and one thing more　173
　That womanhood denies my tongue to tell:　174
　O, keep me from their worse-than-killing lust,
　And tumble me into some loathsome pit,
　Where never man's eye may behold my body!
　Do this, and be a charitable murderer.

TAMORA

　So should I rob my sweet sons of their fee.
　No, let them satisfy their lust on thee.

DEMETRIUS

　Away! For thou hast stayed us here too long.

LAVINIA

　No grace, no womanhood? Ah, beastly creature!
　The blot and enemy to our general name!　183
　Confusion fall—　184

CHIRON

　Nay, then I'll stop your mouth. [*To Demetrius*.] Bring
　thou her husband.
　This is the hole where Aaron bid us hide him.

　　　　　[*Demetrius and Chiron throw the body of
　　　　　　　Bassianus into the pit; then exeunt
　　　　　　　　　Demetrius and Chiron,
　　　　　　　　　　dragging off Lavinia.*]

TAMORA

　Farewell, my sons. See that you make her sure.　187
　Ne'er let my heart know merry cheer indeed
　Till all the Andronici be made away.　189
　Now will I hence to seek my lovely Moor,
　And let my spleenful sons this trull deflower.　[*Exit.*]　191

　　Enter Aaron, with two of Titus' sons [*Quintus
　　and Martius*].

AARON

　Come on, my lords, the better foot before.　192

172 Fond foolish　**173 present** immediate　**174 denies** forbids　**183 our
general name** i.e., women's reputation　**184 Confusion** destruction
187 sure safe, incapable of revenge　**189 made away** murdered
191 spleenful lustful.　**trull** whore, slut　**192 better foot before**
best foot forward

Straight will I bring you to the loathsome pit
Where I espied the panther fast asleep.

QUINTUS
My sight is very dull, whate'er it bodes.

MARTIUS
And mine, I promise you. Were it not for shame,
Well could I leave our sport to sleep awhile.

[He falls into the pit.]

QUINTUS
What, art thou fallen? What subtle hole is this,
Whose mouth is covered with rude-growing briers
Upon whose leaves are drops of new-shed blood
As fresh as morning dew distilled on flowers?
A very fatal place it seems to me.   202
Speak, brother. Hast thou hurt thee with the fall?

MARTIUS
O brother, with the dismal'st object hurt   204
That ever eye with sight made heart lament!

AARON *[Aside]*
Now will I fetch the King to find them here,
That he thereby may have a likely guess
How these were they that made away his brother.

Exit.

MARTIUS
Why dost not comfort me and help me out
From this unhallowed and bloodstainèd hole?

QUINTUS
I am surprisèd with an uncouth fear.   211
A chilling sweat o'erruns my trembling joints;
My heart suspects more than mine eye can see.

MARTIUS
To prove thou hast a true-divining heart,
Aaron and thou look down into this den
And see a fearful sight of blood and death.

QUINTUS
Aaron is gone, and my compassionate heart
Will not permit mine eyes once to behold
The thing whereat it trembles by surmise.   219

---

202 fatal ill-omened   **204 object** sight   **211 surprisèd** overcome.   **uncouth** strange   **219 by surmise** even to imagine

O, tell me who it is! For ne'er till now
Was I a child to fear I know not what.

MARTIUS
Lord Bassianus lies berayed in blood,   222
All on a heap, like to a slaughtered lamb,
In this detested, dark, blood-drinking pit.

QUINTUS
If it be dark, how dost thou know 'tis he?

MARTIUS
Upon his bloody finger he doth wear
A precious ring that lightens all this hole,   227
Which like a taper in some monument   228
Doth shine upon the dead man's earthy cheeks   229
And shows the ragged entrails of this pit.   230
So pale did shine the moon on Pyramus   231
When he by night lay bathed in maiden blood.   232
O brother, help me with thy fainting hand—
If fear hath made thee faint, as me it hath—
Out of this fell devouring receptacle,   235
As hateful as Cocytus' misty mouth.   236

QUINTUS [*Offering to help*]
Reach me thy hand, that I may help thee out,
Or, wanting strength to do thee so much good,   238
I may be plucked into the swallowing womb
Of this deep pit, poor Bassianus' grave.
I have no strength to pluck thee to the brink.

MARTIUS
Nor I no strength to climb without thy help.

QUINTUS
Thy hand once more; I will not loose again
Till thou art here aloft or I below.
Thou canst not come to me—I come to thee.

                   [*He falls in.*]

---

222 berayed in defiled by   **227 ring** (Presumably the carbuncle, which
was believed to emit light.)   **228 monument** tomb   **229 earthy** clay-
colored, pale   **230 ragged entrails** i.e., rough interior   **231 Pyramus** the
lover of Thisbe, who killed himself in the mistaken supposition that
she was dead. (See *A Midsummer Night's Dream*, 1.2, 3.1, and 5.1.)
232 maiden i.e., that of an unmarried person. (Pyramus, who dies first,
lies in his own blood, not that of Thisbe, though she soon joins him in
death.)   **235 fell** savage   **236 Cocytus** one of the rivers of Hades—the
river of lamentations   **238 wanting** lacking

*Enter the Emperor [Saturninus, with attendants],
and Aaron the Moor.*

SATURNINUS
Along with me! I'll see what hole is here,   246
And what he is that now is leapt into it.
                              [*He speaks into the pit.*]
Say, who art thou that lately didst descend
Into this gaping hollow of the earth?
MARTIUS [*From within the pit*]
The unhappy sons of old Andronicus,
Brought hither in a most unlucky hour
To find thy brother Bassianus dead.
SATURNINUS
My brother dead! I know thou dost but jest.
He and his lady both are at the lodge
Upon the north side of this pleasant chase;   255
'Tis not an hour since I left them there.
MARTIUS
We know not where you left them all alive,
But, out alas! Here have we found him dead.   258

Enter Tamora, [Titus] Andronicus, and Lucius.

TAMORA   Where is my lord the King?
SATURNINUS
Here, Tamora, though grieved with killing grief.
TAMORA
Where is thy brother Bassianus?
SATURNINUS
Now to the bottom dost thou search my wound.   262
Poor Bassianus here lies murderèd.
TAMORA
Then all too late I bring this fatal writ,
The complot of this timeless tragedy,   265
And wonder greatly that man's face can fold   266
In pleasing smiles such murderous tyranny.
                              She giveth Saturnine a letter.

---

246 **Along** come along   255 **chase** hunting ground   258 **out alas** alas.
(*Out* intensifies the interjection.)   262 **search** probe   265 **complot** plot.
timeless untimely   266 **fold** hide, enfold

SATURNINUS (*Reads the letter*)
    "An if we miss to meet him handsomely,   268
    Sweet huntsman—Bassianus 'tis we mean—
    Do thou so much as dig the grave for him.
    Thou know'st our meaning. Look for thy reward
    Among the nettles at the elder tree
    Which overshades the mouth of that same pit
    Where we decreed to bury Bassianus.
    Do this, and purchase us thy lasting friends."   275
    O Tamora, was ever heard the like?
    This is the pit, and this the elder tree.
    Look, sirs, if you can find the huntsman out
    That should have murdered Bassianus here.   279
AARON [*Finding the gold*]
    My gracious lord, here is the bag of gold.
SATURNINUS [*To Titus*]
    Two of thy whelps, fell curs of bloody kind,   281
    Have here bereft my brother of his life.—
    Sirs, drag them from the pit unto the prison!
    There let them bide until we have devised
    Some never-heard-of torturing pain for them.
        [*Martius and Quintus are dragged out of the
            pit, and Bassianus' body is raised.*]
TAMORA
    What, are they in this pit? O wondrous thing!
    How easily murder is discoverèd!
TITUS [*Kneeling*]
    High Emperor, upon my feeble knee
    I beg this boon, with tears not lightly shed,
    That this fell fault of my accursèd sons—
    Accursèd if the fault be proved in them—
SATURNINUS
    If it be proved? You see it is apparent.   292
    Who found this letter? Tamora, was it you?
TAMORA
    Andronicus himself did take it up.   294
TITUS
    I did, my lord, yet let me be their bail.

---

268 An if if. **handsomely** conveniently **275 purchase** win **279 should**
was to **281 kind** nature **292 apparent** evident **294 take** pick

For, by my fathers' reverend tomb, I vow   296
They shall be ready at Your Highness' will
To answer their suspicion with their lives.   298

SATURNINUS
Thou shalt not bail them. See thou follow me.
Some bring the murdered body, some the murderers.
Let them not speak a word—the guilt is plain;
For, by my soul, were there worse end than death,
That end upon them should be executed.

TAMORA
Andronicus, I will entreat the King.
Fear not thy sons; they shall do well enough.   305

TITUS [*Rising*]
Come, Lucius, come. Stay not to talk with them.   306
      [*Exeunt bearing the dead body of Bassianus;*
      Martius and Quintus under guard].

✤

2.4   *Enter the Empress' sons with Lavinia, her*
hands cut off, and her tongue cut out, and
ravished.

DEMETRIUS
So, now go tell, an if thy tongue can speak,
Who 'twas that cut thy tongue and ravished thee.

CHIRON
Write down thy mind, bewray thy meaning so,   3
An if thy stumps will let thee play the scribe.

DEMETRIUS
See how with signs and tokens she can scrawl.

CHIRON
Go home, call for sweet water, wash thy hands.   6

DEMETRIUS
She hath no tongue to call, nor hands to wash;
And so let's leave her to her silent walks.

CHIRON
An 'twere my cause, I should go hang myself.   9

---

296 fathers' forefathers'   **298 their suspicion** the suspicion they are
under   **305 Fear not** fear not for   **306 them** i.e., Martius and Quintus

2.4. Location: The forest still.
3 bewray reveal   **6 sweet** perfumed   **9 cause** case

DEMETRIUS

If thou hadst hands to help thee knit the cord.   10
     Exeunt [Chiron and Demetrius].

[Wind horns.] Enter Marcus from hunting.
[Lavinia flees from him.]

MARCUS

Who is this? My niece, that flies away so fast?
Cousin, a word. Where is your husband?   12
      [He sees her injuries.]
If I do dream, would all my wealth would wake me!   13
If I do wake, some planet strike me down,   14
That I may slumber an eternal sleep!
Speak, gentle niece. What stern ungentle hands
Hath lopped and hewed and made thy body bare
Of her two branches, those sweet ornaments
Whose circling shadows kings have sought to sleep in,   19
And might not gain so great a happiness   20
As half thy love? Why dost not speak to me?   21
Alas, a crimson river of warm blood,
Like to a bubbling fountain stirred with wind,
Doth rise and fall between thy rosèd lips,
Coming and going with thy honey breath.
But, sure, some Tereus hath deflowered thee   26
And, lest thou shouldst detect him, cut thy tongue.   27
Ah, now thou turn'st away thy face for shame!
And notwithstanding all this loss of blood,
As from a conduit with three issuing spouts,
Yet do thy cheeks look red as Titan's face   31
Blushing to be encountered with a cloud.
Shall I speak for thee? Shall I say 'tis so?
O, that I knew thy heart, and knew the beast,   34
That I might rail at him to ease my mind!
Sorrow concealèd, like an oven stopped,   36

---

10 s.d. Wind horns blow hunting horns (offstage. The stage direction is
from the Folio.) **12 Cousin** kinswoman **13 would . . . me** i.e., I would
give all my wealth to have this be only a bad dream **14 strike me down**
exert its baleful influence on me **19 shadows** i.e., protection, shelter
20–21 And . . . thy love i.e., and could find nowhere any happiness half
so great as having your love **26 Tereus** i.e., the ravisher of Philomela;
see note to 2.3.43 **27 detect** expose **31 Titan's** the sun god's **34 thy
heart** i.e., what is in your mind **36 stopped** closed too long, plugged up

Doth burn the heart to cinders where it is.
Fair Philomela, why, she but lost her tongue,
And in a tedious sampler sewed her mind;   39
But, lovely niece, that means is cut from thee.
A craftier Tereus, cousin, hast thou met,
And he hath cut those pretty fingers off
That could have better sewed than Philomel.
O, had the monster seen those lily hands
Tremble like aspen leaves upon a lute
And make the silken strings delight to kiss them,
He would not then have touched them for his life!
Or had he heard the heavenly harmony
Which that sweet tongue hath made,
He would have dropped his knife and fell asleep,
As Cerberus at the Thracian poet's feet.   51
Come, let us go and make thy father blind,
For such a sight will blind a father's eye.
One hour's storm will drown the fragrant meads;   54
What will whole months of tears thy father's eyes?
Do not draw back, for we will mourn with thee.
O, could our mourning ease thy misery!   *Exeunt.*

❖

39 tedious sampler laboriously contrived embroidered cloth or tapestry.
(See note to 2.3.43.)   **51 Cerberus . . . feet** (According to legend,
Orpheus' sweet singing charmed even Cerberus, three-headed dog
guarding the entrance to Hades.)   **54 meads** meadows

3.1 *Enter the judges and senators [and tribunes]
with Titus' two sons bound, passing over the
stage to the place of execution, and Titus going
before, pleading.*

TITUS
Hear me, grave fathers! Noble tribunes, stay!
For pity of mine age, whose youth was spent
In dangerous wars whilst you securely slept;
For all my blood in Rome's great quarrel shed;   4
For all the frosty nights that I have watched;   5
And for these bitter tears which now you see
Filling the agèd wrinkles in my cheeks,
Be pitiful to my condemnèd sons,
Whose souls is not corrupted as 'tis thought.
For two-and-twenty sons I never wept,   10
Because they died in honor's lofty bed.
       *[Titus] Andronicus lieth down and the judges
               pass by him. [Titus weeps.]*
For these, tribunes, in the dust I write
My heart's deep languor and my soul's sad tears.   13
Let my tears stanch the earth's dry appetite;   14
My sons' sweet blood will make it shame and blush.   15
               [Exeunt all but Titus.]
O earth, I will befriend thee more with rain
That shall distill from these two ancient urns   17
Than youthful April shall with all his showers.
In summer's drought I'll drop upon thee still;   19
In winter with warm tears I'll melt the snow,
And keep eternal springtime on thy face,
So thou refuse to drink my dear sons' blood.   22

    Enter Lucius, with his weapon drawn.

O reverend tribunes! O gentle, agèd men!
Unbind my sons, reverse the doom of death,   24

3.1. Location: Rome. A street.
4 my blood i.e., the blood of my sons **5 watched** stayed awake **10 two-and-twenty** (Compare 1.1.79, 195.) **13 languor** grief **14 stanch** satisfy **15 shame** be ashamed **17 urns** i.e., eyes **19 still** continually **22 So** so long as **24 doom** sentence

And let me say, that never wept before,
My tears are now prevailing orators.

LUCIUS
O noble Father, you lament in vain.
The tribunes hear you not. No man is by,
And you recount your sorrows to a stone.

TITUS
Ah, Lucius, for thy brothers let me plead.
Grave tribunes, once more I entreat of you—

LUCIUS
My gracious lord, no tribune hears you speak.

TITUS
Why, 'tis no matter, man. If they did hear,
They would not mark me; if they did mark,
They would not pity me; yet plead I must,
And bootless unto them.   36
Therefore I tell my sorrows to the stones,
Who, though they cannot answer my distress,
Yet in some sort they are better than the tribunes,
For that they will not intercept my tale.   40
When I do weep, they humbly at my feet
Receive my tears and seem to weep with me;
And, were they but attirèd in grave weeds,   43
Rome could afford no tribunes like to these.   44
A stone is soft as wax, tribunes more hard than stones;
A stone is silent and offendeth not,
And tribunes with their tongues doom men to death.
                                            [*He rises.*]
But wherefore stand'st thou with thy weapon drawn?

LUCIUS
To rescue my two brothers from their death,
For which attempt the judges have pronounced
My everlasting doom of banishment.   51

TITUS
O happy man! They have befriended thee.
Why, foolish Lucius, dost thou not perceive
That Rome is but a wilderness of tigers?
Tigers must prey, and Rome affords no prey

---

36 bootless in vain   **40 For that** because.   **intercept** interrupt   **43 grave
weeds** sober garments   **44 afford** provide   **51 doom** sentence

But me and mine. How happy art thou then
From these devourers to be banishèd!
But who comes with our brother Marcus here?

Enter Marcus with Lavinia.

MARCUS
Titus, prepare thy agèd eyes to weep,
Or if not so, thy noble heart to break.
I bring consuming sorrow to thine age.
TITUS
Will it consume me? Let me see it, then.
MARCUS
This was thy daughter.
TITUS   Why, Marcus, so she is.
LUCIUS   Ay me, this object kills me!   64
TITUS
Fainthearted boy, arise, and look upon her.   65
Speak, Lavinia. What accursèd hand
Hath made thee handless in thy father's sight?
What fool hath added water to the sea,
Or brought a faggot to bright-burning Troy?
My grief was at the height before thou cam'st,
And now, like Nilus, it disdaineth bounds.   71
Give me a sword, I'll chop off my hands too,   72
For they have fought for Rome, and all in vain;
And they have nursed this woe in feeding life;   74
In bootless prayer have they been held up,
And they have served me to effectless use.
Now all the service I require of them
Is that the one will help to cut the other.
'Tis well, Lavinia, that thou hast no hands,
For hands to do Rome service is but vain.
LUCIUS
Speak, gentle sister. Who hath martyred thee?   81
MARCUS
O, that delightful engine of her thoughts,   82

---

64 object i.e., object of sight   **65 arise** (Evidently Lucius has collapsed
or fallen to his knees in grief.)   **71 Nilus** the Nile   **72 Give** i.e., if you
will give   **74 they . . . life** i.e., in sustaining Lavinia, my hands have
merely prolonged her days to suffer this misery   **81 martyred** mutilated   **82 engine** instrument

That blabbed them with such pleasing eloquence,   83
Is torn from forth that pretty hollow cage
Where, like a sweet melodious bird, it sung
Sweet varied notes, enchanting every ear!

LUCIUS
O, say thou for her, who hath done this deed?

MARCUS
O, thus I found her, straying in the park,
Seeking to hide herself, as doth the deer
That hath received some unrecuring wound.   90

TITUS
It was my dear, and he that wounded her   91
Hath hurt me more than had he killed me dead;
For now I stand as one upon a rock
Environed with a wilderness of sea,
Who marks the waxing tide grow wave by wave,
Expecting ever when some envious surge   96
Will in his brinish bowels swallow him.   97
This way to death my wretched sons are gone;
Here stands my other son, a banished man,
And here my brother, weeping at my woes;
But that which gives my soul the greatest spurn   101
Is dear Lavinia, dearer than my soul.
Had I but seen thy picture in this plight,
It would have madded me; what shall I do
Now I behold thy lively body so?   105
Thou hast no hands to wipe away thy tears,
Nor tongue to tell me who hath martyred thee.
Thy husband he is dead, and for his death   108
Thy brothers are condemned, and dead by this.   109
Look, Marcus! Ah, son Lucius, look on her!
When I did name her brothers, then fresh tears
Stood on her cheeks, as doth the honey-dew   112
Upon a gathered lily almost withered.

---

83 blabbed uttered   **90 unrecuring** incurable   **91 dear** (with a familiar pun on *deer*, l. 89)   **96 Expecting ever when** continually awaiting the moment when.   **envious** spiteful   **97 his** its   **101 spurn** stroke, kick   **105 lively** living, actual (as contrasted with her picture)   **108 husband he** husband   **109 by this** by now   **112 honey-dew** sweet dewlike substance, or the dew itself

MARCUS
Perchance she weeps because they killed her husband;
Perchance because she knows them innocent.

TITUS
If they did kill thy husband, then be joyful,
Because the law hath ta'en revenge on them.
No, no, they would not do so foul a deed;
Witness the sorrow that their sister makes.
Gentle Lavinia, let me kiss thy lips;
Or make some sign how I may do thee ease.   121
Shall thy good uncle, and thy brother Lucius,
And thou, and I, sit round about some fountain,   123
Looking all downwards to behold our cheeks
How they are stained, like meadows yet not dry
With miry slime left on them by a flood?
And in the fountain shall we gaze so long
Till the fresh taste be taken from that clearness,   128
And made a brine pit with our bitter tears?   129
Or shall we cut away our hands, like thine?
Or shall we bite our tongues, and in dumb shows   131
Pass the remainder of our hateful days?
What shall we do? Let us that have our tongues
Plot some device of further misery,   134
To make us wondered at in time to come.

LUCIUS
Sweet Father, cease your tears, for at your grief
See how my wretched sister sobs and weeps.

MARCUS
Patience, dear niece. Good Titus, dry thine eyes.

TITUS
Ah, Marcus, Marcus! Brother, well I wot   139
Thy napkin cannot drink a tear of mine,   140
For thou, poor man, hast drowned it with thine own.   141

LUCIUS
Ah, my Lavinia, I will wipe thy cheeks.

---

121 do thee ease bring you comfort, relief   **123 fountain** spring
128 taken removed, destroyed.   **clearness** i.e., of the pure water
129 And made i.e., and the spring made   **131 bite** bite out.   **dumb**
shows mute pageants, as in dramatic action without dialogue
134 device dramatic representation   **139 wot** know   **140 napkin** hand-
kerchief   **141 drowned** i.e., saturated

TITUS
    Mark, Marcus, mark! I understand her signs.
    Had she a tongue to speak, now would she say
    That to her brother which I said to thee.
    His napkin, with his true tears all bewet,
    Can do no service on her sorrowful cheeks.
    O, what a sympathy of woe is this,   148
    As far from help as Limbo is from bliss!   149

        Enter Aaron the Moor alone.

AARON
    Titus Andronicus, my lord the Emperor
    Sends thee this word: that if thou love thy sons,
    Let Marcus, Lucius, or thyself, old Titus,
    Or any one of you, chop off your hand
    And send it to the King. He for the same
    Will send thee hither both thy sons alive,   155
    And that shall be the ransom for their fault.   156
TITUS
    O gracious Emperor! O gentle Aaron!
    Did ever raven sing so like a lark,
    That gives sweet tidings of the sun's uprise?
    With all my heart I'll send the Emperor my hand.
    Good Aaron, wilt thou help to chop it off?
LUCIUS
    Stay, Father, for that noble hand of thine,
    That hath thrown down so many enemies,
    Shall not be sent. My hand will serve the turn.
    My youth can better spare my blood than you,
    And therefore mine shall save my brothers' lives.
MARCUS
    Which of your hands hath not defended Rome   167
    And reared aloft the bloody battle-ax,
    Writing destruction on the enemy's castle?
    O, none of both but are of high desert.

148 sympathy agreement, sharing   **149 Limbo** region bordering hell,
where were confined the souls of those barred from heaven through no
fault of their own, such as good men who lived before the Christian era
or who died unbaptized   **155 Will . . . alive** (Aaron's secret double
meaning may be, "will send to you here, you being alive, both your
sons.")   **156 that** (Secretly, *that* may refer to the sons being sent here—
dead.)   **167 Which . . . hands** i.e., has either of you a hand that

My hand hath been but idle; let it serve
To ransom my two nephews from their death.
Then have I kept it to a worthy end.

AARON
Nay, come, agree whose hand shall go along,
For fear they die before their pardon come.

MARCUS
My hand shall go.

LUCIUS   By heaven, it shall not go!

TITUS
Sirs, strive no more. Such withered herbs as these
Are meet for plucking up, and therefore mine.   178

LUCIUS
Sweet Father, if I shall be thought thy son,   179
Let me redeem my brothers both from death.

MARCUS
And, for our father's sake and mother's care,
Now let me show a brother's love to thee.

TITUS
Agree between you. I will spare my hand.   183

LUCIUS   Then I'll go fetch an ax.

MARCUS   But I will use the ax.

Exeunt [Lucius and Marcus].

TITUS
Come hither, Aaron. I'll deceive them both.
Lend my thy hand, and I will give thee mine.   187

AARON [*Aside*]
If that be called deceit, I will be honest,
And never whilst I live deceive men so;
But I'll deceive you in another sort,
And that you'll say, ere half an hour pass.

He cuts off Titus' hand.

Enter Lucius and Marcus again.

TITUS
Now stay your strife. What shall be is dispatched.

---

178 meet fit   **179 shall** am to   **183 spare** (In a virtuous deception, Titus
uses a double meaning for *spare*; ostensibly he means "save from being
cut off," but secretly he means "do without.")   **187 Lend . . . mine**
(Another pun, on *hand*: "Give me your assistance, and I'll give you
my hand.")

Good Aaron, give His Majesty my hand.
Tell him it was a hand that warded him   194
From thousand dangers. Bid him bury it.
More hath it merited; that let it have.
As for my sons, say I account of them
As jewels purchased at an easy price,
And yet dear too, because I bought mine own.   199

AARON

I go, Andronicus, and for thy hand
Look by and by to have thy sons with thee.   201
[*Aside.*] Their heads, I mean. O, how this villainy
Doth fat me with the very thoughts of it!   203
Let fools do good, and fair men call for grace;
Aaron will have his soul black like his face.   *Exit.*

TITUS [*Kneeling*]

O, here I lift this one hand up to heaven
And bow this feeble ruin to the earth.
If any power pities wretched tears,
To that I call! [*To Lavinia, who kneels.*] What, wouldst
      thou kneel with me?
Do, then, dear heart, for heaven shall hear our prayers,
Or with our sighs we'll breathe the welkin dim   211
And stain the sun with fog, as sometimes clouds
When they do hug him in their melting bosoms.   213

MARCUS

O brother, speak with possibility,   214
And do not break into these deep extremes.

TITUS

Is not my sorrow deep, having no bottom?
Then be my passions bottomless with them.   217

MARCUS

But yet let reason govern thy lament.   218

TITUS

If there were reason for these miseries,   219

---

194 warded guarded   **199 dear** expensive.   **because . . . own** because
I am buying back what was mine to begin with   **201 Look** expect
203 fat fatten, feed   **211 breathe . . . dim** make cloudy the sky with our
sighs.   **welkin** sky   **213 melting** i.e., dissolving into teardroplike rain
214 speak with possibility speak of things possible.   **with** within the
bounds of   **217 be my passions** let my passionate expressions of grief
be   **218–219 reason . . . reason** rationality . . . necessity

Then into limits could I bind my woes.
When heaven doth weep, doth not the earth o'erflow?
If the winds rage, doth not the sea wax mad,
Threat'ning the welkin with his big-swoll'n face?
And wilt thou have a reason for this coil?   224
I am the sea. Hark how her sighs doth blow!   225
She is the weeping welkin, I the earth.
Then must my sea be movèd with her sighs,
Then must my earth with her continual tears
Become a deluge overflowed and drowned,
Forwhy my bowels cannot hide her woes,   230
But like a drunkard must I vomit them.
Then give me leave, for losers will have leave
To ease their stomachs with their bitter tongues.   233

Enter a Messenger, with two heads and a hand.

MESSENGER
Worthy Andronicus, ill art thou repaid
For that good hand thou sent'st the Emperor.
Here are the heads of thy two noble sons,
And here's thy hand in scorn to thee sent back—
Thy grief their sports, thy resolution mocked,   238
That woe is me to think upon thy woes   239
More than remembrance of my father's death.
        [He sets down the heads and hand, and exit.]

MARCUS
Now let hot Etna cool in Sicily,   241
And be my heart an ever-burning hell!
These miseries are more than may be borne.
To weep with them that weep doth ease some deal,   244
But sorrow flouted at is double death.

LUCIUS
Ah, that this sight should make so deep a wound,
And yet detested life not shrink thereat!   247

---

224 coil noise, fuss   **225 her** i.e., Lavinia's   **230 Forwhy** because.
bowels (Supposed to be the seat of compassion.)   **her** their, my bowels'
233 ease their stomachs relieve their resentments (with a play on *vomit*)
238 sports entertainment   **239 That** so that   **241 Etna** volcanic mountain on the island of Sicily (which will, compared to Marcus' burning heart, seem cool)   **244 some deal** somewhat   **247 shrink** i.e., slip
away

That ever death should let life bear his name,   248
Where life hath no more interest but to breathe!   249
                    [*Lavinia kisses Titus.*]
MARCUS
Alas, poor heart, that kiss is comfortless
As frozen water to a starvèd snake.   251
TITUS
When will this fearful slumber have an end?   252
MARCUS
Now, farewell, flattery! Die, Andronicus.   253
Thou dost not slumber. See thy two sons' heads,
Thy warlike hand, thy mangled daughter here,
Thy other banished son with this dear sight   256
Struck pale and bloodless, and thy brother, I,
Even like a stony image, cold and numb.
Ah, now no more will I control thy griefs!   259
Rend off thy silver hair, thy other hand
Gnawing with thy teeth, and be this dismal sight
The closing up of our most wretched eyes.   262
Now is a time to storm. Why art thou still?
TITUS   Ha, ha, ha!
MARCUS
Why dost thou laugh? It fits not with this hour.
TITUS
Why, I have not another tear to shed.
Besides, this sorrow is an enemy,
And would usurp upon my watery eyes
And make them blind with tributary tears.   269
Then which way shall I find Revenge's cave?
For these two heads do seem to speak to me,
And threat me I shall never come to bliss
Till all these mischiefs be returned again   273
Even in their throats that hath committed them.
Come, let me see what task I have to do.

---

248 bear his name i.e., still be called life   **249 Where . . . breathe** i.e.,
where virtually nothing remains of life except the drawing of breath
251 starvèd i.e., benumbed with cold   **252 fearful slumber** i.e., dreadful
nightmare   **253 flattery** comforting deception   **256 dear** grievous
259 control try to restrain   **262 closing up** closing in death   **269 tributary tears** tears paid as tribute (to sorrow, the usurping enemy)
273 mischiefs evils, injuries

You heavy people, circle me about,   276
That I may turn me to each one of you
And swear unto my soul to right your wrongs.
                    [*They form a circle about Titus,
                                and he pledges each.*]
The vow is made. Come, brother, take a head,
And in this hand the other will I bear.
                              [*They pick up the two heads,
                                and give the hand to Lavinia.*]
And, Lavinia, thou shalt be employed:
Bear thou my hand, sweet wench, between thy teeth.
As for thee, boy, [*To Lucius*] go get thee from my sight;
Thou art an exile, and thou must not stay.
Hie to the Goths and raise an army there.
And if ye love me, as I think you do,
Let's kiss and part, for we have much to do.
        [*They kiss.*] *Exeunt* [*Titus, Marcus, and Lavinia*].
LUCIUS
Farewell, Andronicus, my noble father,
The woefull'st man that ever lived in Rome.
Farewell, proud Rome, till Lucius come again!
He loves his pledges dearer than his life.   291
Farewell, Lavinia, my noble sister.
O, would thou wert as thou tofore hast been!   293
But now nor Lucius nor Lavinia lives
But in oblivion and hateful griefs.
If Lucius live, he will requite your wrongs
And make proud Saturnine and his empress
Beg at the gates, like Tarquin and his queen.   298
Now will I to the Goths and raise a power   299
To be revenged on Rome and Saturnine.   *Exit Lucius.*

❖

276 heavy sorrowing   **291 He . . . life** i.e., his vows are more important
to him than his life, or he loves his family, left behind in Rome as hostages to fortune, more than his life   **293 tofore** heretofore, formerly
298 Tarquin Tarquinius Superbus, seventh king of Rome, who, because
his son had raped a Roman lady, Lucretia, was banished and his kingdom overthrown; a republic was then established   **299 power** army

3.2   *A banquet [set out]. Enter [Titus] Andronicus,*
            Marcus, Lavinia, and the boy [young Lucius].

TITUS

So, so. Now sit, and look you eat no more
Than will preserve just so much strength in us
As will revenge these bitter woes of ours.
Marcus, unknit that sorrow-wreathen knot.   4
Thy niece and I, poor creatures, want our hands   5
And cannot passionate our tenfold grief   6
With folded arms. This poor right hand of mine
Is left to tyrannize upon my breast,   8
Who, when my heart, all mad with misery,   9
Beats in this hollow prison of my flesh,
Then thus I thump it down.   [*He beats his breast.*]
[*To Lavinia.*] Thou map of woe, that thus dost talk
    in signs,   12
When thy poor heart beats with outrageous beating,
Thou canst not strike it thus to make it still.
Wound it with sighing, girl, kill it with groans;   15
Or get some little knife between thy teeth
And just against thy heart make thou a hole,
That all the tears that thy poor eyes let fall
May run into that sink and, soaking in,   19
Drown the lamenting fool in sea-salt tears.   20

MARCUS

Fie, brother, fie! Teach her not thus to lay
Such violent hands upon her tender life.

TITUS

How now, has sorrow made thee dote already?   23
Why, Marcus, no man should be mad but I.
What violent hands can she lay on her life?
Ah, wherefore dost thou urge the name of hands,
To bid Aeneas tell the tale twice o'er   27

3.2. Location: Rome. Titus' house.
s.d. banquet a light repast, here set out on stage as the scene begins,
with appropriate furniture allowing for sitting   **4 sorrow-wreathen knot**
arms folded in a conventional expression of grief   **5 want** lack   **6 pas-**
sionate express passionately   **8 tyrannize** i.e., by beating   **9 Who** which
12 map picture   **15 Wound it with sighing** (Each sigh was believed to
cost the heart a drop of blood.)   **19 sink** receptacle   **20 fool** (Here a
term of pity or endearment.)   **23 dote** be foolish   **27 Aeneas** (See
Aeneid, 2.2.)

How Troy was burnt and he made miserable?
O, handle not the theme, to talk of hands,
Lest we remember still that we have none.   30
Fie, fie, how franticly I square my talk,   31
As if we should forget we had no hands
If Marcus did not name the word of hands!
Come, let's fall to; and, gentle girl, eat this.
Here is no drink! Hark, Marcus, what she says;
I can interpret all her marytred signs.
She says she drinks no other drink but tears,
Brewed with her sorrow, mashed upon her cheeks.   38
Speechless complainer, I will learn thy thought;
In thy dumb action will I be as perfect   40
As begging hermits in their holy prayers.   41
Thou shalt not sigh, nor hold thy stumps to heaven,
Nor wink, nor nod, nor kneel, nor make a sign,   43
But I of these will wrest an alphabet
And by still practice learn to know thy meaning.   45

BOY [*Weeping*]
Good grandsire, leave these bitter deep laments!
Make my aunt merry with some pleasing tale.

MARCUS
Alas, the tender boy, in passion moved,   48
Doth weep to see his grandsire's heaviness.

TITUS
Peace, tender sapling! Thou art made of tears,   50
And tears will quickly melt thy life away.
                    Marcus strikes the dish with a knife.
What dost thou strike at, Marcus, with thy knife?

MARCUS
At that that I have killed, my lord: a fly.

TITUS
Out on thee, murderer! Thou kill'st my heart.
Mine eyes are cloyed with view of tyranny.
A deed of death done on the innocent

---

30 still continually **31 square** shape, regulate **38 mashed** mixed with
hot water in a mash, as for brewing **40 action** gesture. **perfect** thoroughly acquainted **41 As . . . prayers** i.e., as hermits are with the
subject of their prayerful meditation **43 wink** close the eyes **45 still**
continual **48 passion** sorrow **50 made of tears** (See Genesis 3:16: "In
sorrow thou shalt bring forth children." Like a sapling, the child is soft,
unformed.)

Becomes not Titus' brother. Get thee gone!
I see thou art not for my company.

MARCUS
Alas, my lord, I have but killed a fly.

TITUS
"But"? How if that fly had a father and mother?
How would he hang his slender gilded wings   61
And buzz lamenting doings in the air!   62
Poor harmless fly,
That, with his pretty buzzing melody,
Came here to make us merry! And thou hast killed him.

MARCUS
Pardon me, sir. It was a black ill-favored fly,   66
Like to the Empress' Moor. Therefore I killed him.

TITUS   O, O, O!
Then pardon me for reprehending thee,
For thou hast done a charitable deed.
Give me thy knife. I will insult on him,   71
Flattering myself as if it were the Moor   72
Come hither purposely to poison me.—
There's for thyself, and that's for Tamora!
                   [*He takes the knife and strikes.*]
Ah, sirrah!   75
Yet I think we are not brought so low
But that between us we can kill a fly
That comes in likeness of a coal black Moor.

MARCUS
Alas, poor man! Grief has so wrought on him
He takes false shadows for true substances.

TITUS
Come, take away. Lavinia, go with me.   81
I'll to thy closet and go read with thee   82
Sad stories chancèd in the times of old.   83
Come, boy, and go with me. Thy sight is young,
And thou shalt read when mine begin to dazzle.   85
                                    Exeunt.

❖

61 he i.e., the father   62 buzz . . . doings tell sad stories   66 ill-favored
ugly   71 insult on exult over   72 Flattering . . . if deluding myself into
believing   75 sirrah (Ordinary term of address to inferiors.)   81 take
away clear the table. (The "banquet" and furniture are removed from
the stage as the scene ends.)   82 closet private room   83 chancèd that
occurred   85 dazzle become dazzled, unable to see

4.1 *Enter Lucius' son, and Lavinia running after him, and the boy flies from her, with his books under his arm. Enter Titus and Marcus.*

BOY
Help, grandsire, help! My aunt Lavinia
Follows me everywhere, I know not why.
Good uncle Marcus, see how swift she comes.
Alas, sweet aunt, I know not what you mean.
                                    [*He drops his books.*]

MARCUS
Stand by me, Lucius. Do not fear thine aunt.

TITUS
She loves thee, boy, too well to do thee harm.

BOY
Ay, when my father was in Rome she did.   7

MARCUS
What means my niece Lavinia by these signs?

TITUS
Fear her not, Lucius. Somewhat doth she mean.   9

MARCUS
See, Lucius, see how much she makes of thee;
Somewhither would she have thee go with her.
Ah, boy, Cornelia never with more care   12
Read to her sons than she hath read to thee   13
Sweet poetry and Tully's *Orator*.   14
Canst thou not guess wherefore she plies thee thus?   15

BOY
My lord, I know not, I, nor can I guess,
Unless some fit or frenzy do possess her;
For I have heard my grandsire say full oft,
Extremity of griefs would make men mad,
And I have read that Hecuba of Troy   20
Ran mad for sorrow. That made me to fear,
Although, my lord, I know my noble aunt

4.1. Location: Rome. Titus' garden.
7 when . . . Rome i.e., when my father was here to protect me   **9 Somewhat** something   **12 Cornelia** the mother of the Gracchi brothers, the two most famous tribunes in Roman history. (Her success in educating her sons was highly regarded.)   **13 Read** gave instruction   **14 Tully's Orator** Cicero's treatise on rhetoric, *De Oratore*   **15 plies** importunes   **20 Hecuba** (See 1.1.136 and note.)

Loves me as dear as e'er my mother did,
And would not but in fury fright my youth—   24
Which made me down to throw my books and fly,
Causeless, perhaps. But pardon me, sweet aunt,
And, madam, if my uncle Marcus go,   27
I will most willingly attend your ladyship.

MARCUS   Lucius, I will.   29

> [*Lavinia turns over with her stumps the
> books that young Lucius has let fall.*]

TITUS
How now, Lavinia? Marcus, what means this?
Some book there is that she desires to see.
Which is it, girl, of these?—Open them, boy.
[*To Lavinia.*] But thou art deeper read and better skilled;
Come and take choice of all my library,
And so beguile thy sorrow till the heavens
Reveal the damned contriver of this deed.—
Why lifts she up her arms in sequence thus?   37

MARCUS
I think she means that there were more than one
Confederate in the fact. Ay, more there was;   39
Or else to heaven she heaves them for revenge.

TITUS
Lucius, what book is that she tosseth so?   41

BOY
Grandsire, 'tis Ovid's *Metamorphoses;*
My mother gave it me.

MARCUS   For love of her that's gone,
Perhaps, she culled it from among the rest.

TITUS
Soft, so busily she turns the leaves!
Help her.
What would she find? Lavinia, shall I read?
This is the tragic tale of Philomel,   49
And treats of Tereus' treason and his rape;   50

---

24 but in fury except in madness   **27 go** i.e., come with us. (See l. 11.)
The boy doesn't want to be alone with his mad aunt.   **29 Lucius** i.e.,
young Lucius, the boy   **37 in sequence** one after the other   **39 fact**
deed   **41 tosseth** turns the pages of   **49–50 Philomel, Tereus**
(Cf. 2.3.43, note.)

And rape, I fear, was root of thy annoy.   51

MARCUS

See, brother, see! Note how she quotes the leaves.   52

TITUS

Lavinia, wert thou thus surprised, sweet girl,
Ravished and wronged as Philomela was,
Forced in the ruthless, vast, and gloomy woods?   55
See, see!
Ay, such a place there is, where we did hunt—
O, had we never, never hunted there!—
Patterned by that the poet here describes,   59
By nature made for murders and for rapes.

MARCUS

O, why should nature build so foul a den,
Unless the gods delight in tragedies?

TITUS

Give signs, sweet girl—for here are none but friends—
What Roman lord it was durst do the deed.
Or slunk not Saturnine, as Tarquin erst,   65
That left the camp to sin in Lucrece' bed?

MARCUS

Sit down, sweet niece. Brother, sit down by me.

                     [They sit.]

Apollo, Pallas, Jove, or Mercury   68
Inspire me, that I may this treason find!
My lord, look here. Look here, Lavinia.

        He writes his name with his staff,
           and guides it with feet and mouth.

This sandy plot is plain; guide, if thou canst,   71
This after me. I have writ my name   72
Without the help of any hand at all.
Cursed be that heart that forced us to this shift!   74
Write thou, good niece, and here display at last
What God will have discovered for revenge.   76
Heaven guide thy pen to print thy sorrows plain,

---

51 annoy injury   **52 quotes** examines   **55 vast** desolate   **59 Patterned by that** on the pattern of that which   **65 Or . . . Saturnine** or was it Saturnine who slunk.   **Tarquin** (See notes at 2.1.108 and 3.1.298.)   **erst** once   **68 Pallas** Minerva, Athene   **71 plain** level   **72 after me** following my example   **74 shift** expedient   **76 will** wishes to.   **discovered** revealed, uncovered

That we may know the traitors and the truth!
> *She takes the staff in her mouth, and guides
> it with her stumps, and writes.*
O, do ye read, my lord, what she hath writ?

TITUS
"*Stuprum*. Chiron. Demetrius." 80

MARCUS
What, what! The lustful sons of Tamora
Performers of this heinous, bloody deed?

TITUS
Magni Dominator poli, 83
Tam lentus audis scelera? Tam lentus vides? 84

MARCUS
O, calm thee, gentle lord, although I know
There is enough written upon this earth
To stir a mutiny in the mildest thoughts
And arm the minds of infants to exclaims. 88
My lord, kneel down with me; Lavinia, kneel;
And kneel, sweet boy, the Roman Hector's hope. 90
> [*All kneel.*]
And swear with me—as, with the woeful fere 91
And father of that chaste dishonored dame,
Lord Junius Brutus sware for Lucrece' rape— 93
That we will prosecute by good advice 94
Mortal revenge upon these traitorous Goths,
And see their blood or die with this reproach. 96
> [*They rise.*]

TITUS
'Tis sure enough, an you knew how. 97
But if you hunt these bear whelps, then beware:
The dam will wake an if she wind ye once. 99

---

80 Stuprum violation, rape   **83–84 Magni . . . vides?** Ruler of the
mighty heavens, are you so slow to see and hear the crimes that are
committed? (Derived from Seneca, *Hippolytus,* 671–672.)   **88 exclaims**
exclamations   **90 the Roman Hector's hope** i.e., the hope and future
of Lucius, whose deeds compare with those of Hector in Troy   **91 fere**
spouse, husband   **93 Brutus** (After Sextus Tarquinius had raped
Lucretia—see 2.1.108 and Shakespeare's *Rape of Lucrece*—Junius
Brutus led the Romans to expel the Tarquin dynasty; see also 3.1.298
and *Julius Caesar,* 2.1.53–54.)   **sware** swore   **94 by good advice** after
careful deliberation, planning   **96 reproach** disgrace, infamy   **97 an**
if   **99 dam** mother.   **an if** if.   **wind** scent

She's with the lion deeply still in league,   100
And lulls him whilst she playeth on her back,
And when he sleeps will she do what she list.   102
You are a young huntsman, Marcus. Let alone,   103
And come, I will go get a leaf of brass,   104
And with a gad of steel will write these words,   105
And lay it by. The angry northern wind   106
Will blow these sands like Sibyl's leaves abroad,   107
And where's our lesson then? Boy, what say you?

BOY
I say, my lord, that if I were a man,
Their mother's bedchamber should not be safe   110
For these base bondmen to the yoke of Rome.   111

MARCUS
Ay, that's my boy! Thy father hath full oft
For his ungrateful country done the like.   113

BOY
And, uncle, so will I, an if I live.

TITUS
Come, go with me into mine armory.
Lucius, I'll fit thee, and withal my boy   116
Shall carry from me to the Empress' sons
Presents that I intend to send them both.
Come, come. Thou'lt do my message, wilt thou not?

BOY
Ay, with my dagger in their bosoms, grandsire.

TITUS
No, boy, not so. I'll teach thee another course.
Lavinia, come. Marcus, look to my house.
Lucius and I'll go brave it at the court.   123

---

100 still always   **102 list** choose, please   **103 young** inexperienced.
Let alone let it alone, be wary   **104 leaf** sheet   **105 gad** stylus, spike
106 lay it by i.e., put it in safekeeping, where the words will be preserved, unlike the writing in the sand   **107 Sibyl's leaves** (The Cumaean
Sibyl, an inspired woman, wrote her prophecies on leaves which she
placed at the entrance to her cave. Those wishing to consult them had
to do so before they were scattered by the wind.)   **110–111 Their . . .
Rome** i.e., no place of hiding will be held sacred in my seeking to
destroy these men who cravenly thrive under the yoke of Rome's tyranny   **113 done the like** i.e., fought against tyranny   **116 fit thee** provide you with what you need.   **withal** in addition   **123 brave it** put on
a good show, cut a bold figure

Ay, marry, will we, sir, and we'll be waited on.   124
　　　　Exeunt [Titus, Lavinia, and young Lucius].
MARCUS
　O heavens, can you hear a good man groan
　And not relent, or not compassion him?   126
　Marcus, attend him in his ecstasy,   127
　That hath more scars of sorrow in his heart   128
　Than foemen's marks upon his battered shield,
　But yet so just that he will not revenge.
　Revenge the heavens for old Andronicus!   *Exit.* 131

❖

4.2　　*Enter Aaron, Chiron, and Demetrius, at one*
　　　　door, and at the other door young Lucius and
　　　　another, with a bundle of weapons and verses
　　　　writ upon them.

CHIRON
　Demetrius, here's the son of Lucius.
　He hath some message to deliver us.
AARON
　Ay, some mad message from his mad grandfather.
BOY
　My lords, with all the humbleness I may,
　I greet your honors from Andronicus—
　[*Aside*] And pray the Roman gods confound you both!   6
DEMETRIUS
　Gramercy, lovely Lucius. What's the news?   7
BOY [*Aside*]
　That you are both deciphered, that's the news,   8
　For villains marked with rape.—May it please you,
　My grandsire, well advised, hath sent by me   10

---

124 marry (A mild interjection equivalent to "Indeed!"; originally
an oath, "by the Virgin Mary.")　**be waited on** i.e., demand attention
126 compassion have compassion for　**127 ecstasy** madness　**128 That**
who　**131 Revenge the heavens** may the heavens take revenge

4.2. Location: Rome. The Emperor's palace.
s.d. another (Presumably an attendant of Lucius, bearing the weapons
and verses; see l. 16, stage direction.)　**6 confound** destroy　**7 Gramercy**
many thanks　**8 deciphered** detected　**10 well advised** having considered carefully

The goodliest weapons of his armory
To gratify your honorable youth,   12
The hope of Rome; for so he bid me say.
And so I do, and with his gifts present
Your lordships, that, whenever you have need,
You may be armèd and appointed well.   16
           [His attendant presents the bundle.]
And so I leave you both—*[Aside]* like bloody villains.
                 Exit [with attendant].

DEMETRIUS
What's here? A scroll, and written round about?   19
Let's see:
[Reads.] "*Integer vitae, scelerisque purus,*   20
       Non eget Mauri iaculis, nec arcu."   21

CHIRON
O, 'tis a verse in Horace; I know it well.
I read it in the grammar long ago.   23

AARON
Ay, just; a verse in Horace; right, you have it.   24
[Aside.] Now, what a thing it is to be an ass!
Here's no sound jest! The old man hath found their guilt,   26
And sends them weapons wrapped about with lines
That wound, beyond their feeling, to the quick.   28
But were our witty empress well afoot,   29
She would applaud Andronicus' conceit.   30
But let her rest in her unrest awhile.—   31
And now, young lords, was 't not a happy star
Led us to Rome, strangers, and more than so,
Captives, to be advancèd to this height?
It did me good before the palace gate

---

12 gratify grace, please **16 appointed** equipped **19 round about** all
around **20–21 Integer . . . arcu** (The opening lines of perhaps the best
known of the Odes of Horace, l. 22: "He who is spotless in life and free
of crime needs not the Moorish bow and arrow.") **23 grammar** i.e.,
Latin grammar book. (William Lilly's grammar book, containing this
passage, was widely used in Elizabethan England.) **24 just** precisely
26 Here's no sound jest (Said ironically to mean its opposite: Here's a
splendid joke indeed.) **28 beyond their feeling** i.e., far beyond the
capacity of Demetrius and Chiron to be sensitive to the injury. **to the
quick** i.e., to the very life **29 witty** clever. **afoot** up and about, i.e., not
in childbed (as we soon learn) **30 conceit** design **31 her unrest** i.e.,
her labor of delivery

To brave the tribune in his brother's hearing.   36

DEMETRIUS
But me more good to see so great a lord
Basely insinuate and send us gifts.   38

AARON
Had he not reason, Lord Demetrius?
Did you not use his daughter very friendly?

DEMETRIUS
I would we had a thousand Roman dames
At such a bay, by turn to serve our lust.   42

CHIRON
A charitable wish, and full of love!

AARON
Here lacks but your mother for to say amen.

CHIRON
And that would she, for twenty thousand more.   45

DEMETRIUS
Come, let us go and pray to all the gods
For our belovèd mother in her pains.   47

AARON
Pray to the devils. The gods have given us over.   48
                              Trumpets sound [within].

DEMETRIUS
Why do the Emperor's trumpets flourish thus?

CHIRON
Belike for joy the Emperor hath a son.   50

DEMETRIUS
Soft, who comes here?

        *Enter Nurse, with a blackamoor child [in her
        arms].*

NURSE   Good morrow, lords.
O, tell me, did you see Aaron the Moor?

---

36 To . . . hearing i.e., to taunt Marcus in Titus' presence   **38 insinuate**
ingratiate himself by flattery   **42 At such a bay** cornered thus (as in
hunting)   **45 for . . . more** i.e., to pray for 20,000 more Roman *dames*,
or ladies, to be ravished   **47 pains** i.e., labor pains. (Tamora is being
delivered of a child sired by Aaron; see ll. 29–31 above.)   **48 Pray . . .
over** (Said perhaps to Demetrius and Chiron, or as a mocking aside.)
50 Belike probably

AARON

Well, more or less, or ne'er a whit at all,   53
Here Aaron is; and what with Aaron now?   54

NURSE

O gentle Aaron, we are all undone!
Now help, or woe betide thee evermore!

AARON

Why, what a caterwauling dost thou keep!   57
What dost thou wrap and fumble in thy arms?

NURSE

O, that which I would hide from heaven's eye,
Our empress' shame and stately Rome's disgrace!
She is delivered, lords, she is delivered.

AARON   To whom?   62

NURSE   I mean she is brought abed.

AARON

Well, God give her good rest! What hath he sent her?   64

NURSE   A devil.

AARON

Why, then she is the devil's dam. A joyful issue!   66

NURSE

A joyless, dismal, black, and sorrowful issue!   67
Here is the babe, as loathsome as a toad
Amongst the fair-faced breeders of our clime.
The Empress sends it thee, thy stamp, thy seal,   70
And bids thee christen it with thy dagger's point.

AARON

Zounds, ye whore, is black so base a hue?   72
[*To the child.*] Sweet blowze, you are a beauteous
    blossom, sure.   73

DEMETRIUS   Villain, what hast thou done?

53–54 more . . . Aaron is (Punning on *more* and *Moor*, l. 52, with sardonic humor, Aaron suggests that whether he is addressed as Aaron the Great or the Less or by no title at all, he is who he is.) **57 keep** keep up
62 To whom (Aaron plays on *delivered*, l. 61, in the sense of "handed over or transferred to another person," though he of course knows that the Nurse means "delivered of a child.") **64 God . . . rest** (Again Aaron jestingly pretends to misinterpret *brought abed*, l. 63, in its literal sense.)
66 dam mother. **issue** result **67 issue** i.e., child **70 thy stamp, thy seal** i.e., bearing your imprint **72 Zounds** by His (Christ's) wounds
73 blowze red-cheeked one. (Usually addressed to a wench or slattern; here an affectionately abusive term for the child.)

AARON   That which thou canst not undo.
CHIRON   Thou hast undone our mother.
AARON   Villain, I have done thy mother.   77
DEMETRIUS
   And therein, hellish dog, thou hast undone her.
   Woe to her chance, and damned her loathèd choice!   79
   Accurst the offspring of so foul a fiend!   80
CHIRON   It shall not live.
AARON   It shall not die.
NURSE
   Aaron, it must. The mother wills it so.
AARON
   What, must it, Nurse? Then let no man but I
   Do execution on my flesh and blood.
DEMETRIUS
   I'll broach the tadpole on my rapier's point.   86
   Nurse, give it me. My sword shall soon dispatch it.
AARON [*Taking the child and drawing his sword*]
   Sooner this sword shall plow thy bowels up.
   Stay, murderous villains, will you kill your brother?
   Now, by the burning tapers of the sky
   That shone so brightly when this boy was got,   91
   He dies upon my scimitar's sharp point
   That touches this my firstborn son and heir!
   I tell you, younglings, not Enceladus   94
   With all his threatening band of Typhon's brood,   95
   Nor great Alcides, nor the god of war   96
   Shall seize this prey out of his father's hands.
   What, what, ye sanguine, shallow-hearted boys!   98
   Ye white-limed walls! Ye alehouse painted signs!   99
   Coal black is better than another hue
   In that it scorns to bear another hue;

---

77 done i.e., had sexual intercourse with (playing on *undone* in the previous line)   **79 chance** luck.   **damned** damned be   **80 Accurst** accursed be   **86 broach** impale   **91 got** begotten   **94 Enceladus** one of the giants who rose against the gods and were defeated by them; Enceladus was buried under Mount Etna in Sicily   **95 Typhon** a terrible monster who attacked the gods and was flung into Tartarus   **96 Alcides** Hercules, a descendant of Alcaeus   **98 sanguine** red-cheeked (as distinguished from black-complexioned)   **99 white-limed** whitewashed. (The image is of a fair exterior hiding darkness within.)   **alehouse painted signs** i.e., cheap painted imitations of men

For all the water in the ocean
Can never turn the swan's black legs to white,
Although she lave them hourly in the flood.   104
Tell the Empress from me, I am of age
To keep mine own, excuse it how she can.   106

DEMETRIUS
Wilt thou betray thy noble mistress thus?

AARON
My mistress is my mistress, this myself,   108
The vigor and the picture of my youth.
This before all the world do I prefer;
This maugre all the world will I keep safe,   111
Or some of you shall smoke for it in Rome.   112

DEMETRIUS
By this our mother is forever shamed.

CHIRON
Rome will despise her for this foul escape.   114

NURSE
The Emperor in his rage will doom her death.

CHIRON
I blush to think upon this ignomy.   116

AARON
Why, there's the privilege your beauty bears.   117
Fie, treacherous hue, that will betray with blushing
The close enacts and counsels of thy heart!   119
Here's a young lad framed of another leer.   120
Look how the black slave smiles upon the father,
As who should say, "Old lad, I am thine own."   122
He is your brother, lords, sensibly fed   123
Of that self blood that first gave life to you,   124
And from that womb where you imprisoned were

---

104 lave wash. **flood** stream   **106 excuse . . . can** i.e., no matter how she may wish to explain away the circumstance by getting rid of the evidence   **108 this myself** i.e., this child is a part of myself   **111 maugre** in spite of   **112 smoke** i.e., suffer. (The metaphor is from burning at the stake.)   **114 escape** escapade, outrageous transgression   **116 ignomy** ignominy, shame   **117 Why . . . bears** i.e., blushing is one of the benefits of your fair complexion. (Said ironically; Aaron prefers a hue that cannot incriminate itself.)   **119 close enacts** secret purposes   **120 framed** made. **leer** countenance, complexion   **122 As . . . say** as if saying, as if one might say   **123 sensibly** manifestly, or as a creature endowed with feeling (?)   **124 Of** by. **self** same

He is enfranchisèd and come to light.
Nay, he is your brother by the surer side,   127
Although my seal be stampèd in his face.   128

NURSE
Aaron, what shall I say unto the Empress?

DEMETRIUS
Advise thee, Aaron, what is to be done,   130
And we will all subscribe to thy advice.   131
Save thou the child, so we may all be safe.   132

AARON
Then sit we down, and let us all consult.
My son and I will have the wind of you;   134
Keep there. Now talk at pleasure of your safety.
                                        [*They sit.*]

DEMETRIUS [*To the Nurse*]
How many women saw this child of his?

AARON
Why, so, brave lords! When we join in league
I am a lamb; but if you brave the Moor,
The chafèd boar, the mountain lioness,   139
The ocean swells not so as Aaron storms.
[*To the Nurse.*] But say again, how many saw the child?

NURSE
Cornelia the midwife and myself,
And no one else but the delivered Empress.

AARON
The Empress, the midwife, and yourself.
Two may keep counsel when the third's away.
Go to the Empress, tell her this I said.   *He kills her.*
Wheak, wheak!—   147
So cries a pig preparèd to the spit.   148

DEMETRIUS
What mean'st thou, Aaron? Wherefore didst thou this?

AARON
O Lord, sir, 'tis a deed of policy.   150

---

127 surer i.e., mother's   **128 seal be stampèd** (See line 70 above; the child bears the imprint of the father in his looks.)   **130 Advise thee** consider   **131 subscribe** agree   **132 so** so long as   **134 have . . . you** i.e., remain at a safe distance and stay downwind of you (as in hunting, so as not to be scented by the game)   **139 chafèd** enraged   **147 Wheak** (Aaron mimics her dying cry.)   **148 preparèd to the spit** i.e., being spitted for roasting   **150 policy** prudent action

Shall she live to betray this guilt of ours,
A long-tongued babbling gossip? No, lords, no.
And now be it known to you my full intent.
Not far, one Muliteus my countryman   154
His wife but yesternight was brought to bed;   155
His child is like to her, fair as you are.
Go pack with him, and give the mother gold,   157
And tell them both the circumstance of all,   158
And how by this their child shall be advanced
And be receivèd for the Emperor's heir,
And substituted in the place of mine,
To calm this tempest whirling in the court;
And let the Emperor dandle him for his own.
Hark ye, lords, you see I have given her physic,   164
                    [*Pointing to the Nurse*]
And you must needs bestow her funeral.   165
The fields are near, and you are gallant grooms.   166
This done, see that you take no longer days,   167
But send the midwife presently to me.   168
The midwife and the nurse well made away,
Then let the ladies tattle what they please.

CHIRON
Aaron, I see thou wilt not trust the air
With secrets.

DEMETRIUS   For this care of Tamora,
Herself and hers are highly bound to thee.
                Exeunt [Demetrius and Chiron, bearing off
                        the Nurse's body].

AARON
Now to the Goths, as swift as swallow flies,
There to dispose this treasure in mine arms   175
And secretly to greet the Empress' friends.
Come on, you thick-lipped slave, I'll bear you hence,
For it is you that puts us to our shifts.   178
I'll make you feed on berries and on roots,
And feed on curds and whey, and suck the goat,

154–155 one . . . wife the wife of a certain Muliteus, a fellow countryman of mine   157 pack make a deal   158 the circumstance of all
the full details   164 physic medicine   165 bestow provide, furnish
166 grooms fellows   167 days time   168 presently at once   175 dispose
dispose of   178 shifts stratagems, tricks

And cabin in a cave, and bring you up   181
To be a warrior and command a camp.

> *Exit* [*with the child*].

❋

4.3   *Enter Titus, old Marcus, [his son Publius,]*
young Lucius, and other gentlemen
[Sempronius, Caius,] with bows; and Titus
bears the arrows with letters on the ends of
them.

TITUS

Come, Marcus, come. Kinsmen, this is the way.
Sir boy, let me see your archery.
Look ye draw home enough, and 'tis there straight.   3
Terras Astraea reliquit;   4
Be you remembered, Marcus, she's gone, she's fled.   5
Sirs, take you to your tools. You, cousins, shall
Go sound the ocean and cast your nets;
Happily you may catch her in the sea.   8
Yet there's as little justice as at land.   9
No; Publius and Sempronius, you must do it;
'Tis you must dig with mattock and with spade,
And pierce the inmost center of the earth.
Then, when you come to Pluto's region,   13
I pray you, deliver him this petition.
Tell him it is for justice and for aid,
And that it comes from old Andronicus,
Shaken with sorrows in ungrateful Rome.
Ah, Rome! Well, well, I made thee miserable
What time I threw the people's suffrages   19
On him that thus doth tyrannize o'er me.
Go, get you gone, and pray be careful all,

---

181 cabin lodge

4.3. Location: Rome. A public place.
3 home to the full extent (of the bow)   **4 Terras Astraea reliquit** Astraea
(the goddess of justice) has abandoned the earth. (From Ovid, *Metamor-*
phoses, 1.150.)   **5 Be you remembered** remember   **8 Happily** haply,
perhaps   **9 there's** i.e., there in the sea there is   **13 Pluto's region**
the underworld, ruled over by Pluto   **19 What time** when

And leave you not a man-of-war unsearched.
This wicked emperor may have shipped her hence, 23
And, kinsmen, then we may go pipe for justice. 24

MARCUS
O Publius, is not this a heavy case, 25
To see thy noble uncle thus distract? 26

PUBLIUS
Therefore, my lords, it highly us concerns
By day and night t' attend him carefully,
And feed his humor kindly as we may, 29
Till time beget some careful remedy. 30

MARCUS
Kinsmen, his sorrows are past remedy. 31
Join with the Goths, and with revengeful war
Take wreak on Rome for this ingratitude, 33
And vengeance on the traitor Saturnine.

TITUS
Publius, how now? How now, my masters?
What, have you met with her? 36

PUBLIUS
No, my good lord, but Pluto sends you word,
If you will have Revenge from hell, you shall.
Marry, for Justice, she is so employed, 39
He thinks, with Jove in heaven, or somewhere else,
So that perforce you must needs stay a time. 41

TITUS
He doth me wrong to feed me with delays.
I'll dive into the burning lake below 43
And pull her out of Acheron by the heels. 44
Marcus, we are but shrubs, no cedars we,
No big-boned men framed of the Cyclops' size, 46

---

23 her i.e., Justice, the goddess Astraea. (In his madness, Titus imagines that Saturninus may ship Astraea out of the country in an armed naval vessel, a *man-of-war*.) **24 pipe** whistle, i.e., look in vain **25 heavy case** sad situation **26 distract** distracted, crazed **29 feed his humor** humor him **30 careful** showing and requiring care **31 remedy** (In the first quarto, this word is followed by a catch word *But* at the foot of the page that is not repeated in the first line of the next page, possibly suggesting an omission in the text.) **33 wreak** vengeance **36 her** i.e., Justice **39 for** as for **41 stay a time** wait awhile **43 burning lake** i.e., Phlegethon, the burning river of the underworld **44 Acheron** a river in the underworld **46 Cyclops** one-eyed giants in Homer's *Odyssey* (9)

But metal, Marcus, steel to the very back,
Yet wrung with wrongs more than our backs can bear.
And sith there's no justice in earth nor hell,   49
We will solicit heaven and move the gods
To send down Justice for to wreak our wrongs.   51
Come, to this gear. You are a good archer, Marcus.   52
                              He gives them the arrows.
"*Ad Jovem*," that's for you; here, "*Ad Apollinem*";   53
"*Ad Martem*," that's for myself;   54
Here, boy, "to Pallas"; here, "to Mercury";   55
"To Saturn," Caius—not "to Saturnine"!
You were as good to shoot against the wind.   57
To it, boy! Marcus, loose when I bid.   58
Of my word, I have written to effect;   59
There's not a god left unsolicited.

MARCUS
Kinsmen, shoot all your shafts into the court.
We will afflict the Emperor in his pride.

TITUS
Now, masters, draw. [*They shoot.*] O, well said, Lucius!   63
Good boy, in Virgo's lap! Give it Pallas.   64

MARCUS
My lord, I aim a mile beyond the moon;   65
Your letter is with Jupiter by this.

TITUS   Ha, ha!
Publius, Publius, what hast thou done?
See, see, thou hast shot off one of Taurus' horns.   69

MARCUS
This was the sport, my lord: when Publius shot,
The Bull, being galled, gave Aries such a knock   71

---

49 sith since   **51 for to** to   **52 gear** business   **53–54 Ad Jovem, Ad
Apollinem, Ad Martem** to Jove, to Apollo, to Mars   **55 Pallas** Minerva,
Athene   **57 You . . . wind** you would do as much good shooting against
the wind (as you would in appealing to Saturninus)   **58 loose** let fly,
discharge   **59 Of** on   **63 said** done   **64 in Virgo's lap** in the constella-
tion of the Virgin (the zodiacal sign representing Astraea, having fled
from earth).   **Give it Pallas** i.e., shoot the arrow labeled "Pallas" there
65 a mile . . . moon (Marcus' literal meaning is intended to humor Titus'
madness, but his expression also means "wild conjecture, far wide of
the mark," thus commenting on the madness of their proceedings.)
69, 71 Taurus, Aries the Bull, the Ram; signs of the zodiac   **71 galled**
slightly wounded

That down fell both the Ram's horns in the court;   72
And who should find them but the Empress' villain?   73
She laughed, and told the Moor he should not choose   74
But give them to his master for a present.   75

TITUS

Why, there it goes. God give his lordship joy!   76

Enter the Clown, with a basket, and two pigeons
in it.

News, news from heaven! Marcus, the post is come.—
Sirrah, what tidings? Have you any letters?
Shall I have justice? What says Jupiter?

CLOWN   Ho, the gibbet maker? He says that he hath   80
taken them down again, for the man must not be   81
hanged till the next week.

TITUS   But what says Jupiter, I ask thee?

CLOWN   Alas, sir, I know not Jupiter. I never drank with
him in all my life.

TITUS   Why, villain, art not thou the carrier?   86

CLOWN   Ay, of my pigeons, sir; nothing else.

TITUS   Why, didst thou not come from heaven?

CLOWN   From heaven! Alas, sir, I never came there. God
forbid I should be so bold to press to heaven in my
young days. Why, I am going with my pigeons to the
tribunal plebs, to take up a matter of brawl betwixt my   92
uncle and one of the Emperal's men.   93

MARCUS [*To Titus*]   Why, sir, that is as fit as can be to serve
for your oration; and let him deliver the pigeons to the
Emperor from you.

TITUS [*To Clown*]

Sirrah, come hither. Make no more ado,   97

72 horns i.e., signs of being a cuckold, bestowed by Aaron on the Emperor   **73 villain** i.e., Aaron, both servant and villain in the modern sense   **74–75 should . . . But** must   **76 there it goes** (A hunting cry of encouragement.)   **s.d. Clown** rustic   **80 gibbet maker** (The Clown seems to have heard "Jupiter" as "gibbeter.")   **81 them** i.e., the gallows.   **must not be** is not to be   **86 carrier** postman. (But the Clown answers in the sense of "one who carries things.")   **92 tribunal plebs** i.e., *tribunus plebis*, tribune of the plebs.   **take up** settle amicably **93 Emperal's** (Malapropism for *emperor's*.)   **97 Sirrah** (In the early texts, this line is preceded by four lines that appear to be a first draft of ll. 102–103: "TITUS Tell me, can you deliver an oration to the Emperor with a grace? CLOWN Nay, truly, sir, I could never say grace in all my life.")

But give your pigeons to the Emperor.
By me thou shalt have justice at his hands.
Hold, hold; meanwhile here's money for thy charges.   100
                              [*He gives money.*]
Give me pen and ink.
Sirrah, can you with a grace deliver up a supplication?
CLOWN   Ay, sir.
TITUS [*Writing and handing him a supplication*]   Then
  here is a supplication for you. And when you come to
  him, at the first approach you must kneel, then kiss
  his foot, then deliver up your pigeons, and then look
  for your reward. I'll be at hand, sir; see you do it
  bravely.   109
CLOWN   I warrant you, sir. Let me alone.   110
TITUS
  Sirrah, hast thou a knife? Come, let me see it.
             [*He takes the knife and gives it to Marcus.*]
  Here, Marcus, fold it in the oration,
  For thou hast made it like an humble suppliant.—   113
  And when thou hast given it to the Emperor,
  Knock at my door and tell me what he says.
CLOWN   God be with you, sir. I will.   *Exit.*
TITUS   Come, Marcus, let us go. Publius, follow me.
                                              Exeunt.

✤

4.4   *Enter Emperor [Saturninus] and Empress
        [Tamora] and her two sons [and others,
        including guards]. The Emperor brings the
        arrows in his hand that Titus shot at him. [The
        Emperor and Empress sit.]*

SATURNINUS
  Why, lords, what wrongs are these! Was ever seen
  An emperor in Rome thus overborne,   2

---

100 charges expenses **109 bravely** handsomely, stylishly **110 Let me
alone** leave it to me **113 For . . . suppliant** (A puzzling and perhaps
corrupt line. Titus may mean that Marcus has made the supplication
seem humble enough, even though it conceals a knife.)

4.4. Location: Rome. Before or in the palace.
2 overborne oppressed

Troubled, confronted thus, and, for the extent   3
Of equal justice, used in such contempt?
My lords, you know, as know the mightful gods,
However these disturbers of our peace
Buzz in the people's ears, there naught hath passed
But even with law against the willful sons   8
Of old Andronicus. And what an if
His sorrows have so overwhelmed his wits?
Shall we be thus afflicted in his wreaks,   11
His fits, his frenzy, and his bitterness?
And now he writes to heaven for his redress.
See, here's "to Jove," and this "to Mercury,"
This "to Apollo," this to the god of war—
Sweet scrolls to fly about the streets of Rome!
What's this but libeling against the Senate
And blazoning our unjustice everywhere?   18
A goodly humor, is it not, my lords?   19
As who would say, in Rome no justice were.
But if I live, his feignèd ecstasies   21
Shall be no shelter to these outrages;
But he and his shall know that justice lives   23
In Saturninus' health, whom, if he sleep,   24
He'll so awake as he in fury shall   25
Cut off the proud'st conspirator that lives.

TAMORA
My gracious lord, my lovely Saturnine,
Lord of my life, commander of my thoughts,
Calm thee, and bear the faults of Titus' age,
Th' effects of sorrow for his valiant sons,
Whose loss hath pierced him deep and scarred his heart;
And rather comfort his distressèd plight
Than prosecute the meanest or the best   33
For these contempts. [*Aside.*] Why, thus it shall become

---

3 extent exercise   **8 even** conformable   **11 wreaks** revengeful acts   **18 blazoning** making public   **19 humor** whim, caprice   **21 ecstasies** fits of madness   **23 his** i.e., the Andronici   **23–25 justice . . . shall** i.e., justice in Rome depends on Saturninus' thriving, and, if justice be asleep, Saturninus will so rouse him to fury that he will. (The use of male pronouns for justice is unusual; see 4.3.4–5 and 23. Possibly the text should read *she* in ll. 24–25, or the pronouns may refer to Saturninus.)   **33 the meanest or the best** those of low or high station

High-witted Tamora to gloze with all.   35
But, Titus, I have touched thee to the quick;
Thy lifeblood out, if Aaron now be wise,   37
Then is all safe, the anchor in the port.

    Enter Clown.

How now, good fellow, wouldst thou speak with us?
CLOWN   Yea, forsooth, an your mistress-ship be emperial.
TAMORA   Empress I am, but yonder sits the Emperor.
CLOWN   'Tis he. [*He kneels.*] God and Saint Stephen give
  you good e'en. I have brought you a letter and a couple   43
  of pigeons here.   *He [Saturninus] reads the letter.*
SATURNINUS
Go, take him away and hang him presently.   45
CLOWN   How much money must I have?   46
TAMORA   Come, sirrah, you must be hanged.
CLOWN   Hanged! By 'r Lady, then I have brought up a   48
  neck to a fair end.   *Exit [guarded].*
SATURNINUS
Despiteful and intolerable wrongs!
Shall I endure this monstrous villainy?
I know from whence this same device proceeds.
May this be borne?—as if his traitorous sons,
That died by law for murder of our brother,
Have by my means been butchered wrongfully!
Go, drag the villain hither by the hair.
Nor age nor honor shall shape privilege.   57
For this proud mock I'll be thy slaughterman,
Sly frantic wretch, that holp'st to make me great   59
In hope thyself should govern Rome and me.   60

    Enter nuntius, Aemilius.

What news with thee, Aemilius?
AEMILIUS
Arm, my lords! Rome never had more cause.

---

35 High-witted clever.   **gloze** deceive with smooth talk   **37 Thy lifeblood out** once your lifeblood is spilled.   **wise** i.e., wise enough to keep
silent about the baby   **43 good e'en** good afternoon or evening   **45 presently** at once   **46 must I** am I to   **48 By 'r Lady** by Our Lady, the Virgin Mary   **57 shape privilege** make for exemption   **59 holp'st** helped
60 s.d. nuntius messenger

The Goths have gathered head, and with a power   63
Of high-resolvèd men bent to the spoil   64
They hither march amain under conduct   65
Of Lucius, son to old Andronicus,
Who threats in course of this revenge to do
As much as ever Coriolanus did.   68

SATURNINUS
Is warlike Lucius general of the Goths?
These tidings nip me, and I hang the head
As flowers with frost or grass beat down with storms.
Ay, now begins our sorrows to approach.
'Tis he the common people love so much;
Myself hath often heard them say,
When I have walkèd like a private man,   75
That Lucius' banishment was wrongfully,   76
And they have wished that Lucius were their emperor.

TAMORA
Why should you fear? Is not your city strong?

SATURNINUS
Ay, but the citizens favor Lucius
And will revolt from me to succor him.

TAMORA
King, be thy thoughts imperious, like thy name.   81
Is the sun dimmed, that gnats do fly in it?
The eagle suffers little birds to sing
And is not careful what they mean thereby,   84
Knowing that with the shadow of his wings
He can at pleasure stint their melody;   86
Even so mayst thou the giddy men of Rome.   87
Then cheer thy spirit, for know, thou Emperor,
I will enchant the old Andronicus
With words more sweet and yet more dangerous
Than baits to fish or honey-stalks to sheep,   91

---

63 gathered head raised an army.   **power** armed force   **64 bent to the
spoil** intent on plunder   **65 amain** forcefully, swiftly.   **conduct** command   **68 Coriolanus** an early Roman hero turned enemy of Rome,
about whom Shakespeare wrote one of his later tragedies   **75 walkèd
. . . man** i.e., gone in disguise among the commoners, like Henry V or
the Duke in *Measure for Measure*   **76 wrongfully** wrongfully imposed
81 imperious imperial   **84 careful** full of concern   **86 stint** stop
87 giddy changeable in opinion and allegiance   **91 honey-stalks** clover.
(Too much clover can make sheep ill.)

Whenas the one is wounded with the bait,   92
The other rotted with delicious feed.   93

SATURNINUS
But he will not entreat his son for us.

TAMORA
If Tamora entreat him, then he will;
For I can smooth and fill his agèd ears   96
With golden promises, that were his heart
Almost impregnable, his old ears deaf,
Yet should both ear and heart obey my tongue.
[*To Aemilius.*] Go thou before to be our ambassador.
Say that the Emperor requests a parley
Of warlike Lucius, and appoint the meeting   102
Even at his father's house, the old Andronicus.

SATURNINUS
Aemilius, do this message honorably,
And if he stand on hostage for his safety,   105
Bid him demand what pledge will please him best.   106

AEMILIUS
Your bidding shall I do effectually.   *Exit.*

TAMORA
Now will I to that old Andronicus
And temper him with all the art I have   109
To pluck proud Lucius from the warlike Goths.
And now, sweet Emperor, be blithe again
And bury all thy fear in my devices.

SATURNINUS
Then go successantly, and plead to him.   *Exeunt.* 113

❖

92 **Whenas** when   93 **rotted** afflicted by the rot, a liver disease in sheep
96 **smooth** flatter   102 **Of** with   105 **stand** insist   106 **demand** request
109 **temper** work upon   113 **successantly** at once

5.1   [*Flourish.*] *Enter Lucius with an army of Goths, with drums and soldiers.*

LUCIUS
Approvèd warriors and my faithful friends,   1
I have receivèd letters from great Rome   2
Which signifies what hate they bear their emperor
And how desirous of our sight they are.
Therefore, great lords, be as your titles witness,
Imperious, and impatient of your wrongs,
And wherein Rome hath done you any scath   7
Let him make treble satisfaction.

A GOTH
Brave slip, sprung from the great Andronicus,   9
Whose name was once our terror, now our comfort,
Whose high exploits and honorable deeds
Ingrateful Rome requites with foul contempt,
Be bold in us. We'll follow where thou lead'st,   13
Like stinging bees in hottest summer's day
Led by their master to the flowered fields,   15
And be avenged on cursèd Tamora.   16

ALL THE GOTHS
And as he saith, so say we all with him.

LUCIUS
I humbly thank him, and I thank you all.
But who comes here, led by a lusty Goth?   19

Enter a Goth, leading of Aaron with his child in his arms.

ANOTHER GOTH
Renownèd Lucius, from our troops I strayed
To gaze upon a ruinous monastery,   21
And as I earnestly did fix mine eye
Upon the wasted building, suddenly   23

5.1. Location: Near Rome.
s.d. drums drummers   **1 Approvèd** put to proof, tried   **2 letters** a letter
7 scath injury   **9 slip** offspring, scion   **13 bold** confident   **15 their master** (Bees were thought to be led by a king bee.)   **16 cursèd Tamora** (The play permits us to speculate as to why Tamora was not popular in her own country.)   **19 lusty** valiant   **21 ruinous** decayed   **23 wasted** ruined

I heard a child cry underneath a wall.
I made unto the noise, when soon I heard   25
The crying babe controlled with this discourse: 26
"Peace, tawny slave, half me and half thy dam!   27
Did not thy hue bewray whose brat thou art,   28
Had nature lent thee but thy mother's look,
Villain, thou mightst have been an emperor.
But where the bull and cow are both milk white,
They never do beget a coal black calf.
Peace, villain, peace!"—even thus he rates the babe—   33
"For I must bear thee to a trusty Goth,
Who, when he knows thou art the Empress' babe,
Will hold thee dearly for thy mother's sake."
With this, my weapon drawn, I rushed upon him,
Surprised him suddenly, and brought him hither
To use as you think needful of the man.   39

LUCIUS
    O worthy Goth, this is the incarnate devil
    That robbed Andronicus of his good hand!
    This is the pearl that pleased your empress' eye,
    And here's the base fruit of her burning lust.—   43
    Say, walleyed slave, whither wouldst thou convey   44
    This growing image of thy fiendlike face?   45
    Why dost not speak? What, deaf? Not a word?
    A halter, soldiers! Hang him on this tree,
    And by his side his fruit of bastardy.

AARON
    Touch not the boy. He is of royal blood.

LUCIUS
    Too like the sire for ever being good.   50
    First hang the child, that he may see it sprawl—
    A sight to vex the father's soul withal.
    Get me a ladder.
            [*A ladder is brought, which Aaron is made
                            to ascend.*]
AARON   Lucius, save the child,

25 **made unto** approached   26 **controlled** calmed   27 **slave** (Used
affectionately; as also in *brat*, l. 28, and *villain*, ll. 30 and 33.)   **dam**
mother   28 **bewray** reveal   33 **rates** chides   39 **use . . . man** deal with
the man as you think fit   43 **fruit** i.e., the baby   44 **walleyed** glaring
45 **image** likeness   50 **for ever being** ever to be

And bear it from me to the Empress.
If thou do this, I'll show thee wondrous things
That highly may advantage thee to hear.
If thou wilt not, befall what may befall,
I'll speak no more but "Vengeance rot you all!"

LUCIUS

Say on. An if it please me which thou speak'st,   59
Thy child shall live, and I will see it nourished.   60

AARON

An if it please thee! Why, assure thee, Lucius,
'Twill vex thy soul to hear what I shall speak;
For I must talk of murders, rapes, and massacres,
Acts of black night, abominable deeds,
Complots of mischief, treason, villainies,   65
Ruthful to hear, yet piteously performed.   66
And this shall all be buried in my death
Unless thou swear to me my child shall live.

LUCIUS

Tell on thy mind. I say thy child shall live.

AARON

Swear that he shall, and then I will begin.

LUCIUS

Who should I swear by? Thou believest no god.
That granted, how canst thou believe an oath?

AARON

What if I do not? As, indeed, I do not.
Yet, for I know thou art religious   74
And hast a thing within thee callèd conscience,
With twenty popish tricks and ceremonies
Which I have seen thee careful to observe,
Therefore I urge thy oath. For that I know   78
An idiot holds his bauble for a god   79
And keeps the oath which by that god he swears,
To that I'll urge him. Therefore thou shalt vow
By that same god, what god soe'er it be,
That thou adorest and hast in reverence,

---

59 An if if   **60 nourished** cared for   **65 Complots** conspiracies
66 Ruthful lamentable, pitiable.   **piteously** in a way to excite pity
74 for because   **78 urge** insist on.   **For that** because   **79 bauble**
fool's stick

To save my boy, to nourish and bring him up,
Or else I will discover naught to thee.

LUCIUS

Even by my god I swear to thee I will.

AARON

First know thou, I begot him on the Empress.

LUCIUS

O most insatiate and luxurious woman!   88

AARON

Tut, Lucius, this was but a deed of charity
To that which thou shalt hear of me anon.   90
'Twas her two sons that murdered Bassianus;
They cut thy sister's tongue, and ravished her,
And cut her hands, and trimmed her as thou sawest.

LUCIUS

O detestable villain! Call'st thou that trimming?

AARON

Why, she was washed and cut and trimmed, and 'twas
Trim sport for them which had the doing of it.   96

LUCIUS

O barbarous, beastly villains, like thyself!

AARON

Indeed, I was their tutor to instruct them.
That codding spirit had they from their mother,   99
As sure a card as ever won the set;   100
That bloody mind I think they learned of me,
As true a dog as ever fought at head.   102
Well, let my deeds be witness of my worth.
I trained thy brethren to that guileful hole   104
Where the dead corpse of Bassianus lay;
I wrote the letter that thy father found,
And hid the gold within that letter mentioned,
Confederate with the Queen and her two sons;
And what not done, that thou hast cause to rue,
Wherein I had no stroke of mischief in it?

---

88 luxurious lecherous   **90 To** compared to   **96 Trim** fine (with a play
on *trimmed*, ll. 93–95)   **99 codding** lustful   **100 set** game   **102 as . . .
head** as ever went for the bear's head (in bearbaiting)   **104 trained**
lured

I played the cheater for thy father's hand,   111
And when I had it, drew myself apart
And almost broke my heart with extreme laughter.
I pried me through the crevice of a wall   114
When, for his hand, he had his two sons' heads,
Beheld his tears, and laughed so heartily
That both mine eyes were rainy like to his;
And when I told the Empress of this sport,
She swoonèd almost at my pleasing tale,
And for my tidings gave me twenty kisses.

A GOTH
What, canst thou say all this and never blush?

AARON
Ay, like a black dog, as the saying is.   122

LUCIUS
Art thou not sorry for these heinous deeds?

AARON
Ay, that I had not done a thousand more.
Even now I curse the day—and yet, I think,
Few come within the compass of my curse—
Wherein I did not some notorious ill,
As kill a man, or else devise his death,
Ravish a maid, or plot the way to do it,
Accuse some innocent and forswear myself,
Set deadly enmity between two friends,
Make poor men's cattle break their necks,
Set fire on barns and haystacks in the night
And bid the owners quench them with their tears.
Oft have I digged up dead men from their graves
And set them upright at their dear friends' door,
Even when their sorrows almost was forgot,
And on their skins, as on the bark of trees,
Have with my knife carvèd in Roman letters,
"Let not your sorrow die, though I am dead."

---

111 cheater (1) deceiver (2) escheater, one designated to take care of
property forfeited to the crown   **114 pried me** peered   **122 like a black
dog** ("To blush like a black dog" is a proverb with ironic meaning, as
here; at 4.2.117–119, Aaron is proud that, being black, he cannot blush.)

But I have done a thousand dreadful things   141
As willingly as one would kill a fly,
And nothing grieves me heartily indeed
But that I cannot do ten thousand more.

LUCIUS
Bring down the devil, for he must not die
So sweet a death as hanging presently.   146
                    [*Aaron is brought down.*]

AARON
If there be devils, would I were a devil,
To live and burn in everlasting fire,
So I might have your company in hell
But to torment you with my bitter tongue!

LUCIUS
Sirs, stop his mouth, and let him speak no more.
                    [*Aaron is gagged.*]

    Enter Aemilius.

A GOTH
My lord, there is a messenger from Rome
Desires to be admitted to your presence.   153

LUCIUS   Let him come near.
Welcome, Aemilius. What's the news from Rome?

AEMILIUS
Lord Lucius, and you princes of the Goths,
The Roman Emperor greets you all by me;
And, for he understands you are in arms,   158
He craves a parley at your father's house,
Willing you to demand your hostages,
And they shall be immediately delivered.

A GOTH   What says our general?

LUCIUS
Aemilius, let the Emperor give his pledges
Unto my father and my uncle Marcus,
And we will come. March away.   [*Flourish. Exeunt.*]

❖

141 **But** i.e., but why go on with this recital. (Sometimes emended to
Tut, as in the second quarto.)   146 **presently** immediately   153 **Desires**
who desires   158 **for** since

5.2   *Enter Tamora and her two sons, disguised.*

TAMORA

Thus, in this strange and sad habiliment,   1
I will encounter with Andronicus
And say I am Revenge, sent from below
To join with him and right his heinous wrongs.
Knock at his study, where they say he keeps   5
To ruminate strange plots of dire revenge.
Tell him Revenge is come to join with him
And work confusion on his enemies.   8

They knock, and Titus [above] opens his study door.

TITUS

Who doth molest my contemplation?
Is it your trick to make me ope the door,
That so my sad decrees may fly away   11
And all my study be to no effect?
You are deceived, for what I mean to do,
See here, in bloody lines I have set down,
And what is written shall be executed.

[He shows a paper.]

TAMORA

Titus, I am come to talk with thee.

TITUS

No, not a word. How can I grace my talk,
Wanting a hand to give it action?   18
Thou hast the odds of me; therefore no more.   19

TAMORA

If thou didst know me, thou wouldst talk with me.

TITUS

I am not mad; I know thee well enough.
Witness this wretched stump, witness these crimson
lines,   22
Witness these trenches made by grief and care,   23

5.2. Location: Rome. The court of Titus' house.
1 **sad habiliment** somber garments   5 **keeps** dwells   8 **confusion**
destruction   11 **sad decrees** solemn resolutions   18 **Wanting . . . action**
lacking a hand to provide suitable gesture by way of support   19 **odds
of** advantage over   22 **crimson** i.e., bloody (as in l. 14)   23 **trenches** i.e.,
wrinkles

Witness the tiring day and heavy night,
Witness all sorrow, that I know thee well
For our proud empress, mighty Tamora.
Is not thy coming for my other hand?

TAMORA
Know, thou sad man, I am not Tamora;
She is thy enemy, and I thy friend.
I am Revenge, sent from th' infernal kingdom
To ease the gnawing vulture of thy mind
By working wreakful vengeance on thy foes.   32
Come down and welcome me to this world's light;
Confer with me of murder and of death.
There's not a hollow cave or lurking-place,
No vast obscurity or misty vale   36
Where bloody murder or detested rape
Can couch for fear, but I will find them out,   38
And in their ears tell them my dreadful name,
Revenge, which makes the foul offender quake.

TITUS
Art thou Revenge? And art thou sent to me
To be a torment to mine enemies?

TAMORA
I am. Therefore come down and welcome me.

TITUS
Do me some service ere I come to thee.
Lo, by thy side where Rape and Murder stands.
Now give some surance that thou art Revenge: 46
Stab them, or tear them on thy chariot wheels,
And then I'll come and be thy wagoner,
And whirl along with thee about the globe.
Provide thee two proper palfreys, black as jet,   50
To hale thy vengeful wagon swift away   51
And find out murderers in their guilty caves;
And when thy car is loaden with their heads,   53
I will dismount, and by thy wagon wheel
Trot like a servile footman all day long,
Even from Hyperion's rising in the east   56

---

32 wreakful vengeful   **36 obscurity** place of darkness and desolation
38 couch lie hidden   **46 surance** assurance   **50 proper** excellent, handsome.   **palfreys** horses   **51 hale** pull   **53 car** chariot   **56 Hyperion's**
the sun god's

Until his very downfall in the sea;
And day by day I'll do this heavy task,
So thou destroy Rapine and Murder there.   59

TAMORA
These are my ministers, and come with me.

TITUS
Are they thy ministers? What are they called?

TAMORA
Rape and Murder, therefore callèd so
'Cause they take vengeance of such kind of men.   63

TITUS
Good Lord, how like the Empress' sons they are,
And you, the Empress! But we worldly men   65
Have miserable, mad, mistaking eyes.
O sweet Revenge, now do I come to thee,
And if one arm's embracement will content thee,
I will embrace thee in it by and by.   [*Exit above.*]

TAMORA
This closing with him fits his lunacy.   70
Whate'er I forge to feed his brainsick humors   71
Do you uphold and maintain in your speeches,
For now he firmly takes me for Revenge;
And, being credulous in this mad thought,
I'll make him send for Lucius his son,
And whilst I at a banquet hold him sure,
I'll find some cunning practice out of hand   77
To scatter and disperse the giddy Goths
Or at the least make them his enemies.
See, here he comes, and I must ply my theme.

      [*Enter Titus below.*]

TITUS
Long have I been forlorn, and all for thee.
Welcome, dread Fury, to my woeful house.   82
Rapine and Murder, you are welcome too.
How like the Empress and her sons you are!

---

59 So provided that   **63 of . . . men** i.e., upon rapists and murderers
65 worldly mortal   **70 closing** agreeing   **71 forge** invent. **humors**
moods, whims   **77 practice** plot.   **out of hand** on the spur of the moment   **82 Fury** (The Furies were primeval beings devoted to avenging
certain crimes, especially against the ties of kinship.)

Well are you fitted, had you but a Moor.   85
Could not all hell afford you such a devil?
For well I wot the Empress never wags   87
But in her company there is a Moor;
And, would you represent our queen aright,
It were convenient you had such a devil.   90
But welcome as you are. What shall we do?

TAMORA
What wouldst thou have us do, Andronicus?

DEMETRIUS
Show me a murderer, I'll deal with him.

CHIRON
Show me a villain that hath done a rape,
And I am sent to be revenged on him.

TAMORA
Show me a thousand that hath done thee wrong,
And I will be revengèd on them all.

TITUS [*To Demetrius*]
Look round about the wicked streets of Rome,
And when thou find'st a man that's like thyself,
Good Murder, stab him; he's a murderer.
[*To Chiron.*] Go thou with him, and when it is thy hap   101
To find another that is like to thee,
Good Rapine, stab him; he is a ravisher.
[*To Tamora.*] Go thou with them, and in the Emperor's
        court
There is a queen, attended by a Moor;
Well shalt thou know her by thine own proportion,
For up and down she doth resemble thee.   107
I pray thee, do on them some violent death;
They have been violent to me and mine.

TAMORA
Well hast thou lessoned us; this shall we do.
But would it please thee, good Andronicus,
To send for Lucius, thy thrice-valiant son,
Who leads towards Rome a band of warlike Goths,
And bid him come and banquet at thy house,
When he is here, even at thy solemn feast,   115

85 **fitted** i.e., fitted out to resemble the Empress   **87 wags** moves about
90 were convenient would be fitting   **101 hap** chance   **107 up and
down** i.e., from top to toe   **115 solemn** stately

I will bring in the Empress and her sons,
The Emperor himself, and all thy foes,
And at thy mercy shall they stoop and kneel,
And on them shalt thou ease thy angry heart.
What says Andronicus to this device?

TITUS [*Calling*]
Marcus, my brother! 'Tis sad Titus calls.

    Enter Marcus.

Go, gentle Marcus, to thy nephew Lucius;
Thou shalt inquire him out among the Goths.
Bid him repair to me and bring with him   124
Some of the chiefest princes of the Goths.
Bid him encamp his soldiers where they are.
Tell him the Emperor and the Empress too
Feast at my house, and he shall feast with them.
This do thou for my love; and so let him,
As he regards his agèd father's life.

MARCUS
This will I do, and soon return again.   [*Exit.*]

TAMORA
Now will I hence about thy business
And take my ministers along with me.

TITUS
Nay, nay, let Rape and Murder stay with me,
Or else I'll call my brother back again
And cleave to no revenge but Lucius.   136

TAMORA [*Aside to her sons*]
What say you, boys? Will you abide with him
Whiles I go tell my lord the Emperor
How I have governed our determined jest?   139
Yield to his humor, smooth and speak him fair,   140
And tarry with him till I turn again.   141

TITUS [*Aside*]
I knew them all, though they supposed me mad,
And will o'erreach them in their own devices—
A pair of cursèd hellhounds and their dam!

---

124 repair come   **136 but Lucius** i.e., but that which Lucius and his army can provide   **139 governed . . . jest** managed the jest we determined on   **140 smooth . . . fair** flatter and humor him   **141 turn** return

DEMETRIUS
  Madam, depart at pleasure. Leave us here.
TAMORA
  Farewell, Andronicus. Revenge now goes
  To lay a complot to betray thy foes.   147
TITUS
  I know thou dost; and, sweet Revenge, farewell.
                              [*Exit Tamora.*]
CHIRON
  Tell us, old man, how shall we be employed?
TITUS
  Tut, I have work enough for you to do.
  Publius, come hither! Caius and Valentine!

  [*Enter Publius, Caius, and Valentine.*]

PUBLIUS   What is your will?
TITUS   Know you these two?
PUBLIUS
  The Empress' sons, I take them—Chiron, Demetrius.
TITUS
  Fie, Publius, fie! Thou art too much deceived.
  The one is Murder, and Rape is the other's name;
  And therefore bind them, gentle Publius.
  Caius and Valentine, lay hands on them.
  Oft have you heard me wish for such an hour,
  And now I find it. Therefore bind them sure,   160
  And stop their mouths if they begin to cry.   [*Exit.*] 161
              [*Publius, Caius, and Valentine lay hold on
                          Chiron and Demetrius.*]
CHIRON
  Villains, forbear! We are the Empress' sons.
PUBLIUS
  And therefore do we what we are commanded.   163
  Stop close their mouths; let them not speak a word.
              [*They gag and bind the two sons.*]
  Is he sure bound? Look that you bind them fast.

    *Enter Titus Andronicus with a knife, and Lavinia
    with a basin.*

---

147 complot conspiracy   **160 sure** securely   **161 cry** cry out   **163 therefore** for that very reason

TITUS

Come, come, Lavinia. Look, thy foes are bound.
Sirs, stop their mouths. Let them not speak to me,
But let them hear what fearful words I utter.
O villains, Chiron and Demetrius!
Here stands the spring whom you have stained with
    mud,   170
This goodly summer with your winter mixed.
You killed her husband, and for that vile fault
Two of her brothers were condemned to death,
My hand cut off and made a merry jest;
Both her sweet hands, her tongue, and that more dear
Than hands or tongue, her spotless chastity,
Inhuman traitors, you constrained and forced.
What would you say if I should let you speak?
Villains, for shame. You could not beg for grace.   179
Hark, wretches, how I mean to martyr you.   180
This one hand yet is left to cut your throats,
Whiles that Lavinia 'tween her stumps doth hold   182
The basin that receives your guilty blood.
You know your mother means to feast with me,
And calls herself Revenge, and thinks me mad.
Hark, villains, I will grind your bones to dust,
And with your blood and it I'll make a paste,   187
And of the paste a coffin I will rear,   188
And make two pasties of your shameful heads,   189
And bid that strumpet, your unhallowed dam,
Like to the earth swallow her own increase.   191
This is the feast that I have bid her to,
And this the banquet she shall surfeit on;
For worse than Philomel you used my daughter,
And worse than Procne I will be revenged.   195

---

170 spring i.e., Lavinia   **179 for shame . . . grace** i.e., your colossal
shame would not let you beg for mercy, would choke your plea
180 martyr torture, kill cruelly   **182 Whiles that** while   **187 paste**
dough   **188 coffin** pie crust (probably also suggesting the container in
which they will be buried)   **189 pasties** meat pies   **191 Like to the
earth** i.e., just as the earth devours all her children when they have
died.   **increase** offspring   **195 worse than Procne** (An allusion to
Procne's revenge on Tereus for raping her sister Philomel; cf. 2.3.43,
note. She killed her son Itys and served his flesh to Tereus, his father. In
Seneca's *Thyestes*, Atreus similarly sets before Thyestes a dish of his
own children's flesh.)

And now prepare your throats. Lavinia, come.
                              He cuts their throats.
Receive the blood, and when that they are dead,
Let me go grind their bones to powder small,
And with this hateful liquor temper it,   199
And in that paste let their vile heads be baked.
Come, come, be everyone officious   201
To make this banquet, which I wish may prove
More stern and bloody than the Centaurs' feast.   203
So, now bring them in, for I'll play the cook
And see them ready against their mother comes.   205
                    Exeunt [bearing the dead bodies].

❖

5.3   *Enter Lucius, Marcus, and the Goths [with*
            Aaron prisoner, and an attendant bearing his
            child].

LUCIUS
    Uncle Marcus, since 'tis my father's mind
    That I repair to Rome, I am content.   2
A GOTH
    And ours with thine, befall what fortune will.   3
LUCIUS
    Good uncle, take you in this barbarous Moor,   4
    This ravenous tiger, this accursèd devil.
    Let him receive no sustenance. Fetter him
    Till he be brought unto the Empress' face   7
    For testimony of her foul proceedings.   8
    And see the ambush of our friends be strong;   9
    I fear the Emperor means no good to us.

---

199 temper blend, mix   **201 officious** busy   **203 Centaurs' feast** i.e., the
wedding feast of Pirithous and Hippodamia to which the Lapithae
invited the Centaurs, fabulous creatures, half men and half horses. (The
Centaurs attempted to carry off the women but were slaughtered by
their hosts.)   **205 against** by the time that

5.3. Location: The scene appears to take place in a court in Titus'
house; in the opening lines Lucius speaks as if he and his soldiers have
just arrived in Rome.
2 repair return   **3 ours with thine** i.e., our intentions are in agreement
with yours   **4 in** i.e., into Titus' house; see l. 123   **7 unto** before   **8 of**
regarding   **9 ambush** forces lying in wait to attack

AARON
　　Some devil whisper curses in my ear
　　And prompt me that my tongue may utter forth
　　The venomous malice of my swelling heart!
LUCIUS
　　Away, inhuman dog, unhallowed slave!
　　Sirs, help our uncle to convey him in.
　　　　　　　　　　　[*Exeunt Goths, with Aaron.*]
　　　　　　　　　　　　　Sound trumpets [*within*].
　　The trumpets show the Emperor is at hand.

　　　Enter Emperor [*Saturninus*] *and Empress*
　　　[*Tamora*], *with* [*Aemilius,*] *tribunes,* [*senators*],
　　　and others.

SATURNINUS
　　What, hath the firmament more suns than one?   17
LUCIUS
　　What boots it thee to call thyself a sun?   18
MARCUS
　　Rome's emperor, and nephew, break the parle.   19
　　These quarrels must be quietly debated.
　　The feast is ready which the careful Titus   21
　　Hath ordained to an honorable end,
　　For peace, for love, for league, and good to Rome.
　　Please you therefore draw nigh and take your places.
SATURNINUS   Marcus, we will.
　　　　　[*A table is brought in. The company sit down.*]

　　　Trumpets sounding, enter Titus like a cook,
　　　placing the dishes, and Lavinia with a veil over
　　　her face, [*young Lucius, and others*].

TITUS
　　Welcome, my gracious lord; welcome, dread Queen;
　　Welcome, ye warlike Goths; welcome, Lucius;
　　And welcome, all. Although the cheer be poor,   28
　　'Twill fill your stomachs. Please you eat of it.
SATURNINUS
　　Why art thou thus attired, Andronicus?

---

17 What . . . than one i.e., two suns cannot occupy the same heavenly
sphere, and Rome cannot have two kings at once   **18 boots** avails
19 break the parle cease the dispute   **21 careful** full of sorrows; assidu-
ous   **28 cheer** fare

TITUS
　Because I would be sure to have all well
　To entertain Your Highness and your empress.
TAMORA
　We are beholding to you, good Andronicus.   33
TITUS
　An if Your Highness knew my heart, you were.   34
　My lord the Emperor, resolve me this: 35
　Was it well done of rash Virginius   36
　To slay his daughter with his own right hand
　Because she was enforced, stained, and deflowered?
SATURNINUS   It was, Andronicus.
TITUS   Your reason, mighty lord?
SATURNINUS
　Because the girl should not survive her shame,   41
　And by her presence still renew his sorrows.   42
TITUS
　A reason mighty, strong, and effectual;
　A pattern, precedent, and lively warrant
　For me, most wretched, to perform the like.
　Die, die, Lavinia, and thy shame with thee,
　And with thy shame thy father's sorrow die!
　　　　　　　　　　　[He kills Lavinia.]

SATURNINUS
　What hast thou done, unnatural and unkind?   48
TITUS
　Killed her for whom my tears have made me blind.
　I am as woeful as Virginius was,
　And have a thousand times more cause than he
　To do this outrage, and it now is done.
SATURNINUS
　What, was she ravished? Tell who did the deed.
TITUS
　Will 't please you eat? Will 't please Your Highness feed?
TAMORA
　Why hast thou slain thine only daughter thus?

33 beholding beholden   **34 were** would be   **35 resolve** answer   **36 Virginius** Roman centurion who, according to Livy, killed his daughter to prevent her from being raped (rather than killing her afterward to preserve her honor, as told here to accord with Titus' story. The latter version was also current in the Renaissance.)   **41 Because** in order that **42 still** continually   **48 unkind** unnatural

TITUS
    Not I; 'twas Chiron and Demetrius.
    They ravished her and cut away her tongue,
    And they, 'twas they that did her all this wrong.
SATURNINUS
    Go fetch them hither to us presently.   59
TITUS
    Why, there they are, both bakèd in this pie,
    Whereof their mother daintily hath fed,
    Eating the flesh that she herself hath bred.
    'Tis true, 'tis true; witness my knife's sharp point.
                              He stabs the Empress.
SATURNINUS
    Die, frantic wretch, for this accursèd deed!
                              [*He kills Titus.*]
LUCIUS
    Can the son's eye behold his father bleed?
    There's meed for meed, death for a deadly deed!   66
              [*He kills Saturninus. A great tumult, during
                        which Marcus, Lucius, and others
                                          go aloft.*]
MARCUS
    You sad-faced men, people and sons of Rome,
    By uproars severed, as a flight of fowl
    Scattered by winds and high tempestuous gusts,
    O, let me teach you how to knit again
    This scattered corn into one mutual sheaf,   71
    These broken limbs again into one body.
A ROMAN LORD
    Let Rome herself be bane unto herself,   73
    And she whom mighty kingdoms curtsy to,
    Like a forlorn and desperate castaway,
    Do shameful execution on herself,
    But if my frosty signs and chaps of age,   77
    Grave witnesses of true experience,
    Cannot induce you to attend my words.   79

59 presently at once   **66 meed for meed** measure for measure   **s.d. A great . . . aloft** (In ll. 130–134, Marcus and Lucius offer to throw themselves down from where they are speaking.)   **71 corn** grain   **73 s.p. A Roman Lord** (Perhaps Aemilius; compare his speech at ll. 137 ff.)   **bane** poison, death   **77 But if** if.   **frosty signs** i.e., white hair.   **chaps** wrinkles   **79 attend** listen to

[*To Lucius.*] Speak, Rome's dear friend, as erst our
   ancestor,   80
When with his solemn tongue he did discourse
To lovesick Dido's sad-attending ear   82
The story of that baleful burning night
When subtle Greeks surprised King Priam's Troy.
Tell us what Sinon hath bewitched our ears,   85
Or who hath brought the fatal engine in
That gives our Troy, our Rome, the civil wound.   87
My heart is not compact of flint nor steel,   88
Nor can I utter all our bitter grief,
But floods of tears will drown my oratory
And break my utterance, even in the time
When it should move ye to attend me most
And force you to commiseration.
Here's Rome's young captain. Let him tell the tale,
While I stand by and weep to hear him speak.

LUCIUS
Then, gracious auditory, be it known to you
That Chiron and the damned Demetrius
Were they that murderèd our emperor's brother,
And they it were that ravishèd our sister.
For their fell faults our brothers were beheaded,   100
Our father's tears despised, and basely cozened   101
Of that true hand that fought Rome's quarrel out   102
And sent her enemies unto the grave;
Lastly, myself unkindly banishèd,   104
The gates shut on me, and turned weeping out
To beg relief among Rome's enemies,
Who drowned their enmity in my true tears
And oped their arms to embrace me as a friend.
I am the turned-forth, be it known to you,   109
That have preserved her welfare in my blood   110
And from her bosom took the enemy's point,   111

---

80 erst formerly, once. **our ancestor** i.e., Aeneas **82 sad-attending**
seriously listening **85 Sinon** the crafty Greek who persuaded the Trojans
to take the wooden horse (the *fatal engine*) into their city **87 civil**
incurred in civil strife **88 compact** composed **100 fell** savage, cruel
101 and basely cozened and he was basely cheated **102 fought . . . out**
fought to the finish in behalf of Rome's cause **104 unkindly** unnaturally
109 turned-forth exile **110 in** by **111 from . . . point** took in my own
bosom the sword's point aimed at her, Rome's, bosom

Sheathing the steel in my adventurous body.
Alas, you know I am no vaunter, I;
My scars can witness, dumb although they are,   114
That my report is just and full of truth.
But soft, methinks I do digress too much,
Citing my worthless praise. O, pardon me,
For when no friends are by, men praise themselves.

MARCUS
Now is my turn to speak. Behold the child:

> [*Pointing to the child in the
> arms of an attendant*]

Of this was Tamora deliverèd,
The issue of an irreligious Moor,
Chief architect and plotter of these woes.
The villain is alive in Titus' house,
And as he is to witness, this is true.
Now judge what cause had Titus to revenge
These wrongs unspeakable, past patience,   126
Or more than any living man could bear.
Now have you heard the truth. What say you, Romans?
Have we done aught amiss, show us wherein,   129
And from the place where you behold us pleading
The poor remainder of Andronici
Will hand in hand all headlong hurl ourselves,
And on the ragged stones beat forth our souls,   133
And make a mutual closure of our house.   134
Speak, Romans, speak, and if you say we shall,
Lo, hand in hand, Lucius and I will fall.

AEMILIUS
Come, come, thou reverend man of Rome,
And bring our emperor gently in thy hand,
Lucius our emperor; for well I know
The common voice do cry it shall be so.

ALL
Lucius, all hail, Rome's royal emperor!

MARCUS [*To attendants*]
Go, go into old Titus' sorrowful house
And hither hale that misbelieving Moor

---

114 dumb . . . are (The scars are dumb mouths, giving mute testimony.)
126 patience endurance   **129 Have we** if we have   **133 ragged** rough,
rugged   **134 closure** conclusion, death

To be adjudged some direful slaughtering death
As punishment for his most wicked life.
[*Exeunt attendants. Marcus, Lucius,
and the others come down.*]

ALL
Lucius, all hail, Rome's gracious governor!

LUCIUS
Thanks, gentle Romans. May I govern so
To heal Rome's harms and wipe away her woe!
But, gentle people, give me aim awhile,   149
For nature puts me to a heavy task.
Stand all aloof, but, uncle, draw you near
To shed obsequious tears upon this trunk.—   152
O, take this warm kiss on thy pale cold lips,
[*Kissing Titus*]
These sorrowful drops upon thy bloodstained face,
The last true duties of thy noble son!

MARCUS [*Kissing Titus*]
Tear for tear, and loving kiss for kiss,
Thy brother Marcus tenders on thy lips.
O, were the sum of these that I should pay
Countless and infinite, yet would I pay them!

LUCIUS [*To young Lucius*]
Come hither, boy. Come, come, and learn of us
To melt in showers. Thy grandsire loved thee well.
Many a time he danced thee on his knee,
Sung thee asleep, his loving breast thy pillow;
Many a story hath he told to thee,
And bid thee bear his pretty tales in mind
And talk of them when he was dead and gone.

MARCUS
How many thousand times hath these poor lips,
When they were living, warmed themselves on thine!
O, now, sweet boy, give them their latest kiss.   169
Bid him farewell; commit him to the grave;
Do them that kindness, and take leave of them.   171

BOY [*Kissing Titus*]
O grandsire, grandsire! Ev'n with all my heart
Would I were dead, so you did live again!—

---

149 give me aim bear with me, give me encouragement
152 obsequious mourning   **169 latest** last   **171 them** i.e., the lips

O Lord, I cannot speak to him for weeping.
My tears will choke me if I ope my mouth.

[*Enter attendants with Aaron.*]

A ROMAN
　You sad Andronici, have done with woes.   176
　Give sentence on this execrable wretch
　That hath been breeder of these dire events.
LUCIUS
　Set him breast-deep in earth and famish him;
　There let him stand and rave and cry for food.
　If anyone relieves or pities him,
　For the offense he dies. This is our doom.   182
　Some stay to see him fastened in the earth.
AARON
　Ah, why should wrath be mute and fury dumb?
　I am no baby, I, that with base prayers
　I should repent the evils I have done.
　Ten thousand worse than ever yet I did
　Would I perform, if I might have my will.
　If one good deed in all my life I did,
　I do repent it from my very soul.
LUCIUS
　Some loving friends convey the Emperor hence,
　And give him burial in his father's grave.   192
　My father and Lavinia shall forthwith
　Be closèd in our household's monument.
　As for that ravenous tiger, Tamora,
　No funeral rite nor man in mourning weed,
　No mournful bell shall ring her burial;
　But throw her forth to beasts and birds to prey.   198
　Her life was beastly and devoid of pity,
　And being dead, let birds on her take pity.   200
　　　　　　　　Exeunt, [*bearing the dead bodies*].

---

176 s.p. A Roman (The speech is sometimes assigned to Aemilius.)
182 doom decision, judgment　**192 father's** (or possibly *fathers'*, forefathers')　**198 prey** prey upon　**200 pity** (The first quarto text closes the play with this line. The second quarto and subsequent texts add the following four lines:
　See justice done on Aaron, that damned Moor,
　By whom our heavy haps had their beginning.
　Then, afterwards, to order well the state,
　That like events may ne'er it ruinate.)

Date and Text

On February 6, 1594, "a Noble Roman Historye of Tytus Andronicus" was entered in the Stationers' Register, the official record book of the London Company of Stationers (booksellers and printers), to John Danter, along with "the ballad thereof." The entry probably, though not certainly, refers to Shakespeare's play. Later in that same year, at any rate, Danter published a quarto volume with the following title:

> THE MOST LAmentable Romaine Tragedie of Titus Andronicus: As it was Plaide by the Right Honourable the Earle of *Darbie*, Earle of *Pembrooke*, and Earle of *Sussex* their Seruants. LONDON, Printed by Iohn Danter, and are to be sold by *Edward White & Thomas Millington*, at the little North doore of Paules at the signe of the Gunne. 1594.

This text seems to have been set from Shakespeare's foul papers in an unpolished state. A second quarto appeared in 1600, adding the name of the Lord Chamberlain's company to those who had acted the play. It was set up from a slightly damaged copy of the first quarto. Although the second quarto made some improvements, these were probably by the compositor and not the author, or may have been made in a press corrected first quarto no longer extant (since we have only one copy today). A third quarto (1611), set up from the second, contributed new errors. The First Folio text of 1623 was derived from the third quarto, but with an authentic added scene (3.2) from a manuscript source and with additional stage directions that suggest a playhouse promptbook. One theory is that the copy used by the Folio printers, the third quarto, had been corrected from an annotated copy of the second quarto that had been used as a promptbook, or perhaps directly from the promptbook. Despite these improvements, the first quarto clearly remains the authoritative text except for Act 3, scene 2.

The date of *Titus* must be prior to 1594. Philip Henslowe's *Diary* records a performance of a "Titus & Ondronicus" by the Earl of Sussex's men on January 24, 1594, and indicates it was "ne" or new. This could certainly mean a new play, but it could also mean it was newly revised or newly acquired. Since the players on this occasion, Sussex's men, were listed third on the 1594 title page after Derby's and Pembroke's men, they may just have acquired *Titus*. Two allusions may point to an earlier date: *A Knack to Know a Knave* (performed in 1592) and *The Troublesome Reign of King John* (published 1591) may contain echoes of *Titus*. Stylistic considerations favor a date around 1590 or even earlier.

The authorship of *Titus* would appear at first glance to be beyond question. Although the 1594 quarto does not mention Shakespeare's name (a common omission in such early texts, especially since the author was as yet relatively unknown), Francis Meres (in his *Palladis Tamia: Wit's Treasury*, 1598, a slender volume on contemporary literature and art, valuable because it lists most of Shakespeare's plays that existed at that time) assigns the play to Shakespeare, and the Folio editors included it in the 1623 edition. Doubts began to arise, however, when Edward Ravenscroft observed in 1687 that he had been "told by some anciently conversant with the stage that it was not originally his, but brought by a private author to be acted, and he only gave some master touches to one or two of the principal parts or characters." This remark touched off a controversy that continues today; for example, J. Dover Wilson in his New Cambridge Shakespeare (1948) and J. C. Maxwell in his Arden edition (1953) still argue for the presence of Peele, in the first act especially. Nevertheless, Ravenscroft's testimonial is suspect both because it came one hundred years after the fact and because Ravenscroft himself was embarked on an adaptation of *Titus* and so might wish to denigrate the original. The efforts at assigning portions of the play to Shakespeare's contemporaries have generally been motivated by a wish to rescue Shakespeare's reputation from the violent and garish effects of this play. Most recent criticism prefers to regard the play as an interesting experiment in revenge tragedy by a young artist, with many shrewdly characteristic Shakespearean touches. The external evidence of the Elizabethan period, at any rate, is entirely on the side of awarding the play wholly to Shakespeare.

Henslowe's *Diary* records the performance of a "Tittus & Vespacia" on April 11, 1592, a "ne" play by Strange's men. Despite the similarity of the title, this play was probably on an independent subject.

Textual Notes

These textual notes are not a historical collation, either of the early quartos and the early folios or of more recent editions; they are simply a record of departures in this edition from the copy text. The reading adopted in this edition appears in boldface, followed by the rejected reading from the copy text, i.e., the quarto of 1594. Only major alterations in punctuation are noted. Changes in lineation are not indicated, nor are some minor and obvious typographical errors.

Abbreviations used:
F the First Folio
Q the quarto of 1594
s.d. stage direction
s.p. speech prefix

Copy text: the first quarto of 1594, except for 3.2, based on F.

1.1. 14 seat, to virtue consecrate, seate to vertue, consecrate [The punctuation variations from the edited text are considerable in this play and are generally not recorded in these notes.]   **35 the field** [Q follows with a half line and three more lines: "and at this day, / To the Monument of that *Andronicy* / Done sacrifice of expiation, / And slaine the Noblest prisoner of the *Gothes.*"]   **55 s.d. Exeunt** Exit   **64 s.p. Captain** [not in Q]   **69 s.d. three sons** two sonnes   **98 manes** manus   **129 s.d. Exeunt** Exit   **157 s.p. Lavinia** [not in Q]   **227 Titan's** [F] Tytus   **243 Pantheon** Pathan   **265 chance** [F] change   **281 cuique** cuiqum   **300 s.p. [and elsewhere] Saturninus** Emperour   **317 Phoebe** Thebe   **318 gallant'st** [F] gallanst   **359 s.p. Martius** Titus two sonnes speakes   **s.p. Quintus** [not in Q]   **361 s.p. Martius** Titus sonne speakes   **369 s.p. Quintus** 3. Sonne   **370 s.p. Martius** 2. Sonne [also at l. 372]   **389 s.d. They all kneel** they all kneele and say   **390 s.p. All** [not in Q]   **391 s.d. Exeunt** Exit   **392 dreary** dririe [Q] sudden [F]   **399 Marcus. Yes . . . remunerate** [F; not in Q]   **475 s.p. Lucius** [F; not in Q]   **476 mildly** mi'd ie

2.1. 37 s.p. [and elsewhere] Aaron Moore   **110 than** this

2.2. 1 morn [F] Moone   **11** [Q provides a s.p.: Titus]   **24 run** runnes

2.3. 13 snake [F] snakes   **69 try** [F] trie thy   **72 swarthy** swartie [Q] swarth [F]   **88 s.p. [and elsewhere] Tamora** Queene   **131 ye desire** we desire   **150 heard** hard   **153 Some** So me   **160 ears** [F] yeares   **175 their** there   **180 satisfy** satisfice (?)   **192 s.p. Aaron** [not in Q]   **208 s.d. Exit** [at l. 207 in Q]   **210 unhallowed** [F] vnhollow   **222 berayed in blood** bereaud in blood [Q, with marginal correction in contemporary handwriting: "heere reau'd of lyfe"]   **231 Pyramus** [F] Priamus   **236 Cocytus'** Ocitus   **260 s.p. [and elsewhere] Saturninus** King   **276** [Q provides a s.p.: King]   **291 fault** faults

2.4. 5 scrawl scrowle   **11 s.p. Marcus** [not in Q]   **27 him** them   **30 three** their

3.1. 17 urns ruines   **21 on thy** [F] out hy   **67 handless** handles   **146 his** her   **225 blow** flow   **281 employed:** imployde in these Armes [Q] employd in these things [F]

3.2 [the entire scene is missing in Q; copy text is F]   **s.d. banquet** Bnaket [F]
1 s.p. [and throughout scene] Titus An   **39 complainer** complaynet   **52 thy
knife** knife   **53 fly** Flys   **54 thee** the   **55 are cloyed** cloi'd   **72 myself** my
selfes

4.1. 1 s.p. [and throughout] Boy [F] Puer   **10 s.p. Marcus** [not in Q]
19 griefs greeues   **52 quotes** coats   **55 Forced** Frocd   **80 s.p. Titus** [not in
Q]   **90 hope** hop (?) I op (?)

4.2. 15 lordships, that Lordships   **51 Good** God   **96 Alcides** Alciades
125 that [F] your

4.3. 56 Saturn Saturnine, to   **77 News . . . come** [assigned in Q to Clown]
96 from you [Q follows with four lines: *Titus.* Tell mee, can you deliuer an
Oration to the Em- / perour with a grace. / *Clowne.* Nay truelie sir, I could
neuer say grace in all / my life.]

4.4. 5 know, as know know   **48 By 'r** be   **93 feed** seede   **98 ears** [F] yeares
105 on [F] in

5.1. 17 s.p. All the Goths [not in Q]   **20 s.p. Another Goth** Goth   **43 here's** [F]
her's   **53 Get me a ladder** [assigned in Q to Aaron]   **113 extreme** extreanie

5.2. 18 it action [F] that accord   **38 them out** the mout   **49 globe** Globes
52 murderers murder   **caves** cares   **56 Hyperion's** Epeons   **61 they** them
65 worldly wordlie   **121 s.d.** [at l. 120 in Q]   **196 s.d.** [at l. 203 in Q]

5.3. 26 gracious lord [F] Lord   **36 Virginius** Viginius   **125 cause** course
141 s.p. All Marcus   **142 s.p. Marcus** [no s.p. here in Q; see previous note]
144 adjudged [F] adiudge   **146 s.p. All** [not in Q]   **154 bloodstained** blood
slaine   **163 Sung** Song   **172 s.p. Boy** [F] Puer

Shakespeare's Sources

Although we do not today possess any work that Shakespeare could have used for his immediate source in *Titus*, we have an eighteenth-century chapbook called *The History of Titus Andronicus* that may tell us substantially what that source was like. This chapbook is similar to Shakespeare's play. According to Ralph Sargent (*Studies in Philology*, 1949), a closely related prose version, now lost, served as Shakespeare's chief source. This hypothesis is now generally accepted. Some scholars even argue that the Stationers' Register entry in 1594 to the printer John Danter for his publication of "a Noble Roman Historye of Tytus Andronicus" with "the ballad thereof" refers to just such a prose account. Of this we cannot be certain, for Danter did, after all, publish Shakespeare's play in that same year, and the ballad appears to owe some of its details to the play (though based primarily, it would seem, on the lost prose version). All in all, the existence of a prose *History of Titus* when Shakespeare wrote his play seems likely. (A ballad of "Titus Andronicus' Complaint," published in 1620 in Richard Johnson's *The Golden Garland of Princely Pleasures*, attests to the continued currency of the story in the early seventeenth century.)

The prose *History* (a modernized edition of which follows) is a fictitious medley of revenge stories inspired by Seneca and Ovid. It is set in the last days of the Roman Empire, but contains no recognizable historical characters or events. Titus Andronicus is a Roman senator who defends Rome against the Goths in a protracted ten-year struggle, losing twenty-two of his own sons in the conflict. He slays the Gothic King Tottilius in battle and captures the Queen, Attava. When Tottilius' two sons Alaricus and Abonus continue the assault on Rome, the Roman Emperor wearies of the conflict and resolves to marry Attava against the advice of his general, Andronicus. The Queen, naturally regarding Titus as an enemy, proceeds to obtain powerful positions for her own kinsmen. She succeeds in having Titus banished, but he is recalled by popular insistence. Attava has an affair with her nameless Moorish servant and has a black child by him. Discovery of the child leads to the Moor's banishment, but he too is later recalled. Attava opposes the marriage of Titus' daughter Lavinia to the Emperor's only son (by a former marriage), since she desires the possession of the empire for her own sons. The remainder of the story proceeds much as in the play, except that we do not learn what happens to Rome after Titus' death. Shakespeare's chief additions include Titus' candidacy for and rejection of the throne, the struggle between Saturninus and Bassianus, the sacrifice of Tamora's son Alarbus, and a greatly magnified role for Aaron the Moor.

Although the prose version itself made use of Ovid and Seneca, Shakespeare evidently consulted these authors directly as well. The play contains many explicit references to classical authors, most notably when Lavinia turns the pages of Ovid's *Metamorphoses* to the story of Philomela's rape (4.1). In Ovid's famous account (Book 6, 526 ff.), King Tereus of Thrace rapes Philomela, cuts out her tongue (but not her hands) to prevent her from revealing the crime, and keeps her prisoner. She nevertheless manages to weave her story into a tapestry and send it to her sister, Procne, who liberates Philomela and plots with her to serve Tereus and Procne's son Itys to him at a banquet.

A similar grisly feast takes place in Seneca's *Thyestes*, from which Shakespeare may well have drawn some particulars. Atreus, the wronged avenger, murders the two sons of Thyestes and serves them to him. As in Shakespeare's play, there are two sons rather than one. Of these two sons, one is guilty of ambition, whereas Ovid's Itys is an innocent victim. The slayer is a male avenger, not (as in Ovid) the mother of the slain victim. Senecan conventions of underworld spirits of revenge and the like are also present in the play, though they may have reached Shakespeare by way of Thomas Kyd's *The Spanish Tragedy* and other plays of the late 1580s. Both Ovid and Seneca were commonly taught in Elizabethan grammar schools, though both were also available in English translation: Ovid by Arthur Golding (1567) and Seneca by Jasper Heywood (1560). Christopher Marlowe's *Tamburlaine* and *The Jew of Malta* certainly had an influence, especially on Shakespeare's conception of Aaron the Moor.

Two continental plays about Titus, the German *Tragoedia*

von Tito Andronico (1620) and the Dutch *Aran en Titus* by
Jan Vos (1641), were once thought to have been derived from
an English play before 1594, which might then have served
as a source for Shakespeare. In the German play the name
of Titus' son Lucius is Vespasian, and this fact has caused
scholars to wonder if the "Tittus & Vespacia" acted in April
1592 by the acting company known as Lord Strange's men
(as mentioned in Philip Henslowe's *Diary*) was about Titus
Andronicus. Lucius' part is small for such prominence in a
title, however, and the prevailing opinion today is that
Henslowe's play was on an independent subject.

The History of
Titus Andronicus

CHAPTER 1

How, Rome being besieged by the barbarous Goths and be-
ing at the point to yield through famine, it was unexpectedly
rescued by Andronicus, with the utter defeat of the enemy,
for which he was received in triumph.

When the Roman Empire was grown to its height and the
greatest part of the world was subjected to its imperial
throne, in the time of Theodosius,[1] a barbarous northern
people out of Swedeland, Denmark, and Gothland[2] came
into Italy in such numbers under the leading of Tottilius,
their king, that they overran it with fire and sword, plunder-
ing churches, ripping up women with child, and deflower-
ing virgins in so horrid and barbarous a manner that the
people fled before them like flocks of sheep.

To oppose this destroying torrent of the Goths—a barbarous people, strangers to Christianity—the Emperor raised
a mighty army in Greece, Italy, France, Spain, Germany,
and England, and gave battle under the passage of the Al-
pine mountains, but was overthrown with the loss of three-
score thousand of his men, and, flying to Rome, was
besieged in it by a numerous host of these barbarians, who

---

1 Theodosius Roman Emperor from 379 to 395   **2 Gothland** (in modern-
day southern Sweden)

pressed so hard to beat down the walls and enter with a miserable slaughter of the citizens that such as could get over the river Tiber fled in a fearful manner to a distant country. The siege lasting ten months, such a famine arose that no unclean thing was left uneaten; dogs, cats, horses, rats, and mice were curious dainties.[3] Thousands died in the streets of hunger, and most of those that were alive looked more like glass[4] than living creatures. So that, being brought to the last extremity, the vulgar sort[5] came about the Emperor's palace and with piteous cries implored him either to find some means to get them food to stay[6] their fleeting lives or make the best terms he could and open the gates to the enemy.

This greatly perplexed him. The former he could not do, and the latter he knew would not only uncrown him, if he escaped with his life, but be the ruin of the Roman Empire. Yet in the greatest of this extremity he unexpectedly found relief.

Titus Andronicus, a Roman senator and a true lover of his country, hearing in Graecia, where he was governor of the province of Achaia, what straits Rome and his sovereign were brought into by the barbarous nations, got together friends and sold whatever he had of value to hire soldiers. So that with his small army he secretly marched away, and, falling upon the mighty army of the enemy (when they were drowned, as it were, in security, wine, and sleep, resolved to make a general storm the next day,[7] in which they had undoubtedly carried[8] the city), he and his sons, entering their camp and followed by the rest, made such a slaughter that the cry and confusion were exceeding great. Some changed sleep into death, others vomited wine and blood mixed together through the wounds they received; some lost heads at once, other[9] arms. Tottilius, in this confusion being awakened, had his first care to convey away his queen and two sons, who were newly come to the camp, and then labored to rally his flying men; but being desperately charged by Andronicus, he was thrown from his horse and much

---

3 curious dainties rare delicacies   **4 like glass** i.e., emaciated, hollow
5 the vulgar sort the commoners   **6 stay** prolong   **7 resolved . . . day**
having determined to make a general assault on Rome the next day
8 had undoubtedly carried would undoubtedly have won   **9 other**
others

wounded, many lives being lost in remounting him.[10]
Whereupon, seeing the slaughter so great by the pale beams
of the moon and not knowing the number of his adversaries, having caused the retreat to be sounded he fled in great
confusion and left the rich spoils of his camp, the wealth of
many plundered nations, to Andronicus and his soldiers;
who, being expert in war, would not meddle with them that
night, but stood to their arms till the morning.

CHAPTER 2

*How in ten years' war, with the loss of two-and-twenty of
his valiant sons, he won many famous battles, slew Tottilius,
King of the Goths, and did many other brave exploits, etc.*

The watch upon the walls of Rome, having heard a confused
cry and the clashing of arms, were greatly astonished, but
could not think what it should mean, for the camps of the
barbarous Goths extended in a large circuit about the famous city. However, the captains of the guards advertised[1]
the Emperor of it, who sent out scouts. But they, fearful of
approaching too near the enemy in the night, could get certain intelligence only that they heard the groans and cries,
as they thought, of dying men. However, the shades of night
being dispelled and the glorious sun casting forth a cheerful light, the porters of the gate, espying three men coming
towards it, and, soon after being come up, knocked[2] with
great earnestness, they[3] took the courage to demand what
they were and what they required.[4]

"I am," said one of them, "Andronicus, your friend, and
desire admittance to speak with the Emperor, since the
news I bring will no doubt be pleasing to him."

Upon this, lifting[5] up his helmet, they knew him with joy,
knowing him to be a very worthy patriot, thinking he came
to do them good, as he had often done in their great distress

---

10 remounting him getting him back on his horse

1 advertised informed **2 and, soon . . . knocked** i.e., (three men) who,
soon after arriving at the gate, knocked at it **3 they** i.e., the porters of
the gate **4 required** wanted **5 lifting** i.e., Andronicus lifting

when the Huns and Vandals invaded the empire some years before and were beaten out by him.

The Emperor no sooner heard he was come but he ran from his palace to meet him, and would not suffer him to kneel but embraced him tenderly as a brother, saying, "Welcome, Andronicus, in this, the time of our greatest misery! It was thy counsel I wanted, to know how to free us from this barbarous enemy, against whose force the city cannot long hold out."

"May it please Your Majesty," replied Andronicus, "let those fears be banished. The work is done to you unknown. I and my twenty-five sons and what friends and soldiers I could get have this night fallen into[6] their quarters, cut off fifty thousand of them, and their scattered remains with their king are fled."

At this the Emperor was astonished and scarce could believe it, though he very well knew the integrity of Andronicus, till his own captains came and told him the siege was raised, with a miserable[7] slaughter, but by whom they knew not, unless the enemy had fallen out among themselves, and the troops they could yet see in view were but inconsiderable. Now these were those that belonged to Andronicus, who, as soon as it was day, were in pursuit of the enemy under the command of his five-and-twenty sons.

This surprising news was no sooner spread in the city but the joy of the people was exceeding great; and when they knew who was their deliverer they went in procession and sung his praises. After that he rode in a triumphant chariot through the city, crowned with an oaken garland, the people shouting, trumpets sounding, and all other expressions and demonstrations of joy that a grateful people could afford their deliverer, in which he behaved himself so humble that he gained the love of all.

This was no sooner over but he desired the Emperor to join what forces he could with those that he had brought and speedily pursue the enemy before he could gather new strength, that he might beat him out of Italy and his other countries where he yet held strong garrisons. This was embraced as good counsel, and the senators, by the Emperor's

6 fallen into attacked   **7 miserable** devastating, causing misery

mandate, assembled with joy, who chose with one consent
Andronicus their general. He was not slow in mustering his
forces, nor in the speedy pursuit. He found they had passed
the Alps and that their army was increased by new supplies;
yet he gave them battle and, charging through the thickest
of their squadrons hand to hand, slew Tottilius and beat
down his standard.[8] Whereupon the Goths fled and the
slaughter continued for many miles, covering all the lanes
and roads with the bodies of the dead. And in the pursuit he
took the Queen of the Goths captive and brought her to
Rome, for which signal[9] victory he had a second triumph[10]
and was styled[11] the deliverer of his country. But his joy was
a little eclipsed by the loss of five of his sons, who died cou-
rageously fighting in battle.

CHAPTER 3

*How the Emperor, weary of so tedious a war, contrary to
the mind[1] and persuasions of Andronicus, married the
Queen of the Goths and concluded a peace; how she tyran-
nized, and her sons slew the prince that was betrothed to
Andronicus' daughter and hid him in the forest.*

The Goths, having found the pleasantness of these fruitful
countries, resolved not so to give them over, but, encouraged by Tottilius' two sons, Alaricus and Abonus, sent for
fresh forces and made a desolation in the Roman provinces,
continuing a ten years' war, wherein the valiant Andronicus, captain-general of the empire, gained many victories
over them with great effusion of blood on either side. But
those barbarous people still increasing in their numbers,
the Emperor desiring peace, it was agreed to, in consideration he should marry[2] Attava, Queen of the Goths, and in
case he should die without issue, her sons might succeed in
the empire. Andronicus opposed this very much, as did
many other,[3] knowing, through the Emperor's weakness,

---

8 standard flag serving as the army's rallying point   **9 signal** notable
10 triumph triumphal procession   **11 styled** named with an honorific
title

1 mind opinion   **2 he should marry** of his marrying   **3 other** others

that she, being an imperious woman and of a haughty spirit, would govern him as she pleased and enslave the noble empire to strangers.[4] However, it was carried on with a high hand,[5] and great preparations were made for the royal nuptials, though with very little rejoicing among the people; for what they expected soon followed.

The Queen of the Goths, being made Empress, soon began to show her disposition according to the cruelty of her nation and temper, persuading the easy[6] Emperor to place the Goths in the places of his most trusty friends; and having, above all, vowed revenge on Andronicus, who most opposed her proceedings, she procured[7] him to be banished. But the people, whose deliverer he had been in their greatest extremity, calling to mind that and his many other good services, rose unanimously in arms and went clamoring to the palace, threatening to fire it[8] and revenge so base an indignity on the Queen if the decree which had been passed against all reason was not speedily revoked. This put her and the Emperor into such a fear* that their request was granted. And now she plotted by more private ways to bring the effects of revenge and implacable hatred about more secretly.

She had a Moor as revengeful as herself, whom she trusted in many great affairs, and was usually privy to her secrets, so far that from private dalliances she grew pregnant and brought forth a blackamoor child. This grieved the Emperor extremely, but she allayed his anger by telling him it was conceived by the force of imagination, and brought many suborned women and physicians to testify the like had often happened. This made the Emperor send the Moor into banishment, upon pain of death never to return to Rome; but her lust, and the confidence she had put in him as the main engine[9] to bring about her devilish designs, made her plot to have that decree revoked; when, having got the Emperor into a pleasant humor, she feigned herself sick, telling him withal[10] she had seen a vision which commanded her to call back the innocent Moor from banishment or she should never recover of that sickness.

---

4 strangers foreigners   **5 with a high hand** with imperious exercise of power   **6 easy** pliable   **7 procured** caused   **8 fire it** burn it down   **9 engine** means   **10 withal** in addition

The kind, good-natured Emperor, who could not resist her tears and entreaties, with some difficulty consented to it, provided he should be commanded to keep always out of her sight, lest the like mischance might happen as had been before. This she seemingly consented to, and he was immediately sent for, and the former familiarities continued between them, though more privately.

Andronicus, besides his sons, had a very fair and beautiful daughter named Lavinia, brought up in all singular virtues, humble, courteous, and modest, insomuch that the Emperor's only son by a former wife fell extremely in love with her, seeking her favor by all virtuous and honorable ways, insomuch that, after a long courtship, with her father and the Emperor's consent she was betrothed to him.

The Queen of the Goths, hearing this, was much enraged because from such a marriage might spring princes that might frustrate her ambitious designs, which was to make her sons emperors jointly. Wherefore she labored all she could to frustrate it by declaring what a disgrace it would be to the Emperor to marry his son to the daughter of a subject, who[11] might have a queen with a kingdom to her dowry. But, finding the prince constant,[12] she resolved to take him[13] out of the way. So it was plotted between her, the Moor, and her two sons that they should invite him to hunt in the great forest on the banks of the river Tiber and there murder him. This was effected by shooting him through the back with a poisoned arrow, which came out at his breast, of which wound he fell from his horse and immediately died. Then they digged a very deep pit in a pathway and threw him in, covering it lightly with boughs and sprinkling earth on it; and so, returning, reported they had lost the Prince in the forest, and though they had sought and called everywhere, they could not find him.

Chapter 4

How the wicked Moor, who had laid with the Empress and got into her favor above all others, betrayed Andronicus'

11 who he who   12 finding the prince constant finding the Emperor firmly resolved ("The Prince" usually refers to the Emperor's son, but here it probably refers to the Emperor, i.e., "the Emperor, the prince.")
13 him i.e., the Emperor's son

*three sons and charged the Prince's murder on them, for
which they were cast into a dungeon and, after their father
had cut off his hand to save them, were beheaded.*

The fair Lavinia no sooner heard the Prince was missing
but she fell into great sorrow and lamentation, her heart
misgiving her of some treachery, and thereupon she entreated her brothers to go in search of him, which they did
with all speed. But, being dogged by the Moor and the
Queen of Goths' two sons, they unluckily coming in the way
where the pit was digged, they fell both in upon the dead
body and could not, by reason of the great depth, get out.
Their cruel enemies no sooner saw this but they hasted to
the court and sent the guards in search of the murdered
Prince, who found Andronicus' two sons with the dead
body, which[1] they drew up and carried prisoners to the
court, where the Moor and the other two falsely swore
against them that they had often heard them threaten revenge on the Prince because he had put them to the foil[2] in a
tournament at jousting. This, and the circumstances of
their being found, with the vehement aggravation,[3] was a
sufficient ground to the Emperor to believe, who loved his
son entirely and was much grieved for his death. And
though they denied it with all the protestations imaginable
and pleaded their innocence, demanded the combat[4]
against their accusers, which by the law of arms they ought
to have been allowed, they were immediately loaden[5] with
irons and cast into a deep dungeon among noisome[6] creatures, as frogs, toads, serpents, and the like, where, notwithstanding all the intercessions that were made, they
continued,[7] eating the filth that they found in that place.

At last the Queen, designing to work her revenge on Andronicus, sent the Moor in the Emperor's name to tell him,
if he designed[8] to save his sons from the misery and death
that would ensue, he should cut off his right hand and send
it to court. This the good-natured father scrupled not to do;
no, nor had it been his life to ransom them, he would have
freely parted with it. Whereupon, laying his hand on a

1 **which** i.e., the dead body and Andronicus' two sons 2 **put them to
the foil** defeated them 3 **aggravation** accusation 4 **the combat** a trial
by combat 5 **loaden** loaded down 6 **noisome** offensive, noxious
7 **continued** remained 8 **designed** intended, hoped

block, he gave the wicked Moor his sword, who immediately struck it off and inwardly laughed at the villainy. Then, departing with it, he told him his sons should be sent to him in a few hours. But whilst he[9] was rejoicing with the hopes of their delivery, a hearse came to his door with guards, which made his aged heart to tremble. The first thing they presented him was his hand, which they said would not be accepted; and the next was his three sons beheaded. At this woeful sight, overcome with grief, he fainted away on the dead bodies. And when he recovered again, he tore his hoary hair, which age and his lying in winter camps for the defense of his country had made as white as snow, pouring out floods of tears; but found no pity from the hardened villains, who left him with scoffs in the midst of his woeful lamentations with his sorrowful daughter. Yet this was not all, for soon after, another to-be-deplored affliction followed, as shall in the next chapter be shown.

CHAPTER 5

How the two lustful sons of the Empress, with the assistance of the Moor, in a barbarous manner ravished Lavinia, Andronicus' beautiful daughter, and cut out her tongue and cut off her hands to prevent discovery; yet she did it by writing in the dust with a wand,[1] etc.

The fair and beautiful Lavinia for the loss of her lover* and brothers so basely murdered by treachery, tore her golden hair, shed floods of tears, and with her nails offered violence to that lovely face kings had adored and beheld with admiration. She shunned all company, retiring to woods and groves to utter her piteous complaints and cries to the senseless trees. When one day, being watched thither by the Moor, he gave notice of it to the Queen's two sons, who, like the wicked Elders and chaste Susanna, had a long time burned in lust, yet knew her virtues were proof against all temptations, and therefore it could not be obtained but by

9 he i.e., Andronicus
1 wand stick

violence. So, thinking this an opportunity to serve their
turns, immediately repaired to the grove, and setting the
Moor to watch on the outborders, soon found her pensive
and sorrowful, yet comely and beautiful in tears. When, un-
awares, before she saw them, like two ravenous tigers they
seized the trembling lady, who struggled all she could and
cried out piteously for help. And seeing what their wicked
intentions bent at, she offered them her throat, desiring
they would bereave her of her life but not of her honor.
However, in a villainous manner, staking her down by the
hair of her head and binding her hands behind her, they
turned up her nakedness and forced their way into her
closet of chastity, taking it by turns, the elder beginning
first and the younger seconding him as they had before
agreed on. And having tired themselves in satiating their
beastly appetites, they began to consider how they should*
come off[2] when such a villainy was discovered. Whereupon,
calling the Moor to them, they asked his advice, who wickedly counseled them to make all sure, seeing they had gone
thus far, by cutting out her tongue to hinder her telling
tales and her hands off to prevent her writing a discovery.[3]
This cruel wretches did whilst she in vain entreated 'em
to take away her life, since they had bereaved her of her
honor, which was dearer to her. And in this woeful condition they left the lady, who had[4] expired for the loss of blood
had not her uncle Marcus happened accidentally, soon
after, to come in search of her, who, at the woeful sight overcome with sorrow, could hardly keep life in himself; yet, recovering his spirits, he bound up her wounds and conveyed
her home.

Poor Andronicus' grief for this sad disaster was so great
that[5] no pen can write or words express. Much ado they had
to restrain him from doing violence upon himself. He
cursed the day he was born to see such miseries fall on himself and family, entreating her to tell him, if she could any
ways do it by signs, who had so villainously abused her. At
last the poor lady, with a flood of tears gushing from her
eyes, taking a wand between her stumps, wrote these lines:

2 come off avoid detection and punishment   **3 discovery** explanation,
disclosure   **4 had** would have   **5 that** as

The lustful sons of the proud Empress
Are doers of this hateful wickedness.

Hereupon he vowed revenge, at the hazard of his own and
all their lives, comforting his daughter with this when nothing else would do.

CHAPTER 6

*How Andronicus, feigning himself mad, found means to
entrap the Empress' two sons in a forest, where, binding
them to a tree, he cut their throats, made pies of their flesh,
and served them up to the Emperor and Empress, then slew
them, set the Moor quick[1] in the ground, and then killed his
daughter and himself.*

Andronicus, upon these calamities, feigned himself distracted and went raving about the city, shooting his arrows
towards heaven as in defiance, calling to hell for vengeance,
which mainly[2] pleased the Empress and her sons, who
thought themselves now secure. And though his friends required[3] justice of the Emperor against the ravishers, yet
they could have no redress, he rather threatening them if
they insisted on it. So that, finding they were in a bad case
and that in all probability their lives would be the next, they
conspired together to prevent that mischief and revenge
themselves. Lying in ambush in the forest when the two
sons went a-hunting, they surprised them and, binding
them to a tree, pitifully crying out for mercy though they
would give none to others, Andronicus cut their throats
whilst Lavinia, by his command, held a bowl between her
stumps to receive the blood. Then, conveying the bodies
home to his own house privately, he cut the flesh into fit
pieces and ground the bones to powder and made of them
two mighty pasties,[4] and invited the Emperor and Empress
to dinner, who, thinking to make sport with his frantic humor, came. But when they had eat[5] of the pasties he told
them what it was; and thereupon giving the watchword to

1 quick alive   **2 mainly** greatly   **3 required** begged   **4 mighty pasties**
large meat pies   **5 eat** eaten

his friends, they immediately issued out, slew the Emperor's guards, and lastly the Emperor and his cruel wife after they had sufficiently upbraided them with the wicked deeds they had done. Then, seizing on the wicked Moor, the fearful villain fell on his knees, promising to discover[6] all; but when he had told how he had killed the Prince, betrayed the three sons of Andronicus by false accusation, and counseled the abuse to the fair Lavinia, they scarce knew what torments sufficient to devise for him. But at last, digging a hole, they set him in the ground to the middle alive, smeared him over with honey, and so, between the stinging of bees and wasps and starving, he miserably ended his wretched days. After this, to prevent the torments he[7] expected when these things came to be known, at his daughter's request he killed her; and so, rejoicing he had revenged himself on his enemies to the full, fell on his own sword and died.

Text based on *The History of Titus Andronicus, the Renowned Roman General. Who, after he had saved Rome by his valor, etc. Newly translated from the Italian copy printed at Rome. London: printed and sold by C. Dicey in Bow churchyard and at his wholesale warehouse in Northampton*. It is a mid-eighteenth-century text probably derived from a sixteenth-century original.

In the following, departures from the original text appear in boldface; original readings are in roman.

p. 129 *fear Fears   p. 132 *lover Lovers   p. 133 *should should should

---

6 **discover** reveal, tell   7 **he** i.e., Andronicus

Further Reading

Baker, Howard. "Transformations of Medieval Structure: *Titus Andronicus* and the Shakespearian Practice." *Induction to Tragedy: A Study in a Development of Form in "Gorboduc," "The Spanish Tragedy," and "Titus Andronicus,"* 1939. Rpt. New York: Russell and Russell, 1965. Baker denies that *Titus* is a Senecan tragedy. Asserting its greater dependence upon English medieval and Ovidian models, he concludes that *Titus* is an Elizabethan transformation of Ovid's story of Philomel.

Bowers, Fredson Thayer. *Elizabethan Revenge Tragedy 1587–1642*, pp. 110–118. Princeton, N.J.: Princeton Univ. Press, 1940. Bowers examines *Titus* as an example of the Elizabethan revenge play. Though Shakespeare's play follows most of the conventions of this subgenre, it departs from its models with the introduction of Aaron's unmotivated villainy, which, for Bowers, disrupts the clear moral outlines of the play.

Bradbrook, M. C. "Moral Heraldry: *Titus Andronicus, Rape of Lucrece, Romeo and Juliet.*" *Shakespeare and Elizabethan Poetry: A Study of His Earlier Work in Relation to the Poetry of the Time*. London: Chatto and Windus, 1951. For Bradbrook, *Titus* is less a play than a formal pageant. It stylizes the play's violence in its emblematic and heraldic scenes and in a rhetoric drawn from late medieval poetry of "complaint."

Brooke, Nicholas. *"Titus Andronicus." Shakespeare's Early Tragedies*. London: Methuen, 1968. Brooke's essay explores Shakespeare's use of structural and poetic techniques to manipulate our response to the play. *Titus* insists that we are appalled by the spectacle of human nobility degenerating into bestiality, but its stylization is designed to prevent us from responding sympathetically to those who are victimized.

Brower, Reuben A. "Most Lamentable Romaine Tragedie." *Hero and Saint: Shakespeare and the Graeco-Roman Heroic Tradition*. New York and Oxford: Oxford Univ. Press, 1971. Though lacking the structural unity and moral clarity of the great tragedies, *Titus*, Brower finds, initiates Shakespeare's exploration of their controlling themes of justice and human suffering. *Titus* movingly poses "the great questions: why should a noble man suffer, why are his cries for justice unheard, how is he to act?"

Danson, Lawrence N. "Introduction: *Titus Andronicus.*" *Tragic Alphabet: Shakespeare's Drama of Language.* Princeton, N.J.: Princeton Univ. Press, 1974. For Danson, Shakespeare's tragedies are plays about the difficulty of achieving truthful and effective verbal expression. This is powerfully felt in *Titus*, where Titus' need to "wrest an alphabet" from the mute Lavinia is symbolic of the task confronting both Shakespeare and his characters of finding a language able to articulate the complexities of human life.

Ettin, Andrew V. "Shakespeare's First Roman Tragedy." *ELH* 37 (1970): 325–341. Ettin denies that Rome serves as the symbol of civilization in the play. He proposes instead that Shakespeare subjects the values of Rome to intense scrutiny, raising disturbing questions about both the ethical and the literary legacy that Renaissance England inherited from Rome.

Hattaway, Michael. "*Titus Andronicus:* Strange Images of Death." *Elizabethan Popular Theatre.* London: Routledge and Kegan Paul, 1982. Hattaway examines the play as it would have been staged in Shakespeare's playhouse. He examines Shakespeare's use of theatrical space, stage emblems, music, and props, as well as his indebtedness to the theatrical techniques of contemporaries such as Thomas Kyd and Christopher Marlowe, in a play that explores not just the representation of violence but the audience's perception of it.

Hunter, G. K. "Shakespeare's Earliest Tragedies: *Titus Andronicus* and *Romeo and Juliet.*" *Shakespeare Survey* 27 (1974): 1–9. While *Titus* and *Romeo and Juliet* represent the full range of Shakespeare's tragic practice (the former possessing the bleakest view of human potential, the latter often veering toward comedy), the differences between them should not obscure important affinities. The two plays, Hunter argues, are unique among Shakespeare's tragedies as tales of cities: in each, a conflict between rival households threatens civic order; and in each, the use of a family tomb as a central stage prop emphasizes the social and personal aspects of the tragedy.

Metz, G. Harold. "The Stage History of *Titus Andronicus*." *Shakespeare Quarterly* 28 (1977): 154–169. Contrary to critical assertions that *Titus* holds little appeal for modern audiences, Metz's overview of the play's stage history shows that the play has enjoyed a lively presence on the stage in this century with twenty-three separate productions between 1951 and 1974, including outstanding successes directed by Peter Brook (1955) and Gerald Freedman (1967).

Miola, Robert S. "*Titus Andronicus:* Rome and Romans." *Shakespeare's Rome*. Cambridge: Cambridge Univ. Press, 1983. Miola shows how deeply *Titus* is steeped in things Roman: the poetry of Virgil, Seneca, and Ovid; the Roman obsessions with exile, rebellion, civil war, blood ritual, and the code of military honor; and most of all, the inflexible Roman *pietas*, which demands that natural feeling be subordinated to public need.

Sommers, Alan. " 'Wilderness of Tigers': Structure and Symbolism in *Titus Andronicus*." *Essays in Criticism* 10 (1960): 275–289. The opposition of civilization and barbarism, of Rome and primitive nature, is for Sommers the central conflict of the play. Sommers explores the structural and symbolic patterns enforcing this opposition, in which he discovers the play's tragic meaning and Titus' tragic stature.

Spencer, T. J. B. "Shakespeare and the Elizabethan Romans." *Shakespeare Survey* 10 (1957): 27–38. Spencer's essay discusses Shakespeare's Roman plays in terms of the Elizabethan use and understanding of Roman history. *Titus*, he finds, is typical of many Elizabethan treatments of Roman history in that it offers not a true picture of a particular political situation but a generalized portrait of Roman politics and political institutions—a product, perhaps, of Shakespeare's desire "not to get it all right but to get it all in."

Waith, Eugene M. "The Metamorphosis of Violence in *Titus Andronicus*." *Shakespeare Survey* 10 (1957): 39–49. Waith explores the relation between the raw violence enacted in

Titus and the rhetorical style in which it is written. Waith finds that Shakespeare adopts a style and a mode of characterization derived from Ovid and designed to arouse astonishment rather than terror at the spectacle of characters under extraordinary emotional stress.

TIMON
OF
ATHENS

Introduction

Timon of Athens is Shakespeare's most relentless study in misanthropy. It expresses with *King Lear* a moral outrage at human depravity, but refuses to soften anger with compassionate tears. The protagonist learns little other than bitterness from his encounters with avarice and ingratitude. In its mordant vision of human folly, *Timon of Athens* resembles a number of other Roman or classical plays. As in *Julius Caesar, Titus Andronicus, Coriolanus*, and *Troilus and Cressida*, the dominant mood is one of enervation and futility. Political conflicts end in stalemate or a victory for opportunists; the populace and their leaders are fickle and craven; private virtues of noble men must yield to crass considerations of statecraft. Banishment or self-exile is too often the reward of those who have given their lives to public service. Shakespeare's misanthropic vision in *Timon of Athens* is, then, integral to his portrayal of humanity's political and social nature in the ancient classical world. This is a world to which Shakespeare turned often during his writing career, especially during the period from about 1601 to 1608, when he was engaged primarily in writing tragedies. As a group, the Roman and classical plays tend to differ from the great tragedies of evil (*Hamlet, Othello, King Lear, Macbeth*) in that the classical plays naturally make less use of a Christian perspective and focus instead on a sardonic and dispiriting view of life's tragic absurdity. Even in *Antony and Cleopatra*, where Shakespeare offers us an ennobling dream of greatness to offset the worldly failure of his protagonists, the arena of human conflict remains pitiless and disillusioning. *Timon of Athens* offers no compensatory vision; it is bleak to the end, unwavering in its denial.

Timon of Athens appears to have been written between 1605 and 1608, and is often grouped with *King Lear* (c. 1605) on grounds of stylistic and thematic similarity. For its chief source it uses Thomas North's translation of Plutarch's *The Lives of the Noble Grecians and Romans*, a source also for *Julius Caesar, Antony and Cleopatra, Coriolanus*, and parts of other plays. *Timon of Athens* also makes use, through intermediary versions, of the dialogue called *Ti-*

mon, or *The Misanthrope,* by the Greek satirist Lucian. The play may not have been produced; the text, not printed until the 1623 Folio, appears to have been taken from the author's unfinished manuscript, with contradictory uncanceled lines (see Timon's will, 5.4.70–73), unresolved discrepancies as to the amount of money Timon gives or requests, and passages of half-versified prose. Whatever the exact date and circumstance of composition, the play certainly belongs to the period of Shakespeare's most unsparing portrayal of human villainy and corruption.

Like *Troilus and Cressida, Timon of Athens* defies the conventional categories of tragedy, comedy, and history. Generically, the play stands chiefly between tragedy and satire in its preoccupation with dying and sterility. The play is tragic in portraying a fall from greatness, satiric in exposing an unfeeling society. Satire is potentially comic as well, and we are invited to laugh sardonically at the hypocrisies of Timon's fair-weather friends. The play is also a history, drawn from historical sources, as its Folio title, *The Life of Timon of Athens,* suggests. We ought to see or read it with the expectations not simply of tragedy but also of satire and ironic history.

As a genre, in fact, the play most resembles those works that the Painter and the Poet wish to offer Timon himself: a "moral painting" and a "satire against the softness of prosperity" (1.1.95 and 5.1.32–33). Such a genre is deliberately old-fashioned, reminiscent of medieval morality plays and of the "hybrid" morality plays of the 1570s and '80s like Thomas Lupton's *All for Money* (c. 1577) or Thomas Lodge and Robert Greene's *A Looking Glass for London and England* (1587–1591), which inveigh against usury and the neglect of military heroes. John Marston's later quasimorality, *Histriomastix* (c. 1599), proclaims the decline of civilization through worldly insolence. Ben Jonson's *Volpone* (1605–1606), though "comical" rather than "tragical" in its satire, similarly castigates human greed. The *Parnassus* trilogy (1598–1603), a series of three mordantly satirical plays written to be acted by students at Cambridge, indulges in a massive venting of spleen against a philistine culture. *Timon of Athens* follows this tradition of social satire, derived from both English and classical models. Like most satire of the 1600s, both dramatic and

nondramatic, it is crabbed in style, features a railing protagonist, and denounces through exaggerated caricature an
ugly array of types representing a broad social spectrum.
Choice of the satiric morality play as a generic model accords well with the play's acerbic view of decadence and
"softness."

Human greed, with which *Timon of Athens* is so occupied, lends itself readily to satiric treatment. Avarice does
not seem terrifying at first, like the spiritual sins of envy or
prideful ambition as portrayed in *Othello* and *Macbeth;* instead, it is disgusting, ludicrous, and incredibly tenacious.
Avarice is after all one of the Deadly Sins and is often referred to in medieval commentary as the pivotal Sin, the
radix malorum, or root of all evils. Although less vivid in its
manifestation than pride or envy, greed is insidious and all-
embracing. We see its corrupting effects in Timon's friends.
Those who sponge off him and then desert him are quick to
return when he is rumored to have found gold in his exile.
Greed is also self-deceiving. Many are the excuses offered
for failing to come to Timon's aid: one friend rates Timon as
a bad credit risk, another happens to be short of ready cash
at the moment, a third insists that Timon's generosity to
him wasn't as great as people suppose, and so on. No wonder Timon feels he must devise for such hypocrites a suitable comeuppance, consisting of a farewell banquet in
which their crass expectations are rewarded with a mocking litany of curses and a dinner of water and stones.

Appropriately for this satirical depiction of human greed,
the characters are virtually all types or social abstractions
in a generic portrayal of avarice. Several represent the
crafts and professions, and are abstractly labeled as such:
the Poet, the Painter, the Jeweler, the Merchant. Others are
"flattering lords" or "false friends" or "thieves." Seldom
in Shakespeare do we find so many characters without
proper names. They are depersonalized, and we are distanced from them. Apemantus is another type, a "churlish
philosopher," recognizable in all his appearances by this
one feature; we learn little about him other than that he professes to scoff at worldliness with a scabrous wit derived in
part from legends about Diogenes the Cynic philosopher
and other devotees of an extravagantly simple mode of life.
Timon himself becomes a type in his conversion to mis-

anthropy, "infected," as Apemantus says, by "A poor unmanly melancholy sprung / From change of fortune" (4.3.205–206). Apemantus' remark appeals to a view of personality as governed by "humors" or dominant traits such as melancholy or irascibility, which are generated by imbalance in the body of the four "humors," blood, phlegm, bile, and black bile. Images of disease, prominent throughout the play, are often derived from such "humorous" imbalances. The imagery also associates character types, as in Jonson's *Volpone*, with various beasts: the lion, the fox, the ass, the wolf, the bear, and most of all the dog. By means of such techniques, Shakespeare portrays those whom Timon comes to despise with a seemingly intentional onesidedness; the caricatures of avarice are vivid and amusing, with little allowance for subtlety or change. The plot too is, by Shakespeare's standard, unusually lacking in complication: Timon discovers the ingratitude and graspingness of his fellow creatures and retires from a world he can no longer tolerate, breathing upon it his dying curse. The dramatic tension of this uneventful story lies instead in Timon's own tortured spiritual saga, in the painful process of realization, in the revulsion, the refusal to compromise, the spurning even of honest friendship, the bitter renunciation and longing for oblivion. Alcibiades, too, is a complex character, offering as he does the alternatives of vengeful action against an ungrateful world or of successful conciliation; the debate between Alcibiades and Timon is an essential part of Timon's working toward total rejection of hope. The true drama is thus inner, and is increasingly contrasted with a static and superficial society toward which we are asked to feel revulsion and finally indifference.

There are no villains in *Timon of Athens*, only weak and foolish men. What is depressing about greed, in fact, is its insidious normality. Those who desert Timon have many prudent arguments on their side. After all, his original generosity is excessive and reckless. If his friends take advantage of him, they can at least say they have tried to warn him. Even a fool can see what lies in store. Much of Timon's wealth goes into drunken and gluttonous debauchery, into "feasts, pomps, and vainglories" (1.2.247–248). Timon does not know how to use prosperity wisely, and even his loyal servants deplore the "riot" (2.2.3). He is deaf to the friendly counsel of his steward, Flavius. For one who is so open-handed, Timon is surprisingly churlish with his creditors. And is he not presumptuous to assume that his friends will come to his aid when such vast sums are needed? Are they to be blamed for not emulating his prodigal decline into poverty? Clearly Timon expects too much. We readily though sadly perceive, as do all Timon's friends, that commerce is a god worshiped by all; need he be so shocked at this? As bystanders, we share with Timon's choric servants the certainty that his large requests for help will be refused. And yet, no matter how stupid or blind Timon may be, the desertion of him is still monstrous. Timon differs from us chiefly in being an idealist, in expecting that men will repay kindness with gratitude. We know, as do Timon's sympathetic servants, that most men are not like that.

Timon thus tears himself apart in a rage at what we consider the way of the world. We find his misanthropy intemperate, and yet we cannot help being moved by his sweeping indictment of human pettiness and inhumanity. Timon's furor carries him beyond satire. He is, like Lear, all the more clear-sighted for being near to madness. Wisdom and folly exchange places, as Apemantus' friend the Fool has already pointed out (2.2.99–120). In Timon's nearly mad vision beggars and lords are interchangeable, distinguished only by wealth and position. Love of gold, he sees, inverts everything decent in human life, making "Black white, foul fair, wrong right, / Base noble, old young, coward valiant" (4.3.29–30). Thieves and whores are at least more honest than their counterparts in everyday life, the respectable citizens of Athens and their wives, and so Timon mockingly rewards the thieves and insults the hypocrites. Yet Timon also inveighs furiously against women and all sexuality in a way that suggests feelings of betrayal. Though women occupy virtually no place in Timon's life, he himself has sought to displace women by serving as the generous source of comfort for all his friends—a self-created and narcissistic role that is destined to collapse into self-hatred and dread of all human feeling. His curse embraces the cosmos as well as humanity, inverting all semblance of hierarchical order: obedience must turn to rebellion, fidelity to incontinence, virginity to lasciviousness. "Degrees, observances, customs, and laws" must "Decline to your confounding contraries" (4.1.19–20). Clothing and cosmetics must be stripped away, as in *King Lear*, so that humanity's monstrosity may be revealed for what it truly is.

Three persons, Apemantus, Alcibiades, and Flavius, serve as chief foils to Timon in his estrangement from humanity. Apemantus the Cynic, who first taught Timon to rail at greed, now counsels him to find stoic contentment in renunciation of desire, or, conversely, to thrive as a flatterer by preying on those who have undone him (4.3.200–234). Alcibiades, the military commander banished by an ungrateful Athenian Senate for presuming to beg the life of one who had rashly shed blood in a quarrel, offers Timon the example of revenge against his enemies; subsequently, he offers Athens the olive branch with the sword, making "war breed peace" (5.4.83), in an accommodating move that is important for the conclusion of the play and its final mitigating tone. Timon, although resembling both men as railer and as victim of ingratitude, rejects their counsels as too politic, too worldly. His stand is unflinching, absolute, so lacking in compromise that his sole choice can be to curse, die, and hope for oblivion. Only Flavius, his steward, offers brief consolation. Flavius comes to him, like Kent to King Lear, offering love and service in exile. Flavius even speaks in paradoxes reminiscent of *King Lear*, calling Timon "My dearest lord, blest to be most accurst, / Rich only to be wretched" (4.2.43–44). These are precious words, showing that humanity is not utterly irredeemable. Still, this consolation is evidently too late to offset the nightmarish truth that Timon has learned. Timon experiences little of the compassionate love that comes to Lear in his madness, but he at least faces the bleakness of human existence with unbending honesty.

Timon of Athens
in Performance

Timon of Athens onstage suffered the fate of many of Shakespeare's late plays: neglect, followed by adaptation in an attempt to remedy its presumed defects. Not until the mid-nineteenth century was it often seen in anything like its original form. The reasons are not hard to imagine: the bitter misanthropy and caustic satire, the ambiguity as to genre, the distasteful presentation of women (which means, among other things, there are no adequate roles for lead actresses), and above all the absence of romantic interest. No performance is recorded as having occurred during Shakespeare's lifetime, and the text is sufficiently unfinished that we cannot safely assume his company ever acted it. The first certain theatrical event of any kind, in fact, was the performance of Thomas Shadwell's *The History of Timon of Athens, the Man-hater*, at the theater in Dorset Garden in 1678. Thomas Betterton played Timon; his wife (Mary Sanderson) and Mrs. Shadwell (Anne Gibbs) took the roles of two new female characters, Evandra and Melissa. With music by Henry Purcell and a new love plot, the play enjoyed quite a success.

Shadwell's adaptation adroitly supplies the conflicts of love and honor, so necessary to Restoration heroic drama, that Shakespeare had somehow neglected to provide. The two women in Timon's life are Melissa, a coquettish gold digger, and Evandra, his selfless and devoted mistress—both of them Restoration stereotypes. Melissa, when we first see her with her maid Chloe as she makes herself up for a visit from Timon, is flirtatiously trying to balance the attentions of two men, the wealthy Timon and the powerful Alcibiades. She naturally drops Timon when he falls into financial ruin, but then, hearing of his having found gold, seeks him out at his cave. Fittingly, she is rejected by Timon and then by Alcibiades, whom she has also jilted in his time of banishment. Melissa is thus a much-expanded counterpart of Shakespeare's Phrynia and Timandra, suitably punished for her infidelities and heartlessness. Evandra, who embodies the selfless qualities of Shakespeare's loyal steward, Flavius, is contrasted to Melissa in every way. Evandra remains loyal to Timon even when he leaves her for Melissa; she offers all her wealth to assist him in his financial difficulties, follows him into exile after he churlishly turns down her offer of help, and, when Timon despairingly commits suicide, takes her own life rather than outlive him.

Flavius meanwhile is replaced by a self-seeking steward called Demetrius, who warns Timon of impending ruin but is interested only in his own survival. Alcibiades becomes the heroic foe of tyranny and friend of democracy, no doubt with some application to the politics of the 1670s and especially to the high-handed tactics of Charles II and his Catholic brother, later James II. The story of the two added women not only provides love interest but a unified plot, required by neoclassical ideas of form. Shadwell boasted that he had made Shakespeare's original "into a play," though he granted, as his age was ready to do, that Shakespeare's genius provided the main strength of the work, however much it needed to be rescued from oblivion by added refinements. Shadwell managed in fact to save a number of Shakespeare's scenes, including the one in which Timon is approached by the Painter, the Poet, the Jeweler, and the Merchant (1.1), and the colloquy between Timon and Apemantus (4.3).

Shadwell's *Timon* did remarkably well. It was absent from the stage only in nine of the years between 1678 and 1745. After Betterton, Barton Booth was the outstanding Timon of the era. Although Shakespeare's text seems to have been briefly revived in Dublin in 1761, Shadwell's adaptation continued on into the late eighteenth century in a slightly modified version by James Love in 1768 and another by Thomas Hull in 1786.

A script prepared by Richard Cumberland for a production by actor-manager David Garrick at the Theatre Royal, Drury Lane, in 1771, made use of some Shadwell as well, but developed the conflict of selfish and selfless love in a new and, if possible, more sentimental direction. This version replaces Melissa and Evandra with Evanthe, Timon's virtuous daughter. She receives the attentions of three men, of whom two, Lucius and Lucullus, are interested only in her inheritance. They meet their just reward when Lucullus' buried money is found in the woods by Timon and when Lucius' house in Athens is looted by Alcibiades' troops intent upon revenging the wrongs done to Timon. Evanthe's true love is Alcibiades himself, a man of sterling honor who would never dream of keeping mistresses. When Evanthe is delivered to Alcibiades by the Athenian elders as a hostage, he escorts her to Timon's cave and receives a parental blessing on their marriage just before Timon expires on the steps of the ruined Temple of Faunus. Poetic justice having been richly served, virtue is triumphant.

George Lamb began the movement back to Shakespeare's text in a version presented at Drury Lane in 1816, with Edmund Kean as Timon, though even here Cumberland's approach of administering fit punishment to the grasping Lucius and Lucullus is retained, while Alcibiades' whores are left out in the interest of "refinement of manners." The cuts are heavy, but most of what is left is Shakespeare's. Not until actor-manager Samuel Phelps's productions at the Sadler's Wells Theatre in 1851 and 1856 do we hear of a genuine and successful revival. Phelps was attracted to the scenic possibilities of *Timon*'s classical setting, as he had been in his *The Winter's Tale* (1845) and was to be in his *Pericles* (1854), among others. Phelps provided Greek interiors, classical landscapes, and a stirring march of Alcibiades and his army to Athens. The production ran for forty nights in late 1851 and was among Phelps's greatest successes. Yet it did less well in his revival of 1856.

Theater managers of the late nineteenth and early twentieth centuries continued to deal uncertainly with the conflicting demands of scenic realism and restoration of Shakespeare's text. Charles Calvert produced out a version in 1871 in Manchester, England, at the Prince's Theatre, from which Phrynia and Timandra were excluded, but which added an array of dancing sequences to the banqueting scenes (1.2 and 3.6). In Calvert's production, Timon recovers his sanity under the care of his servants and dies in their arms, reconciled with humanity. Frank Benson's production of the play at Stratford-upon-Avon on Shakespeare's birthday, in 1892, emphasized the contrast between the magnificence of Timon's fortune and his subsequent "sour misery." Although Benson claimed to "love the play and the part," his *Timon* was not a success. J. H.

Leigh produced the play in London at the Court Theatre in 1904, and Frederick Warde toured America with it in 1910. Robert Atkins produced it at the Old Vic in 1922.

William Bridges-Adams seems to have been the first to address the bitterness of *Timon* in modern terms; at the Picture House, the temporary home of the Shakespeare Festival Theatre in Stratford-upon-Avon, in 1928, and since that time *Timon* has enjoyed a modest revival of interest. A young Tyrone Guthrie directed the Norwich Players at the Maddermarket Theatre in 1931, and then again some twenty-one years later, in 1952, at the Old Vic, with settings by Tanya Moiseiwitsch. For Nugent Monck's production at London's Westminster Theatre in 1935, Benjamin Britten, then aged twenty-one, provided a musical score that captured a modern sense of disillusionment. The play has readily lent itself to modern dress, as in the Birmingham Repertory Theatre's version of 1947. Michael Benthall directed the Old Vic's third *Timon* in 1956, with Ralph Richardson in the title role.

At Stratford, Canada, in 1963, Peter Coe and Michael Langham produced a modern-dress *Timon* that flashily emphasized the play's disillusioned cynicism. Apemantus was a jaded newspaper reporter with a cigarette constantly dangling from his lips; Timon hosted his banquet, which featured a jazz combo playing Duke Ellington music, in a red brocade dinner jacket. John Schlesinger's production at Stratford-upon-Avon in 1965 was more traditional in its decor but nonetheless deeply persuasive in its denunciation of sham and hypocritical friendship; as Timon (Paul Scofield) moved from an initial exuberant innocence to an appalling rage, "the excess of his misanthropy," as critic Robert Speaight noted, "was also the measure of his growth." At Ashland, Oregon, in 1978, director Jerry Turner returned to an aggressively modern idiom. Timon's flatterers and hangers-on were Texas tycoons in white three-piece suits and ten-gallon hats, amid a set that displayed the vulgar ostentation of a love of wealth. Alcibiades and his whores in Act 4, conversely, were guerrilla fighters with automatic weapons and camouflage outfits. The set articulated the doubleness of Turner's vision by literally turning itself inside out on a revolving platform stage; a decadently sybaritic civilization revealed at its back or underside a skeleton of anarchy and revolution.

Timon's deep cynicism has obviously challenged contemporary actors and directors and intrigued modern audiences. Richard Pasco, at The Other Place in Stratford-upon-Avon in 1980, was secretive and withdrawn as Timon in Ron Daniels's Kabuki-like production of the play in which the vibrant portrait of Timon's aristocratic Athens gave way after the intermission to a bare stage with a single tree. Jonathan Pryce's Timon, in the BBC television version directed by Jonathan Miller in 1981, revealed the strain and compulsive quality of his initial generosity and optimism, thus granting his emotional trajectory clarity and coherence.

Without doubt, the most significant modern production of *Timon* was a French version directed by Peter Brook in Paris in 1974. Brook staged the play in the shell of an abandoned Victorian theater, in an area of the orchestra with the audience around it in bleachers. The scarred backstage walls and the cavity that had formerly held the stage became part of the play's dispiriting vision, prompting *The New York Times*'s reviewer to remark: "Every spectator at once knows that he is sitting inside a symbol of the decline of the West." Brook's production memorably proved that *Timon*, even though it will never be a major work in its unfinished form, can enlist the sympathy of today's audiences by its compelling vision of protest against complacent wealth and venality.

TIMON
OF
ATHENS

The Actors' Names

TIMON OF ATHENS
LUCIUS *and* } *two flattering lords*
LUCULLUS,
SEMPRONIUS, *another flattering lord*
VENTIDIUS, *one of Timon's false friends*
APEMANTUS, *a churlish philosopher*
ALCIBIADES, *an Athenian captain*
[PHRYNIA, } *mistresses of Alcibiades*
TIMANDRA,
AN OLD ATHENIAN]
Certain SENATORS [*and* LORDS]
[FLAVIUS, *steward to Timon*]
POET, PAINTER, JEWELER, [*and*] MERCHANT
FLAMINIUS, *one of Timon's servants*
[LUCILIUS, *another*]
SERVILIUS, *another*
CAPHIS,
PHILOTUS' [SERVANT],
TITUS' [SERVANT],   *several servants*
HORTENSIUS' [SERVANT],   *to usurers*
[ISIDORE'S SERVANT,   [*Timon's creditors*]
Two of] VARRO'S [SERVANTS],
[A PAGE
A FOOL
Three STRANGERS
Two MESSENGERS]
Certain THIEVES [*or* BANDITTI]
CUPID [*and*] *certain* MASKERS [*as Amazons*]

With divers other Servants and Attendants, [*other Lords,
Officers, Soldiers*]

[SCENE: *Athens, and the neighboring woods*]

1.1   *Enter Poet, Painter, Jeweler, and Merchant, at*
       several doors. [The Poet and Painter form one
       group, the Jeweler and Merchant another.]

POET   Good day, sir.
PAINTER   I am glad you're well.
POET
  I have not seen you long. How goes the world?   3
PAINTER
  It wears, sir, as it grows.
POET   Ay, that's well known.   4
  But what particular rarity? What strange,   5
  Which manifold record not matches? See,   6
  Magic of bounty, all these spirits thy power   7
  Hath conjured to attend! I know the merchant.
PAINTER
  I know them both. Th' other's a jeweler.
MERCHANT [*To the Jeweler*]
  O, 'tis a worthy lord!
JEWELER   Nay, that's most fixed.   10
MERCHANT
  A most incomparable man, breathed, as it were,   11
  To an untirable and continuate goodness.   12
  He passes.   13
JEWELER   I have a jewel here—
MERCHANT
  O, pray, let's see 't. For the Lord Timon, sir?
JEWELER
  If he will touch the estimate. But for that—   16
POET [*Reciting to himself*]
  "When we for recompense have praised the vile,

1.1. Location: Athens. Timon's house.
s.d. several separate   **3 long** for a long time.   **How . . . world** i.e., how
are you doing? (But the Painter quibbles on the literal sense.)   **4 wears**
decays.   **grows** ages   **5 rarity** unusual occurrence.   **strange** strange
event   **6 Which . . . matches** i.e., which all recorded history cannot
equal   **7 Magic of bounty** i.e., the powerful attractive power of
generosity.   **spirits** i.e., beings, persons (spoken of as if they were
spirits conjured by magic)   **10 worthy lord** i.e., Timon.   **fixed** certain
11 breathed inspired; or trained through exercise   **12 untirable** inex-
haustible.   **continuate** habitual   **13 passes** surpasses   **16 touch the
estimate** offer or meet the price

It stains the glory in that happy verse   18
  Which aptly sings the good."

MERCHANT [*Looking at the jewel*] 'Tis a good form.   19

JEWELER   And rich. Here is a water, look ye.   20

PAINTER [*To the Poet*]
  You are rapt, sir, in some work, some dedication   21
  To the great lord.

POET   A thing slipped idly from me.   22
  Our poesy is as a gum which oozes
  From whence 'tis nourished. The fire i' the flint
  Shows not till it be struck; our gentle flame
  Provokes itself and like the current flies   26
  Each bound it chafes. What have you there?   27

PAINTER
  A picture, sir. When comes your book forth?

POET
  Upon the heels of my presentment, sir.   29
  Let's see your piece.   [*He examines the painting.*]

PAINTER   'Tis a good piece.

POET
  So 'tis. This comes off well and excellent.

PAINTER
  Indifferent.

POET   Admirable! How this grace   33
  Speaks his own standing! What a mental power   34
  This eye shoots forth! How big imagination   35
  Moves in this lip! To th' dumbness of the gesture   36
  One might interpret.   37

PAINTER
  It is a pretty mocking of the life.   38
  Here is a touch; is 't good?

POET   I will say of it,

---

18 happy felicitous, matching truthful praise to a worthy object
19 form shape, appearance. (Refers to the jewel.)   **20 water** luster
21 dedication (Such works were customarily dedicated to great noblemen.)   **22 idly** casually   **26 Provokes itself** i.e., is self-generating
26–27 flies . . . chafes seeks escape from the riverbanks that confine it
29 Upon . . . presentment as soon as I have presented it (to Lord Timon,
in hopes of obtaining his patronage)   **33 Indifferent** i.e., not bad.   **this
grace** i.e., of the person in the picture   **34 Speaks . . . standing** conveys
the dignity of its subject   **35 big** largely   **36–37 To . . . interpret** i.e., the
very gestures depicted are eloquent   **38 mocking** mirroring

It tutors nature. Artificial strife   40
Lives in these touches, livelier than life.

    Enter certain Senators.

PAINTER   How this lord is followed!
POET
    The senators of Athens. Happy man!
PAINTER   Look, more!
            [*The Senators pass over the stage, and exeunt.*]
POET
    You see this confluence, this great flood of visitors.
                            [*He shows his poem.*]
    I have in this rough work shaped out a man
    Whom this beneath world doth embrace and hug   47
    With amplest entertainment. My free drift   48
    Halts not particularly, but moves itself   49
    In a wide sea of tax. No leveled malice   50
    Infects one comma in the course I hold,   51
    But flies an eagle flight, bold and forth on,   52
    Leaving no tract behind.   53
PAINTER   How shall I understand you?   54
POET   I will unbolt to you.   55
    You see how all conditions, how all minds,   56
    As well of glib and slippery creatures as
    Of grave and austere quality, tender down   58
    Their services to Lord Timon. His large fortune,
    Upon his good and gracious nature hanging,   60
    Subdues and properties to his love and tendance   61
    All sorts of hearts; yea, from the glass-faced flatterer 62

---

40 Artificial strife the striving of art to surpass nature   **47 this beneath
world** i.e., the world itself, beneath the sphere of the moon   **48 entertainment** welcome.   **drift** design   **49 Halts not particularly** doesn't
concern itself with criticizing anyone individually   **50 tax** censure.
leveled aimed, as a gun is aimed at a particular object   **51 comma** i.e.,
detail   **52 forth on** straight on   **53 tract** track, trace   **54 How . . . you**
what do you mean   **55 unbolt** unlock, disclose   **56 conditions** ranks,
temperaments   **58 tender down** tender, offer   **60 hanging** providing
attractive adornment, like rich clothes   **61 properties** appropriates.
tendance tending on him (also in l. 85)   **62 glass-faced** showing in his
look, as by reflection, the looks of his patron

To Apemantus, that few things loves better
Than to abhor himself—even he drops down
The knee before him and returns in peace   65
Most rich in Timon's nod.   66

PAINTER   I saw them speak together.

POET

Sir, I have upon a high and pleasant hill
Feigned Fortune to be throned. The base o' the mount   69
Is ranked with all deserts, all kind of natures,   70
That labor on the bosom of this sphere   71
To propagate their states. Amongst them all   72
Whose eyes are on this sovereign lady fixed
One do I personate of Lord Timon's frame,   74
Whom Fortune with her ivory hand wafts to her,   75
Whose present grace to present slaves and servants   76
Translates his rivals.

PAINTER   'Tis conceived to scope.   77
This throne, this Fortune, and this hill, methinks,
With one man beckoned from the rest below,
Bowing his head against the steepy mount   80
To climb his happiness, would be well expressed   81
In our condition.

POET   Nay, sir, but hear me on.   82
All those which were his fellows but of late—   83
Some better than his value—on the moment   84
Follow his strides, his lobbies fill with tendance,   85
Rain sacrificial whisperings in his ear,   86

65 returns departs   **66 in Timon's nod** for having been acknowledged
by Timon   **69 Feigned** imagined, supposed   **70 ranked . . . deserts** filled
with the ranks of all degrees of merit   **71 this sphere** i.e., the earth
72 propagate enlarge.   **states** fortunes   **74 personate** represent.   **frame**
mold, nature   **75 ivory** white.   **wafts** beckons, waves   **76–77 Whose**
. . . rivals i.e., Fortune, whose gracious favor transforms his (Timon's)
rivals immediately into slaves and servants   **77 to scope** to the purpose   **80 Bowing his head** i.e., bending forward with the effort.   **steepy**
steep   **81 his happiness** i.e., to his good fortune   **81–82 would**
. . . condition would find a striking parallel in the human condition
82 hear me on hear me speak further   **83 but of late** only recently
84 better . . . value his superiors.   **on the moment** immediately   **85 his**
. . . tendance fill the anterooms of his house with their attentive presence   **86 sacrificial whisperings** whispers of sacrifices made in his
honor, or whispers offered with reverential deference as a sacrifice is
offered

Make sacred even his stirrup, and through him   87
Drink the free air.

PAINTER   Ay, marry, what of these?   88

POET

When Fortune in her shift and change of mood
Spurns down her late beloved, all his dependents,   90
Which labored after him to the mountain's top
Even on their knees and hands, let him slip down,
Not one accompanying his declining foot.

PAINTER   'Tis common.

A thousand moral paintings I can show   95
That shall demonstrate these quick blows of Fortune's
More pregnantly than words. Yet you do well
To show Lord Timon that mean eyes have seen   98
The foot above the head.   99

> *Trumpets sound. Enter Lord Timon, addressing*
> *himself courteously to every suitor; [a Messenger*
> *from Ventidius talking with him; Lucilius and*
> *other servants following].*

TIMON   Imprisoned is he, say you?

MESSENGER

Ay, my good lord. Five talents is his debt,   101
His means most short, his creditors most strait.   102
Your honorable letter he desires   103
To those have shut him up, which failing   104
Periods his comfort.

TIMON   Noble Ventidius! Well,   105

---

87 stirrup i.e., as they help him to his horse   **87–88 through . . . air**
seem to breathe the free air only through his bounty   **88 marry** (A mild
oath, originally "By Mary.")   **90 Spurns down** kicks or thrusts down
95 moral paintings allegorical depictions   **98 mean eyes** i.e., of men of
low degree   **99 The foot . . . head** i.e., highest fortune tumbling headlong downward by the turn of Fortune's wheel; or perhaps the foot of
Fortune poised over the head of the once-prosperous man   **101 talents**
units of money today worth $2000 or more. (But Shakespeare was
evidently uncertain about the *talent's* value as he wrote this play. *Talents* is also a Biblical term; see, for example, Matthew 25:14–29.)
102 short limited.   **strait** severe, exacting   **103 Your . . . letter** a letter
from your honor   **104 those** those who   **104–105 which failing Periods**
the lack of which puts an end to

I am not of that feather to shake off   106
My friend when he must need me. I do know him   107
A gentleman that well deserves a help,
Which he shall have. I'll pay the debt and free him.

MESSENGER   Your lordship ever binds him.   110

TIMON
Commend me to him. I will send his ransom;
And being enfranchised, bid him come to me.   112
'Tis not enough to help the feeble up,
But to support him after. Fare you well.   114

MESSENGER   All happiness to your honor!   *Exit.*

Enter an Old Athenian.

OLD ATHENIAN
Lord Timon, hear me speak.

TIMON   Freely, good father.   116

OLD ATHENIAN
Thou hast a servant named Lucilius.

TIMON   I have so. What of him?

OLD ATHENIAN
Most noble Timon, call the man before thee.

TIMON
Attends he here or no? Lucilius!

LUCILIUS [*Coming forward*] Here, at your lordship's service.

OLD ATHENIAN
This fellow here, Lord Timon, this thy creature,   122
By night frequents my house. I am a man
That from my first have been inclined to thrift,
And my estate deserves an heir more raised   125
Than one which holds a trencher.

TIMON   Well, what further?   126

OLD ATHENIAN
One only daughter have I, no kin else
On whom I may confer what I have got.
The maid is fair, o' the youngest for a bride,   129

106 feather i.e., disposition (as in "birds of a feather")   **107 know him**
know him to be   **110 binds him** i.e., to grateful obligation
112 enfranchised set free   **114 But** i.e., but one must continue
116 Freely readily, gladly.   **father** (Respectful term of address to an
old man.)   **122 creature** dependent, hanger-on   **125 more raised** of
higher social position   **126 holds a trencher** i.e., serves at table, handling wooden dishes   **129 o' the . . . bride** just of marriageable age

And I have bred her at my dearest cost   130
In qualities of the best. This man of thine
Attempts her love. I prithee, noble lord,   132
Join with me to forbid him her resort;   133
Myself have spoke in vain.

TIMON   The man is honest.

OLD ATHENIAN   Therefore he will be, Timon.   136
His honesty rewards him in itself;
It must not bear my daughter.   138

TIMON   Does she love him?

OLD ATHENIAN   She is young and apt.   140
Our own precedent passions do instruct us   141
What levity's in youth.

TIMON [*To Lucilius*]   Love you the maid?

LUCILIUS
Ay, my good lord, and she accepts of it.   143

OLD ATHENIAN
If in her marriage my consent be missing,
I call the gods to witness, I will choose
Mine heir from forth the beggars of the world
And dispossess her all.   147

TIMON   How shall she be endowed   148
If she be mated with an equal husband?   149

OLD ATHENIAN
Three talents on the present; in future, all.   150

TIMON
This gentleman of mine hath served me long;
To build his fortune I will strain a little,
For 'tis a bond in men. Give him thy daughter.   153
What you bestow, in him I'll counterpoise,   154
And make him weigh with her.

OLD ATHENIAN   Most noble lord,   155
Pawn me to this your honor, she is his.   156

---

130 bred . . . cost brought her up and educated her at great expense
132 Attempts tries to win   **133 her resort** access to her   **136 Therefore he
will be** i.e., he will be if we forbid him to see my daughter   **138 bear my
daughter** carry off my daughter into the bargain   **140 apt** easily wooed,
impressionable   **141 precedent** former   **143 accepts of** accepts   **147 all**
wholly   **148 How . . . endowed** what dowry will she be given   **149 an
equal husband** one of equal estate   **150 on the present** immediately
153 bond obligation. **in** among   **154 counterpoise** match, counterbal-
ance   **155 weigh with her** be equal to her in estate   **156 Pawn . . . honor**
if you'll pledge your word of honor to do as you have said

TIMON
  My hand to thee; mine honor on my promise.
LUCILIUS
  Humbly I thank your lordship. Never may
  That state or fortune fall into my keeping   159
  Which is not owed to you!   160
                    Exeunt [Lucilius and Old Athenian].
POET [*Presenting his poem*]
  Vouchsafe my labor, and long live your lordship!   161
TIMON
  I thank you; you shall hear from me anon.   162
  Go not away.—What have you there, my friend?
PAINTER
  A piece of painting, which I do beseech   164
  Your lordship to accept.   [*He presents his painting.*]
TIMON   Painting is welcome.
  The painting is almost the natural man;   166
  For since dishonor traffics with man's nature,   167
  He is but outside; these penciled figures are   168
  Even such as they give out. I like your work,   169
  And you shall find I like it. Wait attendance   170
  Till you hear further from me.
PAINTER   The gods preserve ye!
TIMON
  Well fare you, gentleman. Give me your hand;
  We must needs dine together.—Sir, your jewel   173
  Hath suffered under praise.
JEWELER   What, my lord, dispraise?   174
TIMON
  A mere satiety of commendations.   175
  If I should pay you for 't as 'tis extolled,
  It would unclew me quite.
JEWELER   My lord, 'tis rated   177

---

159 **That** i.e., any   160 **owed to you** acknowledged to be from you
161 **Vouchsafe** deign to accept   162 **anon** shortly   164 **piece** example,
specimen   166 **the natural man** man as he truly is, not what he pretends to be   167 **traffics** deals (improperly)   168 **He is but outside** i.e.,
he becomes a mere outward appearance.   **penciled** painted   169 **Even
. . . out** exactly as they appear   170 **Wait** remain in   173 **needs** necessarily, of course   174 **suffered under praise** been overwhelmed by
praise. (But the Jeweler misunderstands.)   175 **mere** utter   177 **unclew**
unwind, i.e., ruin

As those which sell would give; but you well know   178
Things of like value differing in the owners
Are prizèd by their masters. Believe 't, dear lord,   180
You mend the jewel by the wearing it.
                                    [*He presents a jewel.*]
TIMON   Well mocked.   182
MERCHANT
No, my good lord, he speaks the common tongue   183
Which all men speak with him.

        Enter Apemantus.

TIMON   Look who comes here. Will you be chid?   185
JEWELER   We'll bear, with your lordship.   186
MERCHANT   He'll spare none.
TIMON
Good morrow to thee, gentle Apemantus!
APEMANTUS
Till I be gentle, stay thou for thy good morrow—   189
When thou art Timon's dog, and these knaves honest.   190
TIMON
Why dost thou call them knaves? Thou know'st them
   not.
APEMANTUS   Are they not Athenians?
TIMON   Yes.
APEMANTUS   Then I repent not.   194
JEWELER   You know me, Apemantus?
APEMANTUS   Thou know'st I do. I called thee by thy   196
   name.   197
TIMON   Thou art proud, Apemantus.
APEMANTUS   Of nothing so much as that I am not like
   Timon.
TIMON   Whither art going?

178 As . . . give at a price which merchants would pay, i.e., at cost
180 prizèd . . . masters valued as their owners are respected; i.e., the
gem will increase in value because Timon will wear it   182 mocked
performed   183 common tongue general opinion   185 Will you be chid
are you prepared to be scolded   186 We'll . . . lordship i.e., we'll put up
with it if your lordship can   189–190 Till . . . honest i.e., you must wait
for my "good morrow" until I have become free of satirical sharpness
and until men are free of the faults I criticize, something as likely to
happen as Timon changing places with his dog   194 repent not don't
regret what I said   196–197 thy name i.e., knave

APEMANTUS To knock out an honest Athenian's brains.

TIMON That's a deed thou'lt die for.

APEMANTUS Right, if doing nothing be death by the law. 204

TIMON How lik'st thou this picture, Apemantus?

APEMANTUS The best, for the innocence.   206

TIMON Wrought he not well that painted it?

APEMANTUS He wrought better that made the painter, and yet he's but a filthy piece of work.

PAINTER You're a dog.   210

APEMANTUS Thy mother's of my generation. What's she, 211 if I be a dog?

TIMON Wilt dine with me, Apemantus?

APEMANTUS No. I eat not lords.   214

TIMON An thou shouldst, thou'dst anger ladies.   215

APEMANTUS O, they eat lords. So they come by great 216 bellies.

TIMON That's a lascivious apprehension.   218

APEMANTUS So thou apprehend'st it. Take it for thy labor.

TIMON How dost thou like this jewel, Apemantus?

APEMANTUS Not so well as plain dealing, which will not cost a man a doit.   222

TIMON What dost thou think 'tis worth?

APEMANTUS Not worth my thinking.—How now, poet?

POET How now, philosopher?

APEMANTUS Thou liest.

POET Art not one?

APEMANTUS Yes.

POET Then I lie not.

APEMANTUS Art not a poet?

POET Yes.

---

204 doing nothing i.e., since there are no honest Athenians, I will be doing nothing. **death by the law** subject to the death penalty. (Athenians have no brains; therefore to knock out their brains is to do nothing.) **206 innocence** innocuous character, inability to do harm (as real life can) **210 dog** (*Cynic* is derived from the Greek for "dog.") **211 generation** species **214 eat not lords** do not consume the substance of great men. (But in his next speech Apemantus gives the phrase a sexual meaning.) **215 An** if **216 come by** acquire **218 apprehension** (1) interpretation (2) seizure, grasp (with a bawdy suggestion in the idea of seizing physically) **222 doit** half a farthing, coin of slight value

APEMANTUS   Then thou liest. Look in thy last work,   233
    where thou hast feigned him a worthy fellow.   234

POET   That's not feigned. He is so.

APEMANTUS   Yes, he is worthy of thee, and to pay thee
    for thy labor. He that loves to be flattered is worthy o'
    the flatterer. Heavens, that I were a lord!

TIMON   What wouldst do then, Apemantus?

APEMANTUS   E'en as Apemantus does now: hate a lord
    with my heart.

TIMON   What, thyself?

APEMANTUS   Ay.

TIMON   Wherefore?

APEMANTUS   That I had no angry wit to be a lord.—Art   245
    not thou a merchant?

MERCHANT   Ay, Apemantus.

APEMANTUS   Traffic confound thee, if the gods will not!   248

MERCHANT   If traffic do it, the gods do it.

APEMANTUS   Traffic's thy god, and thy god confound
    thee!

     Trumpet sounds. Enter a Messenger.

TIMON   What trumpet's that?

MESSENGER
'Tis Alcibiades and some twenty horse,   253
All of companionship.   254

TIMON
Pray, entertain them; give them guide to us.   255
                   [Exeunt some attendants.]
[To his guests.] You must needs dine with me. Go not
    you hence
Till I have thanked you.—When dinner's done,
Show me this piece.—I am joyful of your sights.   258

     Enter Alcibiades, with the rest.

---

233 Then thou liest (because poets are supposed to feign)   **234 him** i.e.,
Timon   **245 That . . . lord** i.e., that in becoming a lord I had forfeited
the angry wit that only an independent philosopher can enjoy
248 Traffic confound may business or trade ruin   **253 horse** horse-
men   **254 of companionship** belonging to the same party
255 entertain them show them hospitality.   **give them guide** show them
in   **258 of your sights** to see you

Most welcome, sir!

APEMANTUS   So, so, there! Aches contract   259
And starve your supple joints! That there should be   260
Small love amongst these sweet knaves, and all
This courtesy! The strain of man's bred out   262
Into baboon and monkey.

ALCIBIADES
Sir, you have saved my longing, and I feed   264
Most hungerly on your sight.

TIMON   Right welcome, sir!   265
Ere we depart, we'll share a bounteous time   266
In different pleasures. Pray you, let us in.   267
                Exeunt [all except Apemantus].

Enter two Lords.

FIRST LORD   What time o' day is 't, Apemantus?
APEMANTUS   Time to be honest.
FIRST LORD   That time serves still.   270
APEMANTUS   The most accursèd thou, that still omitt'st it.   271
SECOND LORD   Thou art going to Lord Timon's feast?
APEMANTUS   Ay, to see meat fill knaves and wine heat fools.
SECOND LORD   Fare thee well, fare thee well.
APEMANTUS   Thou art a fool to bid me farewell twice.
SECOND LORD   Why, Apemantus?
APEMANTUS   Shouldst have kept one to thyself, for I mean to give thee none.
FIRST LORD   Hang thyself!
APEMANTUS   No, I will do nothing at thy bidding. Make thy requests to thy friend.
SECOND LORD   Away, unpeaceable dog, or I'll spurn thee   283
hence!
APEMANTUS   I will fly, like a dog, the heels o' the ass.   285
                             [Exit.]

---

259 So, so, there well, well, look at that (i.e., all the bowing and scraping) **260 starve** destroy **262 strain** race, stock. **bred out** degenerated **264 saved** anticipated and thus prevented **265 hungerly on your sight** hungrily on the sight of you **266 depart** part company **267 different** various. **in** enter **270 still** always **271 most** i.e., more. **omitt'st** fail to take advantage of **283 unpeaceable** quarrelsome, incessantly barking. **spurn** kick **285 fly** flee

FIRST LORD
  He's opposite to humanity. Come, shall we in   286
  And taste Lord Timon's bounty? He outgoes   287
  The very heart of kindness.   288

SECOND LORD
  He pours it out. Plutus, the god of gold,
  Is but his steward. No meed but he repays   290
  Sevenfold above itself; no gift to him
  But breeds the giver a return exceeding
  All use of quittance.

FIRST LORD   The noblest mind he carries   293
  That ever governed man.

SECOND LORD
  Long may he live in fortunes! Shall we in?

FIRST LORD   I'll keep you company.   *Exeunt.*

❖

1.2   *Hautboys playing loud music. A great banquet
served in, [Flavius and others attending]; and
then enter Lord Timon, the states, the Athenian
Lords, [Alcibiades, and] Ventidius (which
Timon redeemed from prison). Then comes,
dropping after all, Apemantus, discontentedly,
like himself.*

VENTIDIUS   Most honored Timon,
  It hath pleased the gods to remember my father's age
  And call him to long peace.   3
  He is gone happy and has left me rich.   4
  Then, as in grateful virtue I am bound
  To your free heart, I do return those talents,   6
  Doubled with thanks and service, from whose help
  I derived liberty.   [*He offers money.*]

---

286 opposite to (1) antagonistic to (2) the reverse of   **287 outgoes** surpasses   **288 heart** essence   **290 meed** merit; or gift   **293 use of quittance** usual rates of repayment with interest

1.2. Location: A banqueting room in Timon's house.
s.d. Hautboys oboelike instruments.   **states** i.e., rulers of the state,
senators.   **dropping** i.e., "dropping in," arriving casually.   **like himself**
not in finery   **3 long peace** eternal rest   **4 gone** died   **6 free** generous

TIMON   O, by no means,
  Honest Ventidius. You mistake my love.
  I gave it freely ever, and there's none
  Can truly say he gives if he receives.   12
  If our betters play at that game, we must not dare   13
  To imitate them. Faults that are rich are fair.   14
VENTIDIUS   A noble spirit!

                 [They all stand ceremoniously
                           looking at Timon.]

TIMON
  Nay, my lords, ceremony was but devised at first
  To set a gloss on faint deeds, hollow welcomes,   17
  Recanting goodness, sorry ere 'tis shown;   18
  But where there is true friendship, there needs none. 19
  Pray, sit. More welcome are ye to my fortunes
  Than my fortunes to me.   *[They sit.]*
FIRST LORD
  My lord, we always have confessed it.   22
APEMANTUS
  Ho, ho, confessed it? Hanged it, have you not?   23
TIMON
  O, Apemantus, you are welcome.
APEMANTUS   No,
  You shall not make me welcome.
  I come to have thee thrust me out of doors.
TIMON
  Fie, thou'rt a churl. You've got a humor there   27
  Does not become a man; 'tis much to blame.   28
  They say, my lords, *Ira furor brevis est*, but yond   29
  man is ever angry. Go, let him have a table by himself, 30

---

12 gives . . . receives (Cf. Acts 20:35: "It is more blessed to give than to
receive.") **13 betters** superiors. **at that game** i.e., taking in wealth
while seeming to be generous **14 that are rich** i.e., in those who are
rich. **fair** i.e., excused by their wealth **17 set a gloss on** give a spe-
ciously fair appearance to **18 Recanting goodness** generosity that takes
back what it has offered **19 there needs none** there is no need for
ceremony **22 confessed it** acknowledged the truth of what you say
23 Hanged it i.e., killed it instead. (Apemantus replies with a jesting
allusion to the saying, "Confess and be hanged.") **27 churl** surly
person. **humor** disposition **28 Does** that does **29 Ira furor brevis est**
wrath is a brief madness. (Horace's *Epistles*, 1.2.62.) **30 ever** always

for he does neither affect company nor is he fit for 't, 31
indeed.

APEMANTUS   Let me stay at thine apperil, Timon. I come 33
to observe; I give thee warning on 't.

TIMON   I take no heed of thee. Thou'rt an Athenian,
therefore welcome. I myself would have no power; 36
prithee, let my meat make thee silent. 37

APEMANTUS   I scorn thy meat; 'twould choke me, for I 38
should ne'er flatter thee. O you gods, what a number 39
of men eats Timon, and he sees 'em not! It grieves me
to see so many dip their meat in one man's blood; and 41
all the madness is, he cheers them up too. 42
I wonder men dare trust themselves with men.
Methinks they should invite them without knives; 44
Good for their meat, and safer for their lives. 45
There's much example for 't. The fellow that sits next
him, now parts bread with him, pledges the breath of 47
him in a divided draft, is the readiest man to kill 48
him. 'T has been proved. If I were a huge man, I 49
should fear to drink at meals,
Lest they should spy my windpipe's dangerous notes. 51
Great men should drink with harness on their throats. 52

TIMON [*Toasting a Lord who drinks to him*]
My lord, in heart! And let the health go round. 53

SECOND LORD
Let it flow this way, my good lord. 54

---

31 affect (1) like (2) seek, aim at   **33 thine apperil** your peril, risk
36 would . . . power do not wish the power (to silence you)   **37 meat**
food   **38–39 for I . . . thee** (Apemantus implies that Timon's food is to
reward flatterers; Apemantus, being none, would choke on it.)   **41 one
man's blood** (Possible allusion to the Last Supper; the *fellow* in
ll. 46–49, who shares food and drink only to betray his host, is like
Judas.)   **42 all . . . too** the most mad aspect of his behavior is that he
encourages them   **44 without knives** (Refers to the Renaissance custom
of guests bringing their own knives.)   **45 Good . . . meat** i.e., without
knives, the guests would eat less food   **47 parts** shares.   **pledges the
breath** i.e., drinks to the health   **48 a divided draft** a cup that they
share   **49 huge** great in rank and wealth   **51 windpipe's . . . notes**
indications on my throat of where my windpipe is (and hence where it
might be slit) as the head is thrown back. (The *windpipe* also suggests a
bagpipe capable of *notes* or musical sounds.)   **52 harness** armor   **53 in
heart** heartily.   **health** toast, and the cup   **54 flow** circulate

APEMANTUS Flow this way? A brave fellow! He keeps 55
his tides well. Those healths will make thee and thy 56
state look ill, Timon.   59
Here's that which is too weak to be a sinner: 58
Honest water, which ne'er left man i' the mire.   59
This and my food are equals; there's no odds.   60
Feasts are too proud to give thanks to the gods. 61

Apemantus' grace.

Immortal gods, I crave no pelf.   62
I pray for no man but myself.
Grant I may never prove so fond   64
To trust man on his oath or bond,
Or a harlot for her weeping,
Or a dog that seems a-sleeping,
Or a keeper with my freedom,   68
Or my friends, if I should need 'em.
    Amen. So fall to 't.   70
    Rich men sin, and I eat root. [*He eats and drinks.*]
Much good dich thy good heart, Apemantus!   72
TIMON Captain Alcibiades, your heart's in the field 73
now.
ALCIBIADES My heart is ever at your service, my lord.
TIMON You had rather be at a breakfast of enemies than 76
a dinner of friends.   77
ALCIBIADES So they were bleeding new, my lord, 78
there's no meat like 'em. I could wish my best friend
at such a feast.
APEMANTUS Would all those flatterers were thine ene-
mies then, that then thou mightst kill 'em—and bid
me to 'em!   83
FIRST LORD Might we but have that happiness, my lord,

---

55 brave fine. (Said ironically.) **56 tides** times, seasons (with quibbling
reference to *flow* of tides) **57 state** (1) physical condition (2) fortune,
estate **58 a sinner** an incentive to sin **59 i' the mire** i.e., in trouble
60 there's no odds there's nothing to choose between them **61 Feasts**
i.e., partakers of fine feasts **62 pelf** property, possessions **64 fond**
foolish **68 keeper** jailer **70 fall to 't** i.e., begin to eat **72 dich** may it
do. (Originally a contraction of "d' it ye" in the phrase "much good do
it you.") **73 field** battlefield **76 of** consisting of **77 of** among **78 So**
provided that **83 to 'em** i.e., to eat them

that you would once use our hearts, whereby we 85
might express some part of our zeals, we should think 86
ourselves forever perfect. 87

TIMON O, no doubt, my good friends, but the gods
themselves have provided that I shall have much help
from you. How had you been my friends else? Why
have you that charitable title from thousands, did not 91
you chiefly belong to my heart? I have told more of 92
you to myself than you can with modesty speak in 93
your own behalf; and thus far I confirm you. O you 94
gods, think I, what need we have any friends if we 95
should ne'er have need of 'em? They were the most
needless creatures living, should we ne'er have use for 97
'em, and would most resemble sweet instruments 98
hung up in cases, that keeps their sounds to themselves. Why, I have often wished myself poorer, that I
might come nearer to you. We are born to do benefits;
and what better or properer can we call our own than 102
the riches of our friends? O, what a precious comfort
'tis to have so many, like brothers, commanding one 104
another's fortunes! O, joy's e'en made away ere 't can 105
be born! Mine eyes cannot hold out water, methinks. 106
To forget their faults, I drink to you. 107

                    [*He weeps, and drinks a toast.*]
APEMANTUS Thou weep'st to make them drink, Timon.
SECOND LORD [*To Timon*]
   Joy had the like conception in our eyes,
   And at that instant like a babe sprung up. 109
APEMANTUS
   Ho, ho! I laugh to think that babe a bastard. 111
THIRD LORD [*To Timon*]
   I promise you, my lord, you moved me much. 112

---

85 use our hearts make trial of our love   **86 zeals** love   **87 forever perfect**
completely happy   **91 charitable title** beloved name.   **from** from
among   **92 told** (1) recited (2) counted   **92–93 of you** i.e., concerning your
deservings   **94 confirm you** endorse your claim to be my worthy
friends   **95 what** why   **97 needless** useless   **98 instruments** musical
instruments   **102 properer** more fittingly   **104 commanding** having at
their disposal   **105 made away** destroyed, i.e., turned to tears   **106 born**
i.e., expressed   **107 To . . . faults** i.e., to mask my weakness in giving way
to tears   **109 sprung up** (1) leaped from the womb (2) welled up like a
spring of tears   **111 bastard** i.e., illegitimate, without genuine source.
(Refers to the guests' tears.)   **112 promise** assure

APEMANTUS   Much!   *Sound tucket* [*within*].   113
TIMON   What means that trump?

    Enter Servant.

                            How now?   114
SERVANT   Please you, my lord, there are certain ladies
  most desirous of admittance.
TIMON   Ladies? What are their wills?
SERVANT   There comes with them a forerunner, my   118
  lord, which bears that office to signify their pleasures.   119
TIMON   I pray, let them be admitted.   [*Exit Servant.*]

    Enter Cupid.

CUPID
  Hail to thee, worthy Timon, and to all
  That of his bounties taste! The five best senses
  Acknowledge thee their patron, and come freely
  To gratulate thy plenteous bosom. Th' ear,   124
  Taste, touch, and smell, pleased from thy table rise;
  They only now come but to feast thine eyes.   126
TIMON
  They're welcome all. Let 'em have kind admittance.
  Music, make their welcome!
               [*Cupid summons the maskers.*]

FIRST LORD
  You see, my lord, how ample you're beloved.   129

    [*Music.*] *Enter a masque of Ladies* [*as*] *Amazons,*
    with lutes in their hands, dancing and playing.

APEMANTUS   Hoyday!   130
  What a sweep of vanity comes this way!
  They dance? They are madwomen.
  Like madness is the glory of this life   133
  As this pomp shows to a little oil and root.   134

---

113 Much (An expression of contemptuous disbelief; playing on *much* in
the previous line.)   **s.d. tucket** trumpet call   **114 trump** trumpet
blast   **118 forerunner** herald, messenger   **119 which** who.   **office**
function.   **pleasures** wishes   **124 gratulate** greet, salute.   **plenteous
bosom** generous heart   **126 They** i.e., the maskers.   **only now come but**
come only   **129 ample** amply   **130 Hoyday** (Exclamation denoting
surprise; a variety of "heyday.")   **133 Like** similar, equal.   **glory** vain-
glory   **134 As . . . root** i.e., in the same way as this splendid feast appears when compared with the mere necessities of life

We make ourselves fools to disport ourselves   135
And spend our flatteries to drink those men   136
Upon whose age we void it up again   137
With poisonous spite and envy.   138
Who lives that's not depravèd or depraves?   139
Who dies that bears not one spurn to their graves   140
Of their friends' gift?   141
I should fear those that dance before me now
Would one day stamp upon me. 'T has been done;
Men shut their doors against a setting sun.   144

*The Lords rise from table, with much adoring of
Timon; and to show their loves each singles out
an Amazon, and all dance, men with women, a
lofty strain or two to the hautboys, and cease.*

TIMON
You have done our pleasures much grace, fair ladies,
Set a fair fashion on our entertainment,   146
Which was not half so beautiful and kind.   147
You have added worth unto 't and luster,
And entertained me with mine own device.   149
I am to thank you for 't.   150

FIRST LADY
My lord, you take us even at the best.   151

APEMANTUS   Faith, for the worst is filthy and would not   152
hold taking, I doubt me.   153

TIMON
Ladies, there is an idle banquet attends you;   154
Please you to dispose yourselves.   155

---

135 disport entertain   **136–138 And . . . envy** and lavish our flatteries in
drinking the healths of those upon whom, when they are old, we cast up
our surfeit in poisonous spite and malice   **139 depravèd** vilified, slan-
dered.   **depraves** slanders   **140 spurn** injury, insult   **141 gift** giving
144 s.d. hautboys oboelike instruments   **146 Set . . . on** given grace and
elegance to   **147 was not** i.e., before your arrival was not.   **kind** gracious   **149 with . . . device** (The masque appears to have been designed
by Timon to surprise his guests; or, he acknowledges that it was designed especially for him.)   **150 am to** am under obligation to   **151 take
. . . best** i.e., praise us most generously   **152 the worst** i.e., the worst
part of you. (An obscene suggestion.)   **152–153 would . . . taking** i.e.,
(1) would not warrant notice (2) is too rotten with venereal disease
153 doubt me fear   **154 idle** trifling, slight   **155 dispose yourselves** take
your places

ALL LADIES   Most thankfully, my lord.
                              Exeunt [Cupid and Ladies].
TIMON   Flavius!
FLAVIUS
  My lord?
TIMON   The little casket bring me hither.
FLAVIUS   Yes, my lord. [*Aside.*] More jewels yet?
  There is no crossing him in 's humor;   160
  Else I should tell him well, i' faith I should,   161
  When all's spent, he'd be crossed then, an he could.   162
  'Tis pity bounty had not eyes behind,   163
  That man might ne'er be wretched for his mind. *Exit.*   164
FIRST LORD   Where be our men?
SERVANT   Here, my lord, in readiness.
SECOND LORD
  Our horses!

        Enter Flavius [with the casket].

TIMON   O my friends, I have one word
  To say to you. Look you, my good lord,
  I must entreat you honor me so much   169
  As to advance this jewel; accept it and wear it,   170
  Kind my lord.   [*He offers a jewel.*]
FIRST LORD
  I am so far already in your gifts—
ALL   So are we all.

      Enter a Servant.

SERVANT
  My lord, there are certain nobles of the Senate
  Newly alighted and come to visit you.
TIMON
  They are fairly welcome.   [*Exit Servant.*]
FLAVIUS   I beseech your honor,   176
  Vouchsafe me a word; it does concern you near.   177

---

160 humor frame of mind   **161 well** plainly   **162 crossed** (1) wishing to
have his debts canceled (2) thwarted (as in l. 160).   **an** if   **163 bounty**
generosity.   **had not eyes behind** i.e., is not able to be more cautious
164 for his mind on account of his generous inclinations   **169 you
honor** you to honor   **170 advance** make more worthy; i.e., by possessing
it   **176 fairly** sincerely   **177 near** closely

TIMON
  Near? Why then, another time I'll hear thee.
  I prithee, let's be provided to show them entertainment.
FLAVIUS [*Aside*]   I scarce know how.
     Enter another Servant.

SECOND SERVANT
  May it please your honor, Lord Lucius,
  Out of his free love, hath presented to you
  Four milk-white horses trapped in silver.   183
TIMON
  I shall accept them fairly. Let the presents   184
  Be worthily entertained.   [*Exit Servant.*]
     Enter a third Servant.

                 How now? What news?   185
THIRD SERVANT Please you, my lord, that honorable
  gentleman, Lord Lucullus, entreats your company to-
  morrow to hunt with him and has sent your honor
  two brace of greyhounds. ·   189
TIMON
  I'll hunt with him; and let them be received,
  Not without fair reward.   [*Exit Servant.*]
FLAVIUS [*Aside*]   What will this come to?
  He commands us to provide, and give great gifts,
  And all out of an empty coffer;
  Nor will he know his purse, or yield me this,   194
  To show him what a beggar his heart is,
  Being of no power to make his wishes good.   196
  His promises fly so beyond his state   197
  That what he speaks is all in debt; he owes
  For every word. He is so kind that he now
  Pays interest for 't; his land's put to their books.   200
  Well, would I were gently put out of office
  Before I were forced out!
  Happier is he that has no friend to feed

---

183 trapped in silver in silver-mounted trappings **184 fairly** graciously **185 Be worthily entertained** given the reception they deserve
189 brace pair **194 purse** financial situation. **yield me this** grant me
opportunity **196 Being of** i.e., the desires of his heart having
197 state estate **200 put . . . books** i.e., mortgaged to those whom he
has befriended with gifts

　　Than such that do e'en enemies exceed.   204
　　I bleed inwardly for my lord.   *Exit.*
TIMON [*To the Lords*]   You do yourselves
　　Much wrong, you bate too much of your own merits.—   206
　　Here, my lord, a trifle of our love.   [*He offers a gift.*]
SECOND LORD
　　With more than common thanks I will receive it.
THIRD LORD   O, he's the very soul of bounty!
TIMON   And now I remember, my lord, you gave good 210
　　words the other day of a bay courser I rode on. 'Tis 211
　　yours because you liked it.
THIRD LORD
　　O, I beseech you, pardon me, my lord, in that.   213
TIMON
　　You may take my word, my lord: I know no man
　　Can justly praise but what he does affect.   215
　　I weigh my friends' affection with mine own.   216
　　I'll tell you true, I'll call to you.   217
ALL LORDS   O, none so welcome.
TIMON
　　I take all and your several visitations   219
　　So kind to heart, 'tis not enough to give.   220
　　Methinks I could deal kingdoms to my friends
　　And ne'er be weary. Alcibiades,
　　Thou art a soldier, therefore seldom rich.
　　It comes in charity to thee; for all thy living   224
　　Is 'mongst the dead, and all the lands thou hast
　　Lie in a pitched field.   226
ALCIBIADES   Ay, defiled land, my lord.   227

204 Than . . . exceed i.e., than he that feeds so-called "friends" who, by
consuming his wealth, outdo his enemies in ruining him   **206 bate
. . . of** belittle too much   **210–211 gave good words** spoke favorably
211 bay courser dark brown horse with black mane and tail
213 pardon . . . that i.e., forgive my declining the offer; my mentioning
the horse was not meant as a hint   **215 but . . . affect** a thing unless he
likes and desires it   **216 weigh . . . with** give equal weight to . . . as
compared with   **217 call to** call on; or, perhaps, appeal to in time of
need   **219 all . . . several** your joint and individual   **220 kind** kindly.
'tis . . . give there isn't enough wealth in my possession to match my
wish to be generous   **224 It . . . thee** i.e., giving to you is an act of real
charity.   **living** (1) existence (2) property, wealth   **226 pitched field**
battlefield   **227 defiled** (1) with a quibble on *pitched;* cf. *Ecclesiasticus*
13:1: "He that toucheth pitch shall be defiled" (2) arrayed with files or
rows of soldiers

FIRST LORD   We are so virtuously bound—
TIMON   And so am I to you.
SECOND LORD   So infinitely endeared—
TIMON   All to you. [*To servants.*] Lights, more lights!   231
FIRST LORD
  The best of happiness, honor, and fortunes
  Keep with you, Lord Timon!   233
TIMON   Ready for his friends.   234

> *Exeunt lords [and all but*
> *Apemantus and Timon].*

APEMANTUS   What a coil's here!   235
  Serving of becks and jutting-out of bums!   236
  I doubt whether their legs be worth the sums   237
  That are given for 'em. Friendship's full of dregs.
  Methinks false hearts should never have sound legs.   239
  Thus honest fools lay out their wealth on curtsies.   240
TIMON
  Now, Apemantus, if thou wert not sullen,
  I would be good to thee.
APEMANTUS   No, I'll nothing; for if I should be bribed
  too, there would be none left to rail upon thee, and
  then thou wouldst sin the faster. Thou giv'st so long,
  Timon, I fear me thou wilt give away thyself in paper   246
  shortly. What needs these feasts, pomps, and vain-   247
  glories?
TIMON   Nay, an you begin to rail on society once, I am   249
  sworn not to give regard to you. Farewell, and come   250
  with better music.   *Exit.*
APEMANTUS   So.
  Thou wilt not hear me now; thou shalt not then.
  I'll lock thy heaven from thee.   254
  O, that men's ears should be
  To counsel deaf, but not to flattery!   *Exit.*

♣

231 All to you i.e., the obligation is entirely mine; or, all mine is yours
233 Keep dwell, remain   **234 Ready for** ready to assist   **235 coil** fuss
236 Serving of becks bowing   **237 legs** (1) limbs (2) bows, curtsies
239 have sound legs i.e., be disguised by the outwardly healthy appearance of sound legs able to make bows   **240 curtsies** (1) bows (2) courte-
sies   **246 I fear me** I fear.   **paper** bonds, promises to pay   **247 What
needs** what necessity is there for   **249 an** if   **250 give regard** to take
notice of   **254 thy heaven** i.e., my saving advice

2.1 *Enter a Senator [with papers in his hand].*

SENATOR
    And late, five thousand. To Varro and to Isidore   1
    He owes nine thousand, besides my former sum,
    Which makes it five-and-twenty. Still in motion   3
    Of raging waste? It cannot hold; it will not.   4
    If I want gold, steal but a beggar's dog   5
    And give it Timon, why, the dog coins gold.
    If I would sell my horse and buy twenty more
    Better than he, why, give my horse to Timon—
    Ask nothing, give it him—it foals me straight   9
    And able horses. No porter at his gate,   10
    But rather one that smiles and still invites   11
    All that pass by. It cannot hold. No reason   12
    Can sound his state in safety.—Caphis, ho!   13
    Caphis, I say!

        Enter Caphis.

CAPHIS   Here, sir. What is your pleasure?
SENATOR
    Get on your cloak and haste you to Lord Timon.
    Importune him for my moneys. Be not ceased   16
    With slight denial, nor then silenced when   17
    "Commend me to your master" and the cap   18
    Plays in the right hand, thus, but tell him   19
    My uses cry to me; I must serve my turn   20
    Out of mine own. His days and times are past,   21
    And my reliances on his fracted dates   22
    Have smit my credit. I love and honor him,   23

2.1. Location: Athens. A Senator's house.
1 late lately   **3–4 Still . . . waste** perpetually and ceaselessly squandering   **4 hold** hold out, last (also in l. 12)   **5 steal but** I need only steal   **9 foals me straight** at once yields me foals, i.e., more horses (as gifts)   **10 And able horses** i.e., and what's more they are full-grown horses, not literally foals.   **porter** i.e., one who sternly denies entrance   **11 still** constantly   **12 reason** rational inquiry   **13 sound . . . safety** by sounding the depth of Timon's financial position find it to be safe   **16 ceased** silenced, put off   **17 slight** negligent, offhand   **17–19 when . . . thus** i.e., when he offers fair greetings and flattering gestures in lieu of real payment   **20 uses** needs   **21 days and times** i.e., dates for repayment of his loans   **22 fracted** broken (by failure to meet payments on notes due)   **23 smit** smitten, hurt

But must not break my back to heal his finger.
Immediate are my needs, and my relief
Must not be tossed and turned to me in words,   26
But find supply immediate. Get you gone.
Put on a most importunate aspect,
A visage of demand, for I do fear
When every feather sticks in his own wing   30
Lord Timon will be left a naked gull,   31
Which flashes now a phoenix. Get you gone.   32
CAPHIS I go, sir.
SENATOR [*Giving him bonds*]
Ay, go, sir. Take the bonds along with you
And have the dates in compt.
CAPHIS   I will, sir.
SENATOR   Go.   *Exeunt.* 35

❖

2.2   *Enter steward [Flavius] with many bills in his
hand.*

FLAVIUS
No care, no stop! So senseless of expense   1
That he will neither know how to maintain it   2
Nor cease his flow of riot, takes no account   3
How things go from him nor resumes no care   4
Of what is to continue. Never mind   5
Was to be so unwise to be so kind.   6
What shall be done? He will not hear till feel.   7
I must be round with him, now he comes from hunting.   8
Fie, fie, fie, fie!

---

26 tossed and turned i.e., bandied back as in tennis **30 When . . . wing**
i.e., when everything is in the hands of its rightful possessor **31 gull**
(1) unfledged bird (2) dupe **32 Which flashes now** who now showily
displays himself as. **phoenix** mythical bird, one of a kind, i.e., rare and
precious creature **35 in compt** reckoned

2.2. Location: Athens. Before Timon's house.
1 senseless unaware, regardless **2 know** learn **3 riot** reveling
4–5 resumes . . . continue makes no provision for continuing **5–6 Never
. . . kind** never was there a mind so unwise in being so kind, so determined to be stupidly generous **7 till feel** until he suffers feelingly
8 round plainspoken

Enter Caphis [and the Servants of] Isidore and
   Varro.

CAPHIS
   Good even, Varro. What, you come for money?   10
VARRO'S SERVANT   Is 't not your business too?
CAPHIS   It is. And yours too, Isidore?
ISIDORE'S SERVANT   It is so.
CAPHIS   Would we were all discharged!   14
VARRO'S SERVANT   I fear it.   15
CAPHIS   Here comes the lord.

   Enter Timon and his train [with Alcibiades].

TIMON
   So soon as dinner's done we'll forth again,   17
   My Alcibiades.—With me? What is your will?
CAPHIS [*Presenting a bill*]
   My lord, here is a note of certain dues.   19
TIMON   Dues? Whence are you?
CAPHIS   Of Athens here, my lord.
TIMON   Go to my steward.
CAPHIS
   Please it your lordship, he hath put me off
   To the succession of new days this month.   24
   My master is awaked by great occasion   25
   To call upon his own, and humbly prays you   26
   That with your other noble parts you'll suit   27
   In giving him his right.
TIMON   Mine honest friend,
   I prithee but repair to me next morning.   29
CAPHIS
   Nay, good my lord—
TIMON   Contain thyself, good friend.
VARRO'S SERVANT
   One Varro's servant, my good lord—
ISIDORE'S SERVANT
   From Isidore; he humbly prays your speedy payment.

---

10 Good even (A greeting used any time after noon.) **14 discharged**
paid **15 fear it** i.e., am apprehensive about our being paid **17 forth** go
forth **19 dues** debts **24 To . . . month** from one day to another all
month **25 awaked** i.e., forced **26 his own** i.e., that which he has lent
you **27 with . . . parts** in conformity to your other noble qualities
29 repair come

CAPHIS
  If you did know, my lord, my master's wants—   33
VARRO'S SERVANT
  'Twas due on forfeiture, my lord, six weeks and past.   34
ISIDORE'S SERVANT
  Your steward puts me off, my lord, and I
  Am sent expressly to your lordship.
TIMON   Give me breath.—   37
  I do beseech you, good my lords, keep on;   38
  I'll wait upon you instantly.
                  [Exeunt Alcibiades and Lords.]
              [To Flavius.] Come hither. Pray you,   39
  How goes the world, that I am thus encountered
  With clamorous demands of broken bonds
  And the detention of long-since-due debts   42
  Against my honor?
FLAVIUS   Please you, gentlemen,   43
  The time is unagreeable to this business.
  Your importunacy cease till after dinner,   45
  That I may make his lordship understand   46
  Wherefore you are not paid.
TIMON   Do so, my friends.—   47
  See them well entertained.   *[Exit.]*
FLAVIUS   Pray, draw near.   *Exit.*   48

    Enter Apemantus and Fool.

CAPHIS   Stay, stay, here comes the Fool with Apemantus.
  Let's ha' some sport with 'em.   50
VARRO'S SERVANT   Hang him! He'll abuse us.   51
ISIDORE'S SERVANT   A plague upon him, dog!
VARRO'S SERVANT   How dost, Fool?
APEMANTUS   Dost dialogue with thy shadow?
VARRO'S SERVANT   I speak not to thee.

33 wants needs   **34 on forfeiture** on penalty of forfeiting the security
for it if not paid on the date prescribed   **37 breath** breathing space,
time to breathe   **38 keep on** go ahead without me   **39 wait . . . instantly** be with you in a moment   **42 the detention** the charge of withholding payment   **43 Against my honor** contrary to my honorable
reputation   **45 importunacy** persistent demands   **46 That** so that
47 Wherefore why   **48 entertained** received, treated.   **draw near** come
this way. (Said to Timon, or possibly to the creditors' servants, who,
however, decide to remain.)   **50 ha'** have   **51 abuse** vilify

APEMANTUS   No, 'tis to thyself. [*To the Fool*.] Come away.   56
ISIDORE'S SERVANT [*To Varro's Servant*]   There's the fool   57
   hangs on your back already.   58
APEMANTUS   No, thou stand'st single; thou'rt not on him   59
   yet.   60
CAPHIS [*To Isidore's Servant*]   Where's the fool now?   61
APEMANTUS   He last asked the question. Poor rogues   62
   and usurers' men, bawds between gold and want!
ALL THE SERVANTS   What are we, Apemantus?
APEMANTUS   Asses.
ALL THE SERVANTS   Why?
APEMANTUS   That you ask me what you are, and do not
   know yourselves. Speak to 'em, Fool.
FOOL   How do you, gentlemen?
ALL THE SERVANTS   Gramercies, good Fool. How does   70
   your mistress?
FOOL   She's e'en setting on water to scald such chickens   72
   as you are. Would we could see you at Corinth!   73
APEMANTUS   Good! Gramercy.

   Enter Page.

FOOL   Look you, here comes my mistress' page.
PAGE [*To the Fool*]   Why, how now, captain? What
   do you in this wise company?—How dost thou,
   Apemantus?
APEMANTUS   Would I had a rod in my mouth, that I   79
   might answer thee profitably.   80
PAGE   Prithee, Apemantus, read me the superscription   81
   of these letters. I know not which is which.
                              [*He shows two letters*.]

56 **'tis to thyself** i.e., you (Varro's servant) speak to yourself when you say
"fool"   **57–58 There's . . . already** i.e., you (Varro's servant) have been
labeled fool already. (See l. 56.)   **59–60 No . . . yet** i.e., no, you (Isidore's
servant), a fool, are standing by yourself; you're not on the back of Varro's
servant yet   **61 Where's . . . now** i.e., whose back is labeled fool now
62 He he who (i.e., Caphis, who has now been called a fool like the
others)   **70 Gramercies** many thanks   **72 She's . . . scald** (Allusion to the
sweating-tub treatment for venereal disease, a disease that causes loss of
hair just as a chicken loses its feathers through scalding. The Fool also
implies that they are fools deserving to be plucked.)   **73 Corinth** a city
noted for its brothels; hence, a brothel or the district for such houses
79 rod stick (to use for a beating)   **80 profitably** to your profit (by teaching you a lesson)   **81 superscription** address

APEMANTUS   Canst not read?

PAGE   No.

APEMANTUS   There will little learning die then that day thou art hanged. This is to Lord Timon, this to Alcibiades. Go, thou wast born a bastard and thou'lt die a bawd.

PAGE   Thou wast whelped a dog and thou shalt famish 89 a dog's death. Answer not; I am gone.   *Exit.*

APEMANTUS   E'en so thou outrunn'st grace. Fool, I will 91 go with you to Lord Timon's.

FOOL   Will you leave me there?

APEMANTUS   If Timon stay at home.—You three serve 94 three usurers?

ALL THE SERVANTS   Ay. Would they served us!   96

APEMANTUS   So would I—as good a trick as ever hangman served thief.

FOOL   Are you three usurers' men?

ALL THE SERVANTS   Ay, Fool.

FOOL   I think no usurer but has a fool to his servant; my mistress is one, and I am her fool. When men come to borrow of your masters, they approach sadly and go away merry, but they enter my mistress' house merrily and go away sadly. The reason of this?

VARRO'S SERVANT   I could render one.   106

APEMANTUS   Do it then, that we may account thee a whoremaster and a knave; which notwithstanding, thou shalt be no less esteemed.

VARRO'S SERVANT   What is a whoremaster, Fool?

FOOL   A fool in good clothes, and something like thee. 'Tis a spirit; sometimes 't appears like a lord, sometimes 112 like a lawyer, sometimes like a philosopher, with two stones more than 's artificial one. He is very often like 114 a knight; and generally, in all shapes that man goes

---

89 whelped born. **famish** die   **91 E'en so** precisely so.   **thou outrunn'st grace** you run away from profitable teaching and God's grace **94 If . . . home** i.e., while Timon remains at home, a fool is there.   **You three** do you three   **96 Would** we wish   **106 one** (Implies that the Fool's mistress's house is a bawdy house, where men come merrily but leave diseased and poorer.)   **112 spirit** i.e., one that can assume various shapes   **114 stones** testicles.   **than 's** than his, the philosopher's. **artificial one** i.e., the philosopher's stone, supposed to change other metals into gold

up and down in from fourscore to thirteen, this spirit
walks in.

VARRO'S SERVANT   Thou art not altogether a fool.

FOOL   Nor thou altogether a wise man. As much foolery
as I have, so much wit thou lack'st.

APEMANTUS   That answer might have become Apeman-   121
tus.

ALL THE SERVANTS   Aside, aside! Here comes Lord Timon.
                                        [*They stand aside.*]

Enter Timon and Steward [Flavius].

APEMANTUS   Come with me, Fool, come.

FOOL   I do not always follow lover, elder brother, and   125
woman; sometimes the philosopher.   126
                              [*Exeunt Apemantus and Fool.*]

FLAVIUS [*To Servants*]
Pray you, walk near. I'll speak with you anon.   127
                                    Exeunt [Servants].

TIMON
You make me marvel wherefore ere this time   128
Had you not fully laid my state before me,   129
That I might so have rated my expense   130
As I had leave of means.

FLAVIUS   You would not hear me.   131
At many leisures I proposed—

TIMON   Go to!   132
Perchance some single vantages you took   133
When my indisposition put you back,
And that unaptness made your minister   135
Thus to excuse yourself.

FLAVIUS   O my good lord,   136
At many times I brought in my accounts,

---

121 become been fitted for   **125–126 lover . . . woman** i.e., various sorts
of persons proverbially connected with folly; an *elder brother* is the
oldest son, one who will inherit property and hence worth cultivating
127 walk near remain nearby.   **anon** shortly   **128 wherefore** why
129 fully . . . state completely detailed my financial position   **130 rated**
i.e., estimated and regulated   **131 As . . . means** as my means permitted   **132 leisures** times when you were free.   **proposed** conferred,
conversed   **133 single vantages** occasional opportunities   **135–136 that
. . . yourself** i.e., my disinclination to listen on those occasions served as
your excuse thereafter for remaining silent. (*Made your minister* means
"became your agent or means.")

Laid them before you. You would throw them off
And say you found them in mine honesty.   139
When for some trifling present you have bid me
Return so much, I have shook my head and wept;   141
Yea, 'gainst th' authority of manners prayed you   142
To hold your hand more close. I did endure
Not seldom, nor no slight checks, when I have   144
Prompted you in the ebb of your estate   145
And your great flow of debts. My lovèd lord,
Though you hear now too late, yet now's a time;   147
The greatest of your having lacks a half   148
To pay your present debts.

TIMON   Let all my land be sold.

FLAVIUS
'Tis all engaged, some forfeited and gone,   151
And what remains will hardly stop the mouth   152
Of present dues. The future comes apace;   153
What shall defend the interim? And at length
How goes our reckoning?

TIMON
To Lacedaemon did my land extend.   156

FLAVIUS
O my good lord, the world is but a word.
Were it all yours to give it in a breath,
How quickly were it gone!

TIMON   You tell me true.

FLAVIUS
If you suspect my husbandry of falsehood,   160
Call me before th' exactest auditors
And set me on the proof. So the gods bless me,   162
When all our offices have been oppressed   163
With riotous feeders, when our vaults have wept   164

---

139 found . . . honesty i.e., found warrant for believing the books properly kept in knowing me to be honest   **141 Return so much** give as in repayment a large gift   **142 'gainst . . . manners** contrary to what good manners dictated   **144 checks** rebukes   **145 in** in regard to   **147 yet . . . time** i.e., late as it is, it is necessary that you be made acquainted with it   **148 The greatest . . . having** your total wealth at a most optimistic reckoning   **151 engaged** mortgaged   **152–153 stop . . . Of** satisfy   **153 dues** debts.   **apace** quickly   **156 Lacedaemon** Sparta   **160 husbandry** management, stewardship   **162 set . . . proof** put me to the test   **163 offices** rooms, especially the kitchen and pantries   **164 vaults** wine cellars

With drunken spilth of wine, when every room   165
Hath blazed with lights and brayed with minstrelsy,
I have retired me to a wasteful cock   167
And set mine eyes at flow.
TIMON   Prithee, no more.
FLAVIUS
Heavens, have I said, the bounty of this lord!
How many prodigal bits have slaves and peasants   170
This night englutted! Who is not Timon's?   171
What heart, head, sword, force, means, but is Lord
   Timon's?   172
Great Timon, noble, worthy, royal Timon!
Ah, when the means are gone that buy this praise,
The breath is gone whereof this praise is made.
Feast-won, fast-lost; one cloud of winter showers,   176
These flies are couched.   [*He weeps.*]
TIMON   Come, sermon me no further.   177
No villainous bounty yet hath passed my heart;   178
Unwisely, not ignobly, have I given.
Why dost thou weep? Canst thou the conscience lack   180
To think I shall lack friends? Secure thy heart.   181
If I would broach the vessels of my love   182
And try the argument of hearts by borrowing,   183
Men and men's fortunes could I frankly use   184
As I can bid thee speak.
FLAVIUS   Assurance bless your thoughts!   186
TIMON
And in some sort these wants of mine are crowned,   187
That I account them blessings; for by these   188
Shall I try friends. You shall perceive how you   189
Mistake my fortunes; I am wealthy in my friends.—
Within there! Flaminius! Servilius!

---

165 spilth spilling   **167 retired . . . cock** withdrawn to sit beside the
wastefully flowing faucet of a barrel   **170 bits** morsels   **171 is not** i.e.,
does not profess himself to be   **172 means** financial resources
176 fast-lost (1) lost in time of fast (2) lost quickly and for good   **177 are
couched** hide themselves (to avoid Timon's requests for help).   **sermon**
lecture   **178 villainous bounty** generosity that I am ashamed of
180 conscience faith, or judgment   **181 Secure** set at ease   **182 broach**
tap, open   **183 try . . . hearts** test protestations of love   **184 frankly** as
freely   **186 Assurance . . . thoughts** may your hopes prove well
founded   **187 sort** manner, sense.   **crowned** given a special dignity
188 That so that   **189 try** test

Enter three Servants [Flaminius, Servilius, and
another].

SERVANTS   My lord? My lord?
TIMON   I will dispatch you severally: [*To Servilius*] you   193
   to Lord Lucius; [*To Flaminius*] to Lord Lucullus you—
   I hunted with his honor today; [*To the other*] you to
   Sempronius. Commend me to their loves, and, I am
   proud, say, that my occasions have found time to use   197
   'em toward a supply of money. Let the request be fifty   198
   talents.
FLAMINIUS   As you have said, my lord.
                              [*Exeunt Servants.*]
FLAVIUS [*Aside*]   Lord Lucius and Lucullus? Humh!
TIMON   Go you, sir, to the senators,
   Of whom, even to the state's best health, I have   203
   Deserved this hearing. Bid 'em send o' th' instant   204
   A thousand talents to me.
FLAVIUS   I have been bold—
   For that I knew it the most general way—   206
   To them to use your signet and your name,   207
   But they do shake their heads, and I am here
   No richer in return.
TIMON   Is 't true? Can 't be?
FLAVIUS
   They answer, in a joint and corporate voice,   210
   That now they are at fall, want treasure, cannot   211
   Do what they would, are sorry; you are honorable,
   But yet they could have wished—they know not—
   Something hath been amiss—a noble nature
   May catch a wrench—would all were well—'tis pity.   215
   And so, intending other serious matters,   216
   After distasteful looks and these hard fractions,   217

193 severally separately   **197 occasions** needs.   **time** opportunity
198 toward for   **203 to . . . health** i.e., for my services in behalf of the
state's welfare. (Cf. 4.3.93–96, where Alcibiades refers to Timon's sword
and fortune offered in the defense of Athens.)   **204 o' th' instant** at
once   **206 For that** because.   **general** comprehensive, or customary (?)
207 signet signet ring and seal, token of authority   **210 corporate**
united   **211 at fall** at low ebb.   **want** lack   **215 catch a wrench** be
wrenched away from its true bent   **216 intending** turning their attention to, or pretending (?)   **217 hard** harsh.   **fractions** broken sentences

With certain half-caps and cold-moving nods   218
They froze me into silence.

TIMON   You gods, reward them!
Prithee, man, look cheerly. These old fellows   220
Have their ingratitude in them hereditary.
Their blood is caked, 'tis cold, it seldom flows;   222
'Tis lack of kindly warmth they are not kind;   223
And nature, as it grows again toward earth,   224
Is fashioned for the journey dull and heavy.
Go to Ventidius. Prithee, be not sad.
Thou art true and honest—ingeniously I speak—   227
No blame belongs to thee. Ventidius lately
Buried his father, by whose death he's stepped
Into a great estate. When he was poor,   230
Imprisoned, and in scarcity of friends,   231
I cleared him with five talents. Greet him from me.   232
Bid him suppose some good necessity   233
Touches his friend, which craves to be remembered
With those five talents. That had, give 't these fellows   235
To whom 'tis instant due. Ne'er speak or think
That Timon's fortunes 'mong his friends can sink.

FLAVIUS [*Aside*]   I would I could not think it.
That thought is bounty's foe;   239
Being free itself, it thinks all others so.   *Exeunt.*   240

❖

---

218 **half-caps** i.e., salutations halfheartedly given.   **cold-moving** chilling   220 **cheerly** cheerful   222 **caked** congealed   223 **'Tis . . . kind** it is lack of natural warmth that makes them not generous (with pun on *kind*, natural, of humankind)   224 **earth** i.e., the grave   227 **ingeniously** frankly   230–232 **When he was poor**, etc. (These lines echo Matthew 25:34–37 when Jesus discusses the Last Judgment.)   231 **scarcity** need   232 **cleared** freed   233 **good** genuine   235 **That had** when you have that.   **these fellows** to these fellows   239 **That . . . foe** i.e., the naive assumption that friends will remain true in hard times is the undoing of the bounteous impulse   240 **free** generous

3.1   [*Enter*] *Flaminius, waiting to speak with a lord,* [*Lucullus,*] *from his master. Enter a Servant to him.*

LUCULLUS' SERVANT   I have told my lord of you. He is coming down to you.

FLAMINIUS   I thank you, sir.

Enter Lucullus.

LUCULLUS' SERVANT   Here's my lord.

LUCULLUS [*Aside*]   One of Lord Timon's men? A gift, I warrant. Why, this hits right; I dreamt of a silver basin 6 and ewer tonight.—Flaminius, honest Flaminius, you 7 are very respectively welcome, sir. [*To Servant.*] 8 Fill me some wine. [*Exit Servant.*] And how does that honorable, complete, free-hearted gentleman of 10 Athens, thy very bountiful good lord and master?

FLAMINIUS   His health is well, sir.

LUCULLUS   I am right glad that his health is well, sir. And what hast thou there under thy cloak, pretty Flaminius?

FLAMINIUS   Faith, nothing but an empty box, sir, which, in my lord's behalf, I come to entreat your honor to supply; who, having great and instant occa- 18 sion to use fifty talents, hath sent to your lordship to 19 furnish him, nothing doubting your present assistance 20 therein.

LUCULLUS   La, la, la la! "Nothing doubting," says he? Alas, good lord! A noble gentleman 'tis, if he would 23 not keep so good a house. Many a time and often I ha' 24 dined with him and told him on 't, and come again to 25 supper to him of purpose to have him spend less, and 26 yet he would embrace no counsel, take no warning by 27 my coming. Every man has his fault, and honesty is 28 his. I ha' told him on 't, but I could ne'er get him from 't.

3.1. Location: Athens. Lucullus' house.
6 hits right accords perfectly   **7 ewer** pitcher.   **tonight** last night
8 respectively respectfully   **10 complete** accomplished   **18 supply** fill
18–19 instant occasion urgent need   **20 nothing** not at all.   **present**
immediate   **23 'tis** he is   **24 keep . . . house** be so lavish in his enter-
taining   **25 on 't** of it   **26 of** on   **27 by** from   **28 honesty** liberality

Enter [Lucullus'] Servant, with wine.

LUCULLUS' SERVANT   Please your lordship, here is the wine.

LUCULLUS   Flaminius, I have noted thee always wise.
Here's to thee.   [*He offers a toast.*]

FLAMINIUS   Your lordship speaks your pleasure.   34

LUCULLUS   I have observed thee always for a towardly   35
prompt spirit—give thee thy due—and one that   36
knows what belongs to reason, and canst use the time   37
well if the time use thee well. Good parts in thee! [*To*   38
Servant.] Get you gone, sirrah. [*Exit Servant.*] Draw
nearer, honest Flaminius. Thy lord's a bountiful gentleman; but thou art wise, and thou know'st well
enough, although thou com'st to me, that this is no
time to lend money, especially upon bare friendship,   43
without security. Here's three solidares for thee.   44
[*He gives a tip.*] Good boy, wink at me, and say thou   45
sawst me not. Fare thee well.

FLAMINIUS

Is 't possible the world should so much differ,   47
And we alive that lived? Fly, damnèd baseness,   48
To him that worships thee! [*He throws the money back.*]

LUCULLUS   Ha? Now I see thou art a fool, and fit for thy
master.   *Exit Lucullus.*

FLAMINIUS

May these add to the number that may scald thee!   52
Let molten coin be thy damnation,   53
Thou disease of a friend and not himself!   54
Has friendship such a faint and milky heart
It turns in less than two nights? O you gods!   56
I feel my master's passion. This slave   57

---

34 Your . . . pleasure it pleases your lordship to say so   **35–36 towardly
prompt** quick to meet another's thoughts, well-disposed   **37–38 canst . . .
thee well** can make the most of an opportunity when it presents itself
38 parts qualities   **43 bare** mere   **44 solidares** small coins. (A term
invented by Shakespeare, evidently.)   **45 wink** shut the eyes   **47–48 so . . .
lived** i.e., change so much in our lifetime   **52 scald** i.e., roast in hell
53 Let . . . damnation i.e., may you be punished in hell by having molten
metal poured down your throat   **54 Thou . . . himself** you who are no
true friend at all, but only a diseased resemblance   **56 It turns** that it
sours like milk (with quibble on the idea of *turn* as in "turncoat")   **57 feel
. . . passion** i.e., feel angry on my master's behalf, share his anger and his
suffering   **57–58 slave Unto his honor** person slavishly devoted to his own
dignity. (Said ironically.)

Unto his honor has my lord's meat in him.   58
Why should it thrive and turn to nutriment
When he is turned to poison?   60
O, may diseases only work upon 't!   61
And, when he's sick to death, let not that part of nature
Which my lord paid for be of any power
To expel sickness, but prolong his hour!   *Exit.*

❖

3.2   *Enter Lucius, with three Strangers.*

LUCIUS Who, the Lord Timon? He is my very good
friend and an honorable gentleman.

FIRST STRANGER We know him for no less, though we   3
are but strangers to him. But I can tell you one thing,
my lord, and which I hear from common rumors: now   5
Lord Timon's happy hours are done and past, and his
estate shrinks from him.

LUCIUS Fie, no, do not believe it! He cannot want for   8
money.

SECOND STRANGER But believe you this, my lord, that
not long ago one of his men was with the Lord Lucullus to borrow so many talents, nay, urged extremely   12
for 't, and showed what necessity belonged to 't, and   13
yet was denied.

LUCIUS How?

SECOND STRANGER I tell you, denied, my lord.

LUCIUS What a strange case was that! Now, before the
gods, I am ashamed on 't. Denied that honorable man?
There was very little honor showed in 't. For my own
part, I must needs confess, I have received some small
kindnesses from him, as money, plate, jewels, and
suchlike trifles, nothing comparing to his; yet had he   22
mistook him and sent to me, I should ne'er have de-   23
nied his occasion so many talents.

---

58 meat i.e., food of a feast   **60 When . . . poison** when his behavior is
so poisonous   **61 work upon 't** thrive upon it, *my lord's meat in him*

3.2. Location: Athens. A public place.
3 for no less to be no less than you say   **5 which** one which   **8 want for**
lack   **12 urged extremely** begged insistently   **13 what . . . to 't** how
necessary it was   **22 his** i.e., Lucullus' receiving of generosity
23 mistook . . . me i.e., mistakenly sent to me, who owe him less

Enter Servilius.

SERVILIUS See, by good hap, yonder's my lord. I have 25
sweat to see his honor. [*To Lucius.*] My honored lord— 26
LUCIUS Servilius? You are kindly met, sir. Fare thee
well. Commend me to thy honorable virtuous lord,
my very exquisite friend.   [*He starts to go.*] 29
SERVILIUS May it please your honor, my lord hath
sent—
LUCIUS Ha? What has he sent? I am so much endeared 32
to that lord; he's ever sending. How shall I thank him,
think'st thou? And what has he sent now?
SERVILIUS He's only sent his present occasion now, my 35
lord, requesting your lordship to supply his instant 36
use with so many talents. 37

LUCIUS
I know his lordship is but merry with me;
He cannot want fifty—five hundred—talents. 39

SERVILIUS
But in the meantime he wants less, my lord.
If his occasion were not virtuous, 41
I should not urge it half so faithfully.

LUCIUS
Dost thou speak seriously, Servilius?
SERVILIUS Upon my soul, 'tis true, sir.
LUCIUS What a wicked beast was I to disfurnish myself 45
against such a good time, when I might ha' shown 46
myself honorable! How unluckily it happened that I 47
should purchase the day before for a little part, and 48
undo a great deal of honor! Servilius, now before the 49
gods, I am not able to do—the more beast, I say—I
was sending to use Lord Timon myself, these gentle- 51

25 **hap** fortune   25–26 **I have sweat** i.e., I have been hurrying
29 **exquisite** sought after   32 **endeared** obliged   35 **occasion** need
36–37 **supply . . . use** provide for his immediate need   39 **He cannot
. . . talents** (Probably an indication of Shakespeare's uncertainty over the
value of this currency; see also *so many* above in ll. 12, 24, and 37.)
41 **were not virtuous** were due to a fault instead of a virtue, i.e., generosity   45–46 **disfurnish . . . time** leave myself unprepared for such an
excellent opportunity   47–49 **that I . . . honor** i.e., that I just yesterday
laid out a sum of money in a small investment and thus made it impossible now to acquire a great honor by helping Timon   51 **use** borrow from

men can witness; but I would not for the wealth of   52
Athens I had done 't now. Commend me bountifully
to his good lordship, and I hope his honor will con-   54
ceive the fairest of me, because I have no power to be   55
kind. And tell him this from me: I count it one of my
greatest afflictions, say, that I cannot pleasure such an   57
honorable gentleman. Good Servilius, will you befriend me so far as to use mine own words to him?

SERVILIUS   Yes, sir, I shall.

LUCIUS   I'll look you out a good turn, Servilius.   61
                                        Exit Servilius.
True, as you said, Timon is shrunk indeed;   62
And he that's once denied will hardly speed.   *Exit.*   63

FIRST STRANGER   Do you observe this, Hostilius?

SECOND STRANGER   Ay, too well.

FIRST STRANGER   Why, this is the world's soul,   66
And just of the same piece   67
Is every flatterer's sport. Who can call him his friend
That dips in the same dish? For, in my knowing,   69
Timon has been this lord's father   70
And kept his credit with his purse,   71
Supported his estate; nay, Timon's money
Has paid his men their wages. He ne'er drinks
But Timon's silver treads upon his lip.   74
And yet—O, see the monstrousness of man
When he looks out in an ungrateful shape!—   76
He does deny him, in respect of his,   77
What charitable men afford to beggars.

THIRD STRANGER
Religion groans at it.

FIRST STRANGER   For mine own part,
I never tasted Timon in my life,   80

52 would not do not wish   **54–55 conceive the fairest** think the best
55 because i.e., even though   **57 pleasure** satisfy, please   **61 look you
out** seek occasion to do you   **62 shrunk** brought low   **63 speed** pros-
per   **66 soul** real essence, vital principle   **67 just . . . piece** exactly the
same (i.e., cut from the same piece of cloth)   **69 dips . . . dish** (Alludes
to Judas' betrayal of Christ; see Matthew 26:23.)   **70 father** i.e., patron   **71 kept his** i.e., maintained Lucius'.   **his purse** i.e., Timon's
wealth   **74 treads** presses   **76 looks out** appears   **77 He . . . his** i.e.,
Lucius denies Timon an amount that equals, in comparison with Lucius' total wealth   **80 tasted Timon** i.e., sampled Timon's liberality

Nor came any of his bounties over me   81
To mark me for his friend; yet I protest,
For his right noble mind, illustrious virtue,   83
And honorable carriage,   84
Had his necessity made use of me,   85
I would have put my wealth into donation   86
And the best half should have returned to him,   87
So much I love his heart. But I perceive
Men must learn now with pity to dispense,
For policy sits above conscience.   *Exeunt.* 90

❖

3.3 *Enter a third Servant [of Timon's] with*
       Sempronius, another of Timon's friends.

SEMPRONIUS
   Must he needs trouble me in 't? Hum! 'Bove all others? 1
   He might have tried Lord Lucius or Lucullus;
   And now Ventidius is wealthy too,
   Whom he redeemed from prison. All these
   Owe their estates unto him.
SERVANT   My lord,
   They have all been touched and found base metal,   7
   For they have all denied him.
SEMPRONIUS   How? Have they denied him?
   Has Ventidius and Lucullus denied him?
   And does he send to me? Three? Humh!
   It shows but little love or judgment in him.
   Must I be his last refuge? His friends, like physicians,
   Thrive, give him over. Must I take th' cure upon me?   14
   He's much disgraced me in 't. I'm angry at him,
   That might have known my place. I see no sense for 't 16

81 came . . . me was I the recipient of any of his generosity   83 For
because of   84 carriage conduct   85 made use of me i.e., sought my
aid   86 put . . . donation i.e., made a gift of my wealth   87 returned i.e.,
gone to its proper place, where it belongs   90 policy self-interest

3.3. Location: Athens. Sempronius' house.
1 Must . . . me does he have to involve me   7 touched (Metaphor derived from testing metals with a touchstone to see if they are gold.)
14 Thrive . . . over i.e., thrive on his wealth, but now give him up as
beyond help   16 That . . . place who should have acknowledged my
position (among his friends).   sense reason

But his occasions might have wooed me first; 17
For, in my conscience, I was the first man 18
That e'er receivèd gift from him.
And does he think so backwardly of me now 20
That I'll requite it last? No! 21
So it may prove an argument of laughter 22
To th' rest, and I 'mongst lords be thought a fool.
I'd rather than the worth of thrice the sum
He'd sent to me first, but for my mind's sake; 25
I'd such a courage to do him good. But now return, 26
And with their faint reply this answer join:
Who bates mine honor shall not know my coin. 28

　　　　　　　　　　　　　　　　　　Exit.

SERVANT　Excellent! Your lordship's a goodly villain. 29
The devil knew not what he did when he made man
politic; he crossed himself by 't, and I cannot think but 31
in the end the villainies of man will set him clear. 32
How fairly this lord strives to appear foul! Takes vir- 33
tuous copies to be wicked, like those that under hot 34
ardent zeal would set whole realms on fire. 35
Of such a nature is his politic love.
This was my lord's best hope; now all are fled,
Save only the gods. Now his friends are dead, 38
Doors that were ne'er acquainted with their wards 39
Many a bounteous year must be employed 40
Now to guard sure their master. 41
And this is all a liberal course allows: 42
Who cannot keep his wealth must keep his house. 43

　　　　　　　　　　　　　　　　　　Exit.

❖

17 **But his occasions** i.e., but that he, in his need　18 **in my conscience**
to my knowledge　20 **think . . . me** (1) think I am so backward (2) think
of me last　21 **requite** repay　22 **argument of** subject for　25 **but
. . . sake** if only in recognition of my good feeling toward him
26 **courage** desire　28 **Who bates** whoever abates, detracts from
29 **goodly** proper. (Said ironically.)　31 **politic** cunning.　**crossed** foiled
(by making man his rival in treachery)　32 **set him clear** i.e., make even
the devil look innocent　33 **How fairly** with what a plausible appearance of virtue　33–35 **Takes . . . fire** i.e., how this lord models himself
on the virtuous for wicked purposes, like religious bigots who for
zealous purposes would burn down whole kingdoms　38 **Now** now
that　39 **wards** bolts, locks　40 **Many** for many　41 **guard sure** i.e.,
protect from arrest for debt　42 **liberal** generous　43 **keep . . . keep**
preserve . . . stay inside

3.4 *Enter [two of] Varro's Men, meeting [Titus'*
Servant and] others, all [being servants of]
Timon's creditors, to wait for his coming out.
Then enter Lucius' [Servant] and Hortensius'
[Servant].

VARRO'S FIRST SERVANT
  Well met. Good morrow, Titus and Hortensius.
TITUS' SERVANT
  The like to you, kind Varro.
HORTENSIUS' SERVANT   Lucius!   2
  What, do we meet together?
LUCIUS' SERVANT   Ay, and I think
  One business does command us all;
  For mine is money.
TITUS' SERVANT   So is theirs and ours.

    Enter Philotus' [Servant].

LUCIUS' SERVANT
  And Sir Philotus too!
PHILOTUS' SERVANT   Good day at once.   6
LUCIUS' SERVANT   Welcome, good brother.
  What do you think the hour?
PHILOTUS' SERVANT   Laboring for nine.   8
LUCIUS' SERVANT
  So much?
PHILOTUS' SERVANT   Is not my lord seen yet?
LUCIUS' SERVANT   Not yet.   9
PHILOTUS' SERVANT
  I wonder on 't. He was wont to shine at seven.   10
LUCIUS' SERVANT
  Ay, but the days are waxed shorter with him.   11
  You must consider that a prodigal course
  Is like the sun's,
  But not, like his, recoverable. I fear   14
  'Tis deepest winter in Lord Timon's purse;

3.4. Location: Athens. Timon's house.
2 like same   **6 at once** to one and all   **8 Laboring for** moving toward
9 much i.e., late   **10 was . . . shine** used to be up   **11 are waxed** have
grown   **14 But . . . recoverable** i.e., the sun will return from its wintry
path, but Timon cannot recover (since his funds are not *recoverable*)

That is, one may reach deep enough and yet
Find little.

PHILOTUS' SERVANT   I am of your fear for that.   17

TITUS' SERVANT
I'll show you how t' observe a strange event.   18
Your lord sends now for money?

HORTENSIUS' SERVANT   Most true, he does.

TITUS' SERVANT
And he wears jewels now of Timon's gift,
For which I wait for money.   21

HORTENSIUS' SERVANT   It is against my heart.   22

LUCIUS' SERVANT   Mark how strange it shows:
Timon in this should pay more than he owes,
And e'en as if your lord should wear rich jewels   25
And send for money for 'em.   26

HORTENSIUS' SERVANT
I'm weary of this charge, the gods can witness.   27
I know my lord hath spent of Timon's wealth,   28
And now ingratitude makes it worse than stealth.   29

VARRO'S FIRST SERVANT
Yes, mine's three thousand crowns. What's yours?

LUCIUS' SERVANT   Five thousand, mine.

VARRO'S FIRST SERVANT
'Tis much deep, and it should seem by th' sum   32
Your master's confidence was above mine,   33
Else surely his had equaled.   34

     Enter Flaminius.

TITUS' SERVANT   One of Lord Timon's men.

LUCIUS' SERVANT   Flaminius? Sir, a word. Pray, is my
lord ready to come forth?

FLAMINIUS   No, indeed, he is not.

TITUS' SERVANT We attend his lordship. Pray signify so much.   39

FLAMINIUS   I need not tell him that. He knows you are
too diligent.   [*Exit.*]   41

---

17 am of share   **18 observe** i.e., analyze   **21 For . . . money** i.e., while I wait for the money used to buy those jewels   **22 heart** wish, feeling **25–26 e'en . . . for 'em** i.e., it's just as though your master should both wear the jewels Timon gave him and simultaneously demand the money that paid for those jewels   **27 charge** commission   **28 spent** made use **29 stealth** theft   **32 much deep** very great   **33 mine** my master's   **34 his had equaled** i.e., my master's loan would have equaled in amount your master's   **39 attend** are waiting for   **41 diligent** i.e., officious

Enter steward [Flavius] in a cloak, muffled.

LUCIUS' SERVANT
Ha! Is not that his steward muffled so?
He goes away in a cloud. Call him, call him.   43

TITUS' SERVANT [*To Flavius*]   Do you hear, sir?

VARRO'S SECOND SERVANT [*To Flavius*]   By your leave, sir.

FLAVIUS
What do ye ask of me, my friend?

TITUS' SERVANT
We wait for certain money here, sir.

FLAVIUS   Ay,   47
If money were as certain as your waiting,
'Twere sure enough.
Why then preferred you not your sums and bills   50
When your false masters eat of my lord's meat?   51
Then they could smile and fawn upon his debts,
And take down th' interest into their gluttonous maws.   53
You do yourselves but wrong to stir me up.   54
Let me pass quietly.
Believe 't, my lord and I have made an end;   56
I have no more to reckon, he to spend.   57

LUCIUS' SERVANT   Ay, but this answer will not serve.   58

FLAVIUS
If 'twill not serve, 'tis not so base as you,
For you serve knaves.   [*Exit.*]

VARRO'S FIRST SERVANT   How? What does his cashiered   61
worship mutter?

VARRO'S SECOND SERVANT   No matter what; he's poor,
and that's revenge enough. Who can speak broader   64
than he that has no house to put his head in? Such   65
may rail against great buildings.   66

---

43 in a cloud (1) muffled (2) in a state of confusion and ignominy
47 certain certain sums of. (But Flavius puns bitterly in the next line on
the sense of "reliable," "predictable.")   **50 preferred** presented   **51 eat**
ate. (Pronounced *et*.)   **53 th' interest** i.e., the food and drink they consumed as though it were interest on the loans   **54 do yourselves but** only
do yourselves   **56 made an end** severed our relationship   **57 reckon**
keep account of   **58 serve** do. (But Lucius punningly replies in the sense
of "act as servant.")   **61 cashiered** dismissed. (*His cashiered worship*
is offered sardonically as if it were a title of dignity.)   **64 broader** (1) more
freely (2) more in the open, abroad   **65–66 Such . . . buildings** i.e., a man
who is houseless and out of service, like Flavius, has nothing to lose and
can inveigh against injustice and inequality

Enter Servilius.

TITUS' SERVANT   O, here's Servilius. Now we shall know
  some answer.

SERVILIUS   If I might beseech you, gentlemen, to repair   69
  some other hour, I should derive much from 't. For   70
  take 't of my soul, my lord leans wondrously to discon-   71
  tent. His comfortable temper has forsook him; he's   72
  much out of health and keeps his chamber.   73

LUCIUS' SERVANT
  Many do keep their chambers are not sick,   74
  And if it be so far beyond his health,   75
  Methinks he should the sooner pay his debts
  And make a clear way to the gods.

SERVILIUS   Good gods!   77

TITUS' SERVANT
  We cannot take this for answer, sir.

FLAMINIUS (*Within*)   Servilius, help! My lord, my lord!

Enter Timon, in a rage.

TIMON
  What, are my doors opposed against my passage?
  Have I been ever free, and must my house
  Be my retentive enemy, my jail?   82
  The place which I have feasted, does it now,
  Like all mankind, show me an iron heart?

LUCIUS' SERVANT   Put in now, Titus.   85

TITUS' SERVANT   My lord, here is my bill.

LUCIUS' SERVANT   Here's mine.

HORTENSIUS' SERVANT   And mine, my lord.

BOTH VARRO'S SERVANTS   And ours, my lord.

PHILOTUS' SERVANT   All our bills.

TIMON
  Knock me down with 'em! Cleave me to the girdle!   91

LUCIUS' SERVANT   Alas, my lord—

TIMON   Cut my heart in sums!

TITUS' SERVANT   Mine, fifty talents.

---

69 repair return   **70 derive** benefit   **71 take 't . . . soul** i.e., believe I
speak sincerely   **72 comfortable temper** cheerful disposition   **73 keeps**
stays in   **74 are** who are   **75 if . . . health** if his condition is so far from
good health   **77 make . . . gods** i.e., pay all his debts to smooth his way
to heaven   **82 retentive** confining   **85 Put in** i.e., make your claim
91 Knock, Cleave (Timon puns on *bills* as weapons.)   **girdle** belt

TIMON   Tell out my blood!   95
LUCIUS' SERVANT   Five thousand crowns, my lord.
TIMON
  Five thousand drops pays that. What yours? And yours?
VARRO'S FIRST SERVANT   My lord—
VARRO'S SECOND SERVANT   My lord—
TIMON
  Tear me, take me, and the gods fall upon you!   100
                                          Exit Timon.

HORTENSIUS' SERVANT   Faith, I perceive our masters
  may throw their caps at their money. These debts   102
  may well be called desperate ones, for a madman owes   103
  'em.   *Exeunt.*

      Enter Timon [and Flavius].

TIMON
  They have e'en put my breath from me, the slaves.   105
  Creditors? Devils!
FLAVIUS   My dear lord—
TIMON   What if it should be so?   108
FLAVIUS   My lord—
TIMON
  I'll have it so. My steward!
FLAVIUS   Here, my lord.
TIMON
  So fitly? Go, bid all my friends again,   111
  Lucius, Lucullus, and Sempronius—all.
  I'll once more feast the rascals.
FLAVIUS   O my lord,
  You only speak from your distracted soul;
  There's not so much left to furnish out   115
  A moderate table.
TIMON   Be it not in thy care. Go,   117
  I charge thee, invite them all. Let in the tide
  Of knaves once more. My cook and I'll provide.
                                          Exeunt.

                       ❖

95 Tell out count out by the drop   **100 the gods fall upon you** i.e., may
the gods attack you as with an army   **102 throw . . . at** i.e., give up hope
of recovering   **103 desperate** (1) unlikely to be recovered (2) resulting
from desperate madness   **105 e'en . . . me** left me breathless   **108 What
. . . so** i.e., suppose I give it a try. (Timon has thought of the mock
banquet he will serve in 3.6.)   **111 fitly** conveniently   **115 furnish out**
supply   **117 Be . . . care** don't you worry about it

3.5

Enter three Senators at one door, Alcibiades meeting them, with attendants.

FIRST SENATOR [*To another Senator*]
  My lord, you have my voice to 't.   1
  The fault's bloody;   2
  'Tis necessary he should die.
  Nothing emboldens sin so much as mercy.
SECOND SENATOR   Most true. The law shall bruise 'em.   5
ALCIBIADES
  Honor, health, and compassion to the Senate!   6
FIRST SENATOR   Now, Captain?
ALCIBIADES
  I am an humble suitor to your virtues;
  For pity is the virtue of the law,   9
  And none but tyrants use it cruelly.
  It pleases time and fortune to lie heavy   11
  Upon a friend of mine, who in hot blood   12
  Hath stepped into the law, which is past depth   13
  To those that without heed do plunge into 't.   14
  He is a man, setting his fate aside,   15
  Of comely virtues;
  Nor did he soil the fact with cowardice—   17
  An honor in him which buys out his fault—   18
  But with a noble fury and fair spirit,
  Seeing his reputation touched to death,   20
  He did oppose his foe;
  And with such sober and unnoted passion   22
  He did behave his anger, ere 'twas spent,   23
  As if he had but proved an argument.   24
FIRST SENATOR
  You undergo too strict a paradox,   25

3.5. Location: Athens. The Senate House.
1 voice to 't vote in favor of it (the death sentence under consideration)   **2 fault's bloody** crime involved bloodshed   **5 'em** i.e., all such offenders   **6 compassion to the Senate** i.e., may the Senate have compassion   **9 virtue** chief merit, essence   **11–12 lie . . . Upon** oppress **13 stepped into** incurred the penalties of   **13–14 past depth To** over the heads of   **15 setting . . . aside** excluding his ill-fated action   **17 fact** deed   **18 buys out** redeems   **20 touched to death** fatally threatened **22 unnoted** so well under control as to be unobservable   **23 behave** control   **24 but . . . argument** only been testing a philosophical proposition   **25 undergo** undertake

Striving to make an ugly deed look fair.
Your words have took such pains as if they labored
To bring manslaughter into form and set quarreling   28
Upon the head of valor—which indeed   29
Is valor misbegot, and came into the world
When sects and factions were newly born.
He's truly valiant that can wisely suffer
The worst that man can breathe,   33
And make his wrongs his outsides,   34
To wear them like his raiment, carelessly,   35
And ne'er prefer his injuries to his heart,   36
To bring it into danger.
If wrongs be evils and enforce us kill,   38
What folly 'tis to hazard life for ill!   39

ALCIBIADES
My lord—

FIRST SENATOR   You cannot make gross sins look clear. 40
To revenge is no valor, but to bear.   41

ALCIBIADES
My lords, then, under favor, pardon me   42
If I speak like a captain.
Why do fond men expose themselves to battle,   44
And not endure all threats? Sleep upon 't,   45
And let the foes quietly cut their throats
Without repugnancy? If there be   47
Such valor in the bearing, what make we   48
Abroad? Why then, women are more valiant   49
That stay at home, if bearing carry it,   50
And the ass more captain than the lion, the felon
Loaden with irons wiser than the judge,   52

28 **bring . . . form** make manslaughter appear orderly, or according to
form   **28–29 set . . . of** make quarreling the highest kind of, or subdivi-
sion of   **29 which** i.e., quarreling, duelling   **33 breathe** i.e., speak (as
also in l. 61)   **34 his outsides** merely external circumstance   **35 raiment**
clothing.   **carelessly** without anxiety   **36 prefer** present   **38 kill** to
kill   **39 'tis** this is, i.e., this code that obliges one to repay evil with
violence.   **for ill** in a bad cause   **40 clear** innocent   **41 to bear** i.e.,
bearing insults calmly is true valor   **42 under favor** by your leave
44 fond foolish   **45 Sleep** i.e., why do they not sleep   **47 repugnancy**
resistance   **48 the bearing** i.e., putting up with insults.   **make** do
49 Abroad away from home   **50 bearing** putting up with insults (with a
pun on "childbearing" and perhaps on "supporting the man in sexual
intercourse")   **52 Loaden with irons** weighed down with shackles

If wisdom be in suffering. O my lords,
As you are great, be pitifully good.   54
Who cannot condemn rashness in cold blood?
To kill, I grant, is sin's extremest gust,   56
But in defense, by mercy, 'tis most just.   57
To be in anger is impiety,
But who is man that is not angry?   59
Weigh but the crime with this.

SECOND SENATOR   You breathe in vain.

ALCIBIADES   In vain? His service done
  At Lacedaemon and Byzantium
  Were a sufficient briber for his life.

FIRST SENATOR   What's that?

ALCIBIADES
Why, I say, my lords, he's done fair service   66
And slain in fight many of your enemies.
How full of valor did he bear himself
In the last conflict, and made plenteous wounds!

SECOND SENATOR
He has made too much plenty with 'em.   70
He's a sworn rioter; he has a sin that often   71
Drowns him and takes his valor prisoner.
If there were no foes, that were enough   73
To overcome him. In that beastly fury
He has been known to commit outrages
And cherish factions. 'Tis inferred to us   76
His days are foul and his drink dangerous.

FIRST SENATOR
He dies.

ALCIBIADES   Hard fate! He might have died in war.
My lords, if not for any parts in him—   79
Though his right arm might purchase his own time   80
And be in debt to none—yet, more to move you,

---

54 pitifully good good by showing mercy   **56 sin's extremest gust** the
relish of extremest sin. (*Gust* means outburst, indulgence.)   **57 by
mercy** by a merciful interpretation of law   **59 not** i.e., never   **66 fair**
excellent   **70 made . . . 'em** i.e., used them as an excuse for an excess of
riotous pleasure (playing on *plenty, plenteous*)   **71 sworn rioter** inveterate debauchee.   **a sin** i.e., drunkenness   **73 If** even if.   **foes** accusers
76 cherish factions encourage dissension and conspiracy.   **inferred**
alleged   **79 parts** admirable traits   **80 his right . . . time** i.e., his ability
in war should obtain his freedom and let him live out his natural life

Take my deserts to his and join 'em both;   82
And, for I know your reverend ages love   83
Security, I'll pawn my victories, all   84
My honors, to you, upon his good returns.   85
If by this crime he owes the law his life,
Why, let the war receive 't in valiant gore,   87
For law is strict, and war is nothing more.

FIRST SENATOR
   We are for law. He dies; urge it no more,
   On height of our displeasure. Friend or brother,   90
   He forfeits his own blood that spills another.   91

ALCIBIADES
   Must it be so? It must not be. My lords,
   I do beseech you, know me.

SECOND SENATOR   How?

ALCIBIADES   Call me to your remembrances.

THIRD SENATOR   What?

ALCIBIADES
   I cannot think but your age has forgot me.
   It could not else be I should prove so base   98
   To sue and be denied such common grace.   99
   My wounds ache at you.

FIRST SENATOR   Do you dare our anger?
   'Tis in few words, but spacious in effect: 101
   We banish thee forever.

ALCIBIADES   Banish me?
   Banish your dotage, banish usury,
   That makes the Senate ugly.

FIRST SENATOR
   If after two days' shine Athens contain thee,
   Attend our weightier judgment.
                                                              106

82 to in addition to   83 for because   84 Security (1) safety (2) collateral
for a loan (using a financial metaphor found also in *purchase, pawn,
good returns,* etc.)   85 upon . . . returns as a pledge that he will make a
good return on your investment in him, i.e., fight bravely in war   87 let
. . . gore i.e., let him pay his debt by bleeding as a soldier   90 On
. . . our on pain of our highest   91 another i.e., another's   98 else be
otherwise be (that).   prove i.e., be considered   99 To sue as to request
101 spacious in effect of great import (with quibble on the spacious
world to which Alcibiades is banished)   106 Attend . . . judgment
expect our more severe sentence

And, not to swell our spirit,   107
He shall be executed presently.   *Exeunt [Senators].*   108
ALCIBIADES
Now the gods keep you old enough
That you may live
Only in bone, that none may look on you!—   111
I'm worse than mad. I have kept back their foes,
While they have told their money and let out   113
Their coin upon large interest, I myself
Rich only in large hurts. All those for this?   115
Is this the balsam that the usuring Senate   116
Pours into captains' wounds? Banishment!
It comes not ill; I hate not to be banished.   118
It is a cause worthy my spleen and fury,   119
That I may strike at Athens. I'll cheer up
My discontented troops and lay for hearts.   121
'Tis honor with most lands to be at odds.   122
Soldiers should brook as little wrongs as gods.   *Exit.*   123

❖

3.6   [*Music. Tables and seats set out; servants
            attending.*] *Enter divers friends [of Timon] at
            several doors.*

FIRST LORD   The good time of day to you, sir.
SECOND LORD   I also wish it to you. I think this honor-
    able lord did but try us this other day.   3
FIRST LORD   Upon that were my thoughts tiring when   4
    we encountered. I hope it is not so low with him as he   5
    made it seem in the trial of his several friends.

---

107 spirit anger   **108 presently** immediately   **111 Only in bone** i.e.,
mere skeletons   **113 told** reckoned.   **let** lent   **115 hurts** injuries
116 balsam balm, medicine   **118 It . . . ill** it is not such a bad thing
after all   **119 worthy** worthy of   **121 lay for hearts** endeavor to win
their affection   **122 'Tis . . . odds** it's honorable to be at variance with a
country (and its political leaders) in most instances   **123 brook . . . gods**
endure insults as little as the gods do

3.6. Location: Athens. A banqueting room in Timon's house.
s.d. several separate   **3 did but try** was only testing us   **4 tiring** preying, feeding, i.e., busily engaged   **5 encountered** met.   **it is . . . him**
his financial situation is not so desperate

SECOND LORD   It should not be, by the persuasion of his 7
  new feasting.
FIRST LORD   I should think so. He hath sent me an earnest inviting, which many my near occasions did urge 10
  me to put off; but he hath conjured me beyond them, 11
  and I must needs appear.   12
SECOND LORD   In like manner was I in debt to my im- 13
  portunate business, but he would not hear my excuse.
  I am sorry, when he sent to borrow of me, that my
  provision was out.   16
FIRST LORD   I am sick of that grief too, as I understand 17
  how all things go.   18
SECOND LORD   Every man here's so. What would he
  have borrowed of you?
FIRST LORD   A thousand pieces.   21
SECOND LORD   A thousand pieces?
FIRST LORD   What of you?
SECOND LORD   He sent to me, sir— Here he comes.

Enter Timon and attendants. [Music plays.]

TIMON   With all my heart, gentlemen both! And how
  fare you?
FIRST LORD   Ever at the best, hearing well of your lordship.
SECOND LORD   The swallow follows not summer more
  willing than we your lordship.
TIMON [*Aside*]   Nor more willingly leaves winter, such
  summer birds are men.—Gentlemen, our dinner will
  not recompense this long stay. Feast your ears with 33
  the music awhile, if they will fare so harshly o' the 34
  trumpet's sound. We shall to 't presently.
FIRST LORD   I hope it remains not unkindly with your
  lordship that I returned you an empty messenger.
TIMON   O, sir, let it not trouble you.

---

7 persuasion evidence   **10 inviting** invitation.   **many . . . occasions** my
many urgent necessities or business   **11 conjured . . . them** summoned
me so urgently as to overcome my previous commitments   **12 needs**
necessarily   **13 in debt to** obligated to   **16 provision was out** resources
were exhausted   **17–18 as . . . go** particularly as I now understand the
state of affairs. (Perhaps hinting at Timon's seeming ability to entertain
lavishly again.)   **21 pieces** i.e., gold coins   **33 stay** delay   **34 they . . . o'**
they (your ears) will deign to feast on such rough fare as

SECOND LORD   My noble lord—

TIMON   Ah, my good friend, what cheer?

The banquet brought in.

SECOND LORD   My most honorable lord, I am e'en sick 41
of shame that when your lordship this other day sent
to me I was so unfortunate a beggar.   43

TIMON   Think not on 't, sir.

SECOND LORD   If you had sent but two hours before—

TIMON   Let it not cumber your better remembrance.— 46
Come, bring in all together.

SECOND LORD   All covered dishes!   48

FIRST LORD   Royal cheer, I warrant you.   49

THIRD LORD   Doubt not that, if money and the season
can yield it.

FIRST LORD   How do you? What's the news?

THIRD LORD   Alcibiades is banished. Hear you of it?

FIRST AND SECOND LORDS   Alcibiades banished?

THIRD LORD   'Tis so, be sure of it.

FIRST LORD   How? How?

SECOND LORD   I pray you, upon what?   57

TIMON   My worthy friends, will you draw near?

THIRD LORD   I'll tell you more anon. Here's a noble feast 59
toward.   60

SECOND LORD   This is the old man still.   61

THIRD LORD   Will 't hold? Will 't hold?   62

SECOND LORD   It does; but time will—and so—   63

THIRD LORD   I do conceive.   64

TIMON   Each man to his stool, with that spur as he 65
would to the lip of his mistress. Your diet shall be in 66
all places alike. Make not a city feast of it, to let the 67
meat cool ere we can agree upon the first place; sit, sit. 68
[_They sit._] The gods require our thanks.

You great benefactors, sprinkle our society with

---

41 e'en quite   **43 so . . . beggar** so unfortunate as to be out of ready
reserves   **46 cumber . . . remembrance** trouble your happier thoughts,
memories   **48 covered** (Implies particularly elegant fare.)   **49 Royal** fit
for royalty   **57 what** what ground   **59 anon** soon   **60 toward** imminent
61 old man still man we once knew   **62 hold** last   **63 will** i.e., will tell
64 conceive understand   **65 that spur** the same eagerness   **66 diet** food
66–67 in . . . alike the same wherever you sit to eat   **67 city feast** formal
occasion, with seating by rank   **68 first place** place of honor

thankfulness. For your own gifts, make yourselves
praised; but reserve still to give, lest your deities be   72
despised. Lend to each man enough, that one need not
lend to another; for, were your godheads to borrow of
men, men would forsake the gods. Make the meat be
beloved more than the man that gives it. Let no assembly of twenty be without a score of villains. If there sit
twelve women at the table, let a dozen of them be—as
they are. The rest of your fees, O gods—the senators   79
of Athens, together with the common tag of people—   80
what is amiss in them, you gods, make suitable for
destruction. For these my present friends, as they are   82
to me nothing, so in nothing bless them, and to nothing are they welcome.

Uncover, dogs, and lap!
> [*The dishes are uncovered and seen to contain*
> *warm water and stones.*]

SOME SPEAK   What does his lordship mean?
SOME OTHERS   I know not.
TIMON
  May you a better feast never behold,
  You knot of mouth-friends! Smoke and lukewarm water   89
  Is your perfection. This is Timon's last,   90
  Who, stuck and spangled with your flatteries,   91
  Washes it off and sprinkles in your faces
  Your reeking villainy.
> [*He throws the water in their faces.*]
                    Live loathed and long,
  Most smiling, smooth, detested parasites,
  Courteous destroyers, affable wolves, meek bears,
  You fools of fortune, trencher-friends, time's flies,   96
  Cap-and-knee slaves, vapors, and minute-jacks!   97

---

72 reserve still always hold back something   **79 fees** i.e., what is held in
fee from you, your gifts or benefactions (?) or, those who hold their lives
in fee from you (?)   **80 tag** rabble   **82 For** as for   **89 knot** company,
crowd.   **mouth-friends** friends in words only.   **Smoke** i.e., steam, "hot
air"   **90 Is your perfection** suits you perfectly   **91 stuck and spangled**
bespattered and decorated   **96 trencher-friends** friends only while being
fed.   **time's flies** fair-weather insects   **97 Cap-and-knee slaves** men
obsequious with their caps and curtsies.   **vapors** substanceless creatures.   **minute-jacks** mannikins that strike a bell on the outside of a
clock; hence, time-servers

Of man and beast the infinite malady   98
Crust you quite o'er! What, dost thou go?
Soft! Take thy physic first! Thou too, and thou!   100
Stay, I will lend thee money, borrow none.
[*He assaults them and drives them out.*]
What, all in motion? Henceforth be no feast
Whereat a villain's not a welcome guest.
Burn, house! Sink, Athens! Henceforth hated be
Of Timon, man, and all humanity!   *Exit.* 105

Enter the Senators, with other Lords, [returning].

FIRST LORD   How now, my lords?
SECOND LORD   Know you the quality of Lord Timon's 107
fury?
THIRD LORD   Push! Did you see my cap?   109
FOURTH LORD   I have lost my gown.
FIRST LORD   He's but a mad lord, and naught but hu- 111
mors sways him. He gave me a jewel th' other day, 112
and now he has beat it out of my hat. Did you see my
jewel?   [*They search for their belongings.*]
THIRD LORD   Did you see my cap?
SECOND LORD   Here 'tis.
FOURTH LORD   Here lies my gown.
FIRST LORD   Let's make no stay.
SECOND LORD
Lord Timon's mad.
THIRD LORD   I feel 't upon my bones.
FOURTH LORD
One day he gives us diamonds, next day stones.
                        Exeunt the Senators [etc.].

❧

---

98 the infinite malady every loathsome disease   **100 Soft** i.e., wait a
minute.   **physic** medicine   **105 Of** by   **107 quality** occasion   **109 Push**
pshaw   **111–112 humors** caprice

4.1 *Enter Timon.*

TIMON

Let me look back upon thee. O thou wall
That girdles in those wolves, dive in the earth
And fence not Athens! Matrons, turn incontinent!　　3
Obedience fail in children! Slaves and fools,　　4
Pluck the grave wrinkled Senate from the bench
And minister in their steads! To general filths　　6
Convert o' th' instant, green virginity!　　7
Do 't in your parents' eyes. Bankrupts, hold fast;
Rather than render back, out with your knives
And cut your trusters' throats! Bound servants, steal!　　10
Large-handed robbers your grave masters are,　　11
And pill by law. Maid, to thy master's bed!　　12
Thy mistress is o' the brothel. Son of sixteen,
Pluck the lined crutch from thy old limping sire;　　14
With it beat out his brains! Piety, and fear,　　15
Religion to the gods, peace, justice, truth,　　16
Domestic awe, night rest, and neighborhood,　　17
Instruction, manners, mysteries, and trades,　　18
Degrees, observances, customs, and laws,　　19
Decline to your confounding contraries,　　20
And yet confusion live! Plagues, incident to men,　　21
Your potent and infectious fevers heap
On Athens, ripe for stroke! Thou cold sciatica,　　23
Cripple our senators, that their limbs may halt　　24
As lamely as their manners! Lust and liberty　　25
Creep in the minds and marrows of our youth,　　26

4.1. Location: Outside the walls of Athens.
3 fence (1) enclose (2) defend. **incontinent** lascivious　**4 Obedience fail**
let obedience fail　**6 general filths** common prostitutes　**7 green**
young　**10 trusters'** of those who have trusted you, your creditors.
Bound indentured　**11 Large-handed** rapacious　**12 pill** pillage. **to go
to**　**14 lined** stuffed, padded　**15 fear** religious awe　**16 Religion to**
veneration of　**17 Domestic awe** respect for the seniors of a household. **neighborhood** neighborliness　**18 mysteries** crafts　**19 Degrees**
established ranks of society　**20 confounding contraries** opposites that
reduce all to chaos　**21 yet** i.e., in spite of this dissolution, still let
23 cold chilling, or caused by chill. **sciatica** nerve pain in hip and leg
24 halt limp　**25 liberty** licentiousness　**26 marrows** soft tissues filling
the cavities of bone (thought of as the source of vitality and strength)

That 'gainst the stream of virtue they may strive   27
And drown themselves in riot! Itches, blains,   28
Sow all th' Athenian bosoms, and their crop   29
Be general leprosy! Breath infect breath,
That their society, as their friendship, may   31
Be merely poison! Nothing I'll bear from thee   32
But nakedness, thou detestable town!
                         [*He strips off his garments.*]
Take thou that too, with multiplying bans!   34
Timon will to the woods, where he shall find
Th' unkindest beast more kinder than mankind.
The gods confound—hear me, you good gods all—
Th' Athenians both within and out that wall!
And grant, as Timon grows, his hate may grow
To the whole race of mankind, high and low!
Amen.   *Exit.*

❖

4.2   *Enter steward [Flavius], with two or three*
       Servants.

FIRST SERVANT
  Hear you, Master Steward, where's our master?
  Are we undone, cast off, nothing remaining?
FLAVIUS
  Alack, my fellows, what should I say to you?
  Let me be recorded by the righteous gods,   4
  I am as poor as you.
FIRST SERVANT   Such a house broke?
  So noble a master fall'n? All gone, and not
  One friend to take his fortune by the arm   7
  And go along with him?
SECOND SERVANT   As we do turn our backs
  From our companion thrown into his grave,

---

27 stream current   **28 blains** blisters   **29 Sow** fall like seed in
31 society associating with one another   **32 merely** entirely   **34 bans**
curses

4.2. Location: Athens. Timon's house.
4 be recorded by say in the hearing of   **7 his fortune** i.e., Timon in his
misfortune

So his familiars to his buried fortunes   11
Slink all away, leave their false vows with him
Like empty purses picked; and his poor self,
A dedicated beggar to the air,   14
With his disease of all-shunned poverty,
Walks, like contempt, alone. More of our fellows.   16

    Enter other Servants.

FLAVIUS
All broken implements of a ruined house.
THIRD SERVANT
Yet do our hearts wear Timon's livery;   18
That see I by our faces. We are fellows still,
Serving alike in sorrow. Leaked is our bark,   20
And we, poor mates, stand on the dying deck,   21
Hearing the surges threat. We must all part   22
Into this sea of air.
FLAVIUS   Good fellows all,
The latest of my wealth I'll share amongst you.   24
Wherever we shall meet, for Timon's sake,
Let's yet be fellows. Let's shake our heads and say,   26
As 'twere a knell unto our master's fortunes,   27
"We have seen better days." Let each take some.
                [He gives them money.]
Nay, put out all your hands. Not one word more.   29
Thus part we rich in sorrow, parting poor.
      [Servants] embrace, and part several ways.
O, the fierce wretchedness that glory brings us!
Who would not wish to be from wealth exempt,
Since riches point to misery and contempt?   33
Who would be so mocked with glory, or to live
But in a dream of friendship,
To have his pomp and all what state compounds   36

---

11 his familiars . . . fortunes those close to him when he was fortunate,
now perceiving his ruin   **14 dedicated . . . air** beggar having nothing
and nowhere to go   **16 like contempt** as if he were contemptibility
itself   **18 livery** uniform worn by male household servants (here used
metaphorically)   **20 bark** sailing vessel   **21 mates** (1) fellows (2) mates
of a vessel.   **dying** i.e., sinking   **22 surges** waves   **24 latest** last rem-
nant   **26 yet** still.   **shake our heads** (in sorrow)   **27 knell** tolling of a
bell, announcing a death or other misfortune   **29 put out all** all put
out   **33 point to** tend to   **36 what state compounds** that which consti-
tutes dignity and splendor

But only painted, like his varnished friends?   37
Poor honest lord, brought low by his own heart,
Undone by goodness! Strange, unusual blood,   39
When man's worst sin is he does too much good!
Who then dares to be half so kind again?
For bounty, that makes gods, do still mar men.   42
My dearest lord, blest to be most accurst,   43
Rich only to be wretched, thy great fortunes
Are made thy chief afflictions. Alas, kind lord!
He's flung in rage from this ingrateful seat
Of monstrous friends,
Nor has he with him to supply his life,   48
Or that which can command it.   49
I'll follow and inquire him out.
I'll ever serve his mind with my best will;   51
Whilst I have gold, I'll be his steward still.   *Exit.*

❖

4.3   *Enter Timon, in the woods [with a spade].*

TIMON
O blessèd breeding sun, draw from the earth
Rotten humidity; below thy sister's orb   2
Infect the air! Twinned brothers of one womb,
Whose procreation, residence, and birth
Scarce is dividant, touch them with several fortunes,   5
The greater scorns the lesser. Not nature,   6
To whom all sores lay siege, can bear great fortune   7
But by contempt of nature.   8
Raise me this beggar, and deny 't that lord;   9

37 But only nothing more than   **39 blood** nature   **42 bounty** generosity   **43 to be** only to be   **48 Nor . . . life** nor has he anything to maintain himself with   **49 that . . . it** i.e., money   **51 serve his mind** execute his wishes

4.3. Location: Woods and cave, near the seashore; in front of Timon's cave.
2 Rotten humidity rot-causing damp.   **thy sister's** i.e., the moon's
5 dividant separate, divisible.   **touch** if you test.   **several** different
6 The and the result is that the   **6–8 Not . . . nature** i.e., human nature, which suffers so many afflictions, cannot experience good fortune without scorning fellow creatures who are less fortunate   **9 Raise me** raise. (*Me* is a colloquial usage meaning something like "believe me.")

The senator shall bear contempt hereditary,   10
The beggar native honor.   11
It is the pasture lards the brother's sides,   12
The want that makes him lean. Who dares, who dares   13
In purity of manhood stand upright
And say "This man's a flatterer"? If one be,
So are they all, for every grece of fortune   16
Is smoothed by that below. The learnèd pate   17
Ducks to the golden fool. All's obliquy;   18
There's nothing level in our cursèd natures   19
But direct villainy. Therefore, be abhorred
All feasts, societies, and throngs of men!
His semblable, yea, himself, Timon disdains.   22
Destruction fang mankind! Earth, yield me roots!   23
                                        [*He digs.*]
Who seeks for better of thee, sauce his palate   24
With thy most operant poison! [*He finds gold.*] What
  is here?   25
Gold? Yellow, glittering, precious gold?
No, gods, I am no idle votarist.   27
Roots, you clear heavens! Thus much of this will make 28
Black white, foul fair, wrong right,
Base noble, old young, coward valiant.
Ha, you gods! Why this? What this, you gods? Why, this
Will lug your priests and servants from your sides,
Pluck stout men's pillows from below their heads.   33
This yellow slave
Will knit and break religions, bless th' accurst,   35

10 bear contempt hereditary receive contempt as though he were born
low   **11 native honor** (will receive) honor as though born great   **12–13 It
is . . . lean** i.e., it is the inheritance and possessing of pasture that makes
one brother fat, the lack (want) that makes him, the younger brother, lean.
(The Folio reads *leave* for *lean*, which could mean that the younger
brother has to leave in search of riches elsewhere.)   **lards** that fattens.
want lack (of good pasture)   **16 grece** step   **17 smoothed** assiduously
prepared.   **pate** head   **18 Ducks** bows obsequiously.   **golden** rich.   **All's
obliquy** i.e., all's deviating from the right   **19 level** direct. (The contrary to
obliquy.)   **22 His semblable** i.e., his own kind, his own image   **23 fang**
seize   **24 sauce** stimulate, tickle   **25 operant** active, potent   **27 no idle
votarist** no trifler in my vows (of leading a spare existence)   **28 clear**
pure   **33 Pluck . . . heads** i.e., expedite the death of healthy men by
pulling the pillows from beneath their heads as they sleep (supposedly a
way of throttling them)   **35 knit . . . religions** knit men together in religious harmony and then break that harmony apart

Make the hoar leprosy adored, place thieves   36
And give them title, knee, and approbation   37
With senators on the bench. This is it
That makes the wappened widow wed again;   39
She whom the spital house and ulcerous sores   40
Would cast the gorge at, this embalms and spices   41
To th' April day again. Come, damnèd earth,   42
Thou common whore of mankind, that puts odds   43
Among the rout of nations, I will make thee   44
Do thy right nature. (*March afar off.*) Ha? A drum?
  Thou'rt quick,   45
But yet I'll bury thee. Thou'lt go, strong thief,   46
When gouty keepers of thee cannot stand.
                       [*He buries the gold.*]
Nay, stay thou out for earnest. [*He keeps some gold.*]   48

Enter Alcibiades, with drum and fife, in warlike
manner, and Phrynia and Timandra.

ALCIBIADES   What art thou there? Speak.
TIMON
  A beast, as thou art. The canker gnaw thy heart
  For showing me again the eyes of man!
ALCIBIADES
  What is thy name? Is man so hateful to thee
  That art thyself a man?
TIMON
  I am Misanthropos and hate mankind.   54
  For thy part, I do wish thou wert a dog,   55
  That I might love thee something.
ALCIBIADES   I know thee well,   56
  But in thy fortunes am unlearned and strange.   57

---

36 hoar white-skinned. **place** give recognized status and high office
to **37 knee** the bended deferential knee **39 makes** enables. **wappened** worn out **40 spital house** house for the diseased (cf. hospital)
41 cast the gorge vomit **41–42 this . . . again** i.e., money enables the
diseased old woman to embalm herself with cosmetics to look April-like
and marriageable **42 damnèd earth** i.e., gold **43–44 puts . . . nations**
causes strife among various peoples **45 Do . . . nature** i.e., cause strife,
according to your true nature. **quick** (1) swift to act (2) alive **46 go** be
able to walk **48 for earnest** as an installment or pledge **s.d. drum and
fife** i.e., soldiers playing drum and fife **54 Misanthropos** hater of
mankind **55 For thy part** as for you **56 something** somewhat, a
little **57 unlearned and strange** uninformed and ignorant

TIMON
  I know thee too; and more than that I know thee
  I not desire to know. Follow thy drum;   59
  With man's blood paint the ground gules, gules.   60
  Religious canons, civil laws, are cruel;   61
  Then what should war be? This fell whore of thine   62
  Hath in her more destruction than thy sword,
  For all her cherubin look.
PHRYNIA   Thy lips rot off!   64
TIMON
  I will not kiss thee; then the rot returns
  To thine own lips again.
ALCIBIADES
  How came the noble Timon to this change?
TIMON
  As the moon does, by wanting light to give.   68
  But then renew I could not, like the moon;   69
  There were no suns to borrow of.   70
ALCIBIADES   Noble Timon, what friendship may I do thee?
TIMON   None, but to maintain my opinion.
ALCIBIADES   What is it, Timon?
TIMON   Promise me friendship, but perform none. If   74
  thou wilt not promise, the gods plague thee, for thou   75
  art a man! If thou dost perform, confound thee, for   76
  thou art a man!   77
ALCIBIADES
  I have heard in some sort of thy miseries.   78
TIMON
  Thou sawst them when I had prosperity.
ALCIBIADES
  I see them now. Then was a blessèd time.
TIMON
  As thine is now, held with a brace of harlots.   81

---

59 not desire do not desire   **60 gules** (Heraldic name for "red.")
61 canons rules, laws   **62 fell** deadly   **64 cherubin** angelic. **Thy lips**
may thy lips   **68 wanting** lacking   **69 renew** become new again (with a
quibble on the idea of renewing a loan)   **70 suns** (punning on *sons*, i.e.,
men)   **74–77 If . . . a man** i.e., may the gods plague you for being a man
whether you perform your promises or don't even make promises   **78 I
. . . sort** i.e., I have heard something   **81 brace** pair (with a quibble on
the meaning "clamp," one that holds Alcibiades in its grip)

TIMANDRA
  Is this th' Athenian minion whom the world   82
  Voiced so regardfully?
TIMON   Art thou Timandra?
TIMANDRA   Yes.   83
TIMON
  Be a whore still. They love thee not that use thee;
  Give them diseases, leaving with thee their lust.   85
  Make use of thy salt hours. Season the slaves   86
  For tubs and baths; bring down rose-cheeked youth   87
  To the tub-fast and the diet.
TIMANDRA   Hang thee, monster!
ALCIBIADES
  Pardon him, sweet Timandra, for his wits
  Are drowned and lost in his calamities.—
  I have but little gold of late, brave Timon,
  The want whereof doth daily make revolt   92
  In my penurious band. I have heard and grieved   93
  How cursèd Athens, mindless of thy worth,
  Forgetting thy great deeds, when neighbor states,
  But for thy sword and fortune, trod upon them—   96
TIMON
  I prithee, beat thy drum and get thee gone.
ALCIBIADES
  I am thy friend and pity thee, dear Timon.
TIMON
  How dost thou pity him whom thou dost trouble?
  I had rather be alone.
ALCIBIADES
  Why, fare thee well. Here is some gold for thee.
                                  [He offers gold.]
TIMON   Keep it. I cannot eat it.

---

82 Athenian minion darling of Athens   **83 Voiced** spoke of.   **regardfully**
respectfully   **85 leaving** while they are leaving   **86 salt** lecherous.
Season the slaves i.e., pickle and spice the villains as if preparing them
for the pickling tub; make them ready   **87 tubs and baths** (Allusion to
the treatments for venereal diseases, as also in *tub-fast* and *diet* in the
next line.)   **92 want** lack.   **make revolt** provoke mutiny   **93 penurious**
poverty-stricken   **96 But . . . fortune** (A suggestion of Timon's history as
a great military leader, for which Athens ought to be grateful.)   **trod**
would have trod

ALCIBIADES
   When I have laid proud Athens on a heap—
TIMON
   Warr'st thou 'gainst Athens?
ALCIBIADES   Ay, Timon, and have cause.
TIMON
   The gods confound them all in thy conquest,   105
   And thee after, when thou hast conquered!
ALCIBIADES   Why me, Timon?
TIMON   That by killing of villains   108
   Thou wast born to conquer my country.   109
   Put up thy gold. Go on—here's gold—go on.   110
                                  [He offers gold.]
   Be as a planetary plague, when Jove   111
   Will o'er some high-viced city hang his poison   112
   In the sick air. Let not thy sword skip one.
   Pity not honored age for his white beard;
   He is an usurer. Strike me the counterfeit matron;   115
   It is her habit only that is honest,   116
   Herself's a bawd. Let not the virgin's cheek
   Make soft thy trenchant sword; for those milk paps, 118
   That through the window bars bore at men's eyes,   119
   Are not within the leaf of pity writ,   120
   But set them down horrible traitors. Spare not the babe, 121
   Whose dimpled smiles from fools exhaust their mercy; 122
   Think it a bastard, whom the oracle
   Hath doubtfully pronounced thy throat shall cut,   124
   And mince it sans remorse. Swear against objects;   125
   Put armor on thine ears and on thine eyes,

---

105 confound destroy   **108–109 That . . . country** (Timon evidently
applauds the deed but not the doer. His words are obscure and the text
may be corrupt.)   **110 Put up** put away   **111 planetary plague** (Allusion
to the belief in the malignant influence of planets.)   **112 high-viced**
extremely vicious   **115 Strike me** i.e., strike.   **counterfeit** pretending
respectability   **116 habit** costume, outward appearance.   **honest**
chaste   **118 trenchant** sharp.   **milk paps** nipples   **119 window bars** i.e.,
latticework of her bodice (?)   **120 Are . . . writ** i.e., are not written down
on the list of those to whom pity is to be shown   **121 traitors** i.e.,
betrayers of men   **122 exhaust** draw forth   **124 doubtfully** ambiguously.   **thy . . . cut** will cut your throat. (However, the phrase can also
be ambiguously reversed.)   **125 mince** slash, cut in small pieces.   **sans**
without.   **Swear against objects** bind yourself by oath against objec-
tions (to your cruelty)

Whose proof nor yells of mothers, maids, nor babes,   127
Nor sight of priests in holy vestments bleeding,
Shall pierce a jot. There's gold to pay thy soldiers.
Make large confusion; and, thy fury spent,   130
Confounded be thyself! Speak not, begone.

ALCIBIADES
Hast thou gold yet? I'll take the gold thou givest me,
Not all thy counsel.   [*He takes gold.*]

TIMON
Dost thou or dost thou not, heaven's curse upon thee!   134

PHRYNIA AND TIMANDRA
Give us some gold, good Timon. Hast thou more?

TIMON
Enough to make a whore forswear her trade,
And to make whores, a bawd. Hold up, you sluts,   137
Your aprons mountant. [*He throws gold into their
aprons.*] You are not oathable,   138
Although I know you'll swear—terribly swear
Into strong shudders and to heavenly agues—   140
Th' immortal gods that hear you. Spare your oaths;
I'll trust to your conditions. Be whores still;   142
And he whose pious breath seeks to convert you,
Be strong in whore, allure him, burn him up.   144
Let your close fire predominate his smoke,   145
And be no turncoats. Yet may your pains six months   146
Be quite contrary. And thatch your poor thin roofs   147
With burdens of the dead—some that were hanged,   148
No matter; wear them, betray with them. Whore still;   149

---

127 Whose proof the tested strength of which armor. **nor yells** neither
the yells   **130 large confusion** wholesale destruction   **134 Dost . . . not**
whether you do or not   **137 to . . . bawd** i.e., to make a bawd retire from
turning women into whores   **138 mountant** (A heraldic coinage, with
sexual suggestion; see also *erection* in l. 166.)   **oathable** to be believed
on your oath   **140 strong** violent.   **agues** feverish shivers   **142 your
conditions** what you are, your characters   **144 Be . . . whore** be resolute
in whoring.   **burn him up** (1) inflame him with desire (2) infect him
with venereal disease   **145 Let . . . smoke** i.e., let your secret and
disease-carrying passion overcome his pious professions   **146–147 Yet
. . . contrary** i.e., may you suffer intense pain for six months (?) (Perhaps
six months is simply an arbitrary figure, or alludes to the early symp-
toms of syphilis.)   **147–148 thatch . . . dead** i.e., cover your balding
heads (caused by venereal disease) with wigs made of the hair of
corpses   **149 betray with them** i.e., use these wigs to create false beauty
to betray more men

Paint till a horse may mire upon your face.   150
A pox of wrinkles!
PHRYNIA AND TIMANDRA Well, more gold. What then?   151
Believe 't that we'll do anything for gold.
TIMON Consumptions sow   153
In hollow bones of man; strike their sharp shins,
And mar men's spurring. Crack the lawyer's voice,   155
That he may nevermore false title plead,
Nor sound his quillets shrilly. Hoar the flamen,   157
That scolds against the quality of flesh   158
And not believes himself. Down with the nose,   159
Down with it flat; take the bridge quite away
Of him that, his particular to foresee,   161
Smells from the general weal. Make curled-pate
   ruffians bald,   162
And let the unscarred braggarts of the war
Derive some pain from you. Plague all,
That your activity may defeat and quell
The source of all erection. There's more gold.   166
                         [*He gives gold.*]
Do you damn others and let this damn you,
And ditches grave you all!   168
PHRYNIA AND TIMANDRA
More counsel with more money, bounteous Timon.
TIMON
More whore, more mischief first. I have given you
   earnest.   170

---

150 mire upon bog down in. (Timon sardonically urges so thick a
cosmetic covering that even a horse would become mired.) **151 A pox
of wrinkles** i.e., may you be plagued with wrinkles **153 Consumptions
sow** plant wasting diseases such as syphilis. (Addressed to Phrynia and
Timandra.) **155 spurring** i.e., riding (here used as a sexual metaphor)
157 quillets quibbles. **Hoar the flamen** whiten (with leprosy) the
priest (with a pun on *hoar, whore*) **158 quality of flesh** fleshly desire
159 And . . . himself i.e., and doesn't practice what he preaches. **Down
. . . nose** (An effect of syphilis.) **161 his . . . foresee** in order to look out
for his own interests **162 Smells . . . weal** (1) loses the scent of the
common good (2) stinks above the common crowd. **curled-pate** curly-
headed **166 erection** advancement (with bawdy pun) **168 grave** enclose in the grave (with a pun on "ditches" and "damming" continued
from l. 167) **170 whore** whoring. **mischief** destruction. **earnest**
earnest money, token payment

ALCIBIADES
Strike up the drum towards Athens. Farewell, Timon.
If I thrive well, I'll visit thee again.
TIMON
If I hope well, I'll never see thee more.   173
ALCIBIADES   I never did thee harm.
TIMON
Yes, thou spok'st well of me.
ALCIBIADES   Call'st thou that harm?
TIMON
Men daily find it. Get thee away and take   176
Thy beagles with thee.
ALCIBIADES   We but offend him. Strike!   177
                    [Drum beats.] Exeunt [Alcibiades,
                              Phrynia, and Timandra].

TIMON
That nature, being sick of man's unkindness,   178
Should yet be hungry! [He digs.] Common mother, thou   179
Whose womb unmeasurable and infinite breast
Teems and feeds all, whose selfsame mettle   181
Whereof thy proud child, arrogant man, is puffed   182
Engenders the black toad and adder blue,
The gilded newt and eyeless venomed worm,   184
With all th' abhorrèd births below crisp heaven
Whereon Hyperion's quickening fire doth shine: 186
Yield him who all thy human sons do hate,   187
From forth thy plenteous bosom, one poor root!
Ensear thy fertile and conceptious womb;   189
Let it no more bring out ingrateful man!
Go great with tigers, dragons, wolves, and bears;   191
Teem with new monsters, whom thy upward face   192

173 If I hope well if my hopes are realized   **176 find it** i.e., find it
harmful to be spoken well of   **177 beagles** i.e., beagle hounds, fawning
followers—the prostitutes   **178 That** to think that.   **sick of** sickened by,
surfeited with   **179 Common mother** i.e., the earth   **181 Teems** abundantly bears offspring.   **mettle** spirit, essence (with a pun on *metal;* the
words were virtually interchangeable)   **182 Whereof** with which
184 eyeless venomed worm the blindworm (wrongly supposed poisonous)   **186 Hyperion's** i.e., the sun's.   **quickening** life-giving   **187 who
. . . hate** who hates all your human offspring   **189 Ensear** dry up.
conceptious fertile   **191 Go great** be pregnant   **192 upward** upturned

Hath to the marbled mansion all above   193
Never presented! [*He finds a root.*] O, a root! Dear
    thanks!—
Dry up thy marrows, vines, and plow-torn leas,   195
Whereof ingrateful man with liquorish drafts   196
And morsels unctuous greases his pure mind,   197
That from it all consideration slips—   198

    Enter Apemantus.

More man? Plague, plague!

APEMANTUS
I was directed hither. Men report
Thou dost affect my manners and dost use them.   201

TIMON
'Tis, then, because thou dost not keep a dog,
Whom I would imitate. Consumption catch thee!   203

APEMANTUS
This is in thee a nature but infected,   204
A poor unmanly melancholy sprung
From change of fortune. Why this spade? This place?
This slavelike habit and these looks of care?   207
Thy flatterers yet wear silk, drink wine, lie soft,
Hug their diseased perfumes, and have forgot   209
That ever Timon was. Shame not these woods
By putting on the cunning of a carper.   211
Be thou a flatterer now and seek to thrive
By that which has undone thee. Hinge thy knee
And let his very breath whom thou'lt observe   214
Blow off thy cap. Praise his most vicious strain   215
And call it excellent. Thou wast told thus.   216

---

193 the marbled . . . above i.e., the heavens   **195 marrows** i.e., marrow
in the earth's bones, denoting her fecundity.   **plow-torn leas**
plowed-up pastureland   **196 liquorish drafts** sweet, alcoholic drinks
197 unctuous fatty, oily.   **greases his pure mind** makes greasy and vile
his once-pure mind   **198 That** so that.   **consideration** reflection, rationality; regard for others, or for other things than sensual   **201 affect** put
on   **203 would** i.e., would in that case.   **Consumption catch thee** may a
wasting illness lay hold on you   **204 but infected** i.e., not inborn and
philosophical but induced by misery and hence shallow   **207 habit**
garment   **209 perfumes** perfumed mistresses   **211 putting . . . carper**
assuming the manner and profession of a Cynic   **214 observe** bow
obsequiously before   **215 strain** quality   **216 Thou . . . thus** i.e., you
were spoken to flatteringly in exactly this manner

Thou gav'st thine ears, like tapsters that bade welcome,   217
To knaves and all approachers. 'Tis most just
That thou turn rascal; hadst thou wealth again,
Rascals should have 't. Do not assume my likeness.

TIMON
Were I like thee, I'd throw away myself.

APEMANTUS
Thou hast cast away thyself, being like thyself—
A madman so long, now a fool. What, think'st   223
That the bleak air, thy boisterous chamberlain,   224
Will put thy shirt on warm? Will these mossed trees,   225
That have outlived the eagle, page thy heels   226
And skip when thou point'st out? Will the cold brook,   227
Candied with ice, caudle thy morning taste   228
To cure thy o'ernight's surfeit? Call the creatures
Whose naked natures live in all the spite   230
Of wreakful heaven, whose bare unhousèd trunks,   231
To the conflicting elements exposed,
Answer mere nature; bid them flatter thee.   233
O, thou shalt find—

TIMON   A fool of thee. Depart.   234

APEMANTUS
I love thee better now than e'er I did.

TIMON
I hate thee worse.

APEMANTUS   Why?

TIMON   Thou flatter'st misery.

APEMANTUS
I flatter not, but say thou art a caitiff.   237

TIMON   Why dost thou seek me out?

APEMANTUS   To vex thee.

TIMON
Always a villain's office or a fool's.
Dost please thyself in 't?

---

217 ears i.e., attention. **like . . . welcome** i.e., like barkeeps who welcome all comers indiscriminately   **223–225 think'st . . . warm** (Alludes
to the practice of having a servant warm one's garment by the fire.)
226 page thy heels i.e., follow you obediently   **227 skip . . . out** jump to
fulfill your command   **228 Candied** crystalline. **caudle . . . taste** i.e.,
provide you with a caudle, a hot spiced drink   **230 in** exposed to
231 wreakful vengeful. **trunks** i.e., bodies   **233 Answer** cope with,
contend with. **mere** stark, unrelieved   **234 of** in   **237 caitiff** wretch

APEMANTUS   Ay.

TIMON   What, a knave too?   241

APEMANTUS

If thou didst put this sour cold habit on   242
To castigate thy pride, 'twere well, but thou   243
Dost it enforcedly. Thou'dst courtier be again
Wert thou not beggar. Willing misery   245
Outlives incertain pomp, is crowned before: 246
The one is filling still, never complete,   247
The other at high wish. Best state, contentless, 248
Hath a distracted and most wretched being,   249
Worse than the worst, content.   250
Thou shouldst desire to die, being miserable.

TIMON

Not by his breath that is more miserable.   252
Thou art a slave whom Fortune's tender arm
With favor never clasped but bred a dog.   254
Hadst thou, like us from our first swathe, proceeded 255
The sweet degrees that this brief world affords
To such as may the passive drudges of it   257
Freely command, thou wouldst have plunged thyself 258
In general riot, melted down thy youth   259
In different beds of lust, and never learned   260
The icy precepts of respect, but followed
The sugared game before thee. But myself—   262
Who had the world as my confectionary,   263

---

241 a knave too i.e., a fool and a villain to boot (since it is villainous to take pleasure in vexing others) **242 habit** disposition **243 'twere well** it would be a commendable thing **245–246 Willing . . . before** deliberately chosen poverty outlasts the life of insecure ceremony and wealth, and is sooner crowned with spiritual reward **247 The one** i.e., incertain pomp. **is filling still** is never satisfied **248 at high wish** at the height of contentment **248–250 Best . . . content** being at the height of prosperity without contentment means a wretched existence, worse than being at the bottom of prosperity with contentment **252 Not . . . miserable** i.e., not when he who speaks (Apemantus) is more to be pitied than I **254 but bred** i.e., but whom Fortune bred **255 swathe** swaddling clothes. **proceeded** passed through (like a student taking an academic degree) **257–258 To such . . . command** i.e., to those who have the world and its sycophants at command **259 riot** debauchery **260 different** various **262 sugared game** sweet-tasting quarry **263 my confectionary** maker of sweetmeats just for me; a place where such sweetmeats are stored

The mouths, the tongues, the eyes, and hearts of men
At duty, more than I could frame employment,   265
That numberless upon me stuck, as leaves   266
Do on the oak, have with one winter's brush   267
Fell from their boughs and left me open, bare   268
For every storm that blows—I to bear this,   269
That never knew but better, is some burden.   270
Thy nature did commence in sufferance; time   271
Hath made thee hard in 't. Why shouldst thou hate men? 272
They never flattered thee. What hast thou given?
If thou wilt curse, thy father, that poor rag,   274
Must be thy subject, who in spite put stuff   275
To some she-beggar and compounded thee   276
Poor rogue hereditary. Hence, begone!   277
If thou hadst not been born the worst of men,   278
Thou hadst been a knave and flatterer.

APEMANTUS
Art thou proud yet?

TIMON   Ay, that I am not thee.   280

APEMANTUS   I, that I was no prodigal.

TIMON   I, that I am one now.
Were all the wealth I have shut up in thee,   283
I'd give thee leave to hang it. Get thee gone.   284
That the whole life of Athens were in this!   285
Thus would I eat it.   [*He eats a root.*]

APEMANTUS [*Offering food*]   Here, I will mend thy feast.

TIMON
First mend my company: take away thyself.

APEMANTUS
So I shall mend mine own by th' lack of thine.

TIMON
'Tis not well mended so; it is but botched.   289

---

265 At duty subservient to my wishes.   **frame** provide with   **266 stuck**
having stuck   **267 winter's brush** gust of wintry wind   **268 Fell**
fallen.   **open** exposed   **269 I . . . this** that I should bear this   **270 That**
. . . better who have known only better fortune   **271 sufferance** suffering, poverty   **272 hard in 't** hardened to it   **274 rag** i.e., wretch
275 in spite out of malice   **275–276 put stuff To** fornicated with
276 compounded begot   **277 hereditary** by right of inheritance
278 worst lowest in station   **280 yet** still   **283 shut up** contained
284 hang it i.e., hang yourself   **285 That** I wish that   **289 botched** badly
mended (since you remain in your own company)

If not, I would it were.   290
APEMANTUS What wouldst thou have to Athens?   291
TIMON
    Thee thither in a whirlwind. If thou wilt,
    Tell them there I have gold. Look, so I have.
                                    [*He shows his gold.*]
APEMANTUS
    Here is no use for gold.
TIMON   The best and truest,
    For here it sleeps and does no hirèd harm.
APEMANTUS Where liest anights, Timon?   296
TIMON Under that's above me. Where feed'st thou   297
    adays, Apemantus?   298
APEMANTUS Where my stomach finds meat; or, rather,
    where I eat it.
TIMON Would poison were obedient and knew my
    mind!
APEMANTUS Where wouldst thou send it?
TIMON To sauce thy dishes.   304
APEMANTUS The middle of humanity thou never knew-
    est, but the extremity of both ends. When thou wast
    in thy gilt and thy perfume, they mocked thee for too   307
    much curiosity; in thy rags thou know'st none, but art   308
    despised for the contrary. There's a medlar for thee.   309
    Eat it.   [*He gives a fruit.*]
TIMON On what I hate I feed not.
APEMANTUS Dost hate a medlar?
TIMON Ay, though it look like thee.   313
APEMANTUS An thou'dst hated meddlers sooner, thou   314
    shouldst have loved thyself better now. What man
    didst thou ever know unthrift that was beloved after   316
    his means?   317

---

290 If . . . were i.e., even if you don't think things are made worse by having
yourself for a companion, I wish you did (since I'd prefer to see you unhappy); or, even if it's only a botched job, I'd still prefer to see you get away
from here (?)   **291 What . . . have** what would you have me convey. (But
Timon caustically jests in a more literal sense of the phrase.)   **296 anights** at
night   **297 that's** that which is   **298 adays** by day   **304 sauce** flavor
307 gilt fine trappings   **308 curiosity** fastidiousness, refinement   **309 medlar**
fruit like a small brown-skinned apple, eaten when nearly decayed; used here,
as often, for the sake of a quibble on *meddler*, with sexual suggestion
313 like thee i.e., in a state of decay, or as one who meddles   **314 An
thou'dst** if thou hadst   **316 unthrift** to be unthrifty   **316–317 after his
means** (1) after his wealth was gone (2) according to his means

TIMON   Who, without those means thou talk'st of, didst thou ever know beloved?

APEMANTUS   Myself.

TIMON   I understand thee: thou hadst some means to keep a dog. 321
322

APEMANTUS   What things in the world canst thou nearest compare to thy flatterers?

TIMON   Women nearest. But men—men are the things themselves. What wouldst thou do with the world, Apemantus, if it lay in thy power?

APEMANTUS   Give it the beasts, to be rid of the men.

TIMON   Wouldst thou have thyself fall in the confusion 329
of men and remain a beast with the beasts? 330

APEMANTUS   Ay, Timon.

TIMON   A beastly ambition, which the gods grant thee t' attain to! If thou wert the lion, the fox would beguile thee. If thou wert the lamb, the fox would eat thee. If thou wert the fox, the lion would suspect thee when peradventure thou wert accused by the ass. If thou 336
wert the ass, thy dullness would torment thee, and still thou livedst but as a breakfast to the wolf. If thou wert 338
the wolf, thy greediness would afflict thee, and oft thou shouldst hazard thy life for thy dinner. Wert thou the unicorn, pride and wrath would confound thee 341
and make thine own self the conquest of thy fury. Wert thou a bear, thou wouldst be killed by the horse. Wert thou a horse, thou wouldst be seized by the leopard. Wert thou a leopard, thou wert germane to the lion, 345
and the spots of thy kindred were jurors on thy life; all 346
thy safety were remotion and thy defense absence. 347
What beast couldst thou be that were not subject to a

321–322 thou . . . dog i.e., even in your poverty you were able to keep a dog, and it loved you (since all creatures love only in return for favors) **329–330 in . . . men** i.e., in the destruction of mankind you've just wished for   **336 peradventure** by chance   **338 livedst** wouldst live **341 unicorn** (A legendary creature, supposedly caught by being goaded into charging a tree and embedding its horn in the tree trunk.) **345 germane** akin, related   **346 the spots . . . life** i.e., the crimes of those closely related to you would bring down a sentence of death upon you (with a pun on *spots* meaning "leopard's spots" and "stains, crimes")   **346–347 all . . . remotion** your only safety would consist in your constantly going from place to place

beast? And what a beast art thou already, that seest
not thy loss in transformation!   350

APEMANTUS   If thou couldst please me with speaking to   351
me, thou mightst have hit upon it here. The common-   352
wealth of Athens is become a forest of beasts.

TIMON   How, has the ass broke the wall, that thou art   354
out of the city?

APEMANTUS   Yonder comes a poet and a painter. The   356
plague of company light upon thee! I will fear to catch
it, and give way. When I know not what else to do, I'll   358
see thee again.

TIMON   When there is nothing living but thee, thou
shalt be welcome. I had rather be a beggar's dog than
Apemantus.

APEMANTUS
Thou art the cap of all the fools alive.   363

TIMON
Would thou wert clean enough to spit upon!

APEMANTUS
A plague on thee! Thou art too bad to curse.

TIMON
All villains that do stand by thee are pure.   366

APEMANTUS
There is no leprosy but what thou speak'st.

TIMON   If I name thee.
I'll beat thee, but I should infect my hands.   369

APEMANTUS
I would my tongue could rot them off!

TIMON
Away, thou issue of a mangy dog!   371
Choler does kill me that thou art alive;
I swoon to see thee.

APEMANTUS
Would thou wouldst burst!

---

350 in transformation in being changed into a beast   **351–352 If
. . . here** if it were possible for anything you say to please me, what
you've just said (comparing men with beasts) would be pleasing
354 How what is this   **356 Yonder . . . painter** (In fact, they do not
appear until 5.1; this line may give evidence of an incompletely revised manuscript.)   **358 give way** (I will) leave   **363 cap** acme, summit   **366 by** compared to   **369 I'll** I would   **371 issue** offspring

TIMON   Away, thou tedious rogue!
  I am sorry I shall lose a stone by thee.
                        [He throws a stone at Apemantus.]
APEMANTUS   Beast!
TIMON   Slave!
APEMANTUS   Toad!
TIMON   Rogue, rogue, rogue!
  I am sick of this false world, and will love naught
  But even the mere necessities upon 't.   381
  Then, Timon, presently prepare thy grave.   382
  Lie where the light foam of the sea may beat
  Thy gravestone daily. Make thine epitaph,
  That death in me at others' lives may laugh.   385
  [To the gold.] O thou sweet king-killer and dear divorce
  Twixt natural son and sire! Thou bright defiler   387
  Of Hymen's purest bed! Thou valiant Mars!   388
  Thou ever young, fresh, loved, and delicate wooer,
  Whose blush doth thaw the consecrated snow   390
  That lies on Dian's lap! Thou visible god,   391
  That solderest close impossibilities   392
  And mak'st them kiss; that speak'st with every tongue
  To every purpose! O thou touch of hearts!   394
  Think thy slave, man, rebels, and by thy virtue   395
  Set them into confounding odds, that beasts   396
  May have the world in empire!
APEMANTUS   Would 'twere so!
  But not till I am dead. I'll say thou'st gold;   398
  Thou wilt be thronged to shortly.
TIMON   Thronged to?
APEMANTUS   Ay.
TIMON
  Thy back, I prithee.
APEMANTUS   Live, and love thy misery.   400

---

381 But even except **382 presently** immediately **385 That** in order
that. **in** through **387 natural** i.e., born in the course of nature
388 Hymen god of marriage. **Mars** i.e., as the adulterous lover of
Venus **390 blush** i.e., reddish glow of gold **391 Dian** Diana, goddess of
the hunt and patroness of chastity **392 close** tightly together. **impossibilities** things apparently incapable of being united **394 touch** touchstone **395 virtue** power **396 Set . . . odds** set men at self-destroying
conflict with one another **398 thou'st** thou hast **400 Thy back** i.e.,
show me your back

TIMON
    Long live so, and so die! I am quit.   401
APEMANTUS
    More things like men! Eat, Timon, and abhor them.   402
                             Exit Apemantus.

    Enter the Banditti.

FIRST BANDIT   Where should he have this gold? It is 403
some poor fragment, some slender ort of his remain- 404
der. The mere want of gold and the falling-from of his 405
friends drove him into this melancholy.
SECOND BANDIT   It is noised he hath a mass of treasure. 407
THIRD BANDIT   Let us make the assay upon him. If he 408
care not for 't, he will supply us easily. If he covetously
reserve it, how shall 's get it?   410
SECOND BANDIT   True, for he bears it not about him.
'Tis hid.
FIRST BANDIT   Is not this he?
BANDITTI   Where?
SECOND BANDIT   'Tis his description.
THIRD BANDIT   He. I know him.
BANDITTI   Save thee, Timon.   417
TIMON   Now, thieves?
BANDITTI
    Soldiers, not thieves.
TIMON   Both too, and women's sons.   419
BANDITTI
    We are not thieves, but men that much do want.   420
TIMON
    Your greatest want is, you want much of meat.   421
    Why should you want? Behold, the earth hath roots;
    Within this mile break forth a hundred springs;
    The oaks bear mast, the briers scarlet hips.   424
    The bounteous huswife Nature on each bush
    Lays her full mess before you. What? Why want?   426

---

401 quit rid (of Apemantus)   **402 them** i.e., the bandits   **403 should he
have** can he have obtained   **404 ort** fragment   **405 mere** utter
407 noised rumored   **408 assay** trial, test (as one would test gold ore for
its content)   **410 shall 's** shall we   **417 Save** God save   **419 Both too**
both   **420 want** (1) lack (2) desire   **421 Your . . . meat** i.e., your greatest
deficiency is that you crave such rich food (as Timon goes on to explain)
424 mast acorns. **hips** fruit of the rosebush   **426 mess** food, meal

FIRST BANDIT
   We cannot live on grass, on berries, water,
   As beasts and birds and fishes.

TIMON
   Nor on the beasts themselves, the birds and fishes;
   You must eat men. Yet thanks I must you con   430
   That you are thieves professed, that you work not
   In holier shapes; for there is boundless theft
   In limited professions. [*He gives gold.*] Rascal thieves,   433
   Here's gold. Go, suck the subtle blood o' the grape   434
   Till the high fever seethe your blood to froth,   435
   And so scape hanging. Trust not the physician;   436
   His antidotes are poison, and he slays
   More than you rob. Take wealth and lives together.   438
   Do villainy, do, since you protest to do 't,   439
   Like workmen. I'll example you with thievery.   440
   The sun's a thief, and with his great attraction   441
   Robs the vast sea. The moon's an arrant thief,   442
   And her pale fire she snatches from the sun.
   The sea's a thief, whose liquid surge resolves   444
   The moon into salt tears. The earth's a thief,
   That feeds and breeds by a composture stolen   446
   From general excrement. Each thing's a thief.
   The laws, your curb and whip, in their rough power
   Has unchecked theft. Love not yourselves. Away!   449
   Rob one another. There's more gold. Cut throats.
   All that you meet are thieves. To Athens go,
   Break open shops; nothing can you steal
   But thieves do lose it. Steal less for this I give you,   453
   And gold confound you howsoe'er! Amen.   454

430 thanks . . . con I must offer you thanks   **433 limited** regulated,
legal (with a play on *boundless*, l. 432, as the opposite of *limited*)
434 subtle (1) delicate (2) treacherous in its influence   **435 high fever**
(induced by intoxication).   **seethe** boil   **436 scape hanging** i.e., avoid
execution by dying of excess drinking, using a natural substance
438 Take . . . together i.e., murder your robbery victims   **439 protest**
profess   **440 example you with** give you instances of   **441 attraction**
power to draw up   **442 arrant** notorious   **444 resolves** melts, dissolves.
(Alludes to the belief that the moon draws moisture from the air
and deposits it in the sea, thus creating the effect of tides.)
446 composture compost, manure   **449 Has unchecked** provide opportunity for unlimited   **453–454 Steal . . . howsoe'er** if you steal less
because of my giving you this gold, may gold destroy you no matter
what happens

THIRD BANDIT   He's almost charmed me from my profession by persuading me to it.

FIRST BANDIT   'Tis in the malice of mankind that he thus 457
advises us, not to have us thrive in our mystery.   458

SECOND BANDIT   I'll believe him as an enemy, and give 459
over my trade.

FIRST BANDIT   Let us first see peace in Athens. There is 461
no time so miserable but a man may be true.   462

                                        Exeunt Thieves.

    Enter the steward [Flavius] to Timon.

FLAVIUS   O you gods!
    Is yond despised and ruinous man my lord?   464
    Full of decay and failing? O monument   465
    And wonder of good deeds evilly bestowed!   466
    What an alteration of honor has desp'rate want made!
    What viler thing upon the earth than friends,
    Who can bring noblest minds to basest ends!
    How rarely does it meet with this time's guise,   470
    When man was wished to love his enemies!   471
    Grant I may ever love, and rather woo
    Those that would mischief me than those that do!—   473
    He's caught me in his eye. I will present   474
    My honest grief unto him, and as my lord
    Still serve him with my life.—My dearest master!

TIMON
    Away! What art thou?

FLAVIUS   Have you forgot me, sir?

TIMON
    Why dost ask that? I have forgot all men.
    Then, if thou grant'st thou'rt a man, I have forgot thee.

FLAVIUS   An honest poor servant of yours.

---

457 the malice of i.e., his hating of   **458 mystery** trade   **459 as** as I
would   **461–462 Let . . . true** i.e., let's not rush into reformation, at least
not until there is peace in Athens; besides, there will always be time to
repent   **464 ruinous** brought to ruin   **465 failing** weakness, downfall
465–466 monument . . . wonder astonishing memorial.   **evilly bestowed**
wrongly bestowed on the wicked   **470–471 How . . . enemies** i.e., how
perfectly does the commandment to love one's enemies suit this degenerate age (since one's supposed friends are the ones that do greatest
harm)   **473 Those . . . do** i.e., those who openly profess themselves to be
my enemies rather than those who, professing friendship, actually do
the greater harm   **474 caught . . . eye** seen me

TIMON   Then I know thee not.
  I never had honest man about me, I; all
  I kept were knaves, to serve in meat to villains.   483
FLAVIUS   The gods are witness,
  Ne'er did poor steward wear a truer grief
  For his undone lord than mine eyes for you.

                                              [*He weeps.*]

TIMON
  What, dost thou weep? Come nearer, then. I love thee
  Because thou art a woman and disclaim'st
  Flinty mankind, whose eyes do never give   489
  But thorough lust and laughter. Pity's sleeping.   490
  Strange times, that weep with laughing, not with
    weeping!

FLAVIUS
  I beg of you to know me, good my lord,
  T' accept my grief, and whilst this poor wealth lasts
  To entertain me as your steward still.   494

                                              [*He offers money.*]

TIMON   Had I a steward
  So true, so just, and now so comfortable?   496
  It almost turns my dangerous nature mild.   497
  Let me behold thy face. Surely, this man
  Was born of woman.
  Forgive my general and exceptless rashness,   500
  You perpetual-sober gods! I do proclaim   501
  One honest man—mistake me not, but one;
  No more, I pray—and he's a steward.
  How fain would I have hated all mankind,   504
  And thou redeem'st thyself! But all, save thee,
  I fell with curses.   506
  Methinks thou art more honest now than wise,
  For by oppressing and betraying me
  Thou mightst have sooner got another service;   509
  For many so arrive at second masters
  Upon their first lord's neck. But tell me true—
  For I must ever doubt, though ne'er so sure—

---

483 **serve in meat** serve food   489 **Flinty** hardhearted.   **give** give forth
tears   490 **But thorough** except through   494 **entertain** receive, employ
496 **comfortable** comforting   497 **dangerous** savage   500 **exceptless**
making no exception   501 **perpetual-sober** eternally grave and sedate
504 **fain** gladly   506 **fell** cut down   509 **service** position

Is not thy kindness subtle, covetous,
A usuring kindness, and, as rich men deal gifts,
Expecting in return twenty for one?

FLAVIUS
No, my most worthy master, in whose breast
Doubt and suspect, alas, are placed too late.   517
You should have feared false times when you did feast.
Suspect still comes where an estate is least.   519
That which I show, heaven knows, is merely love,   520
Duty, and zeal to your unmatchèd mind,
Care of your food and living; and believe it,   522
My most honored lord,
For any benefit that points to me,   524
Either in hope or present, I'd exchange   525
For this one wish: that you had power and wealth
To requite me by making rich yourself.   527

TIMON
Look thee, 'tis so. Thou singly honest man,   528
Here, take. [*He offers gold.*] The gods out of my misery
Has sent thee treasure. Go, live rich and happy,
But thus conditioned: thou shalt build from men,   531
Hate all, curse all, show charity to none,
But let the famished flesh slide from the bone
Ere thou relieve the beggar. Give to dogs
What thou deniest to men. Let prisons swallow 'em,
Debts wither 'em to nothing. Be men like blasted woods, 536
And may diseases lick up their false bloods!
And so farewell and thrive.

FLAVIUS   O, let me stay
And comfort you, my master.

TIMON   If thou hat'st curses,
Stay not; fly, whilst thou art blest and free.
Ne'er see thou man, and let me ne'er see thee.
                    Exit [*Flavius; Timon retires to his cave*].

517 **suspect** suspicion   519 **still** always   520 **merely** purely   522 **Care of**
concern for.   **living** maintenance   524 **For** as for.   **points to me** appears
in prospect for me   525 **in hope** in the future   527 **requite** repay
528 **singly** (1) uniquely (2) earnestly   531 **thus conditioned** upon this
condition.   **from** away from   536 **Be men** let men be.   **blasted** withered

5.1   *Enter Poet and Painter. [Timon enters at some point to watch them from his cave.]*

PAINTER   As I took note of the place, it cannot be far where he abides.

POET   What's to be thought of him? Does the rumor hold for true that he's so full of gold?

PAINTER   Certain. Alcibiades reports it. Phrynia and Timandra had gold of him. He likewise enriched poor straggling soldiers with great quantity. 'Tis said he gave unto his steward a mighty sum.

POET   Then this breaking of his has been but a try for   9 his friends?

PAINTER   Nothing else. You shall see him a palm in Ath-   11 ens again, and flourish with the highest. Therefore 'tis not amiss we tender our loves to him in this supposed   13 distress of his. It will show honestly in us and is very   14 likely to load our purposes with what they travail for,   15 if it be a just and true report that goes of his having.   16

POET   What have you now to present unto him?

PAINTER   Nothing at this time but my visitation. Only I will promise him an excellent piece.

POET   I must serve him so too, tell him of an intent that's   20 coming toward him.   21

PAINTER   Good as the best. Promising is the very air o'   22 the time; it opens the eyes of expectation. Performance is ever the duller for his act, and but in the plainer   24 and simpler kind of people the deed of saying is quite   25 out of use. To promise is most courtly and fashionable.   26 Performance is a kind of will or testament which argues a great sickness in his judgment that makes it.

   Enter Timon from his cave.

5.1. Location: The woods. Before Timon's cave. The scene is virtually continuous; Timon may well remain visible to the audience.
9 breaking bankruptcy.   **try** test   **11 a palm** a dignitary (probably referring to Psalm 92:12: "The righteous man shall flourish like a palm")   **13 we tender** that we should offer   **14 show honestly** appear to be seemly or worthy   **15 load our purposes** i.e., crown our efforts.
travail labor   **16 goes of his having** is current about his wealth
20 intent project   **21 coming toward** intended for   **22 Good as the best** i.e., that's perfect.   **air** style   **24 for his act** for its being completed.
but in excepting among   **25 deed of saying** actions fulfilling words or promises   **26 use** fashion

TIMON [*Aside*] Excellent workman! Thou canst not
paint a man so bad as is thyself.

POET I am thinking what I shall say I have provided for   31
him. It must be a personating of himself, a satire   32
against the softness of prosperity, with a discovery of   33
the infinite flatteries that follow youth and opulency.

TIMON [*Aside*] Must thou needs stand for a villain in   35
thine own work? Wilt thou whip thine own faults in
other men? Do so, I have gold for thee.

POET Nay, let's seek him.
Then do we sin against our own estate   39
When we may profit meet and come too late.

PAINTER True.
When the day serves, before black-cornered night,   42
Find what thou want'st by free and offered light.   43
Come.

TIMON [*Aside*]
I'll meet you at the turn. What a god's gold,   45
That he is worshiped in a baser temple   46
Than where swine feed!
'Tis thou that rigg'st the bark and plow'st the foam,   48
Settlest admirèd reverence in a slave.   49
To thee be worship, and thy saints for aye
Be crowned with plagues, that thee alone obey!   50
Fit I meet them.   [*He comes forward.*]   52

POET Hail, worthy Timon!

PAINTER Our late noble master!

TIMON
Have I once lived to see two honest men?   55

POET Sir,
Having often of your open bounty tasted,   57
Hearing you were retired, your friends fall'n off,   58

31 **provided** planned 32 **personating of himself** i.e., representation of
his case 33 **discovery** disclosure 35 **needs** necessarily. **stand for**
serve as a model for 39 **estate** worldly well-being 42 **black-cornered
night** night which darkens as in corners 43 **free and offered light** the
light of day, freely offered to all 45 **at the turn** i.e., trick for trick in a
cheating game 46 **a baser temple** i.e., the human body 48 **rigg'st the
bark** sets the ship's sail 49 **admirèd . . . slave** wondering awe in a slave
for his master 50 **thy saints** may your saints. **aye** ever 52 **Fit** it is fit
that 55 **once** actually 57 **open** generous 58 **were retired** had withdrawn. **fall'n off** estranged

Whose thankless natures—O abhorrèd spirits!
Not all the whips of heaven are large enough—
What, to you,
Whose starlike nobleness gave life and influence   62
To their whole being? I am rapt, and cannot cover   63
The monstrous bulk of this ingratitude
With any size of words.

TIMON
Let it go naked; men may see 't the better.
You that are honest, by being what you are
Make them best seen and known.

PAINTER   He and myself   68
Have traveled in the great show'r of your gifts   69
And sweetly felt it.

TIMON   Ay, you are honest men.

PAINTER
We are hither come to offer you our service.

TIMON
Most honest men! Why, how shall I requite you?   72
Can you eat roots and drink cold water? No.

BOTH
What we can do we'll do to do you service.

TIMON
You're honest men. You've heard that I have gold;
I am sure you have. Speak truth; you're honest men.

PAINTER
So it is said, my noble lord, but therefor   77
Came not my friend nor I.

TIMON
Good honest men! [To the Painter.] Thou draw'st a
    counterfeit
                                                      79
Best in all Athens. Thou'rt indeed the best;
Thou counterfeit'st most lively.

PAINTER   So-so, my lord.   81

---

62 Whose . . . influence i.e., whose nobility of character was of such
power as to influence men's destinies. (An astrological metaphor.)
63 rapt i.e., overwhelmed **68 them** i.e., the ungrateful men you condemn, or ungrateful acts **69 traveled** walked (with a suggestion also of
"worked, travailed," as one would labor for a patron) **72 requite**
repay **77 therefor** for that reason **79 counterfeit** picture, likeness
(with quibble on the idea of "fraudulence") **81 So-so** passably

TIMON

E'en so, sir, as I say. [*To the Poet*.] And for thy fiction,   82
Why, thy verse swells with stuff so fine and smooth   83
That thou art even natural in thine art.   84
But for all this, my honest-natured friends,
I must needs say you have a little fault.
Marry, 'tis not monstrous in you, neither wish I   87
You take much pains to mend.

BOTH   Beseech your honor   88
To make it known to us.

TIMON   You'll take it ill.

BOTH   Most thankfully, my lord.

TIMON   Will you, indeed?

BOTH   Doubt it not, worthy lord.

TIMON

There's never a one of you but trusts a knave   93
That mightily deceives you.

BOTH   Do we, my lord?

TIMON

Ay, and you hear him cog, see him dissemble,   95
Know his gross patchery, love him, feed him,   96
Keep in your bosom; yet remain assured   97
That he's a made-up villain.   98

PAINTER   I know none such, my lord.

POET   Nor I.

TIMON

Look you, I love you well. I'll give you gold;
Rid me these villains from your companies,   100
Hang them or stab them, drown them in a draft,   101
Confound them by some course, and come to me,   102
I'll give you gold enough.

BOTH   Name them, my lord, let's know them.

---

82 fiction any creative writing; here, poetry (with connotation of "lying")   **83 swells . . . smooth** (1) is elegantly styled and adorned (2) is a vainglorious concoction of specious fabrication   **84 thou . . . thine art** (1) your art is able to triumph over nature in verisimilitude (2) you're a born fool and a liar in your art   **87 monstrous** unnatural   **88 mend** remedy   **93 There's . . . but** i.e., each of you   **95 cog** cheat   **96 patchery** knavery   **97 Keep** keep him   **98 made-up** utter, complete   **100 Rid me** if you'll rid   **101 draft** privy, cesspool   **102 Confound** destroy. **course** means

TIMON
  You that way and you this, but two in company;   105
  Each man apart, all single and alone,
  Yet an archvillain keeps him company.
  [*To one.*] If where thou art two villains shall not be,   108
  Come not near him. [*To the other.*] If thou wouldst
    not reside   109
  But where one villain is, then him abandon.—
  Hence, pack! There's gold. You came for gold, ye slaves.   111
  [*To one.*] You have work for me; there's payment. Hence!   112
  [*To the other.*] You are an alchemist; make gold of that.   113
  Out, rascal dogs!

                Exeunt [*Poet and Painter, beaten out by*
                Timon, who retires to his cave].

   Enter steward [*Flavius*] *and two Senators.*

FLAVIUS
  It is in vain that you would speak with Timon;
  For he is set so only to himself   116
  That nothing but himself which looks like man
  Is friendly with him.
FIRST SENATOR   Bring us to his cave.   118
  It is our part and promise to th' Athenians   119
  To speak with Timon.
SECOND SENATOR   At all times alike
  Men are not still the same. 'Twas time and griefs   121
  That framed him thus. Time with his fairer hand
  Offering the fortunes of his former days,
  The former man may make him. Bring us to him,   124
  And chance it as it may.
FLAVIUS   Here is his cave.—   125
  Peace and content be here! Lord Timon! Timon!
  Look out, and speak to friends. Th' Athenians,

---

105 You . . . company (Timon riddlingly suggests that if the two of them stand apart from one another with no one else around, each has an *archvillain*—himself—to keep him company.)   **108 shall not be** are not to be   **109 him** i.e., the other one   **111 pack** be off   **112 there's payment** i.e., here's a beating or a thrown stone   **113 that** i.e., a beating or a thrown stone   **116 set . . . himself** so self-absorbed   **118 friendly with** congenial to   **119 our . . . promise** the part we have promised to undertake   **121 still** always   **124 The former . . . him** may turn him into his former self   **125 chance it** let it happen

By two of their most reverend Senate, greet thee.
Speak to them, noble Timon.

    Enter Timon out of his cave.

TIMON
Thou sun that comforts, burn! Speak and be hanged!
For each true word a blister, and each false
Be as a cauterizing to the root o' the tongue,
Consuming it with speaking!
FIRST SENATOR   Worthy Timon—
TIMON
Of none but such as you, and you of Timon.   134
FIRST SENATOR
The senators of Athens greet thee, Timon.
TIMON
I thank them, and would send them back the plague,
Could I but catch it for them.
FIRST SENATOR   O, forget
What we are sorry for ourselves in thee.   138
The senators with one consent of love   139
Entreat thee back to Athens, who have thought
On special dignities which vacant lie
For thy best use and wearing.
SECOND SENATOR   They confess
Toward thee forgetfulness too general gross;   143
Which now the public body, which doth seldom   144
Play the recanter, feeling in itself   145
A lack of Timon's aid, hath sense withal   146
Of its own fail, restraining aid to Timon,   147
And send forth us to make their sorrowed render,   148
Together with a recompense more fruitful
Than their offense can weigh down by the dram—   150
Ay, even such heaps and sums of love and wealth
As shall to thee blot out what wrongs were theirs   152

134 Of . . . Timon i.e., we are worthy of nothing better than being punished by one another **138 What . . . thee** those wrongs that we regret having done you **139 consent** unanimous voice **143 general gross** evident to everyone **144 public body** state **145 Play the recanter** i.e., change its mind and apologize **146 Timon's aid** aid to Timon. (But suggesting also "aid to be given by Timon to Athens.") **withal** in addition **147 fail** failing. **restraining** in withholding **148 sorrowed** sorrowful. **render** rendering, i.e., of their apologies **150 can . . . dram** can outweigh under the most scrupulous measurement **152 theirs** of their making

And write in thee the figures of their love,   153
Ever to read them thine.
TIMON   You witch me in it,   154
Surprise me to the very brink of tears.
Lend me a fool's heart and a woman's eyes,
And I'll beweep these comforts, worthy senators.   157
FIRST SENATOR
Therefore, so please thee to return with us,   158
And of our Athens, thine and ours, to take
The captainship, thou shalt be met with thanks,
Allowed with absolute power, and thy good name   161
Live with authority. So soon we shall drive back   162
Of Alcibiades th' approaches wild,   163
Who, like a boar too savage, doth root up
His country's peace.
SECOND SENATOR   And shakes his threatening sword
Against the walls of Athens.
FIRST SENATOR   Therefore, Timon—
TIMON
Well, sir, I will; therefore I will, sir; thus:
If Alcibiades kill my countrymen,
Let Alcibiades know this of Timon,
That Timon cares not. But if he sack fair Athens
And take our goodly agèd men by the beards,
Giving our holy virgins to the stain   172
Of contumelious, beastly, mad-brained war,   173
Then let him know, and tell him Timon speaks it
In pity of our agèd and our youth,
I cannot choose but tell him that I care not,
And let him take 't at worst—for their knives care not,   177
While you have throats to answer. For myself,   178
There's not a whittle in th' unruly camp   179
But I do prize it at my love before   180

153 **figures** (1) representations (2) numbers written in a ledger
154 **Ever . . . thine** i.e., to provide a perpetual record of the Athenians'
love for you. **witch** bewitch 157 **beweep these comforts** weep gratefully at these comforting tidings 158 **so** if it 161 **Allowed** vested
162 **Live with** continue to exercise 163 **Of . . . wild** the savage attacks
of Alcibiades 172 **stain** pollution 173 **contumelious** insolent
177 **take 't at worst** interpret what I say in the worst manner possible;
or, (let Alcibiades' troops) do their worst destruction 178 **answer**
suffer the consequences 179 **whittle** small clasp-knife 180 **prize**
value. **at** in. **before** above

The reverend'st throat in Athens. So I leave you
To the protection of the prosperous gods,   182
As thieves to keepers.
FLAVIUS [*To Senators*]   Stay not; all's in vain.   183
TIMON
Why, I was writing of my epitaph;
It will be seen tomorrow. My long sickness
Of health and living now begins to mend,
And nothing brings me all things. Go, live still;   187
Be Alcibiades your plague, you his,
And last so long enough!
FIRST SENATOR   We speak in vain.   189
TIMON
But yet I love my country and am not   190
One that rejoices in the common wrack,   191
As common bruit doth put it.
FIRST SENATOR   That's well spoke.   192
TIMON
Commend me to my loving countrymen—
FIRST SENATOR
These words become your lips as they pass thorough
    them.   194
SECOND SENATOR
And enter in our ears like great triumphers   195
In their applauding gates.
TIMON   Commend me to them,   196
And tell them that, to ease them of their griefs,
Their fears of hostile strokes, their aches, losses,
Their pangs of love, with other incident throes   199
That nature's fragile vessel doth sustain   200
In life's uncertain voyage, I will some kindness do them:
I'll teach them to prevent wild Alcibiades' wrath.   202
FIRST SENATOR [*To the Second Senator*]
I like this well. He will return again.

182 prosperous causing prosperity   **183 keepers** jailers   **187 nothing**
oblivion, death   **189 last . . . enough** remain in that state as long as
possible   **190 yet** still   **191 wrack** destruction   **192 bruit** rumor
194 become grace, do credit to.   **thorough** through   **195 triumphers**
those coming in triumph   **196 applauding gates** i.e., gates crowded with
applauding citizens   **199 incident throes** naturally occurring agonies
200 nature's . . . vessel i.e., the body   **202 prevent** frustrate, forestall
(with a quibble on "anticipate")

TIMON

I have a tree, which grows here in my close,   204
That mine own use invites me to cut down,   205
And shortly must I fell it. Tell my friends,   206
Tell Athens, in the sequence of degree   207
From high to low throughout, that whoso please
To stop affliction, let him take his haste,
Come hither ere my tree hath felt the ax,
And hang himself. I pray you, do my greeting.

FLAVIUS [*To Senators*]

Trouble him no further. Thus you still shall find him.

TIMON

Come not to me again. But say to Athens,
Timon hath made his everlasting mansion   214
Upon the beachèd verge of the salt flood,   215
Who once a day with his embossèd froth   216
The turbulent surge shall cover. Thither come,
And let my gravestone be your oracle.   218
Lips, let four words go by and language end!   219
What is amiss, plague and infection mend!
Graves only be men's works and death their gain!
Sun, hide thy beams! Timon hath done his reign.

                         Exit Timon [*into his cave*].

FIRST SENATOR

His discontents are unremovably
Coupled to nature.   224

SECOND SENATOR

Our hope in him is dead. Let us return
And strain what other means is left unto us
In our dear peril.

FIRST SENATOR   It requires swift foot.   *Exeunt.*   227

❖

204 close enclosure **205 use** need **206 fell** cut **207 in . . . degree** in
order of social rank **214 everlasting mansion** i.e., grave **215 verge
. . . flood** boundary or margin of the sea. (See 5.4.66.) **216 Who** whom or
which, i.e., Timon or his grave, his *everlasting mansion* (l. 214), both of
which the foaming tide will cover daily. **his** its. **embossèd** foaming
218 oracle source of wisdom **219 four words** i.e., few words
224 Coupled to nature integrally part of him **227 dear** costly, dire. **foot**
i.e., action

5.2   *Enter two other Senators, with a Messenger.*

THIRD SENATOR
  Thou hast painfully discovered. Are his files   1
  As full as thy report?
MESSENGER   I have spoke the least.   2
  Besides, his expedition promises   3
  Present approach.   4
FOURTH SENATOR
  We stand much hazard if they bring not Timon.   5
MESSENGER
  I met a courier, one mine ancient friend,   6
  Whom, though in general part we were opposed,   7
  Yet our old love made a particular force   8
  And made us speak like friends. This man was riding
  From Alcibiades to Timon's cave
  With letters of entreaty which imported   11
  His fellowship i' the cause against your city,   12
  In part for his sake moved.

     Enter the other Senators [from Timon].

THIRD SENATOR   Here come our brothers.   13
FIRST SENATOR
  No talk of Timon; nothing of him expect.
  The enemies' drum is heard, and fearful scouring   15
  Doth choke the air with dust. In, and prepare.   16
  Ours is the fall, I fear, our foe's the snare.   *Exeunt.*   17

❖

5.2. Location: Before the walls of Athens.
1 **painfully discovered** revealed unsettling news (?) or reconnoitered
with painstaking effort (?). **files** military ranks   2 **spoke the least**
given the lowest estimate   3 **expedition** speed   4 **Present** immediate
5 **stand much hazard** are at great risk. **they** i.e., the senators who were
sent to Timon   6 **one mine ancient friend** a former friend of mine
7 **Whom** on whom. **in general part** on public issues   8 **particular**
personal   11 **imported** (1) concerned, had to do with (2) importuned
12 **fellowship** partnership   13 **In . . . moved** undertaken or initiated
partly on his (Timon's) behalf   15 **scouring** hurrying along, aggressive
movement   16 **In** let us go in   17 **Ours . . . snare** our part, I fear, is to
fall, our foe's part is to set the trap

5.3   *Enter a Soldier in the woods, seeking Timon.*

SOLDIER
By all description this should be the place.
Who's here? Speak, ho! No answer? What is this?
                    [*He finds a rude tomb.*]
"Timon is dead, who hath outstretched his span.
Some beast read this; there does not live a man."   4
Dead, sure, and this his grave. What's on this tomb
I cannot read. The character I'll take with wax.   6
                    [*He makes a wax impression.*]
Our captain hath in every figure skill,   7
An aged interpreter, though young in days.
Before proud Athens he's set down by this,   9
Whose fall the mark of his ambition is.   *Exit.* 10

❖

5.4   *Trumpets sound. Enter Alcibiades with his
powers before Athens.*

ALCIBIADES
Sound to this coward and lascivious town   1
Our terrible approach.   *Sounds a parley.* 2

The Senators appear on the walls.

Till now you have gone on and filled the time

5.3. Location: The woods. Seemingly near Timon's cave, but also at the
edge of the sea; see 5.1.214–217 and 5.4.66. A rude tomb is seen.
4 Some . . . man i.e., whoever reads this will be a beast, since all men
are beasts   **6 I cannot read** (Suggests there is another inscription in
another language, perhaps Latin, or that this scene shows signs of
incomplete revision and hence apparent inconsistency.)   **The . . . wax**
I'll take an impression of the inscription in wax   **7 every figure** all
kinds of writing   **9 Before . . . this** by this time he has laid siege to
proud Athens   **10 Whose fall** the fall of which.   **mark** goal

5.4. Location: Before the walls of Athens. **Appearances *on the walls*** are
presumably located in the gallery, above, to the rear of the stage.
s.d. powers armed forces   **1 Sound** proclaim   **2 terrible** terrifying
s.d. parley trumpet call to a negotiation

With all licentious measure, making your wills   4
The scope of justice. Till now myself and such   5
As slept within the shadow of your power   6
Have wandered with our traversed arms and breathed 7
Our sufferance vainly. Now the time is flush,   8
When crouching marrow in the bearer strong   9
Cries of itself, "No more!" Now breathless wrong   10
Shall sit and pant in your great chairs of ease,
And pursy insolence shall break his wind   12
With fear and horrid flight.
FIRST SENATOR   Noble and young,   13
    When thy first griefs were but a mere conceit,   14
    Ere thou hadst power or we had cause of fear,
    We sent to thee, to give thy rages balm,
    To wipe out our ingratitude with loves   17
    Above their quantity.
SECOND SENATOR   So did we woo   18
    Transformèd Timon to our city's love
    By humble message and by promised means.   20
    We were not all unkind, nor all deserve
    The common stroke of war.
FIRST SENATOR   These walls of ours   22
    Were not erected by their hands from whom
    You have received your grief; nor are they such
    That these great tow'rs, trophies, and schools should
        fall   25
    For private faults in them.
SECOND SENATOR   Nor are they living   26
    Who were the motives that you first went out.   27

---

4 all licentious measure every kind of licentious behavior   **4–5 making
. . . justice** equating justice with your wills   **6 slept** i.e., dwelled
7 traversed arms arms inactive or folded. (A term in military drill.)
7–8 breathed Our sufferance voiced our sufferings   **8 flush** at flood,
ripe   **9 crouching marrow** latent resolution and might   **10 of itself** of its
own accord.   **breathless wrong** wrongdoers who are frightened into
breathlessness   **12 pursy** short-winded.   **break his wind** pant for breath
(perhaps suggesting also to void air from the bowels in fright)   **13 horrid**
terrified   **14 griefs** grievances.   **conceit** fancy, imagined scheme of
action   **17–18 loves . . . quantity** offers of friendship exceeding the quantity of your grievances   **20 means** terms   **22 common** indiscriminate
25 trophies monuments.   **schools** public buildings   **26 private** personal.   **them** i.e., those from whom you have received your injuries
27 motives . . . out instigators that prompted your banishment

Shame, that they wanted cunning, in excess   28
Hath broke their hearts. March, noble lord,
Into our city with thy banners spread.
By decimation and a tithèd death—   31
If thy revenges hunger for that food
Which nature loathes—take thou the destined tenth,
And by the hazard of the spotted die   34
Let die the spotted.

FIRST SENATOR   All have not offended.   35
For those that were, it is not square to take   36
On those that are, revenge. Crimes, like lands,   37
Are not inherited. Then, dear countryman,   38
Bring in thy ranks, but leave without thy rage.   39
Spare thy Athenian cradle and those kin   40
Which in the bluster of thy wrath must fall
With those that have offended. Like a shepherd
Approach the fold and cull th' infected forth,   43
But kill not all together.

SECOND SENATOR   What thou wilt,
Thou rather shalt enforce it with thy smile
Than hew to 't with thy sword.

FIRST SENATOR   Set but thy foot   46
Against our rampired gates and they shall ope,   47
So thou wilt send thy gentle heart before   48
To say thou'lt enter friendly.

SECOND SENATOR   Throw thy glove,   49
Or any token of thine honor else,   50
That thou wilt use the wars as thy redress
And not as our confusion, all thy powers   52
Shall make their harbor in our town till we   53
Have sealed thy full desire.

ALCIBIADES [*Throwing a glove*] Then there's my glove.   54

---

28 Shame . . . excess i.e., an excess of shame for their lack of cunning in
statecraft   **31 decimation, tithèd death** selection of every tenth to die.
(The two phrases mean the same thing.)   **34 die** (Singular of *dice;* with a
play on the verb *die*.)   **35 the spotted** the corrupt, wicked (with a play
on the spots on the dice)   **36 square** just   **37 are** are now alive
37–38 like . . . not are not like lands   **39 without** outside   **40 thy Athenian cradle** Athens, your birthplace   **43 cull . . . forth** pick out the
tainted   **46 hew** cut   **47 rampired** barricaded.   **ope** open   **48 So** if
only   **49 Throw** if you will throw   **50 token** pledge   **52 confusion**
overthrow.   **powers** armed forces   **53 make their harbor** have safe
lodging   **54 sealed** satisfied, ratified

Descend, and open your unchargèd ports.   55
Those enemies of Timon's and mine own
Whom you yourselves shall set out for reproof   57
Fall, and no more; and, to atone your fears   58
With my more noble meaning, not a man   59
Shall pass his quarter or offend the stream   60
Of regular justice in your city's bounds   61
But shall be remedied to your public laws   62
At heaviest answer.

BOTH   'Tis most nobly spoken.   63

ALCIBIADES   Descend, and keep your words.   64
     [*The Senators descend, and open the gates.*]

     *Enter [Soldier as] a Messenger [with a wax
     tablet].*

SOLDIER
My noble general, Timon is dead,
Entombed upon the very hem o' the sea;   66
And on his gravestone this insculpture, which   67
With wax I brought away, whose soft impression
Interprets for my poor ignorance.

ALCIBIADES (*Reads the epitaph*)
"Here lies a wretched corpse, of wretched soul bereft.   70
Seek not my name. A plague consume you wicked
     caitiffs left!   71
Here lie I, Timon, who, alive, all living men did hate.
Pass by and curse thy fill, but pass and stay not here thy
     gait."   73
These well express in thee thy latter spirits.   74
Though thou abhorredst in us our human griefs,
Scornedst our brains' flow and those our droplets which   76

---

55 unchargèd ports unattacked gates   **57 set out for reproof** pick out for
punishment   **58 atone** appease, make "at one"   **59 man** i.e., soldier of
mine   **60 pass his quarter** leave his assigned duty area   **60–61 offend . . .
justice** violate the norms set by established law   **62 But . . . remedied**
without being remanded   **63 At heaviest answer** to receive severest
punishment   **64 s.d. open the gates** (Presumably, the *gates* are a door in
the tiring-house facade representing here the *walls* of Athens; the gallery
above is *on the walls*.)   **66 hem** i.e., edge, shore   **67 insculpture** inscription   **70–73 Here . . . gait** (Of these two inscriptions, both found in Plutarch, Shakespeare would presumably have deleted one, since they
contradict one another.)   **71 caitiffs** wretches   **73 gait** journey   **74 latter
spirits** recent sentiments   **76 brains' flow** i.e., tears

From niggard nature fall, yet rich conceit   77
Taught thee to make vast Neptune weep for aye   78
On thy low grave, on faults forgiven. Dead
Is noble Timon, of whose memory
Hereafter more. Bring me into your city,
And I will use the olive with my sword,   82
Make war breed peace, make peace stint war, make each   83
Prescribe to other as each other's leech.   84
Let our drums strike.   [*Drums.*] *Exeunt.*

77 niggard nature parsimonious human nature (unable to produce quanti-
ties of tears to compete with the sea).   **conceit** imagination, fancy
78 Neptune the god of the sea in Roman mythology.   **aye** ever   **82 olive,
sword** (Symbols of peace and war.)   **83 stint** stop   **84 leech** physician

Date and Text

Timon of Athens first appeared in the First Folio of 1623. The text seems to have been based on an unusually early draft of the author's papers, with manifest inconsistencies still present that would have been straightened out in a final draft. A more controversial hypothesis is that joint authorship (with Thomas Middleton) contributed to the discrepancies about the value of money and the like. The play seems to have been a last-minute substitution in the Folio, to replace *Troilus and Cressida* when for some reason (probably copyright difficulties) that play had to be removed from its original position following *Romeo and Juliet*. The Folio editors possibly had not intended to use *Timon* at all. The manuscript used by the printers seems to have been copied over in places by a second hand, as though the manuscript was too illegible for the printer to use.

Dating of the play is unusually difficult. In its unfinished state the play was probably never acted, and therefore left no trace until it was registered for publication on November 8, 1623. Stylistically it seems close to the late tragedies. Its pessimism reminds us of *King Lear*, and its use of Plutarch suggests *Antony and Cleopatra*. Theories of multiple authorship were once common and have been recently reasserted (see above on Middleton), but have not won general agreement.

Textual Notes

These textual notes are not a historical collation, either of the early folios or of more recent editions; they are simply a record of departures in this edition from the copy text. The reading adopted in this edition appears in boldface, followed by the rejected reading from the copy text, i.e., the First Folio. Only major alterations in punctuation are noted. Changes in lineation are not indicated, nor are some minor and obvious typographical errors.

Abbreviations used:
F the First Folio
s.d. stage direction
s.p. speech prefix

Copy text: the First Folio.

The Actors' Names [F lists also Varro and Lucius as "Seruants to Vsurers," and the order of names has been changed for Apemantus and Ventidius]

1.1. s.d. Merchant Merchant, and Mercer **23 gum** Gowne **oozes** vses **27 chafes** chases **43 man** men **50 tax** wax **77 conceived to scope.** conceyu'd, to scope **92 hands** hand **slip** sit **116 s.p. [and subsequently] Old Athenian** Oldm **160 s.d. Exeunt** Exit **184 s.d. Enter Apemantus** [after l. 182 in F] **222 cost** cast **227 s.p. Apemantus** pe **234 feigned** fegin'd **259 there!** their **286 Come** Comes **287 taste** raste **296 s.p. First Lord** [not in F]

1.2. s.d. [and elsewhere] Ventidius Ventigius **30 ever** verie **105 O, joy's e'en** Oh ioyes, e'ne **107 To forget their faults,** to forget their Faults. **113 s.d. Sound tucket** [F continues: "Enter the Maskers of Amazons with Lutes in their hands, dauncing and playing"] **114 s.d. Enter Servant** [after "How now?" in F] **120 s.d. Enter Cupid** [F continues: "with the Maske of Ladies"] **124 Th' ear** There **125 and smell** all **129 s.p. First Lord** Luc **s.d.** [see notes at ll. 113 and 120 above] **144 s.d. singles** single **151 s.p. First Lady** 1 Lord **167 s.d. Enter Flavius** [at l. 176 in F] **181 s.p. Second Servant** Ser **211 rode** rod **213 s.p. Third Lord** 1. L

2.1. 34 Ay, go, sir. I go sir? **35 in compt** in. Come

2.2. 1 s.p. [and elsewhere] Flavius Stew **4 resumes** resume **11 s.p. [and elsewhere] Varro's Servant** Var **13 s.p. [and elsewhere] Isidore's Servant** Isid **41 broken** debt, broken **64 s.p. [and elsewhere] All the Servants** Al [or All] **75, 104 mistress'** Masters **81 s.p. Page** Boy **96 Ay. Would** I would **132 proposed** propose **139 found** sound **160 of** or **191 Flaminius** Flauius

3.1. s.d. Enter enters **1 s.p. [and elsewhere] Lucullus' Servant** Ser

3.2. 27 s.p. [and elsewhere] Lucius Lucil

3.3. 5 Owe Owes **23 I 'mongst** 'mong'st

3.4. s.d. Men man **1 s.p. [and elsewhere] Varro's First Servant** Var. man **2 s.p. [and elsewhere] Titus' Servant** Tit **Hortensius' Servant** Hort **3 s.p. [and elsewhere] Lucius' Servant** Luci **6 s.p. Philotus' Servant** Phil **14 recoverable. I fear** recouerable, I feare: **15–16 purse; / That is,** purse,

that is: **45 s.p. [and elsewhere] Varro's Second Servant** 2. Varro
88 s.p. Hortensius' Servant 1. Var **89 s.p. Both Varro's Servants** 2. Var
112 Sempronius Sempronius Vllorxa

3.5. 18 An And **23 behave** behooue **51 lion** Lyon? **felon** fellow **52 judge,**
Iudge? **53 suffering.** suffering, **66 Why, I** Why **70 'em** him **85 honors**
Honour

3.6. 1 s.p. First Lord 1 [and so throughout scene] **19 here's** heares
54 s.p. First and Second Lords Both **80 tag** legge **87 s.p. Others** other
91 with your you with **115 s.p. Third Lord** 2 **116 s.p. Second Lord** 3

4.1. 8 fast; fast **9 back,** backe; **13 Son** Some

4.3. 10 senator Senators **12 pasture** Pastour **13 lean** leaue **41 at, this** at.
This **88 tub-fast** Fubfast **119 bars** Barne **124 thy** the **135 s.p. [and
throughout scene] Phrynia and Timandra** Both **158 scolds** scold'st **187 thy
human** the humane **206 fortune** future **225 mossed** moyst **254 clasped**
claspt. **255 swathe, proceeded** swath proceeded, **257 drudges** drugges
258 command command'st **287 my** thy **402 them** then **414 s.p. [and
throughout scene] Banditti** All **439 villainy** Villaine **462 s.d. Exeunt** Exit
479 grant'st grunt'st **man, I** man. I **497 mild** wilde **514 A** If not a

5.1. 5–6 Phrynia and Timandra Phrinica and Timandylo **50 worship**
worship **66 go naked; men** go, / Naked men **70 men** man **115 in vain**
vaine **125 chance** chanc'd **146 sense** since **147 its own fail** it owne fall
181 reverend'st reuerends

5.2. 1 s.p. [and throughout scene] Third Senator 1 **5 s.p. [and throughout
scene] Fourth Senator** 2 **14 s.p. First Senator** 3

5.4. 27 out. out, **28 Shame . . . excess** Shame that they wanted, cunning in
excesse **55 Descend** Defend **65 s.p. Soldier** Mes

Shakespeare's Sources

Shakespeare certainly made use of a brief passage from the "Life of Marcus Antonius" in Thomas North's English translation (from the French of Jacques Amyot) of the first-century Greek biographer Plutarch's *The Lives of the Noble Grecians and Romans* (1579). This passage is a digression used to illustrate Antonius' embittered withdrawal to an Egyptian island after his defeat at Actium, in which he compares himself to the famous misanthrope of Athens, Timon. As Plutarch reports Timon's story, citing Plato and Aristophanes as his sources, Timon is a hater of mankind because he has been victimized by deception and ingratitude. Timon shuns all company but that of young Alcibiades and occasionally that of Apemantus. When asked by Apemantus why he favors this youth, Timon replies that he knows Alcibiades will some day do great mischief to the Athenians. On another occasion, Timon mounts a public rostrum and invites his Athenian listeners to come hang themselves on a fig tree growing in his yard before he cuts it down (see 5.1.204–211). When Timon dies he is buried upon the seashore (5.1.213–217). Plutarch transcribes two epitaphs, one by the poet Callimachus and one by Timon himself, both of which appear virtually word for word in Shakespeare's play (5.4.70–73). (Shakespeare probably meant to cancel one, for dramatically they are inconsistent with one another.) Plutarch thus provides Shakespeare not only with several incidents in the life of Timon but with the link connecting Timon, Alcibiades, and Apemantus. The twenty-eighth novel in William Painter's *The Palace of Pleasure* (1566) retells the events narrated by Plutarch but without adding any new information.

Oddly, Shakespeare seems to have absorbed little from Plutarch's "Life of Alcibiades," though that account does tell how the general leaves Athens in disgrace and sides with her enemies but ultimately relents when he sees that the Athenians are sorry for the injury they have done him. Alcibiades is a handsome young man and fond of women; his concubine Timandra buries him. Despite these scattered hints, however, Plutarch's "Life of Alcibiades" provides no basis for Shakespeare's plot.

The comedy of Timon by Aristophanes, to which Plutarch alludes, has not survived. Nor has Plato's description. Apparently these accounts were based on a historical figure of fifth-century Athens, Timon the son of Echecratides. Allusions to him in classical literature are common enough to suggest that his name had become synonymous with misanthropy. The fullest surviving classical record of this tradition is a dialogue by Lucian of Samosata (c. A.D. 125–180) called *Timon*, or *The Misanthrope*. No English translation was available in Shakespeare's lifetime, but he could have read Lucian in Italian, Latin, or French translation.

The dialogue begins as Timon, impoverished and abandoned by his fair-weather friends, calls upon Zeus to punish such injustice. Zeus hears this diatribe and learns from Hermes the sad tale of Timon's victimization by his ungrateful fellow beings. Aware that he has been neglectful of this case, Zeus orders Hermes to descend with Plutus (Riches) and restore Timon to prosperity. Although Plutus fears he will be treated improvidently as before, Zeus is insistent. Plutus (personifying Riches) confesses to Hermes, as they descend, how he (i.e., wealth) deceives humanity. Hermes and Plutus find Timon digging, accompanied by Poverty, Toil, Endurance, and other such allegorical companions. Poverty and his fellows are reluctant to leave Timon, for they know he has been happier with them than in his former days; and Timon too protests he wants nothing to do with prosperity. Still, the will of the gods must be obeyed, and Timon discovers treasure where he is digging.

Just as he mordantly predicts, opportunists now seek him out. One is Gnathonides the flatterer, a former recipient of Timon's hospitality who only recently has repaid that kindness by offering Timon a noose. Another, Philiades, once received from Timon a farm as a dowry for his daughters, but has spurned Timon in his poverty; now he makes a pretense of offering money, knowing Timon not to be in need. A third petitioner is the orator Demea, whose debt Timon once paid to obtain his release from jail; now, having insulted Timon in his poverty, Demea comes with a fulsome and patently fictitious decree he has composed in Timon's honor. Fourth is Thrasicles, a hypocritical philosopher who preaches self-denial but drinks to excess, and who professes to come now not for his own benefit but for those to whom he will gladly distribute Timon's new wealth. Timon drives them off one by one and then resorts to throwing stones at the ever-increasing crowd of flatterers. (This parade of villains, and their satirical discomfiture, bear an interesting resemblance to Aristophanes' *The Birds*.)

Many details here are suggestive of Shakespeare's play and are not in Plutarch: Timon's generosity to friends (including the payment of a debt and the providing of a marriage dowry), his friends' ungrateful response when he is in need, the finding of gold in the ground followed by the reappearance of his former friends, the insincere offer of money, the flattering composition in praise of Timon. The personified abstractions are parablelike, as in Shakespeare's play. Yet verbal parallels between Shakespeare and Lucian are tenuous at best. Probably Shakespeare knew some later version based on Lucian. Renaissance works inspired by Lucian are not hard to find, but none seems to be the direct source for Shakespeare. He is not likely to have known an Italian play called *Timone* of Matteo Maria Boiardo (c. 1487).

More suggestive of Shakespeare's play is an English academic play written at Cambridge (c. 1581–1600, or perhaps c. 1609–1610?) and preserved in the Dyce manuscript. (The editor Alexander Dyce first published this Elizabethan manuscript in 1842.) In this version, Timon's servant Laches warns against the effects of prodigality. When one friend, Eutrapelus, experiences financial trouble, Timon gives him five talents. Laches is driven out by Timon, but returns disguised as a soldier to serve his master. At a final banquet, Timon mocks his guests with stones painted to resemble artichokes. When he finds gold, Timon's false mistress shows her readiness to take it. Even a farcical comic subplot reminds us that Shakespeare's *Timon* contains an unrelated and perhaps vestigial Fool scene. Yet this academic play may have been written after Shakespeare's play, though surely not based on it (since *Timon* was not published until 1623 and apparently was never acted), and the likeliest explanation for the similarities is a common source. Perhaps Shakespeare knew and used a play now lost.

Apemantus does not have a prominent role in any of the versions here discussed, though he is mentioned in Plutarch.

Apemantus bears a resemblance to many satirical railers and crabbed philosophers in Renaissance literature, such as Diogenes in John Lyly's play of *Campaspe* (1584) and Jaques in Shakespeare's *As You Like It*.

The Lives of the Noble Grecians and Romans Compared Together by . . . Plutarch
Translated by Thomas North

FROM THE LIFE OF MARCUS ANTONIUS

Antonius, he[1] forsook the city and company of his friends and built him a house in the sea by the isle of Pharos[2] upon certain forced mounts which he caused to be cast into the sea,[3] and dwelt there as a man that banished himself from all men's company, saying that he would lead Timon's life because he had the like wrong offered him that was afore offered unto Timon, and that for the unthankfulness of those he had done good unto, and whom he took to be his friends, he was angry with all men and would trust no man.

This Timon was a citizen of Athens that lived about the war of Peloponnesus,[4] as appeareth by Plato and Aristophanes' comedies, in the which they mocked him, calling him a viper and malicious man unto mankind to shun all other men's companies but the company of young Alcibiades—a bold and insolent youth, whom he would greatly feast and make much of, and kissed him very gladly. Apemantus, wondering at it, asked him the cause what[5] he meant to make so much of that young man alone and to hate all others. Timon answered him: "I do it," said he, "because I know that one day he shall do great mischief unto the Athenians."

This Timon sometimes would have Apemantus in his company, because he was much like of[6] his nature and con-

1 **Antonius, he** Antonius   2 **isle of Pharos** (in the harbor of Alexandria, Egypt)   3 **upon . . . sea** (i.e., Antonius built his house out over the water on piers driven into the sea bottom. Timon similarly took refuge from society at the edge of the sea.)   4 **about the war of Peloponnesus** about the time of the prolonged war in the fifth century B.C. between the Athenian empire and the Spartan league, described by Thucydides   5 **cause what** reason why   6 **like of** alike in

ditions[7] and also followed him in manner of life. On a time[8] when they solemnly celebrated the feasts[9] called *Choae* at Athens (to wit, the feasts of the dead where they make sprinklings and sacrifices for the dead) and that they two then feasted together by themselves, Apemantus said unto the other: "O, here is a trim[10] banquet, Timon!" Timon answered again: "Yea," said he, "so [11] thou wert not here."

It is reported of him also that this Timon on a time (the people being assembled in the marketplace about dispatch of some affairs) got up into the pulpit for orations where the orators commonly use[12] to speak unto the people; and, silence being made, every man listening to hear what he would say because it was a wonder to see him in that place, at length he began to speak in this manner: "My lords of Athens, I have a little yard in my house where there groweth a fig tree, on the which many citizens have hanged themselves. And because I mean to make some building upon the place, I thought good to let you all understand it that, before the fig tree be cut down, if any of you be desperate,[13] you may there in time go hang yourselves."

He died in the city of Hales and was buried upon the seaside. Now it chanced so that the sea getting in, it compassed his tomb round about, that no man could come to it; and upon the same was written this epitaph:

> Here lies a wretched corpse, of wretched soul bereft.
> Seek not my name. A plague consume you wicked
>   wretches left!

It is reported that Timon himself, when he lived, made this epitaph. For that which is commonly rehearsed[14] was not his, but made by the poet Callimachus:

> Here lie I, Timon, who, alive, all living men did hate.
> Pass by and curse thy fill, but pass and stay not here
>   thy gate.[15]

Many other things could we tell you of this Timon, but this little shall suffice at this present.

---

7 conditions disposition, cast of mind   **8 On a time** once   **9 feasts** religious festival   **10 trim** fine, spruce   **11 so** provided   **12 use** are accustomed   **13 desperate** in despair   **14 rehearsed** recited   **15 gate** journey

---

Text based on *The Lives of the Noble Grecians and Romans Compared Together by That Grave, Learned Philosopher and Historiographer, Plutarch of Chaeronea. Translated out of Greek into French by James Amyot . . . and out of French into English by Thomas North. . . . Thomas Vautroullier . . . 1579.* Whether Shakespeare read this edition or one of the subsequent editions of 1595 and 1603 (the 1603 text was reprinted in 1612) is not certain, but the differences are minor.

Further Reading

Bayley, John. "The Big Idea: *Timon of Athens*." *Shakespeare and Tragedy*. London: Routledge and Kegan Paul, 1981. Bayley holds that *Timon* is a play that did not fully engage Shakespeare in its emotional possibilities but only in its aesthetic challenge; nonetheless, behind its impersonal and schematic structure the play uncovers a tragic dimension in Timon's poignant unsuitability for his role either as generous lord or misanthrope.

Bradbrook, M. C. *The Tragic Pageant of "Timon of Athens."* Cambridge: Cambridge Univ. Press, 1966. Rpt. in *Shakespeare, the Craftsman*. London: Chatto and Windus, 1969. Bradbrook sees *Timon* as a work of profound and disturbing power, representing Shakespeare's formal response to the demands of the indoor theater he was writing for in 1609. The play is written in an experimental dramatic style based on the example of symbolic court pageants: Timon is a role rather than a character, and the play develops emblematically, not psychologically.

Burke, Kenneth. "*Timon of Athens* and Misanthropic Gold." *Language as Symbolic Action*. Berkeley and Los Angeles: Univ. of California Press, 1966. Using insights derived from both Freud and Marx, Burke explores the unity of the play's design. He examines how Shakespeare's rhetorical strategies are marshaled to reveal Timon's maturation and organize the tragic potential of his nature.

Campbell, Oscar James. "*Timon of Athens*." *Shakespeare's Satire*. London and New York: Oxford Univ. Press, 1943. Campbell asserts that *Timon* is not a tragedy but rather a tragical satire. The play's construction and concerns are satiric, and while Timon's fate suggests the structure of tragedy, his alienation and death are not presented as the suffering of a noble heart but caricatured as the inevitable result of an ignoble and irrational misanthropy.

Ellis-Fermor, Una Mary. "*Timon of Athens*." *Review of English Studies* 18 (1942): 270–283. Rpt. in *Shakespeare the Dramatist and Other Papers*, ed. Kenneth Muir. London: Methuen, 1961. In an influential and provocative essay,

Ellis-Fermor argues that *Timon* is unfinished even in conception. Shakespeare never succeeds in creating a Timon completely responsive to the play's theme or in relating him to the social circumstances that should give rise to action. Nonetheless, if the play is flawed and incomplete, Ellis-Fermor holds, it is a play "such as a great artist might leave behind him."

Empson, William. "Timon's Dog." *The Structure of Complex Words*. London: Chatto and Windus; New York: New Directions, 1951. Empson explores both the play and the nature of metaphor itself in examining the insistent but multivalent use of "dog" in the play. Characters refer to dogs both as symbols of flattery and of cynicism, and this becomes for Empson a means to gauge the paradoxical nature and tone of the misanthropy shared by Apemantus and Timon.

Fly, Richard D. "Confounding Contraries: The Unmediated World of *Timon of Athens*." *Shakespeare's Mediated World*. Amherst, Mass.: Univ. of Massachusetts Press, 1976. For Fly, *Timon* resists all formal and thematic impulses toward wholeness, leaving characters and episodes disturbingly isolated and polarized. The play's disjunctions and discontinuities seem to Fly to be central to the tragedy of Timon who, like the play itself, is unable to discover any possible synthesis or fusion.

Foakes, R. A. "Shakespeare's Later Tragedies." In *Shakespeare 1564–1964: A Collection of Modern Essays by Various Hands*, ed. Edward A. Bloom. Providence, R.I.: Brown Univ. Press, 1964. Foakes understands *Timon* and the other late tragedies as fundamentally different from Shakespeare's major tragedies. Morally diminished and aesthetically distanced, the heroes of the later tragedies are alienated from the audience, becoming not, as in the major tragedies, embodiments of values sanctioned by the play, but characters who, like Timon, are presented critically rather than empathetically.

Handelman, Susan. "*Timon of Athens:* The Rage of Disillusion." *American Imago* 36 (1979): 45–68. In a suggestive psychoanalytic reading of the play, Handelman locates Timon's misanthropy and alienation in his unwillingness to mourn, and his consequent inability to replace, the infantile love object: "one's own body and that of the nurturant mother." This, for Handelman, explains the absence of women in the play and Timon's disabling isolation and rage.

Hazlitt, William. *"Timon of Athens." Characters of Shakespear's Plays*. London: 1817; rpt. London: Oxford Univ. Press, 1966. Hazlitt praises the intensity and unity of *Timon*, which he finds to be "as much a satire as a play." It is "the only play of our author in which spleen is the predominant feeling of the mind." Only Flavius disrupts the "general picture of selfish depravity."

Johnson, Samuel. *"Timon of Athens."* In *Johnson on Shakespeare*, ed. Arthur Sherbo. *The Yale Edition of the Complete Works of Samuel Johnson*, vol. 8. New Haven and London: Yale Univ. Press, 1968. Though he finds the play to be often obscure, Dr. Johnson considers *Timon* a powerful "domestic tragedy." Its characters, he finds, are "various and exact" and its incidents "natural." He concludes that the play "offers a very powerful warning" against an excessive generosity that "buys flattery, but not friendship."

Kahn, Coppélia. " 'Magic of Bounty': *Timon of Athens*, Jacobean Patronage, and Maternal Power." *Shakespeare Quarterly* 38 (1987): 34–57. Psychoanalytic theories of male subjectivity, anthropological studies of gifts and gift-giving, and a historical consideration of the structure and function of patronage in Renaissance England provide Kahn with a rich series of contexts for her suggestive reading of *Timon* as a play that disturbingly explores anxieties produced by social and psychological dependency.

Kernan, Alvin B. "Tragic Satire." *The Cankered Muse: Satire of the English Renaissance*. New Haven, Conn.: Yale Univ. Press, 1959. Kernan argues that in placing the satirist at the center rather than at the margins of the play, Shakespeare in *Timon* offers a penetrating analysis of the satiric vision itself. Timon's rage has a moral force behind it, born not of envy but of agonized self-knowledge; nonetheless, Shakespeare reveals the ultimate failure of the satiric sense of life, as Timon in killing himself exposes satire's compulsive negation.

Knights, L. C. *"Timon of Athens."* In *The Morality of Art: Essays Presented to G. Wilson Knight by his Colleagues and Friends*, ed. D. W. Jefferson. London: Routledge and Kegan Paul, 1969. Though the play clearly does involve a satirical attack on the deforming power of money, Knights argues that Timon's misanthropy results more directly from his rage at the destruction of his idealized sense of self. Stripped of external supports for his ego-ideal, Timon is left with nothing but a vision of an evil world that reflects in part a social reality but also Timon's self-contempt.

Muir, Kenneth. "*Timon of Athens* and the Cash-Nexus." *The Singularity of Shakespeare and Other Essays*. New York: Barnes and Noble, 1977. In an essay first published in 1947, Muir finds that the play's bitterness rests in Shakespeare's growing awareness that money has become the basis of authority in the increasingly capitalistic world of seventeenth-century England. The social order of the play is "divorced from morality" and power is "animated entirely by self-interest."

Soellner, Rolf. *"Timon of Athens": Shakespeare's Pessimistic Tragedy*. Columbus, Ohio: Ohio State Univ. Press, 1979. Soellner's extended study of the play finds its characterization, imagery, and structure informed by a powerful tragic impulse released by its overriding pessimism. Soellner's reading of *Timon* is supplemented with chapters on aspects of its social and intellectual backgrounds, discussions of the play's date, source, and original theatrical circumstances, and a useful appendix by Gary Jay Williams tracing the history of *Timon* onstage from 1816 to 1978.

CORIOLANUS

Introduction

Coriolanus may be Shakespeare's last tragedy. Even though external evidence is scarce as to its actual date, the style suggests a time around 1608. If so, Shakespeare's final statement on humanity's tragic destiny is disillusioned, wry, almost anticlimactic, in the vein of his Roman and classical tragedies rather than of his great tragedies of evil (*Hamlet, Othello, King Lear, Macbeth*). Shakespeare based *Coriolanus* on Plutarch's *The Lives of the Noble Grecians and Romans*, in the translation by Sir Thomas North. As in the presumably earlier Plutarchan plays, *Julius Caesar, Timon of Athens*, and *Antony and Cleopatra*, and in the non-Plutarchan *Titus Andronicus* and *Troilus and Cressida*, Shakespeare's ancient political world is one of constant upheaval. In the clash of ideologies, the plebeian mob turns giddily from one idol to the next, and strong men rise briefly only to be supplanted by a rival. The result of unceasing change is political stalemate. The great men of the ancient world seem fascinatingly alive to us, but they also seem blind to their own limitations, fatally proud, and hemmed in by circumstance. Their virtues and their defects are inseparable and indeed often identical, for private virtues serve these tragic heroes poorly in the amoral and pitiless arena of politics. Their natures cannot easily be moved from a predilection for catastrophe, and so their downfall proceeds inexorably from what Aristotle, writing of Greek tragedy, termed a flaw, or *hamartia*, in their characters. The ending, ironic rather than cathartic in its effect, leaves us with an impression of tragic waste.

Coriolanus admirably captures this conflict dividing personal nobility from political reality. The play returns to a political problem studied before in *Julius Caesar*: the rivalry in ancient Rome between republican and imperial forms of government. *Coriolanus*, although written later than *Julius Caesar*, analyzes an earlier period of Roman history. In *Coriolanus* we witness the birth of republicanism in its distinctively Roman form, a blend of aristocratic and democratic elements; in *Julius Caesar* we see the demise of this delicately balanced regime. Shakespeare views both events with ironic detachment.

Republicanism was potentially a matter of controversy on the Jacobean stage, insofar as spectators might draw analogies between it and parliamentary efforts to curb the power of the English throne. The differences were real, of course, especially as reflected in *Julius Caesar,* where Caesar's claim to absolute rule has no sanction of divine right and Brutus' republicanism is ineffably genteel rather than populist. *Coriolanus,* however, hits closer to home. Here the plebeians are profoundly dissatisfied with aristocratic rule. Popular unrest over famine and high prices leads to rioting and the expression of democratic sentiments such as were heard and feared by the authorities in England. Riots over scarcity of grain occurred in Northamptonshire, Warwickshire, and Leicestershire during the summer of 1607. King James I, who had come to the throne in 1603, adopted a hostile stance toward Puritan efforts to democratize church government and of corresponding challenges in Parliament on behalf of the common law. From the vantage point of ancient Rome, distant in time and place, *Coriolanus* appraises the conflict in terms that bear no precise relation to Jacobean England and yet have a timeless relevance. Without taking sides, the play dwells on the ambiguity of the struggle and on the indecisive, self-defeating results ironically achieved by both parties.

As in *Julius Caesar,* men on both sides are passionately sincere but driven to shortsighted extremism. The tribunes insist on behalf of the mob that the people's voice is to be the ultimate law of Rome. Coriolanus, in angry response, sees the mob and its elected tribunes as the enemies of hierarchical prerogative, threatening the very existence of the state. Which view is correct? Is the people's voice a brave force of resistance against aristocratic hauteur and class privilege, as exemplified by Coriolanus, or is the tribunes' program a grab for power by demagogues willing to risk anarchy and to weaken Rome's military might? Shakespeare seems to offer no unequivocal answer. Like Plutarch, he explores the weaknesses and strengths of both parties. He uses a dramatic structure, as in *Julius Caesar,* of sustained ambiguity. If any conclusion emerges, it is that violent political struggle leads only to an undoing of those civilized institutions that moderate men, caught in the middle, strive vainly to preserve.

The citizens play a dominant role in *Coriolanus*. The action begins, as in *Julius Caesar*, with a mob scene, setting a tone of ominous instability. The mob is too easily swayed. Lacking any consistent political philosophy of its own, it will follow whatever charismatic orator catches its fancy. It despises Coriolanus one moment and adulates him the next. Its own members agree that the mob is a "many-headed multitude," directionless, irresponsible (2.3.10–17). Other characters besides Coriolanus protest the offensive stench of the crowd, "stinking" breaths, "reechy" necks, "stinking greasy caps," and unclean teeth (2.1.208, 235; 4.6.138). The Roman citizens are a "herd," "apron-men," "garlic eaters," curs, hares, foxes, geese, a "cockle of rebellion, insolence, sedition" (3.1.35, 73; 4.6.101–103). This deliberately repulsive portrayal merely intensifies what is true in the other Roman plays and in the English history plays as well. Nowhere in Shakespeare does mob action lead to anything constructive or even politically acceptable. At the same time, the mob does not bear chief responsibility for disaster either, in *Coriolanus* or elsewhere in Shakespeare. Individually its members are good-natured, slow to be aroused, quick to forget injury, too credulous indeed for their own good. In *Coriolanus*, they have to be prompted again and again by the tribunes to press forward with their resentment. Many citizens, left to themselves, are wise and patient. They are a neutral force, dangerous only when whipped up to collective frenzy by demagogic persuasion.

Much blame would seem to fall then on the tribunes, and indeed even the more moderate patricians such as Menenius are deeply mistrustful of Junius Brutus and Sicinius Velutus. These tribunes are willing to risk mob violence to achieve their ends, especially when they urge the "rabble of plebeians" to "bustle about Coriolanus" (3.1.183–188). Ignoring Menenius' pleas that "This is the way to kindle, not to quench," and that "Confusion's near" (ll. 200, 193), the tribunes deliberately goad Coriolanus to anger. Their strategy is to foment clamor, and "with a din confused / Enforce the present execution," shouting down reason with hysteria (3.3.21–22). They carefully stage each confrontation with Coriolanus, rehearsing the citizens in what they are to

do, cannily timing their provocations. They talk like conspirators. Shakespeare's audience, accustomed to govern-
mental warnings against mob violence, would probably
have understood the menace posed by the tribunes, and
would have savored the irony that Rome is weakened rather
than strengthened by their machinations.

Still, Shakespeare's portrayal of the tribunes is remarkably sympathetic. They honestly fear that Coriolanus seeks
"one sole throne, without assistance" (4.6.34), and that as
consul he will do everything he can to suppress the peoples'
liberties. This is no idle fear; Coriolanus' own friends
merely counsel him to attack the tribunes after he has
achieved power, not before. Although the tribunes do
arouse the people to actions they would not otherwise take,
the tribunes believe they are doing so in the people's best
interests, providing leadership for a constituency that has
hitherto lacked a voice. They believe in a government "by
the consent of all" that can hold aristocratic insolence in
check through the "lawful censure" of the commons.
"What is the city but the people?" (3.1.202–204; 3.3.50).
Moreover, they are not revolutionaries by temperament and
abandon mob tactics once they have made their point.
Their achievements mock them when Rome proves defenseless against the return of Coriolanus, but even here they
can argue with some reason that Rome would have achieved
peace had it not been for Coriolanus' lawless vengeance.

Perhaps then Coriolanus must bear the responsibility for
provoking democratic extremism through his contempt of
the citizenry. From his first appearance, he antagonizes us
as well as the populace with his curt, insulting manner. He
addresses the people as "dissentious rogues" itching with
scabby diseases, and dismisses them as "curs" who are
"beneath abhorring" (1.1.163–167). His hatred amounts to
revulsion, and we fear he is all too ready to employ his
sword on "thousands of these quartered slaves" (l. 198).
When denied the consulship by the tribunes, in fact, he
draws his sword in the marketplace, relishing the opportunity for a military solution. His tendency to forget names
betrays a coldness. Although he professes not to speak
merely in anger, he is too easily baited by the tribunes, too
quick to speak his mind. Even those who admire his virtues
concede that "to seem to affect the malice and displeasure

of the people is as bad as that which he dislikes, to flatter them for their love" (2.2.21–23). Coriolanus is glad to hear of the impending Volscian attack on Rome, for he prefers war to peace and sees conscription as a way of channeling revolutionary energies against an outward foe. He professes love of his country, but because his attachment is to an exclusively patrician order he is ready to turn traitor against a Rome that gives a political voice to the plebeians he so abhors.

Nevertheless, the portrayal of Coriolanus, as of the tribunes, is delicately balanced. We admire Coriolanus' hatred of hypocrisy. He is scrupulously honest, refusing all spoils of war except those to which his fellow soldiers are entitled. Despite his pride in family and name, he genuinely dislikes to hear himself praised. Though he disdains to lead cowardly citizen-soldiers and shines most in single deeds of valor rather than in generalship, he is inspiring and even popular among valiant soldiers like himself. He is generous in praising the achievements of his colleagues. Even in matters of state he shows resoluteness and integrity. He has a consistent political philosophy, one bolstered by Menenius' comparison of the state to a body in which the members must harmoniously interact (1.1.94 ff.). Jacobean spectators would recognize in this analogy the orthodox appeal to order and degree they heard regularly from pulpit and throne, even though they might also recognize that it is being self-interestedly applied by one who enjoys the perquisites of noble birth. Coriolanus, at any rate, firmly believes that the established prerogatives of the aristocracy are Rome's only safe bulwark against chaos. By granting power to the tribunes, in his view, the Senate has sealed its doom. He sees the people as their own worst enemies, insatiable and irrational in their demands, unable to comprehend the subtleties of government, instinctively envious of their betters. Such base mortals require subjection to their masters, though they cannot be expected to realize this themselves. Coriolanus knows that his views are out of fashion and that the current trend is to appease popular demands with compromise, but he can see no end to the compromises that will be needed once the tribunes have established their prerogatives. He prefers a battle to the death and welcomes the danger to himself. If his courage and consistency are "too absolute," if he is "too noble for the world" (3.2.41; 3.1.261), he would prefer to believe that the fault lies in that world rather than in him.

Between the extremes of democratic and aristocratic rule, the middle position of compromise offers many attractions. Menenius sanely desires to see "On both sides more respect," and pleads with those who would be "truly your country's friend" to "temperately proceed to what you would / Thus violently redress" (3.1.184, 222–224). Although his sympathies are patrician, he acknowledges the tribunes' power as a political reality that must be dealt with. He finds fault with Coriolanus for not having "temporized" (4.6.17). Menenius is a bluff, honest fellow who directs our sympathies, like the equally outspoken Enobarbus in *Antony and Cleopatra*. Yet compromise always has its ridiculous aspect. Menenius increasingly assumes the self-contradictory and sardonically amusing role of the appeaser, like York of *Richard II*, urging actions that are repugnant to him personally. His seemingly sage advice to the plebeians in his fable of the belly is in part at least a rhetorical strategy calculated to quiet plebeian restiveness without addressing their real demands. At the last, after having denounced the tribunes for betraying Rome, Menenius must go as their ambassador to beg mercy of Coriolanus. When Aufidius' guardsmen scoff at him for having been turned away by Coriolanus, Menenius is beyond caring for their taunts. He does in fact hold to a consistent principle, the survival of his beloved city at whatever cost to his pride. He and Rome pragmatically blunder through, though not without loss of dignity.

Coriolanus' mother Volumnia is caught in an even more ironic dilemma. She of course shares her son's aristocratic pride, having taught him a code of death before dishonor. The emotional bond between mother and son is extraordinarily, even distressingly, close. Emotionally it takes the place of Coriolanus' bloodless marriage to the chaste and retiring Virgilia. Volumnia in fact speaks of Coriolanus metaphorically as her husband, and of his warlike prowess as a vicarious substitute for "the embracements of his bed" (1.3.4–5). Throughout, Coriolanus' deeds of war are love offerings to his mother. Every citizen of Rome knows that whatever Coriolanus has done for his country he also did "to please his mother" (1.1.37). Yet because Volumnia has not been a properly nourishing mother, Coriolanus is poised between two irreconcilable cravings, to please a mother whose demands can never be satisfied and to fashion an identity that is entirely self-made. He needs her approval but also wishes to be beholden to no one, least of all to her.

The conflict reaches its crisis when Volumnia's oppressive demands take the form of insisting that her son achieve fame not only in war but in politics. Here she must, like Menenius, encourage the compromise and "policy" that they all hate. She and Menenius stage Coriolanus' public appearances with as much care as the tribunes rehearse their plebeians. They "prompt" Coriolanus to "perform a part" for which he has no aptitude (3.2.108–111); as he later says, capitulating to his mother for the last time, "Like a dull actor now, / I have forgot my part, and I am out" (5.3.40–41). This integrity has its admirable side but brings disaster to Volumnia's plans. She is defeated by the very pride she has engendered in him, and he is defeated by her overriding ambition for him. To win her praise he must put away his true disposition, becoming effeminate and emasculated like a "harlot" or "an eunuch" (3.2.114–116). To satisfy her quest for fame he must give up his attack on Rome, perjure himself to Aufidius, and die a condemned traitor to the Volscian state. Volumnia's crushing love for her son proves ironically fatal to everything they have cherished.

Coriolanus' relationship to Aufidius is one of love as well as hate, and it too poses a fatal conflict. Despite their rivalry to the death, these two military heroes are singularly attracted to each other. Coriolanus confesses "I sin in envying his nobility," and considers Aufidius "a lion / That I am proud to hunt" (1.1.231–237). Coriolanus' fate is to love his enemy and hate his birthplace. Aufidius, in turn, greets Coriolanus with more joy "Than when I first my wedded mistress saw / Bestride my threshold" (4.5.122–123). Yet Aufidius has always resented Coriolanus' superiority in battle and has planned to overcome him by fair means or foul. In their brief military alliance, Coriolanus proves too attractive a rival, overshadowing the achievements of Aufidius. For these reasons Aufidius secretly exults in Coriolanus' fatal dilemma, since the Volscian general prefers vengeance to victory over Rome. In a final disillusioning scene he stages one more public outcry against Coriolanus, goading him into a proud rage, and then with his fellow conspirators ingloriously performs an execution "whereat valor will weep" (5.6.139). Aufidius' virtues, like those of Coriolanus, have been betrayed by his worst instincts. Throughout, the Volscians have been cunning enemies, lying in wait for Rome to tear herself apart. The laws governing the relations between states are brutally competitive, characterized by the "slippery turns" (4.4.12) of fortune that ironically bring together former enemies as allies and then turn them against one another. In this world of sudden reversals, Coriolanus' last act is something he could never have foreseen: saving the Roman state and its tribunes from a destruction he himself had wished on it. As Coriolanus wryly observes of his own destiny, "The gods look down, and this unnatural scene / They laugh at" (5.3.184–185).

Coriolanus
in Performance

As with other of Shakespeare's Roman plays, productions of *Coriolanus* have often been politically inspired. The lofty contempt of Coriolanus for the plebeians, his extraordinary mixture of military virtues and political liabilities, the vacillations of Rome, and the eventual rejection of the war hero have all served to remind audiences of their own, sometimes parallel, situations, by the light of which they have tended to see Coriolanus as either an unappreciated hero or an enemy of political order. *Coriolanus'* stage history attests to Shakespeare's remarkable ability to seem relevant to audiences of all eras. The relevance has usually been contrived, however, by the transformation of *Coriolanus* into the kind of play that theater managers have supposed their audiences wanted to see.

Nahum Tate, better known for his adaptation of *King Lear* with a happy ending (1681) and for a version of *Richard II* in the same year that was prompted by Charles II's political difficulties, remade *Coriolanus* into a work called *The Ingratitude of a Commonwealth, or The Fall of Caius Martius Coriolanus* (Theatre Royal, Drury Lane, 1682). Tate's political motive is evident in his title and in his frank admission that some passages bear "no small resemblance with the busy faction of our own time." The Coriolanus of this play is by implication Tory and royalist in his persuasions; his overthrow by mob rule recalls both that of Charles I during the mid-century civil war and Charles II's more recent troubles with those who were ready to exclude Charles's Catholic brother James from the English throne. Writing not long after the discovery of a purported "Popish Plot" to murder King Charles, blow up the Houses of Parliament, and establish Catholicism in England, Tate is patently distressed by civil discord and out of sympathy with the meddling tribunes, though he also sees that the protagonist's intractable snobbery, like that of the Stuart kings, has contributed to the impasse.

Tate's transformations of the plot aim accordingly to

heighten the melodramatic plight of a beleaguered royalist hero. In the final scene, Aufidius' role as antagonist is much enlarged: he imprisons Coriolanus' family, fights with and wounds Coriolanus, and threatens to rape Virgilia before her husband's face; only when Virgilia comes before him, mortally self-wounded to preserve her chastity, does he relent and die contritely. Nigridus, a discharged Roman officer who has joined Aufidius' side and has inflamed Aufidius with envy of Coriolanus, tortures Coriolanus' son and flings the mutilated youth into the arms of Volumnia, who goes mad and fatally attacks Nigridus with a broad-bladed weapon. Coriolanus and his son die together in a touching scene. Valeria's role is enlarged; she becomes in Tate's version a talkative and affected lady, who survives to deliver the epilogue. All this seems gratuitous today, but its function in Restoration times was presumably to enhance the tragic portrait of a gifted if arrogant aristocrat cut down by an ungrateful commonwealth. Tate's concluding moral recommends "submission and adherence to established lawful power."

After a brief appearance of Shakespeare's play in a production by John Rich in 1718 at the theater in Lincoln's Inn Fields, London, *Coriolanus* again fell into the hands of adapters bent on contemporary political interpretation. John Dennis's *The Invader of His Country, or The Fatal Resentment* (Drury Lane, 1719) exploited the political resonances of Shakespeare's play in the wake of a failed Jacobite attempt in 1715 to restore the Stuart pretender James (son of James II) to the British throne. Spain, at war with England, sent an abortive expedition to Scotland in 1719 to help the pretender, and Sweden also threatened to invade. Such a time of crisis, Dennis proclaimed to his spectators, called for a new version of *Coriolanus* written "in the cause of their country, in the cause of their sovereign."

Under these circumstances, Dennis's main interest is understandably the dilemma of a charismatic if willful leader rejected by his people and faced with the seeming necessity of attacking his own country. Whatever the sympathies expressed toward various sides of the conflict, the unavoidable fact is that such an invasion of Rome by a Roman threatens the political order. Dennis's supposed improvements (including the omission of Aufidius' lust for Virgilia and of her chaste suicide, both dramatized by Tate) are motivated also by a desire to unify the play to conform to classical standards of decorum, to bring "as much order as we can" to Shakespeare's "master-strokes" that "in wild confusion lie." Hence the whole first act is presented in one scene at the siege of Corioles, while in Act 5 a climactic fight between Coriolanus and Aufidius leads to Coriolanus' triumph over his rival and three of Aufidius' tribunes, until at last Coriolanus is run through the back by a fourth. Virgilia and Volumnia return for a poignant moment of farewell with the dying protagonist, and Cominius too is brought onstage to pronounce the final speech. The humorous Menenius is little in evidence, as befits a unified tragic play.

James Thomson's *Coriolanus* (Theatre Royal, Covent Garden, 1749) was prompted by a second Jacobite rebellion in 1745–1746 on behalf of Prince Charles Edward, the grandson of James II and son of the so-called Old Pretender, James Stuart, a rebellion that penetrated militarily into the north of England. Although Thomson too deplores civil war, the Coriolanus of this play is adorned with many virtues, while the plebeians' hostility to him is unjustified. The characters are renamed for the most part: Aufidius becomes Attius Tullius, Volumnia becomes Veturia, and Virgilia becomes Volumnia. James Quin, Peg Woffington, and George Anne Bellamy took these three roles. David Garrick produced a version close to Shakespeare's text at Drury Lane in 1754, but in that same year an amalgam of Thomson and Shakespeare, attributed to Thomas Sheridan, succeeded at Covent Garden (having been staged earlier, in 1752, in Dublin), and this version was used for some years afterward. A triumphal procession in honor of Coriolanus during the course of Act 1 required no fewer than 118 persons. John Philip Kemble did well with *Coriolanus* throughout much of his managerial career, starting in 1789 at Drury Lane, though always in a text that drew heavily on Thomson's version, as his predecessors had done, especially for the conspiracy of Aufidius and Volusius and the assassination of Coriolanus by Volusius and the other conspirators. Kemble chose to perform the play on the bicentennial of Shakespeare's death in 1816 and again the following year to mark Kemble's retirement from the stage.

Edmund Kean restored Shakespeare's play to the stage at
Drury Lane in 1820, though without success. While *The
Times* admitted that in general Shakespeare's text was pref-
erable to "the interpolations of modern emendators," in
the case of Kean's Shakespearean revival, "as far as the audience and the actors are concerned, it might have been better to have pursued the old course."

To the nineteenth century, *Coriolanus* provided more
than anything else an opportunity for epic grandeur in the
scenic impressions of ancient Rome. Kemble had begun the
trend as early as 1789 by attempting to make himself and
his sister, Sarah Siddons, who played Volumnia, completely
Roman in appearance. For his production in 1811 he studied Roman architecture, dress, and mannerisms in order
to present his viewers with a splendid triumphal arch, a
ceremonial tribute in honor of Coriolanus' return from
Corioles, and various classical architectural details appropriate (anachronistically, to be sure) to the Rome of the
Caesars. Kean's *Coriolanus* of 1820 included a tribute with
a newly composed ode of triumph and several views of
Rome, including the Capitol and the walls of the city.

William Charles Macready, eschewing the common tendency to focus on Coriolanus alone as in Thomson's re-
daction of the play, deliberately "enlarged the historical
canvas to statelier proportions and severer beauties" in his
production at Covent Garden in 1838 (according to *John
Bull*'s review of March 19 of that year). Macready performed Shakespeare's text, though with cuts to permit scenic elaboration. The first scene showed Rome from the
southwest side with the Tiber River in the foreground and
Capitoline Hill beyond, its summit crowned with temples
and its sloping side picturesquely adorned with a rude
winding street. Onstage, an unruly mob carried staves, mat-
tocks, and pickaxes. In the next scene, the atrium of Coriolanus' house was shown with its shining brickwork and
square-linteled doors. The Roman camp for the war scenes
was replete with the walls and ditches of authentic Roman
warfare. Coriolanus' triumphal return from Corioles
brought him through a massive gate as spectators lined the
walls and battlements. At the Senate House, senators assembled in triple rows on stone benches, with a lighted altar in their midst. At Antium, the port and breakwater were

visible by night, with the horizon broken only by a tall, solitary tower, looking, the *Examiner* wrote, "like Coriolanus himself in a less mortal shape, rising in lonely grandeur." In the final scene, the Volscian army filled the stage in thick files, while the matrons in period dress pleaded with Coriolanus to spare the city. Macready was not interested in visual extravagance alone; by giving an expanded role to the mob and the army, he signaled a political shift of interest away from the patrician Coriolanus and toward the people of Rome. The plebeians were "not a mere coward crowd," *John Bull* reported, but "men who have spied their way to equal franchises, and are determined to fight their way to the goal."

Samuel Phelps at the Sadler's Wells Theatre in 1848 and afterward, and Henry Irving at the Lyceum Theatre in 1901, aimed also at scenic impressiveness and the participation of common citizens. Phelps produced the play in five of his eighteen seasons at Sadler's Wells, apparently using the same text that Macready had used at Covent Garden. His acting of Coriolanus achieved what one critic termed a "sublimity of disdain." Irving substantially reduced the number of scenes to accommodate his scenery. As in Macready's production, the crowd became a formidable protagonist in the play, threatening, arguing—"a genuine mob," as *The Times* said, "and no mere pack of 'supernumeraries.'" Frank Benson directed a more complete text of *Coriolanus* in 1901 at the Comedy Theatre, returning to a play he had first directed at Stratford-upon-Avon in 1893. *The Times* was enthusiastic about "the stirring conflict of factions, the sick hurry of popular passions, played upon by the divided aims of the patricians and plebs." Politically, *Coriolanus* offered the nineteenth century a disturbing spectacle of mob violence, in which Macready and his successors nevertheless succeeded in making clear the aspirations of the people, shifting the play's center from Coriolanus' rigid pride to the social tensions of Rome.

Coriolanus has remained a political battleground in the twentieth century, inviting more radical interpretations as new ideologies have emerged in behalf of National Socialism, anarchism, and proletarian revolution. A production of *Coriolanus* in Paris in the winter and spring of 1933–1934 at the Comédie Française caused political rioting when the radical left interpreted the production as a right-wing attack on social democracy in its indictment of the cowardice and political opportunism of the mob and its leaders. The socialist Daladier government closed the play in the spring and replaced the director of the theater, contending, as *The Times* reported, that the production was a "deliberately tendentious and topical version, intended to discredit Parliamentary institutions and to pave the way for a dictatorship in France." In Moscow in 1934, the Maly Theater produced a leftist version of the play in direct response to the notorious Comédie Française production.

Two modern adaptations, revising Shakespeare in the tradition of Tate, Dennis, and Thomson, further illustrate *Coriolanus'* unceasing potential for ideological appropriation. Bertolt Brecht's *Coriolanus*, written in 1951, revises Shakespeare's play to generate sympathy for the citizenry of Rome. Coriolanus is not merely an anachronism in Brecht's Rome, but also a class enemy. Brecht invents a shipload of grain that Coriolanus refuses to distribute, and grants to the people a dignity and responsible concern for the future that the nobility lack. At the end, Menenius' request to the Senate for a tribute to Coriolanus is overruled by a motion calling for a return to "present business." John Osborne's *A Place Calling Itself Rome* (1973) exactly reverses the political valence of Brecht's adaptation, finding only ugliness, brutality, and hostility to excellence in the vision of popular democracy: "I have seen the future . . . here . . . and it doesn't work," Coriolanus spits as he is banished from Rome to seek a "world elsewhere."

Even when viewed in less inflammatory terms, *Coriolanus* has found a receptive audience in a modern world skeptical of both politicians and generals. As his final Shakespearean production, William Poel directed *Coriolanus* in 1931 on a platform stage at London's Chelsea Palace. Abandoning Poel's usual commitment to Elizabethan costuming, this production saw Coriolanus enter first in a leopard skin and later return from battle in the uniform of a nineteenth-century cavalry officer, the purpose being, as the program explained, to "show the ageless spirit of militarism." In Glen Byam Shaw's production at Stratford-upon-Avon in 1952, Anthony Quayle was a blunt, soldierly Coriolanus, finding himself "sandwiched," as critic Kenneth Tynan said, "between the plebs, whom he spurns, and the patricians, whom he despises." John Houseman directed a clear and energetic version of the play in 1954 at New York's Phoenix Theatre with a self-pitying Coriolanus unable to comprehend the fickleness of the people. Richard Burton's Coriolanus, in an Old Vic production of 1954 staged by Michael Benthall, won sympathy for his brusque candor about the tribunes' self-serving ambitions and the plebeians' vacillations, though he was himself deeply flawed in his fanatical old-guard attachment to patrician privilege. Consistency and intelligence in him seemed capable only of self-destructive fury; the political process enabled Rome to muddle through somehow (as epitomized in William Squire's amiable but fence-sitting Menenius), but at the cost of heroic grandeur. Laurence Olivier and Sybil Thorndike at the Old Vic in 1938 (directed by Lewis Casson) and Olivier with Edith Evans at Stratford in 1959 (directed by Peter Hall) similarly explored the self-defeating ironies of a Rome hopelessly mired in competing interests and unable to summon up the greatness of her tradition.

In the 1960s, while some productions of the play sought historical analogies to explore the ironies of political impasse, others shifted the play's emphasis from overtly political concerns to more subtle psychological and social ones. Michael Langham's direction at Stratford, Ontario, in 1961, sought to illuminate the political tensions of the play by setting its action in late eighteenth-century France, an era of cataclysmic shift from outworn aristocracy to revolutionary democracy. Tyrone Guthrie, on the other hand, chose a more personal idiom for his production that opened the Nottingham Playhouse in 1963. Under his direction John Neville and Ian McKellan enacted what the program called "the love-hate between Coriolanus and Aufidius." Gladys Vaughan directed *Coriolanus* for the New York Shakespeare Festival in 1965, using multiracial casting to emphasize ideological class conflict in the play, whereas John Barton's production in 1967 at Stratford-upon-Avon chose instead to focus on Ian Richardson's Coriolanus, "fated to break down," as the *Sunday Telegraph* said, "when the antagonism between his unacknowledged passions and his boasted ideals becomes too strong."

Recent productions have continued the movement away

from overtly partisan political analogies. Trevor Nunn and Buzz Goodbody's monochromatic production at Stratford-upon-Avon in 1972 did emphasize the social tragedy caused by disparities of wealth and power, but focused more upon Coriolanus' emotional immaturity and impatience. Revived the next year in London, with Nicol Williamson replacing Ian Hogg as Coriolanus, the production shifted its emphasis to the tragedy of a man unable to understand himself or his situation, epitomized in Williamson's memorably plaintive cry, "Mother . . . what . . . have . . . you . . . *done*?" Terry Hands's stark, powerful production of the play in 1977 at Stratford-upon-Avon starred Alan Howard as a Coriolanus whom Benedict Nightingale of the *New Statesman* described as "marooned in the heroic myths with which his vulture-mum must endlessly have regaled him in the cot." At the Anspacher Theater in New York in 1979, Michael Langham directed Joseph Papp's Black Shakespeare Ensemble in a production using a simple set with large doors that opened to admit Coriolanus at Corioles as if they were swallowing him. The action powerfully suggested the vulnerability of his heroic energy in a hostile historical world.

Peter Hall's production of *Coriolanus* at London's National Theatre in 1984 illustrated with particular force that the psychological and political aspects of the play coexist in uneasy if fruitful relation to one another, and that the political relevance of Coriolanus' personal tragedy will never lose its appeal for directors in search of contemporaneity. Hall clearly intended analogies to the British miners' strike of that year, with shop stewards and spray-painted slogans. Conversely, the highly personal response of Ian McKellan's Coriolanus was to remove himself from the political fray. He was awkward and unconvincing in his public persona, truly himself only in moments of his romantic isolation. This was a Coriolanus weary of the politics of Rome. In the provocative tension between McKellan's conception of the character and Hall's conception of the play, lamented by some critics, the production brilliantly revealed what the play itself has become on the modern stage: a wry tragedy of impasse, its chief figure at once noble and unfit for political life.

CORIOLANUS

[*Dramatis Personae*

CAIUS MARCIUS, *afterward* CAIUS MARCIUS CORIOLANUS

TITUS LARTIUS, } *Roman generals*
COMINIUS,
MENENIUS AGRIPPA, *friend of Coriolanus*
SICINIUS VELLUTUS, } *Roman tribunes*
JUNIUS BRUTUS,
NICANOR, *a Roman traitor*
Two Roman PATRICIANS
Two Roman SENATORS
An AEDILE
Two Roman OFFICERS
A Roman LIEUTENANT
Roman SOLDIERS
A Roman HERALD
Seven Roman CITIZENS
MESSENGERS

VOLUMNIA, *Coriolanus' mother*
VIRGILIA, *Coriolanus' wife*
Young MARCIUS, *son of Coriolanus and Virgilia*
VALERIA, *friend of Virgilia*
A GENTLEWOMAN, *attending Virgilia*

TULLUS AUFIDIUS, *Volscian general*
Two SENATORS *of Corioles*
Three Volscian LORDS
A Volscian LIEUTENANT
A Volscian SOLDIER
Three CONSPIRATORS
ADRIAN, *a Volscian*
A CITIZEN *of Antium*
Two Volscian WATCHMEN
Three SERVINGMEN *of Aufidius*

Roman and Volscian Senators, Patricians, Aediles, Lictors,
    Captains, Soldiers, Citizens, Messengers, Servingmen, an
    Usher attending Valeria, and Attendants

SCENE: *Rome and the neighborhood; Corioles and the*
    neighborhood; Antium]

1.1 *Enter a company of mutinous Citizens, with staves, clubs, and other weapons.*

FIRST CITIZEN Before we proceed any further, hear me speak.

ALL Speak, speak.

FIRST CITIZEN You are all resolved rather to die than to famish? 5

ALL Resolved, resolved.

FIRST CITIZEN First, you know Caius Marcius is chief enemy to the people.

ALL We know 't, we know 't.

FIRST CITIZEN Let us kill him, and we'll have corn at our 10
own price. Is 't a verdict? 11

ALL No more talking on 't. Let it be done. Away, away! 12

SECOND CITIZEN One word, good citizens.

FIRST CITIZEN We are accounted poor citizens, the patricians good. What authority surfeits on would relieve 15
us. If they would yield us but the superfluity, while it 16
were wholesome, we might guess they relieved us hu- 17
manely. But they think we are too dear. The leanness 18
that afflicts us, the object of our misery, is as an inven- 19
tory to particularize their abundance. Our sufferance is 20
a gain to them. Let us revenge this with our pikes ere 21
we become rakes; for the gods know I speak this in 22
hunger for bread, not in thirst for revenge.

SECOND CITIZEN Would you proceed especially against
Caius Marcius?

ALL Against him first. He's a very dog to the common- 26
alty. 27

1.1. Location: Rome. A street.
5 famish starve **10 corn** grain, such as wheat or barley **11 Is 't a
verdict** are we agreed **12 on 't** of it, about it **15 good** i.e., noble, well-
to-do. **authority** those in authority, the nobility **16 but the superfluity**
merely the excess **17 wholesome** good to eat **17–18 humanely** out of
common humanity **18 too dear** costing more than we are worth (but
also, paradoxically, *a gain;* see l. 21) **19 object** spectacle **19–20 is as
. . . abundance** serves as a catalogue or inventory to point out in
detail (by means of contrast) how rich they are **20 sufferance**
suffering **21 pikes** spears, lances; pitchforks (playing on *rakes*, l. 22)
22 rakes i.e., as lean as rakes **26 a very dog** i.e., inhumanly cruel
26–27 commonalty common people

SECOND CITIZEN Consider you what services he has
done for his country?

FIRST CITIZEN Very well, and could be content to give
him good report for 't, but that he pays himself with
being proud.

SECOND CITIZEN Nay, but speak not maliciously.

FIRST CITIZEN I say unto you, what he hath done fa- 34
mously he did it to that end. Though soft-conscienced 35
men can be content to say it was for his country, he
did it to please his mother and to be partly proud, 37
which he is, even to the altitude of his virtue.   38

SECOND CITIZEN What he cannot help in his nature you
account a vice in him. You must in no way say he is
covetous.

FIRST CITIZEN If I must not, I need not be barren of ac- 42
cusations. He hath faults, with surplus, to tire in repe- 43
tition. (*Shouts within.*) What shouts are these? The 44
other side o' the city is risen. Why stay we prating 45
here? To the Capitol!   46

ALL Come, come!

FIRST CITIZEN Soft, who comes here?   48

Enter Menenius Agrippa.

SECOND CITIZEN Worthy Menenius Agrippa, one that
hath always loved the people.

FIRST CITIZEN He's one honest enough. Would all the
rest were so!

MENENIUS
What work's, my countrymen, in hand? Where go you
With bats and clubs? The matter? Speak, I pray you. 54

FIRST CITIZEN Our business is not unknown to the Senate. They have had inkling this fortnight what we intend to do, which now we'll show 'em in deeds. They
say poor suitors have strong breaths; they shall know 58
we have strong arms too.

34–35 famously achieving fame **35 to that end** i.e., in order to become
famous. **soft-conscienced** weak-minded, lacking real conviction **37 to
be partly proud** partly out of pride **38 even . . . virtue** i.e., he is as
proud as he is brave **42 If** even if **43–44 to tire in repetition** to tire out
the speaker in reporting them **45 prating** talking idly **46 Capitol**
Temple of Jupiter on Capitoline Hill; used here to stand for the Senate
building **48 Soft** stay, stop **54 bats** cudgels **58 suitors** petitioners.
strong strong-smelling (with a play in the next line on *strong*, mighty)

MENENIUS
　Why, masters, my good friends, mine honest neighbors, 60
　Will you undo yourselves? 61

FIRST CITIZEN
　We cannot, sir. We are undone already.

MENENIUS
　I tell you, friends, most charitable care
　Have the patricians of you. For your wants, 64
　Your suffering in this dearth, you may as well 65
　Strike at the heaven with your staves as lift them
　Against the Roman state, whose course will on 67
　The way it takes, cracking ten thousand curbs 68
　Of more strong link asunder than can ever
　Appear in your impediment. For the dearth, 70
　The gods, not the patricians, make it, and
　Your knees to them, not arms, must help. Alack, 72
　You are transported by calamity 73
　Thither where more attends you, and you slander 74
　The helms o' the state, who care for you like fathers, 75
　When you curse them as enemies.

FIRST CITIZEN Care for us? True indeed! They ne'er
　cared for us yet. Suffer us to famish, and their store-
　houses crammed with grain; make edicts for usury, to 79
　support usurers; repeal daily any wholesome act es-
　tablished against the rich, and provide more piercing 81
　statutes daily to chain up and restrain the poor. If the
　wars eat us not up, they will; and there's all the love
　they bear us.

MENENIUS Either you must
　Confess yourselves wondrous malicious,
　Or be accused of folly. I shall tell you
　A pretty tale. It may be you have heard it,
　But, since it serves my purpose, I will venture
　To stale 't a little more. 90

---

60 masters i.e., good sirs. (A term appropriate to ordinary citizens.)
61 undo ruin **64 For** as for (also in l. 70) **65 dearth** famine **67 on**
continue on **68 cracking** breaking. **curbs** restraints. (A term from
horsemanship; the curb is attached to the bit.) **70 in your impediment**
in any hindrance you may be able to offer **72 knees** i.e., prayers (with a
play on *arms* as parts of the body and as weapons) **73 transported**
carried away **74 attends** awaits **75 helms** helmsmen **79 for** permit-
ting **81 piercing** severe **90 stale 't** make it stale by repeating it

FIRST CITIZEN   Well, I'll hear it, sir; yet you must not
   think to fob off our disgrace with a tale. But, an 't   92
   please you, deliver.   93

MENENIUS
   There was a time when all the body's members
   Rebelled against the belly, thus accused it:
   That only like a gulf it did remain   96
   I' the midst o' the body, idle and unactive,
   Still cupboarding the viand, never bearing   98
   Like labor with the rest, where th' other instruments   99
   Did see and hear, devise, instruct, walk, feel,   100
   And, mutually participate, did minister   101
   Unto the appetite and affection common   102
   Of the whole body. The belly answered—

FIRST CITIZEN   Well, sir, what answer made the belly?

MENENIUS
   Sir, I shall tell you. With a kind of smile,
   Which ne'er came from the lungs, but even thus—   106
   For, look you, I may make the belly smile
   As well as speak—it tauntingly replied
   To th' discontented members, the mutinous parts
   That envied his receipt; even so most fitly   110
   As you malign our senators for that   111
   They are not such as you.

FIRST CITIZEN   Your belly's answer—What?
   The kingly-crownèd head, the vigilant eye,
   The counselor heart, the arm our soldier,
   Our steed the leg, the tongue our trumpeter,
   With other muniments and petty helps   117
   In this our fabric, if that they—

MENENIUS   What then?   118
   'Fore me, this fellow speaks! What then? What then?   119

---

92 fob . . . disgrace set aside by a trick our feeling of suffering hard-
ship. **an 't** if it   **93 deliver** tell your tale   **96 gulf** open pit   **98 Still**
always. **cupboarding** stowing away. **viand** food   **99 Like** equal.
where whereas. **instruments** organs   **100 devise** deliberate, think
101 participate participating, taking part   **102 affection** inclination
106 lungs i.e., supposed organ of laughter   **110 his receipt** what it
received. **fitly** fittingly, justly. (Said ironically.)   **111 for that** because
117 muniments furnishings, or defenses. **petty** trifling, minor
118 fabric body formed by the conjunction of various parts   **119 'Fore
me** (An oath.)

FIRST CITIZEN
  Should by the cormorant belly be restrained,   120
  Who is the sink o' the body—

MENENIUS   Well, what then?   121

FIRST CITIZEN
  The former agents, if they did complain,   122
  What could the belly answer?

MENENIUS   I will tell you.
  If you'll bestow a small—of what you have little—   124
  Patience awhile, you'st hear the belly's answer.   125

FIRST CITIZEN
  You're long about it.

MENENIUS   Note me this, good friend;
  Your most grave belly was deliberate,   127
  Not rash like his accusers, and thus answered:
  "True is it, my incorporate friends," quoth he,   129
  "That I receive the general food at first   130
  Which you do live upon; and fit it is,
  Because I am the storehouse and the shop   132
  Of the whole body. But, if you do remember,
  I send it through the rivers of your blood
  Even to the court, the heart, to the seat o' the brain;   135
  And, through the cranks and offices of man,   136
  The strongest nerves and small inferior veins   137
  From me receive that natural competency   138
  Whereby they live. And though that all at once"—
  You, my good friends, this says the belly, mark me—

FIRST CITIZEN
  Ay, sir, well, well.

MENENIUS   "Though all at once cannot
  See what I do deliver out to each,
  Yet I can make my audit up, that all   143

---

120 cormorant ravenous, rapacious (like the voracious seabird known as the cormorant)   **121 sink** cesspool   **122 former** just-named   **124 small** small quantity   **125 you'st** you shall   **127 Your** i.e., this   **129 incorporate** belonging to one body   **130 the general food** the food for everyone   **132 shop** workshop   **135 to the court . . . brain** i.e., to the heart, which is the court and vital center, and to the brain, which is the throne   **136 cranks** winding passages.   **offices** service rooms of a household; kitchen, etc.   **137 nerves** sinews   **138 natural competency** sufficiency for the purposes of nature   **143 audit** balance sheet

From me do back receive the flour of all   144
And leave me but the bran." What say you to 't?   145

FIRST CITIZEN
It was an answer. How apply you this?

MENENIUS
The senators of Rome are this good belly,
And you the mutinous members. For examine
Their counsels and their cares, digest things rightly   149
Touching the weal o' the common, you shall find   150
No public benefit which you receive
But it proceeds or comes from them to you
And no way from yourselves. What do you think,
You, the great toe of this assembly?

FIRST CITIZEN   I the great toe? Why the great toe?

MENENIUS
For that, being one o' the lowest, basest, poorest,
Of this most wise rebellion, thou goest foremost.
Thou rascal, that art worst in blood to run,   158
Lead'st first to win some vantage.   159
But make you ready your stiff bats and clubs.   160
Rome and her rats are at the point of battle;
The one side must have bale.

        Enter Caius Marcius.

                              Hail, noble Marcius!   162

MARCIUS
Thanks. What's the matter, you dissentious rogues,   163
That, rubbing the poor itch of your opinion,
Make yourselves scabs?

FIRST CITIZEN   We have ever your good word.   165

MARCIUS
He that will give good words to thee will flatter   166

---

144 the flour i.e., the nourishing part (with a play on *the flower*, the
pick; spelled *Flowre* in the Folio) **145 bran** chaff **149 digest** analyze,
interpret (with a play on the gastronomic sense) **150 weal o' the common** public welfare **158 rascal** lean deer not worth the hunting. (Hence
the modern meaning. The term is here seemingly applied to a hunting
dog.) **in blood** in vigor, condition. (A hunting term.) **159 Lead'st . . .
vantage** you lead the pack to gain some personal advantage **160 stiff
bats** stout cudgels **162 The one . . . bale** one side or the other must get
the worst of it, receive injury **163 dissentious** rebellious **165 scabs**
(1) scurvy fellows, rascals (2) sores. **ever** always **166 give good words
to** praise

Beneath abhorring. What would you have, you curs,   167
That like nor peace nor war? The one affrights you,   168
The other makes you proud. He that trusts to you,   169
Where he should find you lions, finds you hares;
Where foxes, geese. You are no surer, no,   171
Than is the coal of fire upon the ice,   172
Or hailstone in the sun. Your virtue is   173
To make him worthy whose offense subdues him,   174
And curse that justice did it. Who deserves greatness   175
Deserves your hate; and your affections are   176
A sick man's appetite, who desires most that
Which would increase his evil. He that depends   178
Upon your favors swims with fins of lead
And hews down oaks with rushes. Hang ye! Trust ye?   180
With every minute you do change a mind
And call him noble that was now your hate,   182
Him vile that was your garland. What's the matter,   183
That in these several places of the city   184
You cry against the noble Senate, who,
Under the gods, keep you in awe, which else   186
Would feed on one another?—What's their seeking?   187

MENENIUS
For corn at their own rates, whereof, they say,   188
The city is well stored.

MARCIUS   Hang 'em! They say?
They'll sit by the fire and presume to know
What's done i' the Capitol, who's like to rise,   191
Who thrives and who declines; side factions and give out 192
Conjectural marriages, making parties strong   193

167 abhorring contempt   **168 nor . . . nor** neither . . . nor.   **The one** i.e.,
war   **169 The other** i.e., peace.   **proud** arrogant and demanding
171 no surer no more reliable   **172–173 Than . . . sun** than a pan of
burning coals set down on solid ice or hailstones lying in the warming
sun   **173 virtue** unusual distinction. (Said sardonically.)   **174–175 To
make . . . it** to glorify that person whose wrongdoing subjects him to
punishment and to curse the justice that punishes him   **175 Who
deserves** whoever has a right to   **176 Deserves** acquires, incurs.   **your
affections are** i.e., being loved by you is   **178 evil** malady   **180 rushes**
slender reeds   **182 now** just now   **183 garland** object of highest honor
and praise   **184 several** different, various   **186 which else** who otherwise   **187 seeking** demand   **188 corn** grain.   **rates** prices   **191 like**
likely   **192 side** take sides with.   **give out** report   **193 marriages** i.e.,
political alliances.   **making parties strong** asserting certain parties to
be strong, giving support to them

And feebling such as stand not in their liking   194
Below their cobbled shoes. They say there's grain
    enough?   195
Would the nobility lay aside their ruth   196
And let me use my sword, I'd make a quarry   197
With thousands of these quartered slaves as high   198
As I could pick my lance.   199

MENENIUS
Nay, these are almost thoroughly persuaded,
For though abundantly they lack discretion,
Yet are they passing cowardly. But I beseech you,   202
What says the other troop?

MARCIUS   They are dissolved. Hang 'em!
They said they were an-hungry; sighed forth proverbs, 205
That hunger broke stone walls, that dogs must eat,   206
That meat was made for mouths, that the gods sent not 207
Corn for the rich men only. With these shreds   208
They vented their complainings, which being answered 209
And a petition granted them—a strange one,
To break the heart of generosity   211
And make bold power look pale—they threw their caps
As they would hang them on the horns o' the moon,   213
Shouting their emulation.

MENENIUS   What is granted them?   214

MARCIUS
Five tribunes to defend their vulgar wisdoms,   215
Of their own choice. One's Junius Brutus,
Sicinius Vellutus, and I know not—'Sdeath!   217
The rabble should have first unroofed the city
Ere so prevailed with me. It will in time

---

194 feebling declaring to be weak   **195 Below . . . shoes** i.e., beneath
their feet.   **cobbled** mended   **196 Would the nobility** if only the nobility
would.   **ruth** tenderheartedness   **197 quarry** heap of slain deer
198 quartered cut into quarters, slaughtered like criminals   **199 pick**
pitch   **202 passing** exceedingly   **205 an-hungry** hungry. (The prefix *an*
is an archaic intensifier.)   **206 dogs** i.e., even dogs   **207 meat** food
208 shreds bits, scraps (of wisdom)   **209 vented** discharged, excreted
211 generosity the nobles   **213 As** as if   **214 emulation** rivalry of one
another in shouting; or, envy of superiors   **215 tribunes** official repre-
sentatives of the people's interests   **217 'Sdeath** i.e., by God's death. (An
oath.)

Win upon power and throw forth greater themes	220
For insurrection's arguing.	221

MENENIUS This is strange.

MARCIUS Go get you home, you fragments!   223

Enter a Messenger, hastily.

MESSENGER
Where's Caius Marcius?

MARCIUS   Here. What's the matter?

MESSENGER
The news is, sir, the Volsces are in arms.

MARCIUS

I am glad on 't. Then we shall ha' means to vent	226
Our musty superfluity.—See, our best elders.	227

Enter Sicinius Velutus, Junius Brutus, Cominius,
Titus Lartius, with other Senators.

FIRST SENATOR
Marcius, 'tis true that you have lately told us: 228
The Volsces are in arms.

MARCIUS   They have a leader,
Tullus Aufidius, that will put you to 't.   230
I sin in envying his nobility,
And were I anything but what I am
I would wish me only he.

COMINIUS   You have fought together.   233

MARCIUS

Were half to half the world by the ears and he	234
Upon my party, I'd revolt, to make	235
Only my wars with him. He is a lion	236

That I am proud to hunt.

FIRST SENATOR   Then, worthy Marcius,
Attend upon Cominius to these wars.   238

---

220 Win upon gain advantage over **221 For insurrection's arguing** to
be urged by uprisings **223 fragments** scraps. (A term of contempt.)
226 on 't of it. **vent** discharge, excrete **227 musty superfluity** moldy
excess **228 that** what. **lately** recently **230 to 't** i.e., to the test
233 together against one another **234 by the ears** at variance (with the
other half) **235 Upon my party** on my side **236 with** against
238 Attend upon serve under

COMINIUS
  It is your former promise.
MARCIUS   Sir, it is,
  And I am constant. Titus Lartius, thou   240
  Shalt see me once more strike at Tullus' face.
  What, art thou stiff? Stand'st out?
LARTIUS   No, Caius Marcius,   242
  I'll lean upon one crutch and fight with t'other
  Ere stay behind this business.
MENENIUS   O, true bred!
FIRST SENATOR
  Your company to the Capitol, where, I know,   245
  Our greatest friends attend us.
LARTIUS [*To Cominius*]   Lead you on.
  [*To Marcius.*] Follow Cominius. We must follow you;
  Right worthy you priority.
COMINIUS   Noble Marcius!   248
FIRST SENATOR [*To the Citizens*]
  Hence to your homes, begone!
MARCIUS   Nay, let them follow.
  The Volsces have much corn; take these rats thither
  To gnaw their garners.—Worshipful mutineers,   251
  Your valor puts well forth. Pray, follow.   252
        Exeunt. Citizens steal away. Manent Sicinius
                              and Brutus.

SICINIUS
  Was ever man so proud as is this Marcius?
BRUTUS   He has no equal.
SICINIUS
  When we were chosen tribunes for the people—
BRUTUS
  Marked you his lip and eyes?

---

240 constant true to my promise   **242 stiff** resistant, reluctant. (But
Lartius answers as though the word had meant "stiff with age.")
Stand'st out do you refuse to engage   **245 Your company** let me request
your company   **248 Right . . . priority** you well deserve to take prece-
dence   **251 garners** granaries, storehouses.   **Worshipful mutineers**
worthy mutineers. (Said with mock politeness.)   **252 puts well forth**
begins to bud, shows a fair promise. (Said ironically.)   **s.d. Manent** they
remain onstage

SICINIUS   Nay, but his taunts.
BRUTUS
  Being moved, he will not spare to gird the gods.   257
SICINIUS   Bemock the modest moon.   258
BRUTUS
  The present wars devour him! He is grown   259
  Too proud to be so valiant.
SICINIUS   Such a nature,   260
  Tickled with good success, disdains the shadow   261
  Which he treads on at noon. But I do wonder
  His insolence can brook to be commanded   263
  Under Cominius.
BRUTUS   Fame, at the which he aims,   264
  In whom already he's well graced, cannot   265
  Better be held nor more attained than by
  A place below the first; for what miscarries   267
  Shall be the general's fault, though he perform
  To th' utmost of a man, and giddy censure   269
  Will then cry out of Marcius, "O, if he
  Had borne the business!"
SICINIUS   Besides, if things go well,
  Opinion, that so sticks on Marcius, shall   272
  Of his demerits rob Cominius.
BRUTUS   Come.   273
  Half all Cominius' honors are to Marcius,   274
  Though Marcius earned them not, and all his faults
  To Marcius shall be honors, though indeed
  In aught he merit not.
SICINIUS   Let's hence and hear   277
  How the dispatch is made and in what fashion,   278

---

257 moved angered. **spare to gird** refrain from scoffing at **258 modest** i.e., as representing Diana, goddess of chastity **259 The present** i.e., may the present **260 to be** of being. (Or, Brutus may mean that Marcius' excessive pride makes his valor dangerous.) **261 Tickled with** flattered by, greatly excited by **263 brook** endure **263–264 be commanded Under** be under the command of **265 whom** which **267 miscarries** goes wrong **269 giddy censure** thoughtless popular opinion **272 Opinion . . . on** the fine reputation that adheres so to **273 demerits** merits, deserts **274 are to** belong to **277 aught** anything **278 dispatch** execution of the business

More than his singularity, he goes   279
Upon this present action.
BRUTUS   Let's along.   *Exeunt.* 280

❖

1.2   *Enter Tullus Aufidius with Senators of*
          Corioles.

FIRST SENATOR
So, your opinion is, Aufidius,
That they of Rome are entered in our counsels   2
And know how we proceed.
AUFIDIUS   Is it not yours?
What ever have been thought on in this state   4
That could be brought to bodily act ere Rome
Had circumvention? 'Tis not four days gone   6
Since I heard thence. These are the words—I think   7
I have the letter here. Yes, here it is. [*Finding a letter.*]
[*Reads.*] "They have pressed a power, but it is not known 9
Whether for east or west. The dearth is great,   10
The people mutinous, and it is rumored
Cominius, Marcius your old enemy,
Who is of Rome worse hated than of you,   13
And Titus Lartius, a most valiant Roman,
These three lead on this preparation
Whither 'tis bent. Most likely 'tis for you.   16
Consider of it."
FIRST SENATOR   Our army's in the field.
We never yet made doubt but Rome was ready
To answer us.
AUFIDIUS   Nor did you think it folly
To keep your great pretenses veiled till when   20

---

279 More . . . singularity i.e., with even more than his usual share of
arrogance and idiosyncrasy   **280 along** go, go join

1.2. Location: Corioles (or Corioli), southeast of Rome.
2 entered in acquainted with   **4 What** what things   **6 circumvention**
i.e., warning enabling them to circumvent.   **gone** ago   **7 thence** from
there   **9 pressed a power** raised an army   **10 dearth** famine   **13 of**
by   **16 Whither 'tis bent** against whatever destination it is intended
20 pretenses intentions

They needs must show themselves, which in the
   hatching,   21
It seemed, appeared to Rome. By the discovery   22
We shall be shortened in our aim, which was   23
To take in many towns ere almost Rome   24
Should know we were afoot.

SECOND SENATOR   Noble Aufidius,
Take your commission; hie you to your bands.   26
Let us alone to guard Corioles.
If they set down before 's, for the remove   28
Bring up your army; but I think you'll find
They've not prepared for us.

AUFIDIUS   O, doubt not that;   30
I speak from certainties. Nay more,
Some parcels of their power are forth already,   32
And only hitherward. I leave your honors.   33
If we and Caius Marcius chance to meet,
'Tis sworn between us we shall ever strike   35
Till one can do no more.

ALL   The gods assist you!

AUFIDIUS   And keep your honors safe!

FIRST SENATOR   Farewell.

SECOND SENATOR   Farewell.

ALL   Farewell.
                                        Exeunt omnes. 41

❖

21 needs necessarily   **22 appeared** became evident.   **discovery** disclosure   **23 be shortened in** fall short of   **24 take in** capture.   **ere almost**
even before   **26 hie** hasten.   **bands** companies of soldiers   **28 set down
before 's** lay siege to us.   **remove** raising of the siege   **30 prepared for
us** i.e., laid plans to besiege us   **32 parcels** parts.   **forth** marching
forward   **33 only hitherward** i.e., marching toward this place and this
alone.   **your honors** i.e., you. (Plural and honorific.)   **35 ever strike**
keep on exchanging blows   **41 s.d. omnes** all

1.3   *Enter Volumnia and Virgilia, mother and wife*
to Marcius. They set them down on two low
stools and sew.

VOLUMNIA   I pray you, daughter, sing, or express yourself in a more comfortable sort. If my son were my   2
husband, I should freelier rejoice in that absence   3
wherein he won honor than in the embracements of
his bed where he would show most love. When yet
he was but tender-bodied and the only son of my   6
womb, when youth with comeliness plucked all gaze   7
his way, when for a day of kings' entreaties a mother   8
should not sell him an hour from her beholding, I,   9
considering how honor would become such a person—   10
that it was no better than picturelike to hang by the
wall, if renown made it not stir—was pleased to let him   12
seek danger where he was like to find fame. To a cruel   13
war I sent him, from whence he returned, his brows
bound with oak. I tell thee, daughter, I sprang not   15
more in joy at first hearing he was a man-child than
now in first seeing he had proved himself a man.   17

VIRGILIA   But had he died in the business, madam, how
then?

VOLUMNIA   Then his good report should have been my
son; I therein would have found issue. Hear me pro-   21
fess sincerely: had I a dozen sons, each in my love alike
and none less dear than thine and my good Marcius,
I had rather had eleven die nobly for their country
than one voluptuously surfeit out of action.   25

   Enter a Gentlewoman.

**1.3. Location: Rome. Marcius' house, which may be (as indicated in
Plutarch) his mother's house; see 2.1.194.**
2 comfortable sort cheerful manner   **3 freelier** more readily   **6 tender-
bodied** i.e., young   **7 comeliness** beauty.   **all gaze** the gaze of all   **8 for**
even for   **9 should . . . beholding** i.e., would not let her son out of her
sight even for an hour at any price   **10 such a person** such a fine figure
of a youth   **12 renown made it not stir** desire for fame did not motivate
it   **13 like** likely   **15 bound with oak** i.e., as a badge to signify that he
had saved the life of a Roman citizen. (The *cruel war* was that against
the Latins and Tarquin the Proud; see 2.1.148–149 and note.)   **17 now**
i.e., then   **21 issue** offspring   **25 voluptuously surfeit** live extravagantly
for pleasure

GENTLEWOMAN   Madam, the Lady Valeria is come to visit
you.

VIRGILIA

Beseech you, give me leave to retire myself.   28

VOLUMNIA   Indeed, you shall not.

Methinks I hear hither your husband's drum,   30
See him pluck Aufidius down by the hair;   31
As children from a bear, the Volsces shunning him.   32
Methinks I see him stamp thus, and call thus:
"Come on, you cowards! You were got in fear,   34
Though you were born in Rome." His bloody brow
With his mailed hand then wiping, forth he goes   36
Like to a harvestman that's tasked to mow   37
Or all or lose his hire.   38

VIRGILIA

His bloody brow? O Jupiter, no blood!

VOLUMNIA

Away, you fool! It more becomes a man
Than gilt his trophy. The breasts of Hecuba,   41
When she did suckle Hector, looked not lovelier
Than Hector's forehead when it spit forth blood
At Grecian sword, contemning. Tell Valeria   44
We are fit to bid her welcome.   *Exit Gentlewoman.*   45

VIRGILIA

Heavens bless my lord from fell Aufidius!   46

VOLUMNIA

He'll beat Aufidius' head below his knee
And tread upon his neck.   48

     Enter Valeria, with an usher and a Gentlewoman.

VALERIA   My ladies both, good day to you.

VOLUMNIA   Sweet madam!

VIRGILIA   I am glad to see your ladyship.

---

28 retire myself go in by myself   **30 hither** coming this way, or from
here   **31 See** i.e., methinks I see   **32 As . . . him** (methinks I see) the
Volsces avoiding him as children flee from a bear   **34 got** begot
36 mailed protected by mail, armored   **37 tasked** set the task   **38 Or**
either.   **hire** wages   **41 Than . . . trophy** i.e., than gilding adorns his
monument.   **Hecuba** Queen of Troy, mother of Hector and many other
sons   **44 contemning** scorning (the Grecian sword)   **45 fit** ready
46 bless protect.   **fell** cruel   **48 s.d. an usher** a lady's male attendant

VALERIA How do you both? You are manifest house- 52
keepers. What are you sewing here? A fine spot, in 53
good faith. How does your little son?

VIRGILIA I thank your ladyship; well, good madam.

VOLUMNIA He had rather see the swords and hear a
drum than look upon his schoolmaster.

VALERIA O' my word, the father's son. I'll swear 'tis a 58
very pretty boy. O' my troth, I looked upon him o'
Wednesday half an hour together. H'as such a con- 60
firmed countenance! I saw him run after a gilded but- 61
terfly, and when he caught it, he let it go again, and
after it again, and over and over he comes and up 63
again, catched it again. Or whether his fall enraged 64
him, or how 'twas, he did so set his teeth and tear it! 65
O, I warrant, how he mammocked it! 66

VOLUMNIA One on 's father's moods. 67

VALERIA Indeed, la, 'tis a noble child.

VIRGILIA A crack, madam. 69

VALERIA Come, lay aside your stitchery. I must have
you play the idle huswife with me this afternoon. 71

VIRGILIA No, good madam, I will not out of doors. 72

VALERIA Not out of doors?

VOLUMNIA She shall, she shall.

VIRGILIA Indeed, no, by your patience. I'll not over the 75
threshold till my lord return from the wars.

VALERIA Fie, you confine yourself most unreasonably.
Come, you must go visit the good lady that lies in. 78

VIRGILIA I will wish her speedy strength and visit her
with my prayers, but I cannot go thither.

VOLUMNIA Why, I pray you?

VIRGILIA 'Tis not to save labor, nor that I want love. 82

VALERIA You would be another Penelope. Yet they 83

52–53 manifest housekeepers clearly being stay-at-homes today
53 sewing embroidering.   **spot** pattern, figure   **58 O'** on   **60 H'as** he
has   **60–61 confirmed** resolute   **61 gilded** brilliantly colored   **63 over
and over** head over heels   **64 Or whether** whether   **65 set** clench
66 mammocked tore into fragments   **67 on 's** of his   **69 crack** pert
little imp   **71 huswife** housewife   **72 out** go out   **75 over** step over
78 lies in is expecting a child   **82 want** am deficient in   **83 You would
be** i.e., one might take you for.   **Penelope** faithful wife of Ulysses in
Homer's *Odyssey*, who delayed her suitors by insisting she must finish
the weaving which she then unraveled every night

say all the yarn she spun in Ulysses' absence did but
fill Ithaca full of moths. Come, I would your cambric 85
were sensible as your finger, that you might leave 86
pricking it for pity. Come, you shall go with us.

VIRGILIA No, good madam, pardon me. Indeed, I will
not forth.

VALERIA In truth, la, go with me, and I'll tell you excellent news of your husband.

VIRGILIA O, good madam, there can be none yet.

VALERIA Verily, I do not jest with you. There came
news from him last night.

VIRGILIA Indeed, madam?

VALERIA In earnest, it's true; I heard a senator speak it.
Thus it is: the Volsces have an army forth, against
whom Cominius the general is gone with one part of
our Roman power. Your lord and Titus Lartius are set
down before their city Corioles. They nothing doubt 100
prevailing, and to make it brief wars. This is true, on
mine honor, and so, I pray, go with us.

VIRGILIA Give me excuse, good madam. I will obey you
in everything hereafter.

VOLUMNIA Let her alone, lady. As she is now, she will
but disease our better mirth. 106

VALERIA In troth, I think she would. Fare you well, 107
then. Come, good sweet lady. Prithee, Virgilia, turn
thy solemnness out o' door and go along with us.

VIRGILIA No, at a word, madam. Indeed, I must not. I 110
wish you much mirth.

VALERIA Well, then, farewell.   *Exeunt ladies.*

❧

85 **moths** (1) insects eating the cloth (2) idle courtiers parasitically
consuming her wealth. **would** wish. **cambric** fine white linen
86 **sensible** sensitive. **leave** cease **100 nothing** not at all **106 disease**
. . . **mirth** trouble our mirth which would be greater without her
107 troth truth, faith **110 at a word** once for all

1.4   *Enter Marcius, Titus Lartius, with drum and*
       colors, with captains and soldiers, as before the
       city [of] Corioles. To them a Messenger.

MARCIUS
  Yonder comes news. A wager they have met.
LARTIUS
  My horse to yours, no.
MARCIUS   'Tis done.
LARTIUS   Agreed.   2
MARCIUS
  Say, has our general met the enemy?
MESSENGER
  They lie in view, but have not spoke as yet.   4
LARTIUS
  So, the good horse is mine.
MARCIUS   I'll buy him of you.   5
LARTIUS
  No, I'll nor sell nor give him. Lend you him I will   6
  For half a hundred years.—Summon the town.   7
MARCIUS   How far off lie these armies?
MESSENGER   Within this mile and half.
MARCIUS
  Then shall we hear their 'larum and they ours.   10
  Now, Mars, I prithee, make us quick in work,   11
  That we with smoking swords may march from hence   12
  To help our fielded friends! Come, blow thy blast.   13

       They sound a parley. Enter two Senators, with
       others, on the walls of Corioles.

  Tullus Aufidius, is he within your walls?

1.4. Location: Before Corioles.
2 My horse . . . no i.e., I'll bet my horse against yours that they, Cominius' Roman force and the Volscian army under Aufidius, 1½ miles away,
have not met in battle   **4 in view** i.e., in view of one another.   **spoke**
i.e., encountered   **5 of** (back) from   **6 nor sell** neither sell   **7 Summon
the town** i.e., summon by trumpet, to parley   **10 'larum** call to arms
11 Mars Roman god of war   **12 smoking** steaming   **13 fielded** in the
field of battle   **s.d. on the walls** i.e., in the gallery backstage. (Throughout this scene, the tiring-house facade represents the *walls* of Corioles,
and a door in that facade represents the *gates*.)

FIRST SENATOR

No, nor a man that fears you less than he: 15
That's lesser than a little. (*Drum afar off.*) Hark! Our
  drums   16
Are bringing forth our youth. We'll break our walls   17
Rather than they shall pound us up. Our gates,   18
Which yet seem shut, we have but pinned with rushes; 19
They'll open of themselves. (*Alarum far off.*) Hark you,
  far off!
There is Aufidius. List what work he makes   21
Amongst your cloven army.

MARCIUS   O, they are at it!   22

LARTIUS

Their noise be our instruction. Ladders, ho!   23

    Enter the army of the Volsces [from the city].

MARCIUS

They fear us not, but issue forth their city.   24
Now put your shields before your hearts, and fight
With hearts more proof than shields. Advance, brave
  Titus!   26
They do disdain us much beyond our thoughts,   27
Which makes me sweat with wrath. Come on, my
  fellows!
He that retires, I'll take him for a Volsce,
And he shall feel mine edge.   30

    Alarum. The Romans are beat back to their
    trenches [and thus exeunt].
    Enter Marcius, cursing, [with Soldiers].

MARCIUS

All the contagion of the south light on you,   31

---

15 that fears i.e., but fears. (Since Aufidius doesn't fear Marcius at all,
they are all accordingly fearless.)   **16 lesser than a little** virtually not at
all   **17 break** break out of   **18 pound** shut up as in a pound   **19 rushes**
hollow-stemmed reeds   **21 List** listen to   **22 cloven** split in two, divided, cut to pieces   **23 Their** let their.   **our instruction** a lesson to us,
an example to us   **24 issue forth** rush out of   **26 proof** impenetrable
27 beyond our thoughts more than we thought possible   **30 edge**
sword   **31 south** south wind (as a supposed source of contagion)

You shames of Rome! You herd of—Boils and plagues
Plaster you o'er, that you may be abhorred
Farther than seen, and one infect another   34
Against the wind a mile! You souls of geese,   35
That bear the shapes of men, how have you run
From slaves that apes would beat! Pluto and hell!   37
All hurt behind! Backs red, and faces pale   38
With flight and agued fear! Mend and charge home,   39
Or, by the fires of heaven, I'll leave the foe
And make my wars on you. Look to 't. Come on!
If you'll stand fast, we'll beat them to their wives,
As they us to our trenches. Follow 's!

> *Another alarum; [the Volsces flee back into the
> city,] and Marcius follows them to [the] gates.*

So, now the gates are ope. Now prove good seconds!   44
'Tis for the followers fortune widens them,   45
Not for the fliers. Mark me, and do the like.   46

>   *Enter the gates and is shut in.*

FIRST SOLDIER   Foolhardiness. Not I.
SECOND SOLDIER   Nor I.
FIRST SOLDIER   See, they have shut him in.
ALL   To the pot, I warrant him.   50

>   *Alarum continues.*

Enter Titus Lartius.

LARTIUS
What is become of Marcius?
ALL   Slain, sir, doubtless.
FIRST SOLDIER
Following the fliers at the very heels,
With them he enters, who upon the sudden
Clapped to their gates. He is himself alone,   54

---

34 Farther than seen i.e., before you are even seen   **35 Against . . . mile**
i.e., so greatly that it will carry a mile against the wind   **37 Pluto**
Roman god of the underworld   **38 hurt behind** wounded in the back
(i.e., in cowardly fashion)   **39 agued** trembling as though with an ague
or fever.   **Mend** (1) do better, reform your battle ranks (2) recover from
fever.   **home** to the heart of the enemy's defenses   **44 seconds** supporters   **45 followers** pursuers   **46 the fliers** those pursued   **50 To the
pot** to the cooking pot (i.e., to certain destruction)   **54 Clapped to** shut

To answer all the city.
LARTIUS   O noble fellow!   55
Who sensibly outdares his senseless sword,   56
And, when it bows, stand'st up. Thou art left, Marcius.   57
A carbuncle entire, as big as thou art,   58
Were not so rich a jewel. Thou wast a soldier
Even to Cato's wish, not fierce and terrible   60
Only in strokes, but, with thy grim looks and
The thunderlike percussion of thy sounds,
Thou mad'st thine enemies shake, as if the world
Were feverous and did tremble.

> *Enter Marcius, bleeding, [from the city], assaulted
> by the enemy.*

FIRST SOLDIER   Look, sir.
LARTIUS   O, 'tis Marcius!
Let's fetch him off, or make remain alike.   67

> *They fight, and all enter the city.*

1.5   *Enter certain Romans, with spoils.*

FIRST ROMAN   This will I carry to Rome.
SECOND ROMAN   And I this.
THIRD ROMAN   A murrain on 't! I took this for silver.   3

> *Alarum continues still afar off.*

> *Enter Marcius and Titus [Lartius] with a
> trumpet. Exeunt [Romans with spoils].*

MARCIUS
See here these movers that do prize their hours   4
At a cracked drachma! Cushions, leaden spoons,   5

---

55 answer stand up to, confront   **56–57 Who . . . up** who, though sensitive to pain, dares more than his insensible sword; it might bend to
fear, he would not   **57 left** alone, unique; perhaps also, abandoned
58 carbuncle brilliant, red gemstone.   **entire** flawless   **60 Cato** Marcus
Cato the Censor (234–149 B.C.), celebrated in Plutarch as a staunch
soldier and exponent of Roman ethics   **67 fetch him off** rescue him.
make remain alike remain to share his fate

1.5. Location: The siege of Corioles continues.
3 murrain plague   **s.d. trumpet** trumpeter   **4 movers** active persons.
(Here used ironically.)   **prize their hours** value their time   **5 drachma**
small Greek coin

Irons of a doit, doublets that hangmen would   6
Bury with those that wore them, these base slaves,   7
Ere yet the fight be done, pack up. Down with them!
And hark, what noise the General makes! To him!   9
There is the man of my soul's hate, Aufidius,
Piercing our Romans. Then, valiant Titus, take
Convenient numbers to make good the city,   12
Whilst I, with those that have the spirit, will haste
To help Cominius.
LARTIUS   Worthy sir, thou bleed'st.
Thy exercise hath been too violent
For a second course of fight.
MARCIUS   Sir, praise me not.   16
My work hath yet not warmed me. Fare you well.
The blood I drop is rather physical   18
Than dangerous to me. To Aufidius thus
I will appear, and fight.
LARTIUS   Now the fair goddess Fortune
Fall deep in love with thee, and her great charms   22
Misguide thy opposers' swords! Bold gentleman,
Prosperity be thy page!
MARCIUS   Thy friend no less   24
Than those she placeth highest! So, farewell.   25
LARTIUS   Thou worthiest Marcius!   [Exit Marcius.]
Go sound thy trumpet in the marketplace.
Call thither all the officers o' the town,
Where they shall know our mind. Away!   Exeunt.

❖

6 of a doit worth a coin of small value.   **doublets** tight-fitting coats,
usually quilted and decorated   **6–7 hangmen . . . them** i.e., hangmen,
entitled to the clothes of persons they put to death, would not have
these   **9 the General** i.e., Cominius, fighting Aufidius nearby   **12 make
good** hold, secure   **16 course** bout, engagement. (Perhaps suggesting
also *course* as in a banquet.)   **praise me not** don't praise me yet
18 physical healthful. (Through bloodletting, a standard treatment.)
22 charms spells   **24 Prosperity be thy page** i.e., may success attend on
you.   **Thy . . . less** i.e., may prosperity be no less your friend   **25 those**
i.e., to those

1.6   *Enter Cominius, as it were in retire, with soldiers.*

COMINIUS

Breathe you, my friends. Well fought! We are come off   1
Like Romans, neither foolish in our stands   2
Nor cowardly in retire. Believe me, sirs,
We shall be charged again. Whiles we have struck,   4
By interims and conveying gusts we have heard   5
The charges of our friends. The Roman gods   6
Lead their successes as we wish our own,   7
That both our powers, with smiling fronts encount'ring,   8
May give you thankful sacrifice!

     Enter a Messenger.

                     Thy news?

MESSENGER

The citizens of Corioles have issued   10
And given to Lartius and to Marcius battle.
I saw our party to their trenches driven,
And then I came away.
COMINIUS   Though thou speakest truth,
Methinks thou speak'st not well. How long is 't since?
MESSENGER   Above an hour, my lord.
COMINIUS

'Tis not a mile; briefly we heard their drums.   16
How couldst thou in a mile confound an hour   17
And bring thy news so late?
MESSENGER   Spies of the Volsces   18

**1.6. Location: Near the camp of Cominius. The fighting near Corioles,
heard until now at a short distance, is at a lull.**
s.d. in retire in retreat (also in l. 3)   **1 Breathe** rest.   **are come off** have
left the field of battle   **2 foolish** foolhardy   **4 struck** fought, been
striking blows   **5 By . . . gusts** at intervals and borne to us on the
wind   **6 friends** i.e., the besiegers of Corioles.   **The Roman** may
you, the Roman   **7 successes** fortunes   **8 powers** armies.   **fronts**
(1) foreheads, brows (2) front lines   **10 issued** issued forth   **16 briefly** a
short time ago   **17 confound** consume   **18 Spies** scouts

Held me in chase, that I was forced to wheel   19
Three or four miles about; else had I, sir,   20
Half an hour since brought my report.   [*Exit.*]

    Enter Marcius, [bloody].

COMINIUS   Who's yonder,   21
    That does appear as he were flayed? O gods!   22
    He has the stamp of Marcius, and I have   23
    Before-time seen him thus.
MARCIUS   Come I too late?   24
COMINIUS
    The shepherd knows not thunder from a tabor   25
    More than I know the sound of Marcius' tongue
    From every meaner man.
MARCIUS   Come I too late?   27
COMINIUS
    Ay, if you come not in the blood of others,   28
    But mantled in your own.
MARCIUS   O, let me clip ye   29
    In arms as sound as when I wooed, in heart
    As merry as when our nuptial day was done
    And tapers burnt to bedward!   [*They embrace.*] 32
COMINIUS
    Flower of warriors, how is 't with Titus Lartius?
MARCIUS
    As with a man busied about decrees: 34
    Condemning some to death, and some to exile;
    Ransoming him, or pitying, threat'ning th' other;   36
    Holding Corioles in the name of Rome,
    Even like a fawning greyhound in the leash,
    To let him slip at will.
COMINIUS   Where is that slave   39

19 that so that   19–20 wheel . . . about make a detour of three or four
miles   20 else otherwise   21 since ago   22 as as if   23 stamp bearing,
form   24 Before-time formerly   25 knows distinguishes (also in l. 26).
tabor small drum   27 meaner less noble   28–29 Ay . . . own i.e., if you
yourself are bleeding all that blood, you are presumably too weak to
help, but if it is enemies' blood, you are in time to shed more   29 clip
embrace   32 tapers . . . bedward i.e., candles burned low, indicating the
approach of bedtime, or showing the way to bed   34 busied about
decrees busy with judicial decisions   36 Ransoming him releasing one
man for ransom money.   pitying releasing without ransom   39 let him
slip unleash him

Which told me they had beat you to your trenches?
Where is he? Call him hither.

MARCIUS   Let him alone;
He did inform the truth. But for our gentlemen,   42
The common file—a plague! Tribunes for them!—   43
The mouse ne'er shunned the cat as they did budge   44
From rascals worse than they.

COMINIUS   But how prevailed you?

MARCIUS
Will the time serve to tell? I do not think.
Where is the enemy? Are you lords o' the field?
If not, why cease you till you are so?

COMINIUS
Marcius, we have at disadvantage fought
And did retire to win our purpose.   50

MARCIUS
How lies their battle? Know you on which side   51
They have placed their men of trust?

COMINIUS   As I guess, Marcius,
Their bands i' the vaward are the Antiates,   53
Of their best trust; o'er them Aufidius,   54
Their very heart of hope.

MARCIUS   I do beseech you,   55
By all the battles wherein we have fought,
By th' blood we have shed together, by th' vows we have
    made
To endure friends, that you directly set me   58
Against Aufidius and his Antiates,
And that you not delay the present, but,   60
Filling the air with swords advanced and darts,   61
We prove this very hour.

COMINIUS   Though I could wish   62
You were conducted to a gentle bath
And balms applied to you, yet dare I never   64

---

42 inform report.   **gentlemen** (Said sarcastically of the ordinary soldiers.)   **43 common file** ordinary soldiers, plebeians   **44 budge** flinch
50 to . . . purpose i.e., to regroup   **51 battle** army, battle line   **53 bands**
troops.   **vaward** vanguard.   **Antiates** inhabitants of Antium   **54 Of . . .
trust** their most trustworthy   **55 Their . . . hope** the leader on whom
their hopes depend   **58 endure** continue   **60 not delay the present** do
not delay now   **61 advanced** raised.   **darts** lances   **62 prove** try the
fortunes of   **64 balms** healing ointments

Deny your asking. Take your choice of those
That best can aid your action.

MARCIUS   Those are they
That most are willing. If any such be here—
As it were sin to doubt—that love this painting   68
Wherein you see me smeared; if any fear
Lesser his person than an ill report;   70
If any think brave death outweighs bad life,
And that his country's dearer than himself,
Let him alone, or so many so minded,   73
Wave thus [*Waving his sword*] to express his disposition,
And follow Marcius.

ALL
O, me alone! Make you a sword of me!   76
              They all shout and wave their swords,
              take him up in their arms, and cast up their caps.

MARCIUS
If these shows be not outward, which of you   77
But is four Volsces? None of you but is   78
Able to bear against the great Aufidius
A shield as hard as his. A certain number,
Though thanks to all, must I select from all;
The rest shall bear the business in some other fight,
As cause will be obeyed. Please you to march,   83
And I shall quickly draw out my command,   84
Which men are best inclined.

COMINIUS   March on, my fellows.
Make good this ostentation, and you shall   86
Divide in all with us.   *Exeunt.* 87

❖

68 painting i.e., blood   **70 Lesser . . . report** less for his safety than for
his reputation   **73 Let him alone** let that individual by himself.   **or so**
many or as many as are   **76 O . . . of me** make a sword of me alone,
choose me as your weapon. (Assigned in the Folio to Coriolanus, but
seemingly said by all in response to Coriolanus' *Let him alone* in
l. 73.)   **77 outward** external, deceptive   **78 But is** is not the equal of
83 As . . . obeyed as necessity shall require   **84 draw out my command**
pick out my chosen troop   **86 ostentation** show of zeal   **87 Divide** share

1.7

Titus Lartius, having set a guard upon Corioles,
going with drum and trumpet toward Cominius
and Caius Marcius, enters [from the city] with
a Lieutenant, other soldiers, and a scout.

LARTIUS
So, let the ports be guarded. Keep your duties   1
As I have set them down. If I do send, dispatch
Those centuries to our aid; the rest will serve   3
For a short holding. If we lose the field,   4
We cannot keep the town.
LIEUTENANT   Fear not our care, sir.   5
LARTIUS   Hence, and shut your gates upon 's.   6
[*To the scout.*] Our guider, come; to the Roman camp
conduct us.   7

Exeunt [separately, the Lieutenant
returning into the city].

1.8

Alarum as in battle. Enter Marcius and
Aufidius at several doors.

MARCIUS
I'll fight with none but thee, for I do hate thee
Worse than a promise-breaker.
AUFIDIUS   We hate alike.
Not Afric owns a serpent I abhor
More than thy fame and envy. Fix thy foot.   4
MARCIUS
Let the first budger die the other's slave,   5
And the gods doom him after!

**1.7. Location: Before the gates of Corioles. The military action near
Corioles continues.**
1 ports gates   **3 centuries** companies of a hundred   **4 short holding** i.e.,
brief occupation of the city   **5 Fear not** don't worry ab. ut   **6 Hence** get
a move on   **7 guider** guide

**1.8. Location: A field of battle near the Roman camp. The military
action near Corioles continues.**
s.d. several separate   **4 fame and envy** hated reputation.   **Fix thy foot**
i.e., stand and fight   **5 budger** one who flinches

AUFIDIUS
  If I fly, Marcius, hollo me like a hare.   7
MARCIUS   Within these three hours, Tullus,
  Alone I fought in your Corioles' walls,
  And made what work I pleased. 'Tis not my blood
  Wherein thou seest me masked. For thy revenge
  Wrench up thy power to th' highest.
AUFIDIUS   Wert thou the Hector   12
  That was the whip of your bragged progeny,   13
  Thou shouldst not scape me here.

                           Here they fight,
     and certain Volsces come in the aid of Aufidius.
     Marcius fights till they be driven in breathless.
  Officious, and not valiant, you have shamed me   15
  In your condemnèd seconds.   [*Exeunt.*] 16

1.9   *Flourish. Alarum. A retreat is sounded. Enter,*
        at one door, Cominius with the Romans; at
        another door Marcius, with his arm in a scarf.

COMINIUS
  If I should tell thee o'er this thy day's work,   1
  Thou 't not believe thy deeds. But I'll report it   2
  Where senators shall mingle tears with smiles,
  Where great patricians shall attend and shrug,   4
  I' th' end admire; where ladies shall be frighted   5
  And, gladly quaked, hear more; where the dull tribunes,   6
  That with the fusty plebeians hate thine honors,   7
  Shall say against their hearts, "We thank the gods   8

7 hollo cry in pursuit of **12 Wrench up** strain, wrest, pull **13 the whip . . . progeny** the champion among your boasted (Trojan) ancestors. (Alludes to the supposed descent of the Romans from the Trojans via Aeneas.) **15 Officious** meddling, offering unwanted help **16 condemnèd seconds** futile and despised efforts at assistance

1.9. Location: Scene continues. The Roman camp. The military action near Corioles continues.
s.d. retreat trumpet signal to call off pursuit. **scarf** sling **1 If . . . work** if I should recount to you (*tell thee o'er*) this day's work of yours **2 Thou 't** thou wouldst **4 attend** listen. **shrug** i.e., indicate incredulity **5 admire** marvel **6 gladly quaked** glad to be frightened **7 fusty** moldy, ill-smelling **8 against their hearts** unwillingly

Our Rome hath such a soldier."
Yet cam'st thou to a morsel of this feast,   10
Having fully dined before.

    Enter Titus [Lartius] with his power, from the
    pursuit.

LARTIUS   O General,   11
Here is the steed, we the caparison.   12
Hadst thou beheld—
MARCIUS   Pray now, no more. My mother,
Who has a charter to extol her blood,   14
When she does praise me grieves me. I have done
As you have done—that's what I can;
Induced as you have been—that's for my country.
He that has but effected his good will   18
Hath overta'en mine act.
COMINIUS   You shall not be   19
The grave of your deserving. Rome must know   20
The value of her own. 'Twere a concealment
Worse than a theft, no less than a traducement,   22
To hide your doings and to silence that
Which, to the spire and top of praises vouched,   24
Would seem but modest. Therefore, I beseech you—   25
In sign of what you are, not to reward   26
What you have done—before our army hear me.
MARCIUS
I have some wounds upon me, and they smart
To hear themselves remembered.
COMINIUS   Should they not,   29
Well might they fester 'gainst ingratitude   30
And tent themselves with death. Of all the horses—   31

10–11 Yet cam'st . . . before i.e., this battle was just a small skirmish in
comparison with the major battle you had already fought. **of** in the
form of **11 s.d. power** army **12 steed** i.e., Marcius. **caparison** mere
trappings of a steed **14 charter . . . blood** right to praise her child
18 effected manifested in action. **will** intention **19 overta'en** sur-
passed **19–20 You . . . deserving** you shall not conceal your merit (by
your modesty) **22 traducement** calumny, slander **24 to . . . praises**
i.e., in the highest possible terms of praise. **vouched** affirmed, proclaimed **25 modest** moderate, barely sufficient (in relation to all you
did) **26 sign** token merely. **reward** amply compensate **29 not** i.e., not
be praised **30 'gainst** i.e., being infected by **31 tent** cure by probing
(i.e., the wounds would find no help other than death)

Whereof we have ta'en good and good store—of all   32
The treasure in this field achieved and city,
We render you the tenth, to be ta'en forth   34
Before the common distribution
At your only choice.

MARCIUS   I thank you, General,   36
But cannot make my heart consent to take
A bribe to pay my sword. I do refuse it,
And stand upon my common part with those   39
That have beheld the doing.   *A long flourish.* 40
                    They all cry "Marcius! Marcius!"
                    cast up their caps and lances.
                    Cominius and Lartius stand bare.
May these same instruments, which you profane,
Never sound more! When drums and trumpets shall
I' the field prove flatterers, let courts and cities be
Made all of false-faced soothing! When steel grows   44
Soft as the parasite's silk, let him be made   45
An overture for th' wars. No more, I say!   46
For that I have not washed my nose that bled,   47
Or foiled some debile wretch—which without note   48
Here's many else have done—you shout me forth   49
In acclamations hyperbolical,
As if I loved my little should be dieted   51
In praises sauced with lies.

COMINIUS   Too modest are you,   52
More cruel to your good report than grateful
To us that give you truly. By your patience,   54
If 'gainst yourself you be incensed, we'll put you,
Like one that means his proper harm, in manacles,   56
Then reason safely with you. Therefore be it known,

---

32 good and good store excellent ones and plenty of them   **34 the tenth**
one tenth   **36 At . . . choice** exactly as you choose   **39 stand . . . part**
insist on having only my regular share   **40 beheld the doing** seen the
action   **s.d. bare** bareheaded   **44 Made . . . soothing** given over utterly
to hypocritical flattery   **44–46 When . . . wars** i.e., when steel armor
grows soft with peace, like the silks of flatterers, let it (this softened
steel) be made an overture to war, an invitation to invasion by foreign
enemies (? Various emendations proposed.)   **47 For that** because
48 foiled have overthrown.   **debile** weak.   **note** notice taken   **49 else**
others.   **shout me forth** acclaim me   **51 my little** that the little I have
done.   **dieted** fed   **52 In** on, by.   **sauced** seasoned   **54 give** report
56 means . . . harm intends to injure himself

As to us, to all the world, that Caius Marcius
Wears this war's garland, in token of the which   59
My noble steed, known to the camp, I give him,
With all his trim belonging; and from this time,   61
For what he did before Corioles, call him,
With all th' applause and clamor of the host,
Caius Marcius Coriolanus! Bear
Th' addition nobly ever!   65
            Flourish. Trumpets sound, and drums.

ALL   Caius Marcius Coriolanus!
CORIOLANUS   I will go wash,
And when my face is fair you shall perceive   68
Whether I blush or no. Howbeit, I thank you.   69
I mean to stride your steed, and at all times   70
To undercrest your good addition   71
To th' fairness of my power.
COMINIUS   So, to our tent,   72
Where, ere we do repose us, we will write
To Rome of our success. You, Titus Lartius,
Must to Corioles back. Send us to Rome
The best, with whom we may articulate   76
For their own good and ours.
LARTIUS   I shall, my lord.
CORIOLANUS
The gods begin to mock me. I, that now
Refused most princely gifts, am bound to beg   79
Of my lord general.
COMINIUS   Take 't, 'tis yours. What is 't?   80
CORIOLANUS
I sometime lay here in Corioles   81
At a poor man's house; he used me kindly.   82
He cried to me; I saw him prisoner;   83
But then Aufidius was within my view,

---

59 garland (An emblem of victory.)   **61 his trim belonging** the equipment that goes with him   **65 addition** title   **68 fair** clean   **69 Howbeit**
nevertheless   **70 stride** bestride   **71 undercrest** adopt and support,
bear up (as a heraldic crest)   **72 fairness of my power** best of my
ability   **76 best** i.e., best in blood among the Volscians.   **articulate**
come to terms (about the return of Corioles to the Volscians)   **79 bound**
obliged   **80 Of** from   **81 sometime lay** once lodged   **82 used** treated
83 cried cried out (at the time of the battle just ended)

And wrath o'erwhelmed my pity. I request you
To give my poor host freedom.
COMINIUS   O, well begged!
    Were he the butcher of my son, he should
    Be free as is the wind. Deliver him, Titus.   88
LARTIUS
    Marcius, his name?
CORIOLANUS   By Jupiter, forgot!
    I am weary; yea, my memory is tired.
    Have we no wine here?
COMINIUS   Go we to our tent.
    The blood upon your visage dries; 'tis time
    It should be looked to. Come.
                          A flourish. Cornets. Exeunt.

❖

1.10   *Enter Tullus Aufidius, bloody, with two or
              three Soldiers.*

AUFIDIUS   The town is ta'en.
A SOLDIER
    'Twill be delivered back on good condition.   2
AUFIDIUS   Condition?
    I would I were a Roman, for I cannot,
    Being a Volsce, be that I am. Condition?   5
    What good condition can a treaty find   6
    I' the part that is at mercy? Five times, Marcius,   7
    I have fought with thee; so often hast thou beat me,   8
    And wouldst do so, I think, should we encounter
    As often as we eat. By th' elements,
    If e'er again I meet him beard to beard,
    He's mine or I am his. Mine emulation   12
    Hath not that honor in 't it had; for where   13
    I thought to crush him in an equal force,   14

---

88 Deliver release

1.10. Location: Outside of Corioles, after the battle.
2 condition terms **5 be . . . am** i.e., be honorable, proud **6 good
condition** state of well-being (with a play on "favorable terms," as in
l. 2) **7 I' . . . mercy** for the side that lies at the mercy of the winner
8 so just so **12 emulation** rivalry **13 where** whereas **14 in an equal
force** on equal terms

True sword to sword, I'll potch at him some way   15
Or wrath or craft may get him.

A SOLDIER   He's the devil.   16

AUFIDIUS
Bolder, though not so subtle. My valor's poisoned
With only suffering stain by him; for him   18
Shall fly out of itself. Nor sleep nor sanctuary,   19
Being naked, sick, nor fane nor Capitol,   20
The prayers of priests nor times of sacrifice,   21
Embarquements all of fury, shall lift up   22
Their rotten privilege and custom 'gainst   23
My hate to Marcius. Where I find him, were it   24
At home, upon my brother's guard, even there,   25
Against the hospitable canon, would I   26
Wash my fierce hand in 's heart. Go you to th' city;
Learn how 'tis held, and what they are that must   28
Be hostages for Rome.

A SOLDIER   Will not you go?   29

AUFIDIUS
I am attended at the cyprus grove. I pray you—   30
'Tis south the city mills—bring me word thither   31
How the world goes, that to the pace of it   32
I may spur on my journey.

A SOLDIER   I shall, sir.

                                  [*Exeunt separately.*]

❖

15 **potch** thrust   16 **Or . . . craft** in which either wrath or craftiness
18 **stain** disgrace, eclipse   19 **Shall . . . itself** (my valor) shall deviate
from its own natural course   19–24 **Nor . . . Marcius** i.e., neither his
being asleep nor protected by sanctuary, nor any other circumstances
that would normally ensure Marcius' safety, will protect him from me
next time. (*Sanctuary* provides immunity from law or attack to those
who take refuge in a church or temple.)   20 **naked** unarmed.   **fane**
temple, shrine   22 **Embarquements** embargoes, restraints   23 **rotten**
corrupt, worn out.   **privilege and custom** traditional immunity   25 **At
home** in my own house.   **upon** under.   **guard** protection   26 **hospitable
canon** law of hospitality   28–29 **what . . . Rome** i.e., who they are that
are to be taken to Rome as hostages during the negotiations about the
return of Corioles to the Volscians; see 1.9.76   30 **attended** waited for
31 **south** south of.   **mills** i.e., grain mills.   **thither** there   32 **to the pace
of it** in accordance with the speed of events

2.1 *Enter Menenius with the two tribunes of the*
people, Sicinius and Brutus.

MENENIUS The augurer tells me we shall have news tonight.

BRUTUS Good or bad?

MENENIUS Not according to the prayer of the people, 4
for they love not Marcius.

SICINIUS Nature teaches beasts to know their friends. 6

MENENIUS Pray you, who does the wolf love?

SICINIUS The lamb.

MENENIUS Ay, to devour him, as the hungry plebeians
would the noble Marcius.

BRUTUS He's a lamb indeed, that baas like a bear.

MENENIUS He's a bear indeed, that lives like a lamb.
You two are old men; tell me one thing that I shall
ask you.

BOTH Well, sir.

MENENIUS In what enormity is Marcius poor in, that 16
you two have not in abundance?

BRUTUS He's poor in no one fault, but stored with all. 18

SICINIUS Especially in pride.

BRUTUS And topping all others in boasting.

MENENIUS This is strange now. Do you two know how
you are censured here in the city, I mean of us o' the 22
right-hand file? Do you? 23

BOTH Why, how are we censured?

MENENIUS Because you talk of pride now—will you not
be angry?

BOTH Well, well, sir, well.

MENENIUS Why, 'tis no great matter; for a very little 28
thief of occasion will rob you of a great deal of pa- 29
tience. Give your dispositions the reins and be angry 30
at your pleasures—at the least, if you take it as a plea-

**2.1. Location: Rome. The ovation prepared for Coriolanus is probably to
be imagined as beginning outside the city and moving toward the
Capitol (see l. 203).**
4 according to in accordance with **6 beasts** i.e., even beasts **16 enormity** wickedness **18 stored** well stocked **22 censured** judged
23 right-hand file i.e., party of aristocrats (who took the honorable right-
hand position in battle) **28–30 a very . . . patience** any slight pretext
will rob you of your patience

sure to you in being so. You blame Marcius for being proud?

BRUTUS   We do it not alone, sir.

MENENIUS   I know you can do very little alone, for your helps are many, or else your actions would grow wondrous single. Your abilities are too infantlike for 37 doing much alone. You talk of pride. O, that you could turn your eyes toward the napes of your necks and 39 make but an interior survey of your good selves! O, that you could!

BOTH   What then, sir?

MENENIUS   Why, then you should discover a brace of 43 unmeriting, proud, violent, testy magistrates, alias 44 fools, as any in Rome.

SICINIUS   Menenius, you are known well enough too.

MENENIUS   I am known to be a humorous patrician, and 47 one that loves a cup of hot wine with not a drop of allaying Tiber in 't; said to be something imperfect in 49 favoring the first complaint, hasty and tinderlike 50 upon too trivial motion; one that converses more with 51 the buttock of the night than with the forehead of the 52 morning. What I think I utter, and spend my malice in 53 my breath. Meeting two such wealsmen as you are— 54 I cannot call you Lycurguses—if the drink you give 55 me touch my palate adversely, I make a crooked face 56 at it. I cannot say your worships have delivered the 57 matter well, when I find the ass in compound with the 58 major part of your syllables; and though I must be con- 59

---

37 single poor, feeble   **39 turn . . . necks** i.e., turn your gaze in order to see within   **43 brace** pair   **44 testy** headstrong   **47 humorous** whimsical, governed by humors   **49 allaying Tiber** water used to dilute
49–50 something . . . complaint somewhat at fault for deciding in favor of the complainant before hearing the other side of the case   **50 tinderlike** quick-tempered   **51 motion** cause   **51–53 one . . . morning** i.e., one who is better acquainted with the late hours of the night than with the early hours of the morning   **53 spend** expend   **54 breath** words.
wealsmen statesmen   **55 Lycurguses** (Said ironically; Lycurgus was the famous Spartan lawgiver.)   **55–56 drink you give me** (with a suggestion also of "things you tell me")   **56 make . . . face** i.e., show displeasure
57 delivered reported   **58–59 I find . . . syllables** i.e., I find assininity in nearly everything you say (with a pun on *ass in compound* meaning legal phrases ending in -*as*, like *whereas*)

tent to bear with those that say you are reverend grave
men, yet they lie deadly that tell you you have good   61
faces. If you see this in the map of my microcosm,   62
follows it that I am known well enough too? What   63
harm can your bisson conspectuities glean out of this   64
character, if I be known well enough too?   65

BRUTUS Come, sir, come, we know you well enough.

MENENIUS You know neither me, yourselves, nor anything. You are ambitious for poor knaves' caps and   68
legs. You wear out a good wholesome forenoon in   69
hearing a cause between an orange-wife and a faucet-   70
seller, and then rejourn the controversy of threepence   71
to a second day of audience. When you are hearing a   72
matter between party and party, if you chance to be   73
pinched with the colic, you make faces like mummers,   74
set up the bloody flag against all patience, and, in roar- 75
ing for a chamber pot, dismiss the controversy bleed-   76
ing, the more entangled by your hearing. All the peace   77
you make in their cause is calling both the parties   78
knaves. You are a pair of strange ones.   79

BRUTUS Come, come, you are well understood to be a
perfecter giber for the table than a necessary bencher   81
in the Capitol.   82

MENENIUS Our very priests must become mockers if
they shall encounter such ridiculous subjects as you   84
are. When you speak best unto the purpose, it is not   85

61 deadly excessively. **tell you** say **62 this** i.e., all that I have freely
admitted. **the map of my microcosm** my face, or chart of my little
world (as opposed to the macrocosm or great world) **63 known . . . too**
(Menenius mocks their phrase, l. 46, and its implication that they "see
through" him.) **64 bisson conspectuities** blind faculty of sight
65 character character sketch **68–69 caps and legs** doffing caps and
making obeisances to indicate respect **69 wholesome forenoon** morning that might be put to better use **70 cause** law case. **orange-wife**
woman who sells oranges and other fruit **70–71 faucet-seller** one who
sells taps for drawing liquor from barrels **71 rejourn** adjourn, post-
pone. **of** about **72 audience** hearing **73 party and party** the two
parties in a dispute **74 mummers** masqueraders, performers in dumb
shows **75 set . . . flag** i.e., declare violent war **76–77 bleeding** un-
healed, unsettled **77–79 peace . . . knaves** (Perhaps a reference to the
song "Hold thy peace, thou knave"; see *Twelfth Night,* 2.3.63–70.)
81–82 perfecter . . . Capitol i.e., better at dinner-table jesting than at
sitting in the Senate as a counselor **84 subjects** (1) topics (2) citizens
85 When i.e., even when

worth the wagging of your beards, and your beards
deserve not so honorable a grave as to stuff a botcher's 87
cushion or to be entombed in an ass's packsaddle.
Yet you must be saying Marcius is proud; who, in a 89
cheap estimation, is worth all your predecessors since 90
Deucalion, though peradventure some of the best of 91
'em were hereditary hangmen. Good e'en to your wor- 92
ships. More of your conversation would infect my 93
brain, being the herdsmen of the beastly plebeians. I 94
will be bold to take my leave of you.

                  Brutus and Sicinius [*stand*] *aside.*
      Enter Volumnia, Virgilia, and Valeria.

How now, my as fair as noble ladies—and the moon, 96
were she earthly, no nobler—whither do you follow 97
your eyes so fast?   98

VOLUMNIA   Honorable Menenius, my boy Marcius approaches. For the love of Juno, let's go.

MENENIUS   Ha? Marcius coming home?

VOLUMNIA   Ay, worthy Menenius, and with most pros- 102
perous approbation.   103

MENENIUS   Take my cap, Jupiter, and I thank thee.
[*He tosses his cap.*] Hoo! Marcius coming home?

VALERIA, VIRGILIA   Nay, 'tis true.

VOLUMNIA   Look, here's a letter from him. [*Showing a letter.*] The state hath another, his wife another, and I
think there's one at home for you.

MENENIUS   I will make my very house reel tonight. A
letter for me?

VIRGILIA   Yes, certain, there's a letter for you. I saw 't.

MENENIUS   A letter for me! It gives me an estate of seven 113
years' health, in which time I will make a lip at the 114

---

87 botcher one who patches old clothes or boots   **89–90 in a cheap
estimation** even at the lowest estimation of his worth   **91 Deucalion** the
Noah of classical story, survivor of a great flood.   **peradventure** perhaps   **92 hereditary hangmen** men serving as executioners (a very
ignoble occupation) generation after generation.   **Good e'en** good
evening (used for any time after noon)   **93 conversation** society
94 being you being   **96 the moon** i.e., Diana, goddess of chastity
97–98 whither . . . fast where are you going so eagerly in hopes of some
sight   **102–103 prosperous approbation** success and good reputation
113 estate (1) endowment (2) condition   **114 make a lip** make a contemptuous face, mock

physician. The most sovereign prescription in Galen 115
is but empiricutic and, to this preservative, of no bet- 116
ter report than a horse drench. Is he not wounded? He 117
was wont to come home wounded.   118

VIRGILIA   O, no, no, no.

VOLUMNIA   O, he is wounded, I thank the gods for 't.

MENENIUS   So do I too, if it be not too much. Brings 'a 121
victory in his pocket, the wounds become him.

VOLUMNIA   On 's brows, Menenius. He comes the third 123
time home with the oaken garland.

MENENIUS   Has he disciplined Aufidius soundly?   125

VOLUMNIA   Titus Lartius writes they fought together,
but Aufidius got off.

MENENIUS   And 'twas time for him too, I'll warrant him
that. An he had stayed by him, I would not have been 129
so fidiused for all the chests in Corioles and the gold 130
that's in them. Is the Senate possessed of this?   131

VOLUMNIA   Good ladies, let's go.—Yes, yes, yes; the
Senate has letters from the General, wherein he gives
my son the whole name of the war. He hath in this 134
action outdone his former deeds doubly.

VALERIA   In troth, there's wondrous things spoke of 136
him.

MENENIUS   Wondrous? Ay, I warrant you, and not
without his true purchasing.   139

VIRGILIA   The gods grant them true!

VOLUMNIA   True? Pow waw.   141

MENENIUS   True? I'll be sworn they are true. Where is
he wounded? [*To the tribunes.*] God save your good
worships! Marcius is coming home. He has more
cause to be proud.—Where is he wounded?

115 sovereign efficacious.   **Galen** Greek physician and authority on
medicine (born considerably after the time of Coriolanus)   **116 empiricutic** quacklike.   **to** compared to   **117 report** reputation, standing.
horse drench dose of medicine for horses   **118 wont** accustomed
121 Brings 'a if he brings   **123 On 's brows** i.e., the *victory* is *on his
brows* (in the form of a garland) rather than *in his pocket* as Menenius
suggests. (Said as a pleasantry.)   **125 disciplined** beaten   **129 An** if
130 fidiused (Menenius' coined word meaning "treated as Aufidius
deserves, beaten.")   **131 possessed** informed   **134 name** credit, reputation   **136 troth** truth, faith   **139 his true purchasing** deserving on his
part   **141 Pow waw** i.e., pish

VOLUMNIA   I' the shoulder and i' the left arm. There will
be large cicatrices to show the people when he shall   147
stand for his place. He received in the repulse of Tar-   148
quin seven hurts i' the body.   149

MENENIUS   One i' the neck and two i' the thigh—there's
nine that I know.

VOLUMNIA   He had, before this last expedition, twenty-
five wounds upon him.

MENENIUS   Now it's twenty-seven. Every gash was an
enemy's grave. (*A shout and flourish.*) Hark, the trumpets.

VOLUMNIA   These are the ushers of Marcius. Before him
he carries noise, and behind him he leaves tears.
Death, that dark spirit, in 's nervy arm doth lie,   159
Which, being advanced, declines, and then men die.   160

> *A sennet. Trumpets sound. Enter Cominius the*
> *general, and Titus Lartius; between them,*
> *Coriolanus, crowned with an oaken garland; with*
> *captains and soldiers, and a Herald.*

HERALD
Know, Rome, that all alone Marcius did fight
Within Corioles gates, where he hath won,
With fame, a name to Caius Marcius; these   163
In honor follows "Coriolanus."
Welcome to Rome, renownèd Coriolanus!
                              Sound flourish.

ALL
Welcome to Rome, renownèd Coriolanus!

CORIOLANUS
No more of this. It does offend my heart.
Pray now, no more.

COMINIUS   Look, sir, your mother.

CORIOLANUS   O,

---

147 cicatrices scars   **148 stand for his place** i.e., seek the consulship
148–149 repulse of Tarquin (Plutarch reports that Marcius fought his
first battle against King Tarquin the Proud in 499 B.C. on the occasion
of Tarquin's last attempt to regain the kingdom; see 1.3.13–15 and note,
and 2.2.88 ff.)   **159 in 's** in his.   **nervy** sinewy   **160 advanced** raised.
declines descends   **s.d. A sennet** a trumpet call accompanying an
entrance   **163 With** in addition to.   **to** added to

You have, I know, petitioned all the gods
For my prosperity!   *Kneels.*
VOLUMNIA   Nay, my good soldier, up,   170
  My gentle Marcius, worthy Caius, and
  By deed-achieving honor newly named—   172
  What is it? Coriolanus must I call thee?—
  But, O, thy wife!
CORIOLANUS [*Rising*]   My gracious silence, hail!
  Wouldst thou have laughed had I come coffined home,
  That weep'st to see me triumph? Ah, my dear,
  Such eyes the widows in Corioles wear,
  And mothers that lack sons.
MENENIUS   Now, the gods crown thee!
CORIOLANUS [*To Menenius*]
  And live you yet? [*To Valeria.*] O my sweet lady, pardon.
VOLUMNIA
  I know not where to turn. O, welcome home!
  [*To Cominius.*] And welcome, General! And you're
    welcome all.
MENENIUS
  A hundred thousand welcomes! I could weep
  And I could laugh; I am light and heavy. Welcome.   183
  A curse begin at very root on 's heart   184
  That is not glad to see thee! You are three
  That Rome should dote on; yet, by the faith of men,
  We have some old crab trees here at home that will not   187
  Be grafted to your relish. Yet welcome, warriors!   188
  We call a nettle but a nettle, and   189
  The faults of fools but folly.   190
COMINIUS   Ever right.
CORIOLANUS   Menenius ever, ever.   192
HERALD
  Give way there, and go on!

---

170 prosperity success   **172 deed-achieving** achieved by deeds
183 light and heavy merry and sad   **184 on 's** of his   **187 old crab trees**
old crab apple trees, i.e., sour-natured old men (such as the tribunes)
188 grafted to your relish implanted with a liking for you (something
that would sweeten their sourness)   **189–190 We . . . folly** i.e., some
unpleasant things cannot be changed and must be acknowledged for
what they are   **192 Menenius ever** same old Menenius

CORIOLANUS [*To Volumnia and Virgilia*]
                       Your hand, and yours.
Ere in our own house I do shade my head,   194
The good patricians must be visited,
From whom I have received not only greetings,
But with them change of honors.
VOLUMNIA   I have lived   197
To see inherited my very wishes   198
And the buildings of my fancy. Only   199
There's one thing wanting, which I doubt not but   200
Our Rome will cast upon thee.
CORIOLANUS   Know, good Mother,   201
I had rather be their servant in my way
Than sway with them in theirs.
COMINIUS   On, to the Capitol!   203
      Flourish. Cornets. Exeunt in state, as before.
           Brutus and Sicinius [come forward].
BRUTUS
All tongues speak of him, and the blearèd sights   204
Are spectacled to see him. Your prattling nurse   205
Into a rapture lets her baby cry   206
While she chats him. The kitchen malkin pins   207
Her richest lockram 'bout her reechy neck,   208
Clamb'ring the walls to eye him. Stalls, bulks, windows,   209
Are smothered up, leads filled, and ridges horsed   210
With variable complexions, all agreeing   211
In earnestness to see him. Seld-shown flamens   212
Do press among the popular throngs and puff   213

---

194 shade rest   **197 change of honors** promotion   **198 inherited** realized   **199 fancy** imagination   **200 wanting** lacking   **201 cast upon** offer   **203 sway with** rule over   **204–205 bleared . . . spectacled** people with dimmed vision put on spectacles   **205 Your prattling nurse** the typical chattering nurse, the kind of nurse people talk about, your average nurse   **206 rapture** fit   **207 chats him** i.e., gossips about Coriolanus.   **malkin** untidy servantmaid   **208 lockram** coarse linen fabric.   **reechy** dirty, filthy   **209 Clamb'ring** climbing.   **bulks** structures projecting from the front of a shop   **210 leads** leaded roofs.   **ridges** rooftops.   **horsed** bestridden (as a horse)   **211 variable** various. **complexions** types.   **agreeing** alike   **212 Seld-shown** seldom seen. **flamens** priests (of ancient Rome)   **213 popular** plebeian, vulgar.   **puff** pant, exert themselves

To win a vulgar station. Our veiled dames   214
Commit the war of white and damask in   215
Their nicely-gauded cheeks to the wanton spoil   216
Of Phoebus' burning kisses—such a pother   217
As if that whatsoever god who leads him   218
Were slyly crept into his human powers   219
And gave him graceful posture.
SICINIUS   On the sudden   220
I warrant him consul.
BRUTUS   Then our office may,
During his power, go sleep.   222
SICINIUS
He cannot temperately transport his honors   223
From where he should begin and end, but will   224
Lose those he hath won.
BRUTUS   In that there's comfort.
SICINIUS   ˙ Doubt not
The commoners, for whom we stand, but they   226
Upon their ancient malice will forget   227
With the least cause these his new honors—which   228
That he will give them make I as little question   229
As he is proud to do 't.
BRUTUS   I heard him swear,   230
Were he to stand for consul, never would he
Appear i' the marketplace nor on him put
The napless vesture of humility,   233
Nor showing, as the manner is, his wounds
To the people, beg their stinking breaths.
SICINIUS   'Tis right.   235

---

214 vulgar station place in the crowd   **215 damask** red or pink, like the
damask rose   **216 nicely-gauded** daintily adorned or made up.   **wanton
spoil** (1) ravages (2) amorous despoiling   **217 Phoebus'** i.e., the sun's.
pother hubbub   **218 him** i.e., Coriolanus   **219 human powers** i.e.,
body   **220 On the sudden** suddenly   **222 power** term of authority
223 temperately transport carry in a temperate and self-controlled
way   **224 and end** i.e., to a proper conclusion   **226 for whom we stand**
whom we represent.   **but they** but that they   **227 Upon . . . malice**
because of their long-standing hostility   **228 With . . . cause** upon the
slightest provocation.   **which** i.e., which provocation   **229 make . . .
question** I have as little doubt   **230 As** as that   **233 napless vesture**
threadbare garment   **235 breaths** i.e., voices, votes

BRUTUS
It was his word. O, he would miss it rather   236
Than carry it but by the suit of the gentry to him   237
And the desire of the nobles.
SICINIUS   I wish no better
Than have him hold that purpose and to put it
In execution.
BRUTUS   'Tis most like he will.   240
SICINIUS
It shall be to him then as our good wills,   241
A sure destruction.
BRUTUS   So it must fall out
To him or our authorities, for an end.   243
We must suggest the people in what hatred   244
He still hath held them; that to 's power he would   245
Have made them mules, silenced their pleaders, and   246
Dispropertied their freedoms, holding them   247
In human action and capacity
Of no more soul nor fitness for the world
Than camels in their war, who have their provand   250
Only for bearing burdens, and sore blows
For sinking under them.
SICINIUS   This—as you say, suggested
At some time when his soaring insolence
Shall touch the people, which time shall not want   254
If he be put upon 't, and that's as easy   255
As to set dogs on sheep—will be his fire   256
To kindle their dry stubble; and their blaze   257
Shall darken him forever.

     Enter a Messenger.

BRUTUS   What's the matter?   258

236 miss it i.e., go without the consulship   **237 carry it but** win it
otherwise than   **240 like** likely   **241 as . . . wills** as we would have it
243 authorities offices.   **for an end** ultimately   **244 suggest** insinuate
to   **245 still** always.   **to 's power** to the extent of his power   **246 mules**
i.e., beasts of burden.   **pleaders** i.e., the tribunes   **247 Dispropertied**
alienated, deprived (them) of   **250 provand** provender, food   **254 want**
be lacking   **255 put upon 't** urged, incited to it   **256 his fire** i.e., the
spark that kindles his hatred   **257 To kindle . . . stubble** (Coriolanus'
fiery wrath will in turn kindle the inflammable emotions of the
plebeians.)   **258 darken** eclipse, deprive of authority or renown

MESSENGER
  You are sent for to the Capitol. 'Tis thought
  That Marcius shall be consul. I have seen
  The dumb men throng to see him, and the blind
  To hear him speak. Matrons flung gloves,
  Ladies and maids their scarves and handkerchiefs,
  Upon him as he passed. The nobles bended
  As to Jove's statue, and the commons made
  A shower and thunder with their caps and shouts.
  I never saw the like.
BRUTUS   Let's to the Capitol,
  And carry with us ears and eyes for the time,   268
  But hearts for the event.
SICINIUS   Have with you.   *Exeunt.* 269

❖

2.2 *Enter two Officers, to lay cushions, as it were
in the Capitol.*

FIRST OFFICER Come, come, they are almost here. How
  many stand for consulships?
SECOND OFFICER Three, they say; but 'tis thought of 3
  everyone Coriolanus will carry it.
FIRST OFFICER That's a brave fellow, but he's vengeance 5
  proud and loves not the common people.
SECOND OFFICER Faith, there hath been many great men
  that have flattered the people who ne'er loved them; 8
  and there be many that they have loved, they know
  not wherefore; so that, if they love they know not 10
  why, they hate upon no better a ground. Therefore,
  for Coriolanus neither to care whether they love or
  hate him manifests the true knowledge he has in their 13

---

268 time present situation **269 hearts . . . event** i.e., deeper desires and
purposes for what is to follow. **Have with you** I'm with you, let's go

2.2. Location: Rome. The Capitol.
3 of by **5 vengeance** terribly **8 who** i.e., the people **10 wherefore**
why **13 in** of

disposition, and out of his noble carelessness lets them   14
plainly see 't.

FIRST OFFICER   If he did not care whether he had their
love or no, he waved indifferently twixt doing them   17
neither good nor harm; but he seeks their hate with
greater devotion than they can render it him, and
leaves nothing undone that may fully discover him   20
their opposite. Now, to seem to affect the malice and   21
displeasure of the people is as bad as that which he
dislikes, to flatter them for their love.

SECOND OFFICER   He hath deserved worthily of his coun-   24
try, and his ascent is not by such easy degrees as those   25
who, having been supple and courteous to the people,
bonneted, without any further deed to have them at   27
all into their estimation and report. But he hath so   28
planted his honors in their eyes and his actions in
their hearts that for their tongues to be silent and not
confess so much were a kind of ingrateful injury. To
report otherwise were a malice that, giving itself the   32
lie, would pluck reproof and rebuke from every ear   33
that heard it.

FIRST OFFICER   No more of him; he's a worthy man.
Make way, they are coming.   36

> *A sennet. Enter the Patricians and the tribunes of*
> *the people, lictors before them; Coriolanus,*
> *Menenius, Cominius the consul. Sicinius and*
> *Brutus take their places by themselves.*
> *Coriolanus stands.*

MENENIUS
Having determined of the Volsces and   37
To send for Titus Lartius, it remains,

---

14 noble carelessness patrician indifference to public opinion
17 waved indifferently would waver impartially   **20–21 discover . . .
opposite** reveal him to be their adversary   **21 affect** seek out, desire
24 deserved worthily of justifiably merited much from   **25 degrees**
steps   **27 bonneted** took their hats off.   **have them** gain their way
28 estimation and report esteem and good opinion   **32–33 giving . . . lie**
manifesting its own falsehood   **36 s.d. lictors** officials attendant upon
Roman magistrates   **37 determined of** i.e., reached a decision concerning (the terms for returning Corioles, etc.)

As the main point of this our after-meeting,   39
To gratify his noble service that   40
Hath thus stood for his country. Therefore please you,   41
Most reverend and grave elders, to desire
The present consul and last general   43
In our well-found successes to report   44
A little of that worthy work performed
By Caius Marcius Coriolanus, whom
We met here both to thank and to remember
With honors like himself.   [*Coriolanus sits.*]

FIRST SENATOR   Speak, good Cominius.   48
Leave nothing out for length, and make us think
Rather our state's defective for requital   50
Than we to stretch it out. [*To the tribunes.*] Masters o' the
    people,   51
We do request your kindest ears and, after,   52
Your loving motion toward the common body   53
To yield what passes here.

SICINIUS   We are convented   54
Upon a pleasing treaty, and have hearts   55
Inclinable to honor and advance
The theme of our assembly.

BRUTUS   Which the rather   57
We shall be blest to do, if he remember   58
A kinder value of the people than   59
He hath hereto prized them at.

MENENIUS   That's off, that's off!   60
I would you rather had been silent. Please you
To hear Cominius speak?

BRUTUS   Most willingly;
But yet my caution was more pertinent   63
Than the rebuke you give it.

---

39 after-meeting follow-up meeting   **40 gratify** reward, requite
41 stood for fought for, defended   **43 last** late, recent   **44 well-found**
fortunately met with   **48 like himself** i.e., worthy of his greatness
50–51 Rather . . . out that our state lacks means to reward adequately
rather than that we are defective in intention to extend what reward we
have at our disposal   **52 after** in addition to that   **53 loving . . . body**
friendly intervention with the common people   **54 yield** assent to,
grant.   **passes** is voted.   **convented** summoned, convened   **55 Upon**
in order to consider.   **treaty** proposal   **57 theme** business.   **rather**
sooner   **58 blest** happy   **59 kinder value** more favorable estimation
60 off jarring, not pertinent   **63 pertinent** appropriate

MENENIUS   He loves your people;
But tie him not to be their bedfellow.—   65
Worthy Cominius, speak.

Coriolanus rises and offers to go away.
       Nay, keep your place.   66

FIRST SENATOR
Sit, Coriolanus. Never shame to hear
What you have nobly done.

CORIOLANUS   Your honors' pardon.
I had rather have my wounds to heal again
Than hear say how I got them.

BRUTUS   Sir, I hope
My words disbenched you not?

CORIOLANUS   No, sir. Yet oft,   71
When blows have made me stay, I fled from words.
You soothed not, therefore hurt not. But your people,   73
I love them as they weigh.—

MENENIUS   Pray now, sit down.   74

CORIOLANUS
I had rather have one scratch my head i' the sun   75
When the alarum were struck than idly sit   76
To hear my nothings monstered.   *Exit Coriolanus.*

MENENIUS   Masters of the people,   77
Your multiplying spawn how can he flatter—   78
That's thousand to one good one—when you now see   79
He had rather venture all his limbs for honor   80
Than one on 's ears to hear it?—Proceed, Cominius.   81

COMINIUS
I shall lack voice. The deeds of Coriolanus
Should not be uttered feebly. It is held
That valor is the chiefest virtue and
Most dignifies the haver; if it be,
The man I speak of cannot in the world

---

65 tie oblige   **66 s.d. offers** starts   **71 disbenched you not** did not make
you leave your seat   **73 soothed** flattered   **74 as they weigh** according
to their deserts   **75–76 have . . . struck** i.e., engage in idle pleasure
when the battle signal is sounded.   **alarum** call to arms   **77 monstered**
pointed out as wonderful   **78 multiplying spawn** fast-breeding commoners   **79 That's . . . one** in which there are a thousand bad ones to one
good one; or, a thousand bad ones contrasted to the noble Coriolanus
80 venture risk   **81 on 's** of his.   **it** i.e., praise of his honor

Be singly counterpoised. At sixteen years,   87
When Tarquin made a head for Rome, he fought   88
Beyond the mark of others. Our then dictator,   89
Whom with all praise I point at, saw him fight,   90
When with his Amazonian chin he drove   91
The bristled lips before him. He bestrid   92
An o'erpressed Roman, and i' the Consul's view   93
Slew three opposers. Tarquin's self he met,
And struck him on his knee. In that day's feats,   95
When he might act the woman in the scene,   96
He proved best man i' the field, and for his meed   97
Was brow-bound with the oak. His pupil age   98
Man-entered thus, he waxèd like a sea,   99
And in the brunt of seventeen battles since   100
He lurched all swords of the garland. For this last,   101
Before and in Corioles, let me say,
I cannot speak him home. He stopped the fliers,   103
And by his rare example made the coward
Turn terror into sport. As weeds before
A vessel under sail, so men obeyed
And fell below his stem. His sword, death's stamp,   107
Where it did mark, it took; from face to foot   108
He was a thing of blood, whose every motion
Was timed with dying cries. Alone he entered   110
The mortal gate o' the city, which he painted   111

---

87 singly counterpoised equaled by any other individual   **88 made . . . for** raised a force to attack (and reconquer)   **89 mark** ability, reach. **dictator** leader constitutionally given absolute authority to deal with a specific emergency such as a war   **90 point at** i.e., refer to. (The unnamed dictator of those earlier times, probably Aulus Posthumus Regillensis, is not present.)   **91 Amazonian** i.e., beardless (like the female warriors, the Amazons)   **92 bristled lips** i.e., bearded warriors. **bestrid** stood over in battle, protected   **93 o'erpressed** overwhelmed **95 on** to   **96 he . . . scene** i.e., he was young enough not to have been blamed for cowardice (with an allusion to boys playing women's roles in the theater)   **97 meed** reward   **98 brow-bound** i.e., presented with a garland as an emblem of victory   **99 Man-entered** initiated into manhood   **100 brunt** violence, shock   **101 lurched** robbed, cheated.   **For** as for   **103 speak him home** praise him adequately.   **the fliers** those who tried to flee the battle   **107 stem** main timber of the prow of a ship. **stamp** tool for imprinting a design or pattern   **108 took** took possession, slew   **110 Was timed** kept time, was accompanied   **111 mortal** deadly.   **which** (Refers to the *city*.)   **painted** i.e., stained

With shunless destiny; aidless came off,   112
And with a sudden reinforcement struck   113
Corioles like a planet. Now all's his,   114
When by and by the din of war 'gan pierce   115
His ready sense; then straight his doubled spirit   116
Requickened what in flesh was fatigate,   117
And to the battle came he, where he did
Run reeking o'er the lives of men as if   119
'Twere a perpetual spoil; and till we called   120
Both field and city ours, he never stood   121
To ease his breast with panting.

MENENIUS   Worthy man!

FIRST SENATOR
He cannot but with measure fit the honors   123
Which we devise him.

COMINIUS   Our spoils he kicked at,   124
And looked upon things precious as they were
The common muck of the world. He covets less
Than misery itself would give, rewards   127
His deeds with doing them, and is content   128
To spend the time to end it.

MENENIUS   He's right noble.   129
Let him be called for.

FIRST SENATOR   Call Coriolanus.

OFFICER   He doth appear.

    Enter Coriolanus.

MENENIUS
The Senate, Coriolanus, are well pleased
To make thee consul.

---

112 shunless destiny i.e., the blood of those who could not escape their
doom   **113 reinforcement** fresh assault   **114 like a planet** (Refers to the
power of striking or blasting, believed in astrology to belong to the
planets.)   **114–115 Now . . . When** no sooner was everything his than
115 'gan began to   **116 ready sense** i.e., alert sense of hearing.   **straight**
at once.   **doubled** renewed, twice what it was before   **117 Requickened**
revivified.   **fatigate** fatigued   **119 reeking** steaming (with enemies'
blood)   **120 perpetual spoil** endless slaughter   **121 stood** stopped
123 He . . . fit he can't help but measure up to   **124 devise** devise for.
kicked at spurned   **127 misery** poverty   **127–128 rewards . . . doing
them** finds reward for his actions in the satisfaction that comes from
having acted well   **128–129 is content . . . end it** is satisfied to be repaid
for his time spent with the pleasure of having spent his time thus

CORIOLANUS   I do owe them still   134
  My life and services.
MENENIUS   It then remains
  That you do speak to the people.
CORIOLANUS   I do beseech you,
  Let me o'erleap that custom, for I cannot
  Put on the gown, stand naked, and entreat them   138
  For my wounds' sake to give their suffrage. Please you
  That I may pass this doing.
SICINIUS   Sir, the people   140
  Must have their voices; neither will they bate   141
  One jot of ceremony.
MENENIUS   Put them not to 't.   142
  Pray you, go fit you to the custom and
  Take to you, as your predecessors have,
  Your honor with your form.
CORIOLANUS   It is a part   145
  That I shall blush in acting, and might well
  Be taken from the people.
BRUTUS [*To Sicinius*]   Mark you that?
CORIOLANUS
  To brag unto them, "Thus I did, and thus!"
  Show them th' unaching scars which I should hide,
  As if I had received them for the hire   150
  Of their breath only!
MENENIUS   Do not stand upon 't.—   151
  We recommend to you, tribunes of the people,   152
  Our purpose to them, and to our noble consul   153
  Wish we all joy and honor.
SENATORS
  To Coriolanus come all joy and honor!   155
    Flourish cornets. Then exeunt. Manent Sicinius
                             and Brutus.

BRUTUS
  You see how he intends to use the people.

---

134 still ever   **138 naked** exposed   **140 pass** disregard, omit
141 voices votes.   **bate** abate, do without   **142 Put . . . to 't** i.e., do not
force the issue   **145 with your form** i.e., with the accompanying formal-
ities   **150 hire** wages   **151 breath** i.e., votes.   **stand upon 't** make a
point of it   **152 recommend** commit, consign   **153 purpose** proposal
155 s.d. Manent they remain onstage

SICINIUS

May they perceive 's intent! He will require them 157
As if he did contemn what he requested 158
Should be in them to give.

BRUTUS   Come, we'll inform them 159
Of our proceedings here. On the marketplace 160
I know they do attend us.   [*Exeunt.*] 161

❖

2.3   *Enter seven or eight Citizens.*

FIRST CITIZEN   Once, if he do require our voices, we 1
ought not to deny him.

SECOND CITIZEN   We may, sir, if we will.

THIRD CITIZEN   We have power in ourselves to do it, but
it is a power that we have no power to do; for if he 5
show us his wounds and tell us his deeds, we are to
put our tongues into those wounds and speak for 7
them; so, if he tell us his noble deeds, we must also
tell him our noble acceptance of them. Ingratitude is
monstrous, and for the multitude to be ingrateful were
to make a monster of the multitude; of the which we,
being members, should bring ourselves to be monstrous members.

FIRST CITIZEN   And to make us no better thought of, a 14
little help will serve; for once we stood up about the 15
corn, he himself stuck not to call us the many-headed 16
multitude.

THIRD CITIZEN   We have been called so of many; not that 18
our heads are some brown, some black, some abram, 19
some bald, but that our wits are so diversely colored;
and truly I think if all our wits were to issue out of one
skull, they would fly east, west, north, south, and their

---

157 require ask, solicit   **158 contemn** scorn (that)   **159 in them** theirs
160 On in   **161 attend** wait for

2.3. Location: Rome. The Forum, or marketplace.
1 Once once and for all   **5 no power to do** i.e., no moral right to exercise   **7 put . . . wounds** i.e., let the wounds inspire our tongues
14–15 a little . . . serve a small amount of effort on our part will suffice   **15 once** when   **16 stuck not** did not hesitate   **18 of** by.   **that**
because   **19 abram** auburn

consent of one direct way should be at once to all the 23
points o' the compass.

SECOND CITIZEN Think you so? Which way do you
judge my wit would fly?

THIRD CITIZEN Nay, your wit will not so soon out as 27
another man's will; 'tis strongly wedged up in a blockhead. But if it were at liberty, 'twould, sure, south- 29
ward. 30

SECOND CITIZEN Why that way?

THIRD CITIZEN To lose itself in a fog, where being three
parts melted away with rotten dews, the fourth would 33
return for conscience' sake, to help to get thee a wife.

SECOND CITIZEN You are never without your tricks. You 35
may, you may. 36

THIRD CITIZEN Are you all resolved to give your voices?
But that's no matter, the greater part carries it. I say, if 38
he would incline to the people, there was never a wor- 39
thier man.

> *Enter Coriolanus in a gown of humility, with*
> *Menenius.*

Here he comes, and in the gown of humility. Mark his
behavior. We are not to stay all together, but to come
by him where he stands, by ones, by twos, and by
threes. He's to make his requests by particulars, 44
wherein every one of us has a single honor, in giving him 45
our own voices with our own tongues. Therefore follow me, and I'll direct you how you shall go by him. 47

ALL Content, content.   [*Exeunt Citizens.*]

MENENIUS
O sir, you are not right. Have you not known
The worthiest men have done 't?

CORIOLANUS   What must I say?
"I pray, sir"—Plague upon 't! I cannot bring
My tongue to such a pace. "Look, sir, my wounds!

---

23 consent of agreement upon   **27 out** go out   **29–30 southward** (The
south wind was believed to bring pestilence.)   **33 rotten** unwholesome   **35–36 You may** i.e., go on, say what you like   **38 greater part**
majority   **39 incline to** sympathize with   **44 by particulars** to individ-
uals, one by one   **45 single** separate, individual   **47 go by** appear before

I got them in my country's service, when
Some certain of your brethren roared and ran
From the noise of our own drums."

MENENIUS   O me, the gods!
You must not speak of that. You must desire them
To think upon you.

CORIOLANUS   Think upon me? Hang 'em!   57
I would they would forget me, like the virtues   58
Which our divines lose by 'em.

MENENIUS   You'll mar all.   59
I'll leave you. Pray you speak to 'em, I pray you,
In wholesome manner.   *Exit.*

    Enter three of the Citizens.

CORIOLANUS   Bid them wash their faces   61
And keep their teeth clean. So, here comes a brace.—   62
You know the cause, sir, of my standing here.

THIRD CITIZEN
We do, sir. Tell us what hath brought you to 't.

CORIOLANUS   Mine own desert.

SECOND CITIZEN   Your own desert?

CORIOLANUS   Ay, but not mine own desire.

THIRD CITIZEN   How, not your own desire?

CORIOLANUS   No, sir, 'twas never my desire yet to trouble the poor with begging.

THIRD CITIZEN   You must think, if we give you anything, we hope to gain by you.

CORIOLANUS   Well then, I pray, your price o' the consul- 73
ship?

FIRST CITIZEN   The price is to ask it kindly.

CORIOLANUS   Kindly, sir, I pray, let me ha 't. I have
wounds to show you, which shall be yours in private.— 77
Your good voice, sir. What say you?

SECOND CITIZEN   You shall ha 't, worthy sir.

CORIOLANUS   A match, sir. There's in all two worthy 80
voices begged. I have your alms. Adieu.

---

57 think upon think kindly of   **58 I would** I wish   **59 divines** priests.
lose by 'em vainly seek to instill in them (by preaching)   **61 wholesome**
calculated to do good. (But Coriolanus answers sarcastically to the
sense of "healthful.")   **62 brace** pair. (Used contemptuously here.)
73 o' the for the   **77 yours** available for your inspection   **80 match**
deal, bargain

THIRD CITIZEN   But this is something odd.   82
SECOND CITIZEN   An 'twere to give again—but 'tis no   83
matter.   *Exeunt [the three Citizens].*

Enter two other Citizens.

CORIOLANUS   Pray you now, if it may stand with the   85
tune of your voices that I may be consul, I have here
the customary gown.
FOURTH CITIZEN   You have deserved nobly of your country, and you have not deserved nobly.
CORIOLANUS   Your enigma?   90
FOURTH CITIZEN   You have been a scourge to her ene-   91
mies; you have been a rod to her friends. You have not   92
indeed loved the common people.
CORIOLANUS   You should account me the more virtuous
that I have not been common in my love. I will, sir,   95
flatter my sworn brother, the people, to earn a dearer   96
estimation of them; 'tis a condition they account gen-   97
tle. And since the wisdom of their choice is rather to   98
have my hat than my heart, I will practice the insin-   99
uating nod and be off to them most counterfeitly. That   100
is, sir, I will counterfeit the bewitchment of some pop-   101
ular man and give it bountiful to the desirers. There-   102
fore, beseech you I may be consul.
FIFTH CITIZEN   We hope to find you our friend, and
therefore give you our voices heartily.
FOURTH CITIZEN   You have received many wounds for
your country.
CORIOLANUS   I will not seal your knowledge with show-   108
ing them. I will make much of your voices and so
trouble you no farther.

82 something somewhat   **83 An 'twere** if it were   **85 stand with** be
consistent with   **90 enigma** riddle   **91 scourge** instrument of punishment   **92 rod** stick or whip used to inflict punishment   **95 common**
vulgar, promiscuous (playing on *common* in l. 93)   **96 sworn brother**
one of two friends bound by oath to each other   **96–97 dearer . . .
them** higher esteem on their part   **97 condition** quality   **97–98 gentle**
aristocratic   **99 my hat** i.e., my hat in my hand as a gesture of
courtesy   **99–100 insinuating** ingratiating   **100 be off** doff my hat.
counterfeitly hypocritically   **101 bewitchment** sorcery, bewitching
powers   **101–102 popular man** demagogue   **102 bountiful** bountifully
108 seal confirm

BOTH CITIZENS The gods give you joy, sir, heartily!
[*Exeunt Citizens.*]

CORIOLANUS Most sweet voices!
Better it is to die, better to starve,
Than crave the hire which first we do deserve. 114
Why in this woolvish toge should I stand here 115
To beg of Hob and Dick, that does appear, 116
Their needless vouches? Custom calls me to 't. 117
What custom wills, in all things should we do 't, 118
The dust on antique time would lie unswept 119
And mountainous error be too highly heaped
For truth to o'erpeer. Rather than fool it so, 121
Let the high office and the honor go
To one that would do thus. I am half through;
The one part suffered, the other will I do.

Enter three Citizens more.

Here come more voices.— 125
Your voices! For your voices I have fought;
Watched for your voices; for your voices bear 127
Of wounds two dozen odd. Battles thrice six
I have seen and heard of; for your voices have 129
Done many things, some less, some more. Your voices!
Indeed, I would be consul.

SIXTH CITIZEN He has done nobly, and cannot go without any honest man's voice.

SEVENTH CITIZEN Therefore let him be consul. The gods give him joy, and make him good friend to the people!

ALL Amen, amen. God save thee, noble Consul!
[*Exeunt Citizens.*]

CORIOLANUS Worthy voices!

Enter Menenius, with Brutus and Sicinius.

114 **crave . . . deserve** beg the reward or wages we have already earned 115 **woolvish toge** wolf's toga (like a wolf in sheep's clothing ?), or woolen toga (?) 116 **Hob and Dick** (Typical names for rustics.) **that does appear** as they come forward 117 **needless vouches** unnecessary confirmations of approval 118 **in . . . do 't** if we should obey custom indiscriminately 119 **antique** ancient 121 **o'erpeer** overtop, be visible over or be able to see over. **fool it** play the fool 125 **voices** votes 127 **Watched** kept watch (in camp) 129 **heard of** heard, i.e., been present at

MENENIUS

You have stood your limitation, and the tribunes   139
Endue you with the people's voice. Remains   140
That, in th' official marks invested, you   141
Anon do meet the Senate.

CORIOLANUS   Is this done?   142

SICINIUS

The custom of request you have discharged.   143
The people do admit you, and are summoned
To meet anon, upon your approbation.   145

CORIOLANUS

Where? At the Senate House?

SICINIUS   There, Coriolanus.

CORIOLANUS

May I change these garments?

SICINIUS   You may, sir.

CORIOLANUS

That I'll straight do and, knowing myself again,
Repair to the Senate House.   149

MENENIUS

I'll keep you company.—Will you along?

BRUTUS

We stay here for the people.

SICINIUS   Fare you well.

                    Exeunt Coriolanus and Menenius.

He has it now, and by his looks methinks
'Tis warm at 's heart.

BRUTUS   With a proud heart he wore
His humble weeds. Will you dismiss the people?

    Enter the Plebeians.

SICINIUS

How now, my masters, have you chose this man?

FIRST CITIZEN   He has our voices, sir.

BRUTUS

We pray the gods he may deserve your loves.

---

139 limitation allotted time   **140 Endue** endow.   **Remains** it remains
141 official marks insignia of office.   **invested** dressed   **142 Anon**
immediately   **143 custom of request** i.e., custom of asking the people's
voices.   **discharged** performed   **145 upon your approbation** to confirm
your having been elected   **149 Repair** go

SECOND CITIZEN

   Amen, sir. To my poor unworthy notice,   158
He mocked us when he begged our voices.

THIRD CITIZEN

   Certainly he flouted us downright.

FIRST CITIZEN

   No, 'tis his kind of speech. He did not mock us.

SECOND CITIZEN

   Not one amongst us, save yourself, but says
He used us scornfully. He should have showed us
His marks of merit, wounds received for 's country.

SICINIUS   Why, so he did, I am sure.

ALL   No, no. No man saw 'em.

THIRD CITIZEN

   He said he had wounds, which he could show in private,
And with his hat, thus waving it in scorn,
"I would be consul," says he. "Agèd custom,
But by your voices, will not so permit me;
Your voices therefore." When we granted that,
Here was "I thank you for your voices. Thank you.
Your most sweet voices! Now you have left your voices,
I have no further with you." Was not this mockery?   174

SICINIUS

   Why either were you ignorant to see 't,   175
Or, seeing it, of such childish friendliness
To yield your voices?

BRUTUS   Could you not have told him
As you were lessoned? When he had no power,   178
But was a petty servant to the state,
He was your enemy, ever spake against   180
Your liberties and the charters that you bear   181
I' the body of the weal; and now, arriving   182
A place of potency and sway o' the state,
If he should still malignantly remain
Fast foe to the plebii, your voices might   185
Be curses to yourselves. You should have said
That as his worthy deeds did claim no less

---

158 notice observation   **174 further with** further use for   **175 ignorant**
too dull   **178 lessoned** instructed   **180 ever** always   **181 charters**
privileges   **182 body of the weal** commonwealth.   **arriving** attaining
185 plebii plebeians

Than what he stood for, so his gracious nature   188
Would think upon you for your voices and   189
Translate his malice towards you into love,   190
Standing your friendly lord.

SICINIUS   Thus to have said,   191
As you were fore-advised, had touched his spirit   192
And tried his inclination; from him plucked
Either his gracious promise, which you might,
As cause had called you up, have held him to;   195
Or else it would have galled his surly nature,   196
Which easily endures not article   197
Tying him to aught. So putting him to rage,
You should have ta'en th' advantage of his choler   199
And passed him unelected.

BRUTUS   Did you perceive
He did solicit you in free contempt   201
When he did need your loves, and do you think
That his contempt shall not be bruising to you
When he hath power to crush? Why, had your bodies
No heart among you? Or had you tongues to cry   205
Against the rectorship of judgment?

SICINIUS   Have you   206
Ere now denied the asker? And now   207
Again, of him that did not ask but mock,   208
Bestow your sued-for tongues?

THIRD CITIZEN   He's not confirmed.
We may deny him yet.

SECOND CITIZEN   And will deny him.
I'll have five hundred voices of that sound.

FIRST CITIZEN
I twice five hundred, and their friends to piece 'em.   212

---

188 what . . . for the office he was seeking   **189 Would think upon**
should esteem   **190 Translate** transform   **191 Standing . . . lord** i.e.,
acting on your behalf   **192 had touched** would have tested (as gold and
silver were tested with the touchstone)   **195 cause** occasion.   **called
you up** aroused you (during his consulship)   **196 galled** irritated,
rubbed sore   **197 article** stipulated condition   **199 choler** anger
201 free frank   **205 heart** i.e., as a seat of courage and wisdom.   **to cry**
only to rebel   **206 rectorship** guidance.   **judgment** common sense
206–207 Have . . . asker haven't you on previous occasions denied one
asking for your support   **208 of** upon   **212 piece** add to, reinforce

BRUTUS

Get you hence instantly, and tell those friends
They have chose a consul that will from them take
Their liberties, make them of no more voice
Than dogs that are as often beat for barking
As therefor kept to do so.

SICINIUS   Let them assemble,   217
And on a safer judgment all revoke   218
Your ignorant election. Enforce his pride   219
And his old hate unto you. Besides, forget not   220
With what contempt he wore the humble weed,   221
How in his suit he scorned you; but your loves,
Thinking upon his services, took from you
Th' apprehension of his present portance,   224
Which most gibingly, ungravely, he did fashion   225
After the inveterate hate he bears you.

BRUTUS   Lay   226
A fault on us, your tribunes, that we labored,   227
No impediment between, but that you must   228
Cast your election on him.

SICINIUS   Say you chose him
More after our commandment than as guided
By your own true affections, and that your minds,
Preoccupied with what you rather must do
Than what you should, made you against the grain   233
To voice him consul. Lay the fault on us.

BRUTUS

Ay, spare us not. Say we read lectures to you,
How youngly he began to serve his country,   236
How long continued, and what stock he springs of,
The noble house o' the Marcians, from whence came
That Ancus Marcius, Numa's daughter's son,   239
Who after great Hostilius here was king;

---

217 therefor for that purpose **218 safer** sounder **219 Enforce** lay
stress upon **220 forget not** don't forget to mention **221 weed** garment **224 apprehension** perceiving, comprehending. **portance** behavior **225 gibingly** jeeringly. **ungravely** not seriously **226 After** in
accord with **227 A fault** the blame **228 No impediment between**
without allowing any impediment **233 against the grain** i.e., against
your natural inclination **236 youngly** early (in his life) **239 Numa**
legendary successor of Romulus as King of Rome

Of the same house Publius and Quintus were,
That our best water brought by conduits hither;   242
.   .   .   .   243
And nobly namèd so, twice being censor,   244
Was his great ancestor.
SICINIUS   One thus descended,
That hath besides well in his person wrought   246
To be set high in place, we did commend
To your remembrances; but you have found,
Scaling his present bearing with his past,   249
That he's your fixèd enemy, and revoke
Your sudden approbation.
BRUTUS   Say you ne'er had done 't—   251
Harp on that still—but by our putting on.   252
And presently, when you have drawn your number,   253
Repair to the Capitol.
ALL   We will so. Almost all   254
Repent in their election.   *Exeunt Plebeians.*
BRUTUS   Let them go on.   255
This mutiny were better put in hazard   256
Than stay, past doubt, for greater.   257
If, as his nature is, he fall in rage
With their refusal, both observe and answer   259
The vantage of his anger.
SICINIUS   To the Capitol, come.   260
We will be there before the stream o' the people;
And this shall seem, as partly 'tis, their own,
Which we have goaded onward.   *Exeunt.*

❖

242 **conduits** aqueducts   243 (A line is evidently missing here. From
Plutarch, editors guess that the line may have read something like "And
Censorinus, that was so surnamed.")   244 **censor** Roman magistrate
charged also with the supervision of the census   246 **That . . . wrought**
who in addition has well deserved by his own actions   249 **Scaling**
estimating, weighing   251 **sudden** hasty   252 **putting on** urging
253 **presently** immediately.   **drawn** assembled, collected   254 **Repair**
go, proceed   255 **in** of   256 **put in hazard** risked   257 **Than . . . greater**
than wait for the chance of a greater uprising in which the outcome
would be more certain   259–260 **answer The vantage** make use

3.1 *Cornets. Enter Coriolanus, Menenius, all the gentry, Cominius, Titus Lartius, and other Senators.*

CORIOLANUS
Tullus Aufidius then had made new head?   1
LARTIUS
He had, my lord; and that it was which caused
Our swifter composition.   3
CORIOLANUS
So then the Volsces stand but as at first,
Ready, when time shall prompt them, to make road   5
Upon 's again.
COMINIUS   They are worn, Lord Consul, so,   6
That we shall hardly in our ages see   7
Their banners wave again.
CORIOLANUS   Saw you Aufidius?
LARTIUS
On safeguard he came to me, and did curse   9
Against the Volsces for they had so vilely   10
Yielded the town. He is retired to Antium.   11
CORIOLANUS
Spoke he of me?
LARTIUS   He did, my lord.
CORIOLANUS   How? What?
LARTIUS
How often he had met you, sword to sword;
That of all things upon the earth he hated
Your person most; that he would pawn his fortunes
To hopeless restitution, so he might   16
Be called your vanquisher.
CORIOLANUS   At Antium lives he?
LARTIUS   At Antium.

3.1. Location: Rome. A street. The procession is on its way to the marketplace; see l. 33.
1 made new head raised another army   **3 composition** coming to terms (about the return of Corioles to the Volscians)   **5 road** inroad, attack
6 worn i.e., militarily weakened   **7 ages** lifetimes   **9 On safeguard** under safe-conduct   **10 for** because   **11 is retired** has returned   **16 To . . . restitution** beyond hope of recovery.   **so** provided that

CORIOLANUS
    I wish I had a cause to seek him there,
    To oppose his hatred fully. Welcome home.

    Enter Sicinius and Brutus.

    Behold, these are the tribunes of the people,
    The tongues o' the common mouth. I do despise them,
    For they do prank them in authority   24
    Against all noble sufferance.   25
SICINIUS [*Advancing*]   Pass no further.
CORIOLANUS   Ha? What is that?
BRUTUS
    It will be dangerous to go on. No further.
CORIOLANUS   What makes this change?
MENENIUS   The matter?
COMINIUS
    Hath he not passed the noble and the common?   31
BRUTUS
    Cominius, no.
CORIOLANUS   Have I had children's voices?
FIRST SENATOR
    Tribunes, give way. He shall to the marketplace.
BRUTUS
    The people are incensed against him.
SICINIUS   Stop,
    Or all will fall in broil.
CORIOLANUS   Are these your herd?   35
    Must these have voices, that can yield them now   36
    And straight disclaim their tongues? What are your
        offices?   37
    You being their mouths, why rule you not their teeth?
    Have you not set them on?
MENENIUS   Be calm, be calm.
CORIOLANUS
    It is a purposed thing, and grows by plot,   40

---

24 prank them dress themselves up   **25 Against . . . sufferance** beyond
the power of nobility to tolerate   **31 passed . . . common** been approved
by the nobility and the common people   **35 broil** tumult   **36 yield**
grant, bestow.   **now** one instant   **37 straight** immediately afterward.
offices duties   **40 purposed** prearranged

To curb the will of the nobility.
Suffer 't, and live with such as cannot rule   42
Nor ever will be ruled.

BRUTUS   Call 't not a plot.
The people cry you mocked them; and of late,   44
When corn was given them gratis, you repined,   45
Scandaled the suppliants for the people, called them   46
Timepleasers, flatterers, foes to nobleness.

CORIOLANUS
Why, this was known before.

BRUTUS   Not to them all.

CORIOLANUS
Have you informed them sithence?

BRUTUS   How? I inform them?   49

COMINIUS
You are like to do such business.   50

BRUTUS
Not unlike, each way, to better yours.   51

CORIOLANUS
Why then should I be consul? By yond clouds,
Let me deserve so ill as you, and make me
Your fellow tribune.

SICINIUS   You show too much of that   54
For which the people stir. If you will pass   55
To where you are bound, you must inquire your way,   56
Which you are out of, with a gentler spirit,   57
Or never be so noble as a consul,
Nor yoke with him for tribune.

MENENIUS   Let's be calm.   59

COMINIUS
The people are abused, set on. This paltering   60
Becomes not Rome, nor has Coriolanus   61

---

42 live i.e., you will have to live   **44 of late** lately   **45 repined** expressed
regret   **46 Scandaled** defamed   **49 sithence** since   **50 like** likely
51 Not . . . yours not unlikely to prove, in any case, a better way than
yours   **54 that** i.e., that quality   **55 stir** are aroused, angry   **55–56 If
. . . bound** i.e., if you wish to attain the consulship   **57 are out of** have
strayed from   **59 yoke** be joined. (Sicinius insults Coriolanus by treating
his sarcastic offer to be a tribune, ll. 52–54, as though it were serious.)   **60 abused** deceived.   **set on** incited.   **paltering** equivocation,
ruse   **61 Becomes not** is not appropriate or suitably dignified for

Deserved this so dishonored rub, laid falsely   62
I' the plain way of his merit.
CORIOLANUS   Tell me of corn!   63
This was my speech, and I will speak 't again.
MENENIUS   Not now, not now.
FIRST SENATOR   Not in this heat, sir, now.
CORIOLANUS   Now, as I live, I will.
My nobler friends, I crave their pardons. For   68
The mutable, rank-scented meiny, let them   69
Regard me as I do not flatter, and   70
Therein behold themselves. I say again,   71
In soothing them, we nourish 'gainst our Senate
The cockle of rebellion, insolence, sedition,   73
Which we ourselves have plowed for, sowed, and
    scattered
By mingling them with us, the honored number,   75
Who lack not virtue, no, nor power, but that
Which they have given to beggars.
MENENIUS   Well, no more.
FIRST SENATOR
No more words, we beseech you.
CORIOLANUS   How? No more?
As for my country I have shed my blood,
Not fearing outward force, so shall my lungs
Coin words till their decay against those measles   81
Which we disdain should tetter us, yet sought   82
The very way to catch them.
BRUTUS   You speak o' the people   83
As if you were a god to punish, not
A man of their infirmity.
SICINIUS   'Twere well   85
We let the people know 't.
MENENIUS   What, what? His choler?

---

62 dishonored dishonoring.   **rub** obstacle (as in the game of bowls).
laid falsely treacherously placed   **63 plain way** clear path (as in
bowls)   **68–71 For . . . themselves** as for the changeable, foul-smelling
multitude, let them see themselves in the unflattering truth I show to
them   **73 cockle** weed   **75 honored** honorable   **81 till their decay** i.e.,
until my lungs are no more.   **measles** loathsome disease spots
82 tetter infect with tetter (skin eruption).   **sought** have sought
83 catch (As one would catch a disease.)   **85 of their infirmity** sharing
their human imperfections

CORIOLANUS   Choler?
  Were I as patient as the midnight sleep,
  By Jove, 'twould be my mind.

SICINIUS   It is a mind   89
  That shall remain a poison where it is,
  Not poison any further.

CORIOLANUS   Shall remain?
  Hear you this Triton of the minnows? Mark you   92
  His absolute "shall"?

COMINIUS   'Twas from the canon.

CORIOLANUS   "Shall"?   93
  O good but most unwise patricians! Why,
  You grave but reckless senators, have you thus
  Given Hydra here to choose an officer,   96
  That with his peremptory "shall," being but
  The horn and noise o' the monster's, wants not spirit   98
  To say he'll turn your current in a ditch   99
  And make your channel his? If he have power,   100
  Then vail your ignorance; if none, awake   101
  Your dangerous lenity. If you are learned,   102
  Be not as common fools; if you are not,
  Let them have cushions by you. You are plebeians   104
  If they be senators; and they are no less   105
  When, both your voices blended, the great'st taste   106
  Most palates theirs. They choose their magistrate,   107
  And such a one as he, who puts his "shall,"
  His popular "shall," against a graver bench   109
  Than ever frowned in Greece. By Jove himself,   110

---

89 mind opinion   **92 Triton of the minnows** i.e., god of the little fish. (Triton was Neptune's son and trumpeter.)   **93 from the canon** i.e., not according to proper form, exceeding the authority granted the tribunes   **96 Given** permitted.   **Hydra** many-headed monster slain by Hercules; here, the mob   **98 horn and noise** noisy horn. (See allusion to Triton above.)   **wants** lacks   **99 turn** divert.   **current** stream (of power).   **in** into   **100 make your channel his** i.e., preempt for himself your channel of authority   **101 vail your ignorance** bow down to him in your ignorant yielding   **101–102 awake . . . lenity** arouse yourselves from your dangerous mildness   **102 learned** wise   **104 cushions** i.e., seats in the Senate   **105–107 and . . . theirs** and they are to all intents and purposes senators if, when their voices are mingled with yours, the resulting action savors of them rather than of you   **109 popular** on behalf of the populace.   **graver bench** more august deliberative body   **110 frowned** looked austere in judgment.   **Greece** (Famous for its law-giving institutions.)

It makes the consuls base! And my soul aches
To know, when two authorities are up,   112
Neither supreme, how soon confusion   113
May enter twixt the gap of both and take   114
The one by th' other.

COMINIUS   Well, on to the marketplace.   115

CORIOLANUS
Whoever gave that counsel to give forth
The corn o' the storehouse gratis, as 'twas used   117
Sometime in Greece—

MENENIUS   Well, well, no more of that.   118

CORIOLANUS
Though there the people had more absolute power,
I say they nourished disobedience, fed
The ruin of the state.

BRUTUS   Why shall the people give
One that speaks thus their voice?

CORIOLANUS   I'll give my reasons,
More worthier than their voices. They know the corn
Was not our recompense, resting well assured   124
They ne'er did service for 't. Being pressed to the war, 125
Even when the navel of the state was touched,   126
They would not thread the gates. This kind of service   127
Did not deserve corn gratis. Being i' the war,
Their mutinies and revolts, wherein they showed
Most valor, spoke not for them. Th' accusation   130
Which they have often made against the Senate,
All cause unborn, could never be the native   132
Of our so frank donation. Well, what then?   133
How shall this bosom multiplied digest   134
The Senate's courtesy? Let deeds express
What's like to be their words: "We did request it;   136

112 up established, in action   113 confusion chaos   114 gap of both
space between the two.   take destroy   115 by by means of   117 used
practiced, customary   118 Sometime formerly   124 our recompense
reward from us   125 pressed conscripted, enlisted   126 navel vital
center.   touched threatened   127 thread pass through   130 spoke not
did not speak well   132 All cause unborn unjustifiably.   native natural
source or origin   133 frank freely granted and generous   134 bosom
multiplied multiple stomach.   digest i.e., consider, regard (with also the
literal sense of eating the grain)   136 like likely

We are the greater poll, and in true fear   137
They gave us our demands." Thus we debase
The nature of our seats and make the rabble
Call our cares fears, which will in time   140
Break ope the locks o' the Senate and bring in
The crows to peck the eagles.
MENENIUS   Come, enough.
BRUTUS
Enough, with overmeasure.
CORIOLANUS   No, take more!
What may be sworn by, both divine and human,   144
Seal what I end withal! This double worship—   145
Where one part does disdain with cause, the other
Insult without all reason, where gentry, title, wisdom,   147
Cannot conclude but by the yea and no   148
Of general ignorance—it must omit   149
Real necessities, and give way the while   150
To unstable slightness. Purpose so barred, it follows   151
Nothing is done to purpose. Therefore, beseech you—   152
You that will be less fearful than discreet,   153
That love the fundamental part of state   154
More than you doubt the change on 't, that prefer   155
A noble life before a long, and wish
To jump a body with a dangerous physic   157
That's sure of death without it—at once pluck out
The multitudinous tongue; let them not lick   159
The sweet which is their poison. Your dishonor   160

---

137 greater poll majority, greater number of heads   **140 cares** concern
(for them and for the state).   **which** i.e., which insubordination
144 What (may) whatever   **145 Seal** confirm.   **withal** with.   **double
worship** divided authority   **147 Insult** behave insolently.   **without**
beyond.   **gentry** noble birth   **148 conclude** come to a final decision
149 general popular, common.   **omit** neglect   **150 the while** in the
meanwhile   **151 slightness** vacillation, trifling.   **Purpose so barred**
sound policy and planning being thus obstructed   **152 purpose** any
effect   **153 less . . . discreet** actuated less by fear than by foresight
154–155 That . . . on 't i.e., that love the essentials of our government
more than you fear changes in it (such as getting rid of the tribunes)
157 jump risk (treating).   **physic** cure   **159 The multitudinous tongue**
the voice of the populace, i.e., the tribunes   **160 sweet . . . poison** i.e.,
power which in their hands will undo them as well as Rome.   **dishonor**
present dishonorable state

Mangles true judgment and bereaves the state
Of that integrity which should become 't,   162
Not having the power to do the good it would
For th' ill which doth control 't.
BRUTUS   He's said enough.   164
SICINIUS
He's spoken like a traitor and shall answer   165
As traitors do.
CORIOLANUS   Thou wretch, despite o'erwhelm thee!   166
What should the people do with these bald tribunes,   167
On whom depending, their obedience fails
To the greater bench? In a rebellion,   169
When what's not meet, but what must be, was law,   170
Then were they chosen. In a better hour,
Let what is meet be said it must be meet,   172
And throw their power i' the dust.
BRUTUS   Manifest treason!
SICINIUS   This a consul? No!
BRUTUS
The aediles, ho!

          Enter an Aedile.

                    Let him be apprehended.   176
SICINIUS
Go, call the people [*Exit Aedile*], in whose name myself
Attach thee as a traitorous innovator,   178
A foe to the public weal. Obey, I charge thee,   179
And follow to thine answer.
CORIOLANUS   Hence, old goat!   180
ALL PATRICIANS
We'll surety him.
COMINIUS   Aged sir, hands off.   181

---

162 integrity unity   **164 For** because of.   **ill** i.e., tribunal, popular
power   **165 answer** answer for it   **166 despite** scorn   **167 bald** petty
169 greater bench i.e., senators collectively   **170 When . . . was law**
when "might makes right" prevailed   **172 Let . . . be meet** i.e., let us
openly say that what is right is what should be done   **176 aediles**
officers attached to the tribunes   **178 Attach** arrest.   **innovator** revolutionary   **179 weal** welfare   **180 answer** defense, answer to a charge
181 surety go bail for

CORIOLANUS
Hence, rotten thing! Or I shall shake thy bones
Out of thy garments.
SICINIUS   Help, ye citizens!

Enter a rabble of plebeians, with the aediles.

MENENIUS   On both sides more respect.   184
SICINIUS
Here's he that would take from you all your power.
BRUTUS   Seize him, aediles!
ALL PLEBEIANS   Down with him! Down with him!
SECOND SENATOR   Weapons, weapons, weapons!
                They all bustle about Coriolanus.
ALL
Tribunes!—Patricians!—Citizens!—What, ho!—
Sicinius!—Brutus!—Coriolanus!—Citizens!—
Peace, peace, peace!—Stay, hold, peace!
MENENIUS
What is about to be? I am out of breath.
Confusion's near; I cannot speak. You, tribunes
To th' people! Coriolanus, patience!
Speak, good Sicinius.
SICINIUS   Hear me, people. Peace!
ALL PLEBEIANS
Let's hear our tribune. Peace! Speak, speak, speak.
SICINIUS
You are at point to lose your liberties.   197
Marcius would have all from you—Marcius,
Whom late you have named for consul.
MENENIUS   Fie, fie, fie!   199
This is the way to kindle, not to quench.
FIRST SENATOR
To unbuild the city and to lay all flat.
SICINIUS
What is the city but the people?
ALL PLEBEIANS   True,
The people are the city.

---

184 respect consideration   **197 at point to lose** on the verge of losing
199 late recently

BRUTUS
By the consent of all, we were established
The people's magistrates.

ALL PLEBEIANS   You so remain.

MENENIUS   And so are like to do.   207

COMINIUS
That is the way to lay the city flat,
To bring the roof to the foundation,
And bury all, which yet distinctly ranges,   210
In heaps and piles of ruin.

SICINIUS   This deserves death.

BRUTUS
Or let us stand to our authority   212
Or let us lose it. We do here pronounce,
Upon the part o' the people, in whose power   214
We were elected theirs, Marcius is worthy
Of present death.

SICINIUS   Therefore lay hold of him!   216
Bear him to th' rock Tarpeian, and from thence   217
Into destruction cast him.

BRUTUS   Aediles, seize him!

ALL PLEBEIANS
Yield, Marcius, yield!

MENENIUS   Hear me one word.
Beseech you, tribunes, hear me but a word.

AEDILES   Peace, peace!

MENENIUS [To the Tribunes]
Be that you seem, truly your country's friend,
And temperately proceed to what you would
Thus violently redress.

BRUTUS   Sir, those cold ways,
That seem like prudent helps, are very poisonous   225
Where the disease is violent.—Lay hands upon him
And bear him to the rock.

                    Coriolanus draws his sword.

207 like likely   210 distinctly ranges stretches out in proper order
212 Or either.   stand to maintain   214 Upon the part o' on behalf of.
in by   216 present immediate   217 rock Tarpeian famous precipice on
the Capitoline Hill in ancient Rome from which persons condemned for
offenses against the state were thrown down   225 helps remedies

CORIOLANUS   No, I'll die here.
There's some among you have beheld me fighting.
Come, try upon yourselves what you have seen me.
MENENIUS
Down with that sword! Tribunes, withdraw awhile.
BRUTUS
Lay hands upon him.
MENENIUS   Help Marcius, help!
You that be noble, help him, young and old!
ALL PLEBEIANS   Down with him, down with him!   233
                    In this mutiny, the tribunes, the aediles,
                              and the people are beat in.
MENENIUS [*To Coriolanus*]
Go, get you to your house. Begone, away!
All will be naught else.
SECOND SENATOR   Get you gone.
CORIOLANUS   Stand fast!   235
We have as many friends as enemies.
MENENIUS
Shall it be put to that?
FIRST SENATOR   The gods forbid!
I prithee, noble friend, home to thy house;
Leave us to cure this cause.   239
MENENIUS   For 'tis a sore upon us
You cannot tent yourself. Begone, beseech you.   241
COMINIUS   Come, sir, along with us.
CORIOLANUS
I would they were barbarians, as they are,
Though in Rome littered; not Romans, as they are not,
Though calved i' the porch o' the Capitol.
MENENIUS   Begone!
Put not your worthy rage into your tongue.
One time will owe another.
CORIOLANUS   On fair ground   247
I could beat forty of them.
MENENIUS   I could myself
Take up a brace o' the best of them; yea, the two tribunes.   249

---

233 s.d. beat in i.e., driven offstage   **235 naught else** ruined otherwise
239 cause disease   **241 tent** treat (by probing a wound), cure   **247 One
. . . another** i.e., our time will come   **249 Take up** cope with.   **brace**
pair

COMINIUS

But now 'tis odds beyond arithmetic,   250
And manhood is called foolery when it stands   251
Against a falling fabric. Will you hence   252
Before the tag return, whose rage doth rend   253
Like interrupted waters and o'erbear   254
What they are used to bear?

MENENIUS   Pray you, begone.   255
I'll try whether my old wit be in request   256
With those that have but little. This must be patched   257
With cloth of any color.   258

COMINIUS   Nay, come away.

                    Exeunt Coriolanus and Cominius
                                [with others].

A PATRICIAN   This man has marred his fortune.

MENENIUS

His nature is too noble for the world.
He would not flatter Neptune for his trident   262
Or Jove for 's power to thunder. His heart's his mouth. 263
What his breast forges, that his tongue must vent,   264
And, being angry, does forget that ever
He heard the name of death.   *A noise within.*
                              Here's goodly work!

A PATRICIAN   I would they were abed!

MENENIUS

I would they were in Tiber! What the vengeance!
Could he not speak 'em fair?

          Enter Brutus and Sicinius, with the rabble again.

SICINIUS   Where is this viper   269
That would depopulate the city and
Be every man himself?

MENENIUS   You worthy tribunes—

---

250 'tis . . . arithmetic i.e., we are thoroughly outnumbered
251 manhood manliness. foolery folly   252 fabric building. hence
leave 253 tag rabble 254 interrupted waters waves breaking over
their banks. o'erbear overwhelm 255 bear endure 256 try test.
request demand 257–258 patched . . . color i.e., mended in any way
possible 262 trident three-pronged spear, the symbol of Neptune,
classical god of the sea 263 His . . . mouth i.e., what he feels is exactly
what he speaks 264 vent express 269 'em fair to them courteously

SICINIUS
　He shall be thrown down the Tarpeian rock
　With rigorous hands. He hath resisted law,　　　　273
　And therefore law shall scorn him further trial　　274
　Than the severity of the public power
　Which he so sets at naught.
FIRST CITIZEN　　　　　　　　　He shall well know　276
　The noble tribunes are the people's mouths,
　And we their hands.
ALL PLEBEIANS　He shall, sure on 't.　　　　279
MENENIUS　Sir, sir—
SICINIUS　Peace!
MENENIUS
　Do not cry havoc where you should but hunt　　282
　With modest warrant.
SICINIUS　　　　　　　Sir, how comes 't that you　283
　Have holp to make this rescue?
MENENIUS　　　　　　　　Hear me speak.　284
　As I do know the Consul's worthiness,
　So can I name his faults.
SICINIUS　Consul? What consul?
MENENIUS
　The Consul Coriolanus.
BRUTUS　He consul!
ALL PLEBEIANS　No, no, no, no, no.
MENENIUS
　If, by the tribunes' leave and yours, good people,　291
　I may be heard, I would crave a word or two,
　The which shall turn you to no further harm
　Than so much loss of time.
SICINIUS　　　　　　　Speak briefly, then,
　For we are peremptory to dispatch　　　　295
　This viperous traitor. To eject him hence　　296
　Were but one danger, and to keep him here

273 rigorous severe　**274 scorn** refuse.　**further** any further　**276 sets at naught** views as worthless　**279 sure on 't** be sure of it　**282 cry havoc** give the order for general slaughter　**283 modest warrant** limited license　**284 holp** helped.　**make this rescue** (*Make rescue* is a technical legal term for the forcible removal of a prisoner from custody.)　**291 leave** permission　**295 peremptory** determined　**296 eject him hence** exile him

Our certain death; therefore it is decreed
He dies tonight.
MENENIUS   Now the good gods forbid
That our renownèd Rome, whose gratitude
Towards her deservèd children is enrolled   301
In Jove's own book, like an unnatural dam   302
Should now eat up her own!
SICINIUS
He's a disease that must be cut away.
MENENIUS
O, he's a limb that has but a disease—
Mortal, to cut it off; to cure it, easy.   306
What has he done to Rome that's worthy death?
Killing our enemies, the blood he hath lost—
Which I dare vouch is more than that he hath   309
By many an ounce—he dropped it for his country;
And what is left, to lose it by his country   311
Were to us all that do 't and suffer it
A brand to th' end o' the world.
SICINIUS   This is clean kam.   313
BRUTUS
Merely awry. When he did love his country,   314
It honored him.
SICINIUS   The service of the foot,
Being once gangrened, is not then respected   316
For what before it was.
BRUTUS   We'll hear no more.
Pursue him to his house and pluck him thence,
Lest his infection, being of catching nature,   319
Spread further.
MENENIUS   One word more, one word.
This tiger-footed rage, when it shall find
The harm of unscanned swiftness, will too late   323
Tie leaden pounds to 's heels. Proceed by process,   324

301 **deservèd** deserving   302 **dam** mother   306 **Mortal** fatal   309 **vouch**
declare   311 **by** at the hands of   313 **brand** i.e., brand of infamy,
stigma.   **clean kam** quite perverse, wrong   314 **Merely** completely
316 **gangrened** infected by gangrene (a rotting disease of the tissue
caused by a failure in the circulation of the blood)   319 **of catching
nature** infectious   323 **unscanned** unconsidered   324 **pounds**
weights.   **to 's** to its.   **process** legal method

Lest parties—as he is beloved—break out   325
And sack great Rome with Romans.

BRUTUS   If it were so—   326

SICINIUS What do ye talk?   327
Have we not had a taste of his obedience?
Our aediles smote? Ourselves resisted? Come.

MENENIUS
Consider this: he has been bred i' the wars
Since 'a could draw a sword, and is ill schooled
In bolted language; meal and bran together   332
He throws without distinction. Give me leave;
I'll go to him and undertake to bring him
Where he shall answer, by a lawful form,   335
In peace, to his utmost peril.

FIRST SENATOR   Noble tribunes,   336
It is the humane way. The other course
Will prove too bloody, and the end of it
Unknown to the beginning.

SICINIUS   Noble Menenius,
Be you then as the people's officer.—
Masters, lay down your weapons.

BRUTUS   Go not home.

SICINIUS
Meet on the marketplace. We'll attend you there,   342
Where, if you bring not Marcius, we'll proceed
In our first way.

MENENIUS   I'll bring him to you.
   [To the Senators.] Let me desire your company. He must
      come,
Or what is worst will follow.

FIRST SENATOR   Pray you, let's to him. 347
                                        Exeunt omnes.

❖

325 parties factions   **326 with** by means of   **327 What** why   **332 bolted**
sifted, refined.   **meal and bran** flour and husks   **335–336 answer . . .**
peril stand trial peacefully even though his life is at stake   **342 attend**
await   **347 s.d. omnes** all

3.2   *Enter Coriolanus, with Nobles.*

CORIOLANUS
   Let them pull all about mine ears, present me   1
   Death on the wheel or at wild horses' heels,   2
   Or pile ten hills on the Tarpeian rock,
   That the precipitation might down stretch   4
   Below the beam of sight, yet will I still   5
   Be thus to them.
A PATRICIAN   You do the nobler.
CORIOLANUS   I muse my mother   8
   Does not approve me further, who was wont   9
   To call them woolen vassals, things created   10
   To buy and sell with groats, to show bare heads   11
   In congregations, to yawn, be still, and wonder   12
   When one but of my ordinance stood up   13
   To speak of peace or war.

     Enter Volumnia.

                  I talk of you.
   Why did you wish me milder? Would you have me
   False to my nature? Rather say I play
   The man I am.
VOLUMNIA   O, sir, sir, sir,
   I would have had you put your power well on   18
   Before you had worn it out.
CORIOLANUS   Let go.   20
VOLUMNIA
   You might have been enough the man you are
   With striving less to be so. Lesser had been
   The thwartings of your dispositions if

3.2. Location: Rome. Coriolanus' house.
1 present me i.e., sentence me to   **2 wheel** instrument of torture and
death by which the victim's limbs were broken   **4 precipitation** precipi-
tousness   **5 beam** range   **8 muse** wonder that   **9 approve me further**
approve more of my conduct.   **was wont** used   **10 woolen** coarsely
clad   **11 To . . . groats** i.e., to be nothing more than petty traders.
groats fourpenny pieces   **12 congregations** assemblies.   **yawn** i.e., gape
with amazement   **13 ordinance** rank   **18 I would . . . well on** I would
have preferred that you had learned to achieve and use your authority
well   **20 Let go** enough

You had not showed them how ye were disposed
Ere they lacked power to cross you.
CORIOLANUS   Let them hang!   25
VOLUMNIA   Ay, and burn too.

    Enter Menenius with the Senators.

MENENIUS
Come, come, you have been too rough, something too
   rough;   27
You must return and mend it.
FIRST SENATOR   There's no remedy,
Unless, by not so doing, our good city
Cleave in the midst and perish.
VOLUMNIA   Pray be counseled.   30
I have a heart as little apt as yours,   31
But yet a brain that leads my use of anger
To better vantage.
MENENIUS   Well said, noble woman!
Before he should thus stoop to the herd, but that   34
The violent fit o' the time craves it as physic   35
For the whole state, I would put mine armor on,
Which I can scarcely bear.
CORIOLANUS   What must I do?   37
MENENIUS
Return to the tribunes.
CORIOLANUS   Well, what then? What then?
MENENIUS   Repent what you have spoke.
CORIOLANUS
For them? I cannot do it to the gods.
Must I then do 't to them?
VOLUMNIA   You are too absolute,   41
Though therein you can never be too noble,
But when extremities speak. I have heard you say   43
Honor and policy, like unsevered friends,   44

---

25 Ere . . . you before they lost their power to thwart you. (As consul,
Coriolanus would be beyond their control.)   **27 something** somewhat
30 Cleave in the midst split down the middle   **31 apt** compliant   **34 but**
were it not   **35 fit** (1) convulsion (2) fever.   **craves** demands.   **physic**
medicine   **37 bear** bear the weight of   **41 absolute** uncompromising
43 But . . . speak except when necessity requires   **44 policy** the proper
consideration of stratagem and craft.   **unsevered** inseparable

I' the war do grow together. Grant that, and tell me
In peace what each of them by th' other lose
That they combine not there.

CORIOLANUS   Tush, tush!

MENENIUS   A good demand.

VOLUMNIA
If it be honor in your wars to seem
The same you are not, which for your best ends
You adopt your policy, how is it less or worse   50
That it shall hold companionship in peace
With honor as in war, since that to both
It stands in like request?

CORIOLANUS   Why force you this?   53

VOLUMNIA
Because that now it lies you on to speak   54
To th' people, not by your own instruction,   55
Nor by th' matter which your heart prompts you,
But with such words that are but roted in   57
Your tongue, though but bastards and syllables
Of no allowance to your bosom's truth.   59
Now, this no more dishonors you at all
Than to take in a town with gentle words,   61
Which else would put you to your fortune and   62
The hazard of much blood.
I would dissemble with my nature where   64
My fortunes and my friends at stake required   65
I should do so in honor. I am in this   66
Your wife, your son, these senators, the nobles;   67
And you will rather show our general louts   68
How you can frown than spend a fawn upon 'em   69
For the inheritance of their loves and safeguard   70
Of what that want might ruin.

MENENIUS   Noble lady!—   71

50 adopt adopt as   53 It . . . request it is equally needed.   force urge
54 lies you on is your duty   55 instruction i.e., conviction, inner
prompting   57 are but roted in have been learned merely by rote in
59 Of . . . to unacknowledged by   61 take in capture   62 else . . . fortune otherwise would force you to take your chance (in battle)
64 dissemble . . . nature pretend to be other than I was   65 stake risk
66 in honor in compliance with the requirements of honor   66–67 I am
. . . wife in this I represent your wife   68 general common, vulgar
69 fawn flattering appeal   70 inheritance obtaining   71 that want i.e.,
the lack of their loves

Come, go with us; speak fair. You may salve so,   72
Not what is dangerous present, but the loss   73
Of what is past.
VOLUMNIA   I prithee now, my son,   74
Go to them, with this bonnet in thy hand,   75
And thus far having stretched it—here be with them—   76
Thy knee bussing the stones—for in such business   77
Action is eloquence, and the eyes of th' ignorant
More learnèd than the ears—waving thy head,   79
Which often thus correcting thy stout heart,   80
Now humble as the ripest mulberry   81
That will not hold the handling. Or say to them   82
Thou art their soldier, and being bred in broils   83
Hast not the soft way which, thou dost confess,
Were fit for thee to use as they to claim,   85
In asking their good loves; but thou wilt frame   86
Thyself, forsooth, hereafter theirs, so far   87
As thou hast power and person.
MENENIUS   This but done,   88
Even as she speaks, why, their hearts were yours;   89
For they have pardons, being asked, as free   90
As words to little purpose.
VOLUMNIA   Prithee now,
Go, and be ruled; although I know thou hadst rather
Follow thine enemy in a fiery gulf   93
Than flatter him in a bower.
        Enter Cominius.

                        Here is Cominius.   94
COMINIUS
I have been i' the marketplace; and, sir, 'tis fit   95

72 salve remedy   **73–74 Not . . . past** not only the present danger but
what has been lost already   **75 bonnet** cap   **76 And . . . them** i.e., and go
to them holding your hat out thus—do it this way for them. (She ges-
tures.)   **77 bussing** kissing   **79 learnèd** i.e., receptive.   **waving** bowing up
and down   **80 Which** (Referring perhaps to *thy head;* sometimes emended
to *with* or *while.*)   **correcting** chastening.   **stout** proud   **81–82 Now . . .
handling** i.e., now is as soft and malleable as overripe fruit. (Or *humble*
may mean "abase, let droop.")   **hold** bear, tolerate   **83 broils** battles
85 fit as fit.   **as they** as for them   **86 In asking** in your asking for.   **frame**
conform   **87 theirs** to suit their wish   **87–88 so far . . . person** to the full
extent of your ability and authority   **89 Even** exactly.   **were** would be
90 as free i.e., which they will grant as freely   **93 in** into   **94 bower** arbor,
orchard   **95 fit** appropriate

You make strong party, or defend yourself   96
By calmness or by absence. All's in anger.

MENENIUS
  Only fair speech.

COMINIUS   I think 'twill serve, if he
  Can thereto frame his spirit.

VOLUMNIA   He must, and will.
  Prithee, now, say you will, and go about it.

CORIOLANUS
  Must I go show them my unbarbed sconce? Must I   101
  With my base tongue give to my noble heart
  A lie that it must bear? Well, I will do 't.
  Yet, were there but this single plot to lose,   104
  This mold of Marcius, they to dust should grind it   105
  And throw 't against the wind. To the marketplace!
  You have put me now to such a part which never
  I shall discharge to the life.

COMINIUS   Come, come, we'll prompt you.   108

VOLUMNIA
  I prithee now, sweet son, as thou hast said
  My praises made thee first a soldier, so,
  To have my praise for this, perform a part
  Thou hast not done before.

CORIOLANUS   Well, I must do 't.
  Away, my disposition, and possess me
  Some harlot's spirit! My throat of war be turned,   114
  Which choirèd with my drum, into a pipe   115
  Small as an eunuch or the virgin voice   116
  That babies lulls asleep! The smiles of knaves   117
  Tent in my cheeks, and schoolboys' tears take up   118
  The glasses of my sight! A beggar's tongue   119
  Make motion through my lips, and my armed knees,
  Who bowed but in my stirrup, bend like his

---

96 make strong party support your side strongly, or gather a strong
faction around you   **101 unbarbed sconce** unhelmeted head   **104 this
single plot** this piece of earth only (i.e., my own person)   **105 mold**
(1) bodily form (2) earth   **108 discharge to the life** perform convinc-
ingly   **114 harlot's** (1) rascal's (2) whore's.   **throat of war** i.e., soldier's
voice   **115 choirèd** harmonized, sang in tune   **116 Small** high-pitched
117 babies lulls lulls babies or dolls   **118 Tent** lodge, set up camp.
take up fill up, occupy   **119 glasses of my sight** my eyeballs

That hath received an alms! I will not do 't,   122
Lest I surcease to honor mine own truth   123
And by my body's action teach my mind
A most inherent baseness.
VOLUMNIA   At thy choice, then.   125
To beg of thee, it is my more dishonor
Than thou of them. Come all to ruin. Let
Thy mother rather feel thy pride than fear
Thy dangerous stoutness, for I mock at death   129
With as big heart as thou. Do as thou list.   130
Thy valiantness was mine, thou suck'st it from me,
But owe thy pride thyself.
CORIOLANUS   Pray, be content.   132
Mother, I am going to the marketplace.
Chide me no more. I'll mountebank their loves,   134
Cog their hearts from them, and come home beloved   135
Of all the trades in Rome. Look, I am going.
Commend me to my wife. I'll return consul,
Or never trust to what my tongue can do
I' the way of flattery further.
VOLUMNIA   Do your will.

Exit Volumnia.

COMINIUS
Away! The tribunes do attend you. Arm yourself   140
To answer mildly; for they are prepared
With accusations, as I hear, more strong
Than are upon you yet.
CORIOLANUS
The word is "mildly." Pray you, let us go.   144
Let them accuse me by invention; I   145
Will answer in mine honor.
MENENIUS   Ay, but mildly.   146
CORIOLANUS
Well, mildly be it, then. Mildly!   *Exeunt.*

❧

122 an alms a gift of charity   123 surcease cease   125 inherent irre-
movable, fixed   129 Thy dangerous stoutness the dangers resulting
from your obstinate pride   130 big heart noble courage.   list please
132 owe own   134 mountebank win over as with the tricks of a quack
medicine salesman   135 Cog cheat, beguile   140 attend await.   Arm
prepare   144 word watchword   145 accuse . . . invention invent
charges against me to their heart's desire   146 in in accordance with

3.3   *Enter Sicinius and Brutus.*

BRUTUS
　In this point charge him home, that he affects   1
　Tyrannical power. If he evade us there,
　Enforce him with his envy to the people,   3
　And that the spoil got on the Antiates   4
　Was ne'er distributed.

　　　Enter an Aedile.

　　　　　　　　　What, will he come?   5
AEDILE   He's coming.
BRUTUS   How accompanied?
AEDILE
　With old Menenius, and those senators
　That always favored him.
SICINIUS   Have you a catalogue
　Of all the voices that we have procured
　Set down by the poll?
AEDILE   I have. 'Tis ready.   11
SICINIUS
　Have you collected them by tribes?
AEDILE   I have.   12
SICINIUS
　Assemble presently the people hither;   13
　And when they hear me say "It shall be so
　I' the right and strength o' the commons," be it either
　For death, for fine, or banishment, then let them,
　If I say "Fine," cry "Fine!"—if "Death," cry "Death!"
　Insisting on the old prerogative   18
　And power i' the truth o' the cause.
AEDILE   I shall inform them. 19
BRUTUS
　And when such time they have begun to cry,   20

3.3. Location: Rome. The Forum or marketplace.
1 charge him home press charges against him all the way.   **affects**
aspires to   **3 Enforce . . . to** urge against him his inveterate malice
toward   **4 spoil got on** property taken from   **5 s.d. Aedile** (See note at
3.1.176.)   **11 by the poll** by individual names, by head count   **12 tribes**
divisions of the Roman populace   **13 presently** immediately   **18 old**
prerogative traditional privilege or position   **19 truth** justice.   **cause**
case   **20 cry** cry out, shout

Let them not cease, but with a din confused
Enforce the present execution   22
Of what we chance to sentence.
AEDILE   Very well.
SICINIUS
Make them be strong, and ready for this hint
When we shall hap to give 't them.
BRUTUS   Go about it.   25
                                    [*Exit Aedile.*]
Put him to choler straight. He hath been used   26
Ever to conquer and to have his worth   27
Of contradiction. Being once chafed, he cannot   28
Be reined again to temperance; then he speaks
What's in his heart, and that is there which looks   30
With us to break his neck.   31

    Enter Coriolanus, Menenius, and Cominius, with
    others [Senators and patricians].

SICINIUS   Well, here he comes.
MENENIUS   Calmly, I do beseech you.
CORIOLANUS
Ay, as an hostler, that for th' poorest piece   34
Will bear the knave by the volume.—Th' honored gods 35
Keep Rome in safety and the chairs of justice
Supplied with worthy men! Plant love among 's!
Throng our large temples with the shows of peace,   38
And not our streets with war!
FIRST SENATOR   Amen, amen.
MENENIUS   A noble wish.

    Enter the Aedile, with the plebeians.

SICINIUS   Draw near, ye people.

---

22 Enforce insist upon.   **present execution** immediate performance
25 hap happen   **26 choler** anger.   **straight** straightway.   **used** accustomed   **27 Ever** always.   **worth** i.e., full quota or portion   **28 contradiction** prerogative of answering back. (Coriolanus is accustomed to giving as good as he gets.)   **30 looks** promises, tends   **31 With us** from our point of view, in terms of our interest   **34 hostler** caretaker of horses.   **piece** coin, piece of money   **35 bear . . . by the volume** endure being called knave to any extent or any number of times.   **Th' honored** may the honored   **38 Throng our large temples** let our large temples be crowded.   **shows** ceremonies

AEDILE
    List to your tribunes. Audience! Peace, I say!   43
CORIOLANUS   First, hear me speak.
BOTH TRIBUNES   Well, say.—Peace, ho!
CORIOLANUS
    Shall I be charged no further than this present?   46
    Must all determine here?
SICINIUS   I do demand   47
    If you submit you to the people's voices,   48
    Allow their officers, and are content   49
    To suffer lawful censure for such faults   50
    As shall be proved upon you?
CORIOLANUS   I am content.
MENENIUS
    Lo, citizens, he says he is content.
    The warlike service he has done, consider. Think
    Upon the wounds his body bears, which show
    Like graves i' the holy churchyard.
CORIOLANUS   Scratches with briers,
    Scars to move laughter only.
MENENIUS   Consider further,
    That when he speaks not like a citizen,
    You find him like a soldier. Do not take
    His rougher accents for malicious sounds,
    But, as I say, such as become a soldier
    Rather than envy you.
COMINIUS   Well, well, no more.   61
CORIOLANUS   What is the matter
    That, being passed for consul with full voice,
    I am so dishonored that the very hour
    You take it off again?
SICINIUS   Answer to us.   66
CORIOLANUS   Say, then. 'Tis true, I ought so.   67
SICINIUS
    We charge you that you have contrived to take

---

43 List listen. **Audience** listen, give heed **46 this present** this present
occasion, the matter in hand **47 determine** come to an end, be concluded. **demand** ask **48 If** whether **49 Allow** acknowledge the
authority of **50 censure** judgment **61 Rather . . . you** rather than such
as show malice toward you **66 Answer to us** i.e., we'll do the asking,
not you **67 so** to do so

From Rome all seasoned office and to wind   69
Yourself into a power tyrannical,
For which you are a traitor to the people.

CORIOLANUS
How? Traitor?

MENENIUS   Nay, temperately! Your promise.

CORIOLANUS
The fires i' the lowest hell fold in the people!   73
Call me their traitor? Thou injurious tribune!   74
Within thine eyes sat twenty thousand deaths,   75
In thy hands clutched as many millions, in   76
Thy lying tongue both numbers, I would say   77
"Thou liest" unto thee with a voice as free   78
As I do pray the gods.

SICINIUS   Mark you this, people?

ALL PLEBEIANS   To the rock, to the rock with him!

SICINIUS   Peace!
We need not put new matter to his charge.   83
What you have seen him do and heard him speak,
Beating your officers, cursing yourselves,
Opposing laws with strokes, and here defying   86
Those whose great power must try him—even this,
So criminal and in such capital kind,   88
Deserves th' extremest death.

BRUTUS   But since he hath
Served well for Rome—

CORIOLANUS   What do you prate of service?   90

BRUTUS   I talk of that that know it.

CORIOLANUS   You?

MENENIUS
Is this the promise that you made your mother?

COMINIUS   Know, I pray you—

CORIOLANUS   I'll know no further.
Let them pronounce the steep Tarpeian death,

---

69 seasoned established. **wind** insinuate **73 fold in** enclose, encircle
74 their traitor a traitor to them. **injurious** insulting **75–77 Within
. . . numbers** (Understand "although" before each of the three
clauses.) **78 free** unrestrained **83 put new matter** add new particulars **86 strokes** blows **88 capital** death-deserving **90 prate** talk idly

Vagabond exile, flaying, pent to linger   97
But with a grain a day, I would not buy   98
Their mercy at the price of one fair word,
Nor check my courage for what they can give,   100
To have 't with saying "Good morrow."
SICINIUS   For that he has,   101
As much as in him lies, from time to time   102
Envied against the people, seeking means   103
To pluck away their power, as now at last   104
Given hostile strokes, and that not in the presence   105
Of dreaded justice, but on the ministers
That doth distribute it; in the name o' the people
And in the power of us the tribunes, we,
Ev'n from this instant, banish him our city,
In peril of precipitation   · 110
From off the rock Tarpeian, nevermore
To enter our Rome gates. I' the people's name,
I say it shall be so.
ALL PLEBEIANS
It shall be so, it shall be so! Let him away!
He's banished, and it shall be so!
COMINIUS
Hear me, my masters, and my common friends—
SICINIUS
He's sentenced. No more hearing.
COMINIUS   Let me speak.
I have been consul, and can show for Rome
Her enemies' marks upon me. I do love
My country's good with a respect more tender,   120
More holy and profound, than mine own life,
My dear wife's estimate, her womb's increase,   122
And treasure of my loins. Then if I would
Speak that—

97–98 pent . . . day imprisoned to starve with but a small particle of
food a day   **100 check** restrain.   **courage** spirit   **101 To have 't** if I
might have it.   **with saying** merely by saying.   **For that** because   **102 in
him lies** he could   **103 Envied against** showed malice toward   **104 as**
i.e., and inasmuch as (he has)   **105 not** not merely   **110 precipitation**
being thrown   **120 respect** regard, feeling   **122 estimate** reputation

SICINIUS We know your drift. Speak what?
BRUTUS
 There's no more to be said, but he is banished   126
 As enemy to the people and his country.
 It shall be so.
ALL PLEBEIANS It shall be so, it shall be so!
CORIOLANUS
 You common cry of curs, whose breath I hate   130
 As reek o' the rotten fens, whose loves I prize   131
 As the dead carcasses of unburied men
 That do corrupt my air, I banish you!
 And here remain with your uncertainty!   134
 Let every feeble rumor shake your hearts!
 Your enemies, with nodding of their plumes,   136
 Fan you into despair! Have the power still   137
 To banish your defenders, till at length
 Your ignorance—which finds not till it feels,   139
 Making but reservation of yourselves,   140
 Still your own foes—deliver you   141
 As most abated captives to some nation   142
 That won you without blows! Despising
 For you the city, thus I turn my back.   144
 There is a world elsewhere.
                    Exeunt Coriolanus, Cominius, [Menenius,
                                Senators, and patricians].
AEDILE The people's enemy is gone, is gone!
ALL PLEBEIANS
 Our enemy is banished! He is gone! Hoo! Hoo!
                They all shout and throw up their caps.
SICINIUS
 Go see him out at gates, and follow him,
 As he hath followed you, with all despite;   149

---

126 but but that   **130 cry** pack   **131 reek** vapor   **134 remain** may you remain.   **uncertainty** inconstancy, fickleness; also, insecurity (as explained in the following lines)   **136 Your** may your.   **with** merely with   **137 Have** may you have   **139 finds . . . feels** learns only through experience   **140 Making . . . yourselves** seeking only to preserve yourselves, or excepting no one but yourselves from banishment   **141 Still your own foes** always your own worst enemies   **142 abated** humbled   **144 For** because of   **149 despite** disdain, contempt

Give him deserved vexation. Let a guard   150
Attend us through the city.

ALL PLEBEIANS

Come, come, let's see him out at gates! Come.
The gods preserve our noble tribunes! Come.

                                           Exeunt.

❖

---

150 **vexation** torment

4.1 *Enter Coriolanus, Volumnia, Virgilia, Menenius, Cominius, with the young nobility of Rome.*

CORIOLANUS
Come, leave your tears. A brief farewell. The beast   1
With many heads butts me away. Nay, Mother,
Where is your ancient courage? You were used   3
To say extremities was the trier of spirits;   4
That common chances common men could bear;
That when the sea was calm all boats alike
Showed mastership in floating; fortune's blows   7
When most struck home, being gentle wounded craves   8
A noble cunning. You were used to load me   9
With precepts that would make invincible
The heart that conned them.   11

VIRGILIA
O heavens! O heavens!

CORIOLANUS   Nay, I prithee, woman—

VOLUMNIA
Now the red pestilence strike all trades in Rome,   13
And occupations perish!

CORIOLANUS   What, what, what!   14
I shall be loved when I am lacked. Nay, Mother,   15
Resume that spirit when you were wont to say,   16
If you had been the wife of Hercules,
Six of his labors you'd have done and saved   18
Your husband so much sweat. Cominius,
Droop not. Adieu. Farewell, my wife, my mother.
I'll do well yet. Thou old and true Menenius,
Thy tears are salter than a younger man's,
And venomous to thine eyes. My sometime general,   23
I have seen thee stern, and thou hast oft beheld
Heart-hardening spectacles; tell these sad women

4.1. Location: Rome, near the gates of the city (see l. 47).
1 leave cease, leave off   **3 ancient** former.   **used** accustomed   **4 extremities** crisis   **7–9 fortune's . . . cunning** i.e., when fortune strikes her hardest blows, to bear one's afflictions like a true gentleman requires great wisdom and nobility   **11 conned** studied, memorized   **13 red pestilence** (Red spots presaged death to those stricken with the plague.)   **14 occupations** trades, handicrafts   **15 lacked** missed   **16 wont** accustomed   **18 Six of his labors** i.e., half of the twelve labors of Hercules   **23 sometime** former

'Tis fond to wail inevitable strokes   26
As 'tis to laugh at 'em. My Mother, you wot well   27
My hazards still have been your solace, and—   28
Believe 't not lightly—though I go alone,
Like to a lonely dragon that his fen   30
Makes feared and talked of more than seen, your son
Will or exceed the common or be caught   32
With cautelous baits and practice.

VOLUMNIA   My first son,   33
Whither wilt thou go? Take good Cominius
With thee awhile. Determine on some course
More than a wild exposture to each chance   36
That starts i' the way before thee.

VIRGILIA   O the gods!   37

COMINIUS
I'll follow thee a month, devise with thee   38
Where thou shalt rest, that thou mayst hear of us
And we of thee; so if the time thrust forth
A cause for thy repeal, we shall not send   41
O'er the vast world to seek a single man,
And lose advantage, which doth ever cool   43
I' th' absence of the needer.

CORIOLANUS   Fare ye well.   44
Thou hast years upon thee, and thou art too full
Of the wars' surfeits to go rove with one   46
That's yet unbruised. Bring me but out at gate.   47
Come, my sweet wife, my dearest Mother, and
My friends of noble touch; when I am forth,   49
Bid me farewell, and smile. I pray you, come.
While I remain above the ground, you shall
Hear from me still, and never of me aught
But what is like me formerly.

MENENIUS   That's worthily

---

26 **fond** foolish   27 **wot** know   28 **still** always   30 **fen** lurking place,
marsh   32 **or . . . common** either exceed the ordinary deeds of men
33 **cautelous** crafty, deceitful.   **practice** treacherous methods   36 **exposture** exposure   37 **starts** breaks from cover, darts across your path
38 **follow** go with   41 **repeal** recall from banishment   43 **advantage** the
opportune moment   44 **the needer** the person who needs to seize the
moment   46 **wars' surfeits** wearing effects of military service
47 **Bring** conduct   49 **noble touch** approved nobility. (From the use of
the touchstone with precious metal.)

As any ear can hear. Come, let's not weep.
If I could shake off but one seven years
From these old arms and legs, by the good gods,
I'd with thee every foot.
CORIOLANUS   Give me thy hand.
Come.   *Exeunt.*

❖

4.2   *Enter the two tribunes, Sicinius and Brutus,*
       with the Aedile.

SICINIUS [*To the Aedile*]
Bid them all home. He's gone, and we'll no further.   1
The nobility are vexed, whom we see have sided
In his behalf.
BRUTUS   Now we have shown our power,
Let us seem humbler after it is done
Than when it was a-doing.
SICINIUS   Bid them home.
Say their great enemy is gone, and they
Stand in their ancient strength.
BRUTUS   Dismiss them home.   7
                                    [*Exit Aedile.*]
Here comes his mother.

       Enter Volumnia, Virgilia, and Menenius.

SICINIUS   Let's not meet her.
BRUTUS   Why?
SICINIUS   They say she's mad.
BRUTUS
They have ta'en note of us. Keep on your way.
                                [*They start to leave.*]
VOLUMNIA
O, you're well met. Th' hoarded plague o' the gods   13
Requite your love!
MENENIUS   Peace, peace! Be not so loud.   14

4.2. Location: Rome. A street.
1 home go home   **7 ancient** former   **13 hoarded** stored up   **14 Requite**
repay

VOLUMNIA
    If that I could for weeping, you should hear—
    Nay, and you shall hear some. Will you be gone?
VIRGILIA
    You shall stay too. I would I had the power   17
    To say so to my husband.
SICINIUS   Are you mankind?   18
VOLUMNIA
    Ay, fool, is that a shame?—Note but this fool.—   19
    Was not a man my father? Hadst thou foxship   20
    To banish him that struck more blows for Rome
    Than thou hast spoken words?
SICINIUS   O blessèd heavens!
VOLUMNIA
    More noble blows than ever thou wise words,
    And for Rome's good. I'll tell thee what—yet go.
    Nay, but thou shalt stay too. I would my son   25
    Were in Arabia and thy tribe before him,   26
    His good sword in his hand.
SICINIUS   What then?
VIRGILIA   What then?
    He'd make an end of thy posterity.   28
VOLUMNIA   Bastards and all.
    Good man, the wounds that he does bear for Rome!
MENENIUS   Come, come, peace.
SICINIUS
    I would he had continued to his country
    As he began, and not unknit himself   33
    The noble knot he made.
BRUTUS   I would he had.   34
VOLUMNIA
    "I would he had"? 'Twas you incensed the rabble—
    Cats, that can judge as fitly of his worth   36

---

17 You shall stay too (Sometimes read as if addressed to the second of the two tribunes, but it may mean "you shall too stay," i.e., whether you want to or not. See l. 25.) **18 mankind** masculine (i.e., railing like a man), or infuriated. (Volumnia responds as though it meant "of the human race.") **19 Note but this fool** (The line could read, "Note but this, fool," addressed to Sicinius.) **20 foxship** craftiness **25 would** wish **26 Arabia** i.e., a deserted spot, with no place to hide. **tribe** family, fraternity, set **28 posterity** descendants **33–34 unknit . . . made** i.e., untied the knot binding him and Rome together **36 Cats** (A term of contempt.)

As I can of those mysteries which heaven
Will not have earth to know!

BRUTUS
Pray, let's go.

VOLUMNIA   Now, pray, sir, get you gone.
You have done a brave deed. Ere you go, hear this:
As far as doth the Capitol exceed
The meanest house in Rome, so far my son—   42
This lady's husband here, this, do you see?—
Whom you have banished, does exceed you all.

BRUTUS
Well, well, we'll leave you.

SICINIUS   Why stay we to be baited   45
With one that wants her wits?   *Exeunt tribunes.*

VOLUMNIA   Take my prayers with you.   46
I would the gods had nothing else to do
But to confirm my curses! Could I meet 'em   48
But once a day, it would unclog my heart   49
Of what lies heavy to 't.

MENENIUS   You have told them home,   50
And, by my troth, you have cause. You'll sup with me?   51

VOLUMNIA
Anger's my meat. I sup upon myself,
And so shall starve with feeding. [*To Virgilia.*] Come,
     let's go.
Leave this faint puling and lament as I do,   54
In anger, Juno-like. Come, come, come.   55
                    Exeunt [Volumnia and Virgilia].
MENENIUS   Fie, fie, fie!   *Exit.*

♣

---

42 meanest poorest   **45–46 baited With** harassed by   **48 'em** i.e., the
tribunes   **49 unclog** unburden   **50 to 't** upon it.   **told them home**
berated them thoroughly   **51 sup** dine   **54 puling** whimpering
55 Juno-like resembling Juno, chief goddess of the Romans (whose
unforgiving anger is mentioned by Virgil in *Aeneid* 1.4)

4.3 *Enter [Nicanor,] a Roman, and [Adrian,] a*
       Volsce.

ROMAN I know you well, sir, and you know me. Your
name, I think, is Adrian.

VOLSCE It is so, sir. Truly, I have forgot you.

ROMAN I am a Roman; and my services are, as you are,
against 'em. Know you me yet?   5

VOLSCE Nicanor, no?

ROMAN The same, sir.

VOLSCE You had more beard when I last saw you, but
your favor is well approved by your tongue. What's the   9
news in Rome? I have a note from the Volscian state   10
to find you out there. You have well saved me a day's
journey.

ROMAN There hath been in Rome strange insurrections:
the people against the senators, patricians, and nobles.

VOLSCE Hath been? Is it ended, then? Our state thinks
not so. They are in a most warlike preparation, and
hope to come upon them in the heat of their division.

ROMAN The main blaze of it is past, but a small thing
would make it flame again; for the nobles receive so to
heart the banishment of that worthy Coriolanus that
they are in a ripe aptness to take all power from the
people and to pluck from them their tribunes forever.
This lies glowing, I can tell you, and is almost mature   23
for the violent breaking out.

VOLSCE Coriolanus banished?

ROMAN Banished, sir.

VOLSCE You will be welcome with this intelligence, Nicanor.

ROMAN The day serves well for them now. I have heard   29
it said the fittest time to corrupt a man's wife is when
she's fallen out with her husband. Your noble Tullus
Aufidius will appear well in these wars, his great op-

4.3. Location: A road between Rome and Antium.
5 against 'em i.e., on behalf of the Volsces against Rome   **9 your . . .**
tongue your face and appearance are well confirmed by your voice
10 note instruction   **23 glowing** smoldering   **29 them** i.e., the Volscians

poser, Coriolanus, being now in no request of his 33
country.

VOLSCE   He cannot choose. I am most fortunate thus 35
accidentally to encounter you. You have ended my
business, and I will merrily accompany you home.

ROMAN   I shall, between this and supper, tell you most 38
strange things from Rome, all tending to the good of
their adversaries. Have you an army ready, say you?

VOLSCE   A most royal one: the centurions and their 41
charges, distinctly billeted, already in th' entertain- 42
ment, and to be on foot at an hour's warning.   43

ROMAN   I am joyful to hear of their readiness, and am
the man, I think, that shall set them in present action. 45
So, sir, heartily well met, and most glad of your company.

VOLSCE   You take my part from me, sir; I have the most 48
cause to be glad of yours.

ROMAN   Well, let us go together.   *Exeunt.*

❖

4.4   *Enter Coriolanus in mean apparel, disguised
and muffled.*

CORIOLANUS
  A goodly city is this Antium. City,
  'Tis I that made thy widows. Many an heir
  Of these fair edifices 'fore my wars   3
  Have I heard groan and drop. Then know me not,

---

33 in no request of unvalued by   **35 choose** do otherwise (than appear
well)   **38 this** this present time   **41 centurions** officers each in command of a hundred men or "century"   **41–42 their charges** the men
under their command   **42 distinctly billeted** separately enrolled
42–43 in th' entertainment mobilized, on the payroll   **45 present** immediate   **48 my part** i.e., the words I should say

4.4. Location: Antium. Before Aufidius' house.
3 'fore my wars in the face of my onslaught

Lest that thy wives with spits and boys with stones   5
In puny battle slay me.

     Enter a Citizen.

                    Save you, sir.   6

CITIZEN
And you.
CORIOLANUS   Direct me, if it be your will,
Where great Aufidius lies. Is he in Antium?   8
CITIZEN
He is, and feasts the nobles of the state
At his house this night.
CORIOLANUS   Which is his house, beseech you?
CITIZEN
This, here before you.
CORIOLANUS   Thank you, sir. Farewell.
                         Exit Citizen.
O world, thy slippery turns! Friends now fast sworn,   12
Whose double bosom seems to wear one heart,
Whose hours, whose bed, whose meal and exercise
Are still together, who twin, as 'twere, in love   15
Unseparable, shall within this hour,   16
On a dissension of a doit, break out   17
To bitterest enmity; so fellest foes,   18
Whose passions and whose plots have broke their sleep   19
To take the one the other, by some chance,   20
Some trick not worth an egg, shall grow dear friends   21
And interjoin their issues. So with me: 22
My birthplace hate I, and my love's upon
This enemy town. I'll enter. If he slay me,
He does fair justice; if he give me way,   25
I'll do his country service.   *Exit.*

---

5 spits pointed rods on which meat is held over a fire **6 puny** petty.
Save God save **8 lies** dwells **12 slippery turns** fickle shifts of fortune. **fast** firmly **15 still** ever **16 this hour** an hour **17 dissension of
a doit** i.e., paltry dispute. (A *doit* is a small coin.) **18 fellest** fiercest
19–20 Whose . . . other whose passions and whose plotting to undo each
other have kept them awake at night **21 trick** trifle **22 issues** children
(by marriage ?); fortunes (?) **25 give me way** accede to my request

4.5 *Music plays. Enter a Servingman.*

FIRST SERVINGMAN Wine, wine, wine! What service is
here? I think our fellows are asleep. [*Exit.*] 2

Enter another Servingman.

SECOND SERVINGMAN Where's Cotus? My master calls
for him. Cotus! *Exit.*

Enter Coriolanus.

CORIOLANUS
A goodly house. The feast smells well, but I
Appear not like a guest.

Enter the First Servingman.

FIRST SERVINGMAN What would you have, friend?
Whence are you? Here's no place for you. Pray go to the 8
door. *Exit.* 9

CORIOLANUS
I have deserved no better entertainment 10
In being Coriolanus.

Enter Second Servingman.

SECOND SERVINGMAN Whence are you, sir? Has the
porter his eyes in his head, that he gives entrance
to such companions? Pray, get you out. 14

CORIOLANUS Away!

SECOND SERVINGMAN Away? Get you away.

CORIOLANUS Now thou'rt troublesome.

SECOND SERVINGMAN Are you so brave? I'll have you 18
talked with anon. 19

Enter Third Servingman. The First, [*entering,*]
meets him.

THIRD SERVINGMAN What fellow's this?

4.5. Location: Antium. The house of Aufidius. The sense of time here is
virtually continuous; the stage is imaginatively transformed from the
outside to the inside of Aufidius' house.
2 fellows fellow servants 8 Whence from where 8–9 go to the door
get out 10 entertainment reception 14 companions rascals, base
persons 18 brave insolent 19 anon immediately

FIRST SERVINGMAN   A strange one as ever I looked on. I
   cannot get him out o' the house. Prithee, call my
   master to him.

THIRD SERVINGMAN   What have you to do here, fellow?
   Pray you, avoid the house.   25

CORIOLANUS   Let me but stand. I will not hurt your
   hearth.

THIRD SERVINGMAN   What are you?

CORIOLANUS   A gentleman.

THIRD SERVINGMAN   A marvelous poor one.

CORIOLANUS   True, so I am.

THIRD SERVINGMAN   Pray you, poor gentleman, take
   up some other station; here's no place for you. Pray
   you, avoid. Come.

CORIOLANUS   Follow your function, go, and batten on   35
   cold bits.   *Pushes him away from him.*

THIRD SERVINGMAN   What, you will not?—Prithee, tell
   my master what a strange guest he has here.

SECOND SERVINGMAN   And I shall.
                                        Exit Second Servingman.

THIRD SERVINGMAN   Where dwell'st thou?

CORIOLANUS   Under the canopy.   41

THIRD SERVINGMAN   Under the canopy?

CORIOLANUS   Ay.

THIRD SERVINGMAN   Where's that?

CORIOLANUS   I' the city of kites and crows.   45

THIRD SERVINGMAN   I' the city of kites and crows? What
   an ass it is! Then thou dwell'st with daws too?   47

CORIOLANUS   No, I serve not thy master.

THIRD SERVINGMAN   How, sir? Do you meddle with my   49
   master?

CORIOLANUS   Ay, 'tis an honester service than to meddle
   with thy mistress. Thou prat'st and prat'st. Serve with
   thy trencher. Hence!   53
                          Beats him away. [Exit Third Servingman.]

---

25 avoid leave   **35 Follow your function** go back to your ordinary
business.   **batten** grow fat   **41 canopy** i.e., of heaven   **45 kites and
crows** i.e., scavengers and birds of prey   **47 daws** jackdaws. (Conventional emblems of foolishness.)   **49 meddle** concern yourself with. (But
Coriolanus answers in the sense of "have sexual intercourse with.")
53 trencher wooden plate

Enter Aufidius with the [Second] Servingman.

AUFIDIUS   Where is this fellow?

SECOND SERVINGMAN   Here, sir. I'd have beaten him like
a dog, but for disturbing the lords within.   56
                    [*He and First Servingman stand aside.*]

AUFIDIUS
Whence com'st thou? What wouldst thou? Thy name?
Why speak'st not? Speak, man. What's thy name?

CORIOLANUS [*Unmuffling*]   If, Tullus,
Not yet thou know'st me, and, seeing me, dost not
Think me for the man I am, necessity
Commands me name myself.

AUFIDIUS   What is thy name?

CORIOLANUS
A name unmusical to the Volscians' ears,
And harsh in sound to thine.

AUFIDIUS   Say, what's thy name?
Thou hast a grim appearance, and thy face
Bears a command in 't; though thy tackle's torn,   66
Thou show'st a noble vessel. What's thy name?   67

CORIOLANUS
Prepare thy brow to frown. Know'st thou me yet?

AUFIDIUS   I know thee not. Thy name?

CORIOLANUS
My name is Caius Marcius, who hath done
To thee particularly and to all the Volsces   71
Great hurt and mischief; thereto witness may   72
My surname, Coriolanus. The painful service,   73
The extreme dangers, and the drops of blood
Shed for my thankless country are requited
But with that surname—a good memory,   76
And witness of the malice and displeasure
Which thou shouldst bear me. Only that name remains.
The cruelty and envy of the people,
Permitted by our dastard nobles, who
Have all forsook me, hath devoured the rest,

---

56 but for except for (fear of)   **66 a command** authority.   **tackle** rigging
of a ship (i.e., Coriolanus' clothing)   **67 show'st** appear to be.   **vessel**
(1) ship (2) body containing the soul   **71 particularly** personally
72 mischief injury   **73 painful** arduous   **76 memory** reminder

And suffered me by the voice of slaves to be
Whooped out of Rome. Now this extremity   83
Hath brought me to thy hearth; not out of hope—
Mistake me not—to save my life, for if
I had feared death, of all the men i' the world
I would have 'voided thee, but in mere spite,   87
To be full quit of those my banishers,   88
Stand I before thee here. Then if thou hast
A heart of wreak in thee, that wilt revenge   90
Thine own particular wrongs and stop those maims   91
Of shame seen through thy country, speed thee straight   92
And make my misery serve thy turn. So use it
That my revengeful services may prove
As benefits to thee, for I will fight
Against my cankered country with the spleen   96
Of all the under fiends. But if so be   97
Thou dar'st not this, and that to prove more fortunes   98
Thou'rt tired, then, in a word, I also am
Longer to live most weary, and present
My throat to thee and to thy ancient malice;   101
Which not to cut would show thee but a fool,
Since I have ever followed thee with hate,
Drawn tuns of blood out of thy country's breast,   104
And cannot live but to thy shame, unless
It be to do thee service.

AUFIDIUS   O Marcius, Marcius!
Each word thou hast spoke hath weeded from my heart
A root of ancient envy. If Jupiter   108
Should from yond cloud speak divine things
And say "'Tis true," I'd not believe them more
Than thee, all-noble Marcius. Let me twine
Mine arms about that body, whereagainst
My grainèd ash an hundred times hath broke   113

---

83 Whooped driven with hoots   **87 mere** utter   **88 full quit of** fully
even with   **90 wreak** vengeance   **91 stop** close up   **91–92 maims Of
shame** dishonoring injuries   **92 through** throughout.   **speed** hasten.
straight straightway   **96 cankered** infected with evils (as from the
action of the cankerworm)   **97 under fiends** fiends of the underworld
98 prove more fortunes try your fortunes further   **101 ancient** long-
standing   **104 tuns** large barrels   **108 envy** malice   **113 grainèd ash**
spear with ashen shaft

And scarred the moon with splinters. [*They embrace.*]
  Here I clip   114
The anvil of my sword, and do contest   115
As hotly and as nobly with thy love
As ever in ambitious strength I did
Contend against thy valor. Know thou first,
I loved the maid I married; never man
Sighed truer breath. But that I see thee here,
Thou noble thing, more dances my rapt heart   121
Than when I first my wedded mistress saw
Bestride my threshold. Why, thou Mars, I tell thee   123
We have a power on foot, and I had purpose   124
Once more to hew thy target from thy brawn,   125
Or lose mine arm for 't. Thou hast beat me out   126
Twelve several times, and I have nightly since   127
Dreamt of encounters twixt thyself and me—
We have been down together in my sleep,   129
Unbuckling helms, fisting each other's throat—   130
And waked half dead with nothing. Worthy Marcius,   131
Had we no other quarrel else to Rome but that
Thou art thence banished, we would muster all   133
From twelve to seventy and, pouring war   134
Into the bowels of ungrateful Rome,
Like a bold flood o'erbeat. O, come, go in,   136
And take our friendly senators by the hands,
Who now are here, taking their leaves of me,
Who am prepared against your territories,   139
Though not for Rome itself.
CORIOLANUS   You bless me, gods!
AUFIDIUS
  Therefore, most absolute sir, if thou wilt have   141

---

114 clip embrace **115 anvil** i.e., Coriolanus, on whom Aufidius' sword
has beaten as on an anvil **121 dances** makes to dance. **rapt** enrap-
tured **123 Bestride** step across **124 power on foot** force in the field
125 hew cut, strike. **target** shield. **brawn** i.e., muscular arm **126 out**
thoroughly **127 several** distinct **129 down together** fighting on the
ground. **sleep** i.e., dreams **130 helms** helmets. **fisting** clutching
131 waked (I have) awakened **133 muster all** enlist everyone
134 twelve i.e., aged twelve **136 o'erbeat** overflow, surge over, beat
down **139 am prepared** i.e., have forces ready to move **141 absolute**
perfect

The leading of thine own revenges, take
Th' one half of my commission; and set down—   143
As best thou art experienced, since thou know'st
Thy country's strength and weakness—thine own ways,
Whether to knock against the gates of Rome
Or rudely visit them in parts remote
To fright them ere destroy. But come in.
Let me commend thee first to those that shall   149
Say yea to thy desires. A thousand welcomes!
And more a friend than e'er an enemy;
Yet, Marcius, that was much. Your hand. Most welcome!
                    Exeunt [Coriolanus and Aufidius].
                    Two of the Servingmen [come forward].

FIRST SERVINGMAN   Here's a strange alteration!

SECOND SERVINGMAN   By my hand, I had thought to
have strucken him with a cudgel; and yet my mind gave   155
me his clothes made a false report of him.

FIRST SERVINGMAN   What an arm he has! He turned
me about with his finger and his thumb as one would
set up a top.   159

SECOND SERVINGMAN   Nay, I knew by his face that there
was something in him. He had, sir, a kind of face,
methought—I cannot tell how to term it.

FIRST SERVINGMAN   He had so, looking as it were—
Would I were hanged but I thought there was more   164
in him than I could think.

SECOND SERVINGMAN   So did I, I'll be sworn. He is simply the rarest man i' the world.   167

FIRST SERVINGMAN   I think he is. But a greater soldier
than he you wot one.   169

SECOND SERVINGMAN   Who, my master?

FIRST SERVINGMAN   Nay, it's no matter for that.   171

SECOND SERVINGMAN   Worth six on him.

---

143 commission command. **set down** determine upon   **149 commend**
present   **155 gave** told   **159 set up** set going   **164 but I thought** if I
didn't think   **167 rarest** most remarkable   **169 you wot one** you know
one who is greater, i.e., Aufidius. (Perhaps the phrase should read *you
wot on,* you know of, know who I mean.)   **171 Nay . . . that** i.e., never
mind about names

FIRST SERVINGMAN   Nay, not so neither. But I take him 173
to be the greater soldier.

SECOND SERVINGMAN   Faith, look you, one cannot tell
how to say that. For the defense of a town our general
is excellent.

FIRST SERVINGMAN   Ay, and for an assault too.

Enter the Third Servingman.

THIRD SERVINGMAN   O slaves, I can tell you news—
news, you rascals!

FIRST AND SECOND SERVINGMEN   What, what, what? Let's
partake.

THIRD SERVINGMAN   I would not be a Roman, of all nations; I had as lief be a condemned man.   184

FIRST AND SECOND SERVINGMEN   Wherefore? Wherefore?   185

THIRD SERVINGMAN   Why, here's he that was wont to 186
thwack our general, Caius Marcius.

FIRST SERVINGMAN   Why do you say "thwack our general"?

THIRD SERVINGMAN   I do not say "thwack our general,"
but he was always good enough for him.

SECOND SERVINGMAN   Come, we are fellows and friends.
He was ever too hard for him; I have heard him say
so himself.

FIRST SERVINGMAN   He was too hard for him, directly to
say the truth on 't, before Corioles; he scotched him 195
and notched him like a carbonado.   196

SECOND SERVINGMAN   An he had been cannibally given, 197
he might have boiled and eaten him too.

FIRST SERVINGMAN   But, more of thy news.

THIRD SERVINGMAN   Why, he is so made on here within 200
as if he were son and heir to Mars; set at upper end o' 201
the table; no question asked him by any of the senators but they stand bald before him. Our general him- 203

---

173 him i.e., Aufidius. (Some commentators argue that *him* is Coriolanus;
the servingmen tend to contradict themselves in their newfound admiration for Coriolanus and their loyalty toward their own general.)   **184 as
lief** as soon   **185 Wherefore** why   **186 was wont** used   **195 on 't** of it.
scotched scored, gashed   **196 carbonado** meat scored across for broil-
ing   **197 An** if   **200 made on** made much of   **201 at upper end** i.e., at the
place of honor   **203 but** unless.   **bald** bareheaded

self makes a mistress of him, sanctifies him- 204
self with 's hand, and turns up the white o' the eye to his 205
discourse. But the bottom of the news is, our general is 206
cut i' the middle and but one half of what he was
yesterday, for the other has half by the entreaty and grant
of the whole table. He'll go, he says, and sowl the 209
porter of Rome gates by th' ears. He will mow all down
before him, and leave his passage polled.   211

SECOND SERVINGMAN   And he's as like to do 't as any man
I can imagine.

THIRD SERVINGMAN   Do 't? He will do 't! For look you, sir,
he has as many friends as enemies; which friends, sir,
as it were, durst not, look you, sir, show themselves,
as we term it, his friends whilst he's in directitude.   217

FIRST SERVINGMAN   Directitude? What's that?

THIRD SERVINGMAN   But when they shall see, sir, his crest
up again, and the man in blood, they will out of their 220
burrows like coneys after rain and revel all with him.   221

FIRST SERVINGMAN   But when goes this forward?

THIRD SERVINGMAN   Tomorrow, today, presently. You 223
shall have the drum struck up this afternoon. 'Tis,
as it were, a parcel of their feast, and to be executed 225
ere they wipe their lips.

SECOND SERVINGMAN   Why, then we shall have a stirring 227
world again. This peace is nothing but to rust iron,
increase tailors, and breed ballad makers.

FIRST SERVINGMAN   Let me have war, say I. It exceeds
peace as far as day does night. It's spritely walking,
audible, and full of vent. Peace is a very apoplexy, 232
lethargy; mulled, deaf, sleepy, insensible; a getter of 233
more bastard children than war's a destroyer of men.

SECOND SERVINGMAN   'Tis so. And as wars in some

204–205 sanctifies . . . hand touches his (Coriolanus') hand as though
it were a holy relic   **206 bottom** last item, gist   **209 sowl** drag
211 polled stripped (as one would strip branches or foliage)
217 directitude (A blunder for something like *discretitude* or *discredit*.)   **220 in blood** in full vigor. (Usually said of hounds.)   **will out**
will come out   **221 coneys** rabbits   **223 presently** immediately
225 parcel part   **227 stirring** active   **232 audible** keen of hearing, or
heard as it makes its cry. (War is here seen as a hunting animal.)   **full
of vent** full of activity and vitality, quick to pick up the scent.   **apoplexy**
paralysis   **233 mulled** insipid, drowsy.   **getter** begetter

sort may be said to be a ravisher, so it cannot be
denied but peace is a great maker of cuckolds.

FIRST SERVINGMAN Ay, and it makes men hate one
another.

THIRD SERVINGMAN   Reason: because they then less need
one another. The wars for my money! I hope to see
Romans as cheap as Volscians.—They are rising, 242
they are rising.

FIRST AND SECOND SERVINGMEN   In, in, in, in!

Exeunt.

❖

4.6   *Enter the two tribunes, Sicinius and Brutus.*

SICINIUS
  We hear not of him, neither need we fear him.
  His remedies are tame: the present peace   2
  And quietness of the people, which before
  Were in wild hurry. Here do we make his friends   4
  Blush that the world goes well, who rather had,
  Though they themselves did suffer by 't, behold
  Dissentious numbers pestering streets than see   7
  Our tradesmen singing in their shops and going
  About their functions friendly.   9

BRUTUS
  We stood to 't in good time.

        Enter Menenius.

                              Is this Menenius?   10

SICINIUS
  'Tis he, 'tis he. O, he is grown most kind
  Of late.—Hail, sir!

242 rising i.e., rising from table

4.6. Location: Rome. A public place.
2 His . . . tame the remedies against Coriolanus, the antidotes to him,
are to be found in tameness; or, perhaps, his means of redress are tame.
(Sicinius argues that the quietness of the populace affords no opportunity for those who hope to foment further trouble and thereby bring
about Coriolanus' return.) **4 hurry** commotion **7 pestering** crowding,
blocking **9 functions** activities **10 stood to 't** i.e., stood up against
Coriolanus

MENENIUS   Hail to you both!

SICINIUS
Your Coriolanus is not much missed
But with his friends. The commonwealth doth stand,   14
And so would do were he more angry at it.   15

MENENIUS
All's well, and might have been much better if
He could have temporized.   17

SICINIUS   Where is he, hear you?

MENENIUS   Nay, I hear nothing.
His mother and his wife hear nothing from him.

Enter three or four Citizens.

ALL CITIZENS
The gods preserve you both!

SICINIUS   Good e'en, our neighbors.

BRUTUS
Good e'en to you all, good e'en to you all.

FIRST CITIZEN
Ourselves, our wives, and children, on our knees
Are bound to pray for you both.

SICINIUS   · Live and thrive!

BRUTUS
Farewell, kind neighbors. We wished Coriolanus
Had loved you as we did.

ALL CITIZENS   Now the gods keep you!

BOTH TRIBUNES   Farewell, farewell.   *Exeunt Citizens.*

SICINIUS
This is a happier and more comely time   28
Than when these fellows ran about the streets
Crying confusion.

BRUTUS   Caius Marcius was
A worthy officer i' the war, but insolent,
O'ercome with pride, ambitious, past all thinking
Self-loving.

SICINIUS
And affecting one sole throne, without assistance.   34

MENENIUS   I think not so.

---

14 But with except among   **15 were** even were   **17 temporized** compromised   **28 comely** gracious   **34 affecting . . . throne** desiring to rule alone.   **assistance** partnership (in rule)

SICINIUS
  We should by this, to all our lamentation,   36
  If he had gone forth consul, found it so.
BRUTUS
  The gods have well prevented it, and Rome
  Sits safe and still without him.

    Enter an Aedile.

AEDILE   Worthy tribunes,
  There is a slave, whom we have put in prison,
  Reports the Volsces with two several powers   41
  Are entered in the Roman territories,
  And with the deepest malice of the war
  Destroy what lies before 'em.
MENENIUS   'Tis Aufidius,
  Who, hearing of our Marcius' banishment,
  Thrusts forth his horns again into the world,   46
  Which were inshelled when Marcius stood for Rome, 47
  And durst not once peep out.
SICINIUS Come, what talk you of Marcius?   49
BRUTUS
  Go see this rumorer whipped. It cannot be
  The Volsces dare break with us.
MENENIUS   Cannot be?   51
  We have record that very well it can,
  And three examples of the like hath been
  Within my age. But reason with the fellow   54
  Before you punish him, where he heard this,
  Lest you shall chance to whip your information   56
  And beat the messenger who bids beware
  Of what is to be dreaded.
SICINIUS   Tell not me.
  I know this cannot be.
BRUTUS   Not possible.

    Enter a Messenger.

36 should should have. **this** this time **41 several powers** separate
armed forces **46 Thrusts . . . again** (i.e., like a snail) **47 inshelled** i.e.,
drawn in the shell like a snail's horns. **stood** fought **49 what** why
51 break break their treaty **54 age** lifetime. **reason** discuss **56 information** source of information

MESSENGER
  The nobles in great earnestness are going
  All to the Senate House. Some news is come
  That turns their countenances.
SICINIUS   'Tis this slave—   62
  Go whip him 'fore the people's eyes—his raising,   63
  Nothing but his report.
MESSENGER   Yes, worthy sir,
  The slave's report is seconded, and more,   65
  More fearful, is delivered.
SICINIUS   What more fearful?   66
MESSENGER
  It is spoke freely out of many mouths—
  How probable I do not know—that Marcius,
  Joined with Aufidius, leads a power 'gainst Rome,
  And vows revenge as spacious as between   70
  The young'st and oldest thing.
SICINIUS   This is most likely!   71
BRUTUS
  Raised only that the weaker sort may wish   72
  Good Marcius home again.
SICINIUS   The very trick on 't.
MENENIUS   This is unlikely.
  He and Aufidius can no more atone   76
  Than violent'st contrariety.   77

    Enter [a Second] Messenger.

SECOND MESSENGER
  You are sent for to the Senate.
  A fearful army, led by Caius Marcius   79
  Associated with Aufidius, rages
  Upon our territories, and have already
  O'erborne their way, consumed with fire, and took   82
  What lay before them.

    Enter Cominius.

---

62 turns changes   **62–63 slave . . . his raising** slave's incitement,
for which let him be publicly whipped   **65 seconded** confirmed
66 delivered reported   **70–71 as spacious . . . thing** comprehensive
enough to embrace every living person   **72 Raised** invented, stirred
up. (See *raising,* l. 63 above.)   **76 atone** come to a reconciliation
77 violent'st contrariety most extreme opposites   **79 fearful** frighten-
ing   **82 O'erborne their way** carried all before them

COMINIUS　O, you have made good work!

MENENIUS　What news? What news?

COMINIUS

You have holp to ravish your own daughters and　86
To melt the city leads upon your pates,　87
To see your wives dishonored to your noses—　88

MENENIUS　What's the news? What's the news?

COMINIUS

Your temples burnèd in their cement, and　90
Your franchises, whereon you stood, confined　91
Into an auger's bore.

MENENIUS　　　　　　Pray now, your news?—　92
You have made fair work, I fear me.—Pray, your news?
If Marcius should be joined wi' the Volscians—

COMINIUS　　　　　　　　　　　　　If?
He is their god. He leads them like a thing
Made by some other deity than Nature,
That shapes man better; and they follow him
Against us brats with no less confidence　98
Than boys pursuing summer butterflies
Or butchers killing flies.

MENENIUS　　　　　　You have made good work,
You and your apron-men, you that stood so much　101
Upon the voice of occupation and　102
The breath of garlic eaters!

COMINIUS　He'll shake your Rome about your ears.

MENENIUS

As Hercules did shake down mellow fruit.　105
You have made fair work!

BRUTUS　But is this true, sir?

COMINIUS　Ay, and you'll look pale
Before you find it other. All the regions　109
Do smilingly revolt, and who resists　110
Are mocked for valiant ignorance

---

86 holp helped　**87 leads** roofs of lead.　**pates** heads　**88 to** before
90 in their cement i.e., to their foundations　**91 franchises** political
rights.　**stood** insisted　**92 auger's bore** hole drilled by an auger, i.e.,
narrow space　**98 brats** mere children　**101 apron-men** artisans (who
wore aprons)　**102 voice of occupation** votes of the laboring men
105 Hercules . . . fruit (Hercules' eleventh labor was to carry off the
golden apples of the Hesperides.)　**109 other** otherwise　**110 who**
whoever

And perish constant fools. Who is 't can blame him?   112
Your enemies and his find something in him.   113
MENENIUS   We are all undone, unless
   The noble man have mercy.
COMINIUS   Who shall ask it?
   The tribunes cannot do 't for shame; the people
   Deserve such pity of him as the wolf
   Does of the shepherds. For his best friends, if they   118
   Should say "Be good to Rome," they charged him even 119
   As those should do that had deserved his hate
   And therein showed like enemies.
MENENIUS   'Tis true   121
   If he were putting to my house the brand   122
   That should consume it, I have not the face
   To say "Beseech you, cease." You have made fair hands, 124
   You and your crafts! You have crafted fair!
COMINIUS   You have brought   125
   A trembling upon Rome such as was never
   S' incapable of help.
BOTH TRIBUNES   Say not we brought it.   127
MENENIUS
   How? Was 't we? We loved him, but, like beasts
   And cowardly nobles, gave way unto your clusters,   129
   Who did hoot him out o' the city.
COMINIUS   But I fear
   They'll roar him in again. Tullus Aufidius,   131
   The second name of men, obeys his points   132
   As if he were his officer. Desperation
   Is all the policy, strength, and defense
   That Rome can make against them.

   Enter a troop of Citizens.

112 **constant** loyal   113 **Your . . . him** i.e., both your enemies, the patricians, and his enemies, the Volscians, find cause to ally themselves with
him   118 **For** as for   119 **they . . . even** they would be enjoining him
just   121 **showed** would appear   122 **brand** torch   124 **made fair
hands** done fine work. (Said ironically.)   125 **crafted fair** (1) cleverly
advanced the interests of the crafts or occupations (2) shown your
expert craft or cunning   127 **S'** so   129 **clusters** mobs   131 **roar . . .
again** i.e., roar with pain when he returns   132 **second . . . men** second
greatest name among men.   **his points** Coriolanus' instructions

MENENIUS   Here come the clusters.—
And is Aufidius with him? You are they
That made the air unwholesome when you cast
Your stinking greasy caps in hooting at
Coriolanus' exile. Now he's coming,
And not a hair upon a soldier's head
Which will not prove a whip. As many coxcombs   141
As you threw caps up will he tumble down,
And pay you for your voices. 'Tis no matter;
If he could burn us all into one coal,   144
We have deserved it.

ALL CITIZENS   Faith, we hear fearful news.

FIRST CITIZEN   For mine own part,
When I said banish him, I said 'twas pity.

SECOND CITIZEN   And so did I.

THIRD CITIZEN   And so did I; and, to say the truth, so   151
did very many of us. That we did, we did for the best;
and though we willingly consented to his banishment,
yet it was against our will.

COMINIUS   You're goodly things, you voices!

MENENIUS   You have made good work,
You and your cry!—Shall 's to the Capitol?   156

COMINIUS   O, ay, what else?

                    Exeunt both [Cominius and Menenius].

SICINIUS
Go, masters, get you home, be not dismayed.
These are a side that would be glad to have   159
This true which they so seem to fear. Go home,
And show no sign of fear.

FIRST CITIZEN   The gods be good to us! Come, masters,
let 's home. I ever said we were i' the wrong when we
banished him.

SECOND CITIZEN   So did we all. But come, let's home.

                              Exeunt Citizens.

BRUTUS   I do not like this news.

SICINIUS   Nor I.

---

141 coxcombs i.e., fools' heads   **144 into one coal** into one cindery
mass   **151 That** what   **156 cry** pack.   **Shall 's** i.e., shall we go
159 side party, faction

BRUTUS
Let's to the Capitol. Would half my wealth   168
Would buy this for a lie!
SICINIUS   Pray, let's go.   169
                                        Exeunt tribunes.

❖

4.7   *Enter Aufidius with his Lieutenant.*

AUFIDIUS   Do they still fly to the Roman?
LIEUTENANT
I do not know what witchcraft's in him, but
Your soldiers use him as the grace 'fore meat,
Their talk at table, and their thanks at end;
And you are darkened in this action, sir,   5
Even by your own.
AUFIDIUS   I cannot help it now,   6
Unless by using means I lame the foot   7
Of our design. He bears himself more proudlier,
Even to my person, than I thought he would
When first I did embrace him. Yet his nature
In that's no changeling, and I must excuse   11
What cannot be amended.
LIEUTENANT   Yet I wish, sir—
I mean for your particular—you had not   13
Joined in commission with him, but either
Have borne the action of yourself or else   15
To him had left it solely.
AUFIDIUS
I understand thee well, and be thou sure,
When he shall come to his account, he knows not   18
What I can urge against him. Although it seems—   19

168–169 Would . . . lie I would give half of my fortune if this could be proven a lie

4.7. Location: A camp, at a small distance from Rome.
5 you . . . action your glory is dimmed in this undertaking   **6 your own** i.e., your followers, or your own action   **7 means** remedies
11 changeling i.e., fickle thing   **13 for your particular** regarding your self-interest   **15 Have . . . yourself** had led the campaign yourself
18 account judgment   **19 urge against him** accuse him of

And so he thinks, and is no less apparent
To th' vulgar eye—that he bears all things fairly 21
And shows good husbandry for the Volscian state, 22
Fights dragonlike, and does achieve as soon 23
As draw his sword, yet he hath left undone 24
That which shall break his neck or hazard mine
Whene'er we come to our account.

LIEUTENANT
Sir, I beseech you, think you he'll carry Rome? 27

AUFIDIUS
All places yield to him ere he sits down, 28
And the nobility of Rome are his;
The senators and patricians love him too.
The tribunes are no soldiers, and their people
Will be as rash in the repeal as hasty 32
To expel him thence. I think he'll be to Rome
As is the osprey to the fish, who takes it 34
By sovereignty of nature. First he was
A noble servant to them, but he could not
Carry his honors even. Whether 'twas pride, 37
Which out of daily fortune ever taints 38
The happy man; whether defect of judgment, 39
To fail in the disposing of those chances 40
Which he was lord of; or whether nature, 41
Not to be other than one thing, not moving 42
From th' casque to th' cushion, but commanding peace 43
Even with the same austerity and garb 44
As he controlled the war; but one of these—
As he hath spices of them all, not all, 46
For I dare so far free him—made him feared, 47

---

21 vulgar common. **bears** carries out **22 husbandry for** management
of **23 achieve** accomplish his goals **24 As draw** i.e., as he does draw
27 carry capture **28 sits down** besieges **32 repeal** recall from exile
34 osprey fish hawk, said to have had the power to fascinate fishes so by
his kingly *sovereignty* (l. 35) that they would allow themselves to be
taken without a struggle **37 Carry . . . even** bear his honors temperately **38–39 out of . . . man** as a result of continuous success always
corrupts the fortunate man **40 disposing** clever using **41 nature** (his)
character **42 Not . . . thing** i.e., always rigidly the same, in peace as in
war **43 casque** helmet (as symbolic of the warrior). **cushion** i.e., seat
for a senator **44 austerity and garb** austere behavior **46 spices** tastes,
traces. **not all** not all in full measure **47 free** free from blame

So hated, and so banished. But he has a merit   48
To choke it in the utterance. So our virtues   49
Lie in th' interpretation of the time;   50
And power, unto itself most commendable,   51
Hath not a tomb so evident as a chair   52
T' extol what it hath done.   53
One fire drives out one fire; one nail, one nail;
Rights by rights falter, strengths by strengths do fail.   55
Come, let's away. When, Caius, Rome is thine,
Thou art poor'st of all; then shortly art thou mine.

Exeunt.

❖

48 So . . . banished because he was feared he was hated, and because he
was hated he was banished   **48–49 he . . . utterance** i.e., his merit is of
the perverse sort that undoes the praise it should receive; it *chokes*
itself by its very *utterance*. (Also interpreted as meaning, "He has so
many counterbalancing good points that the words stick in my
throat.")   **50 the time** i.e., our contemporaries   **51–53 power . . . done**
i.e., however much power may be valued for its own sake, its effective-
ness depends more on what people say publicly about its accomplishments than on any intrinsic merit. **chair** public rostrum or magistrate's
chair   **55 by rights falter** i.e., are made to seem less by other rights.
(The point is that great deeds, eclipsed by the subsequent deeds of
others, are soon forgotten.)

5.1   *Enter Menenius, Cominius; Sicinius, Brutus,*
the two tribunes; with others.

MENENIUS
No, I'll not go. You hear what he hath said   1
Which was sometime his general, who loved him   2
In a most dear particular. He called me father;   3
But what o' that? Go you that banished him;
A mile before his tent fall down and knee   5
The way into his mercy. Nay, if he coyed   6
To hear Cominius speak, I'll keep at home.
COMINIUS
He would not seem to know me.
MENENIUS   Do you hear?   8
COMINIUS
Yet one time he did call me by my name.
I urged our old acquaintance, and the drops
That we have bled together. "Coriolanus"
He would not answer to; forbade all names.
He was a kind of nothing, titleless,
Till he had forged himself a name o' the fire
Of burning Rome.
MENENIUS   Why, so; you have made good work!
A pair of tribunes that have wracked for Rome   16
To make coals cheap! A noble memory!   17
COMINIUS
I minded him how royal 'twas to pardon   18
When it was less expected. He replied,
It was a bare petition of a state   20
To one whom they had punished.
MENENIUS   Very well.
Could he say less?

5.1. Location: Rome. A public place.
1 he i.e., Cominius   2 Which who.   sometime formerly   3 In . . .
particular with warmest personal affection.   He i.e., Coriolanus
5 knee crawl on your knees (like penitents approaching shrines)
6 coyed showed reluctance, disdained   8 would not seem pretended
not   16 wracked for brought ruin to (with a play on "striven for")
17 coals charcoal (which will be cheap because Rome will be burnt to
cinders; see 4.6.144).   memory memorial   18 minded reminded
20 bare barefaced, paltry

COMINIUS
   I offered to awaken his regard   23
   For 's private friends. His answer to me was,   24
   He could not stay to pick them in a pile   25
   Of noisome musty chaff. He said 'twas folly,   26
   For one poor grain or two, to leave unburnt
   And still to nose th' offense.   28
MENENIUS   For one poor grain or two!
   I am one of those! His mother, wife, his child,
   And this brave fellow too, we are the grains;
   You are the musty chaff, and you are smelt
   Above the moon. We must be burnt for you.
SICINIUS
   Nay, pray, be patient. If you refuse your aid
   In this so-never-needed help, yet do not   35
   Upbraid 's with our distress. But sure, if you   36
   Would be your country's pleader, your good tongue,
   More than the instant army we can make,   38
   Might stop our countryman.
MENENIUS   No, I'll not meddle.
SICINIUS
   Pray you, go to him.
MENENIUS   What should I do?
BRUTUS
   Only make trial what your love can do
   For Rome, towards Marcius.
MENENIUS
   Well, and say that Marcius return me,   43
   As Cominius is returned, unheard—what then?
   But as a discontented friend, grief-shot   45
   With his unkindness? Say 't be so?
SICINIUS   Yet your good will
   Must have that thanks from Rome after the measure   48
   As you intended well.
MENENIUS   I'll undertake 't.   49

---

23 offered attempted **24 For 's private** for his personal **25 stay . . . them** take time to pick them out **26 noisome** evil-smelling **28 nose th' offense** smell the offensive stuff **35 In . . . help** in this strait where help is needed as never before **36 sure** certainly **38 instant army** army we can raise at this instant **43 say that** i.e., what if **45 But as** i.e., what if I return only as. **grief-shot** grief-stricken **48–49 after . . . As** in proportion that

I think he'll hear me. Yet, to bite his lip   50
And hum at good Cominius much unhearts me.   51
He was not taken well; he had not dined.   52
The veins unfilled, our blood is cold, and then
We pout upon the morning, are unapt   54
To give or to forgive; but when we have stuffed
These pipes and these conveyances of our blood   56
With wine and feeding, we have suppler souls
Than in our priestlike fasts. Therefore I'll watch him
Till he be dieted to my request,   59
And then I'll set upon him.

BRUTUS
You know the very road into his kindness,
And cannot lose your way.

MENENIUS   Good faith, I'll prove him,   62
Speed how it will. I shall ere long have knowledge   63
Of my success.   *Exit.*

COMINIUS   He'll never hear him.

SICINIUS   Not?   64

COMINIUS
I tell you, he does sit in gold, his eye   65
Red as 'twould burn Rome, and his injury   66
The jailer to his pity. I kneeled before him;
'Twas very faintly he said "Rise"; dismissed me   68
Thus, with his speechless hand. What he would do
He sent in writing after me; what he would not,   70
Bound with an oath to yield to his conditions;   71
So that all hope is vain
Unless his noble mother and his wife,   73
Who, as I hear, mean to solicit him

---

50 to bite his lip (An expression of anger, like humming in l. 51; see
below, 5.4.21.) **51 unhearts** disheartens, discourages **52 taken well**
approached at the right time **54 pout upon** are out of temper with
56 conveyances channels **59 dieted to** fed properly so as to be in a
mood for **62 prove** attempt **63 Speed** turn out, succeed **64 success**
outcome **65 in gold** in a golden chair **66 Red** i.e., with anger; also the
color normally used to describe gold. **his injury** his sense of having
been wronged **68 faintly** coldly, indifferently **70–71 what . . . conditions** i.e., what terrible actions he would not take against Rome if we
bound ourselves under oath to agree to his terms. (See 5.3.14.) Or
Cominius may mean that Coriolanus is bound by his own oath not to
relent. **73 Unless** unless in, except for

For mercy to his country. Therefore, let's hence
And with our fair entreaties haste them on.   *Exeunt.*

❖

5.2   *Enter Menenius to the Watch, or Guard.*

FIRST WATCH   Stay! Whence are you?   1
SECOND WATCH   Stand, and go back.   2
MENENIUS
    You guard like men; 'tis well. But, by your leave,
    I am an officer of state, and come
    To speak with Coriolanus.
FIRST WATCH   From whence?
MENENIUS   From Rome.
FIRST WATCH
    You may not pass; you must return. Our general
    Will no more hear from thence.
SECOND WATCH
    You'll see your Rome embraced with fire before
    You'll speak with Coriolanus.
MENENIUS   Good my friends,
    If you have heard your general talk of Rome
    And of his friends there, it is lots to blanks   13
    My name hath touched your ears. It is Menenius.
FIRST WATCH
    Be it so; go back. The virtue of your name   15
    Is not here passable.
MENENIUS   I tell thee, fellow,   16
    Thy general is my lover. I have been   17
    The book of his good acts, whence men have read
    His fame unparalleled happily amplified;   19
    For I have ever verified my friends—   20
    Of whom he's chief—with all the size that verity   21
    Would without lapsing suffer. Nay, sometimes,   22
    Like to a bowl upon a subtle ground,   23

5.2. Location: The Volscian camp before Rome.
1 Whence are you where are you from   **2 Stand** stop   **13 lots to blanks**
prize-winning tickets compared to valueless ones (i.e., all the world to
nothing)   **15 virtue** strength   **16 passable** current (like a coin), and able
to provide passage   **17 lover** friend   **19 happily** aptly, felicitously; or
haply, perhaps   **20 verified** testified to the worth of   **21 size** amplifica-
tion.   **verity** truth   **22 lapsing** erring, distorting.   **suffer** allow
23 bowl ball used in bowls.   **subtle** deceptively irregular

I have tumbled past the throw, and in his praise   24
Have almost stamped the leasing. Therefore, fellow,   25
I must have leave to pass.   26

FIRST WATCH   Faith, sir, if you had told as many lies in   27
his behalf as you have uttered words in your own, you
should not pass here; no, though it were as virtuous   29
to lie as to live chastely. Therefore go back.   30

MENENIUS   Prithee, fellow, remember my name is
Menenius, always factionary on the party of your gen-   32
eral.

SECOND WATCH   Howsoever you have been his liar, as
you say you have, I am one that, telling true under   35
him, must say you cannot pass. Therefore go back.   36

MENENIUS   Has he dined, canst thou tell? For I would
not speak with him till after dinner.

FIRST WATCH   You are a Roman, are you?

MENENIUS   I am, as thy general is.

FIRST WATCH   Then you should hate Rome, as he does.
Can you, when you have pushed out your gates the   42
very defender of them and in a violent popular ig-   43
norance given your enemy your shield, think to front   44
his revenges with the easy groans of old women, the   45
virginal palms of your daughters, or with the palsied   46
intercession of such a decayed dotant as you seem to   47
be? Can you think to blow out the intended fire your
city is ready to flame in with such weak breath as
this? No, you are deceived; therefore, back to Rome
and prepare for your execution. You are condemned;
our general has sworn you out of reprieve and pardon.   52

MENENIUS   Sirrah, if thy captain knew I were here, he   53
would use me with estimation.   54

FIRST WATCH   Come, my captain knows you not.

---

24 tumbled . . . throw overshot the mark   **25 stamped the leasing** given
the stamp of truth to lying (i.e., overstated praise of him)   **26 leave**
permission   **27 if** even if   **29 though** even if   **30 chastely** honestly (but
with a sexual quibble, taking *lie* in a sexual sense)   **32 factionary** active
as a partisan   **35–36 telling . . . him** telling the truth in his service
42 out out at; out of   **43–44 violent popular ignorance** folly of mob
violence   **44 shield** defender, i.e., Coriolanus.   **front** meet   **45 easy
groans** i.e., groans that are easily provoked   **46 virginal . . . daughters**
uplifted hands of your virgin daughters   **47 dotant** dotard   **52 out of**
beyond the reach of   **53 Sirrah** (Term of address to inferiors.)   **54 use**
treat.   **estimation** esteem

MENENIUS   I mean thy general.

FIRST WATCH   My general cares not for you. Back, I say,
go, lest I let forth your half-pint of blood. Back! That's
the utmost of your having. Back!   59

MENENIUS   Nay, but, fellow, fellow—

Enter Coriolanus with Aufidius.

CORIOLANUS   What's the matter?

MENENIUS   Now, you companion, I'll say an errand for   62
you. You shall know now that I am in estimation; you   63
shall perceive that a Jack guardant cannot office me   64
from my son Coriolanus. Guess but by my entertain-   65
ment with him if thou stand'st not i' the state of hang-   66
ing or of some death more long in spectatorship and   67
crueller in suffering; behold now presently, and   68
swoon for what's to come upon thee. [*To Coriolanus.*]
The glorious gods sit in hourly synod about thy partic-   70
ular prosperity and love thee no worse than thy old
father Menenius does! O my son, my son! Thou art
preparing fire for us; look thee, here's water to quench
it. I was hardly moved to come to thee; but being as-   74
sured none but myself could move thee, I have been
blown out of your gates with sighs, and conjure thee   76
to pardon Rome and thy petitionary countrymen. The   77
good gods assuage thy wrath, and turn the dregs of it
upon this varlet here—this, who, like a block, hath   79
denied my access to thee.

CORIOLANUS   Away!

MENENIUS   How? Away?

CORIOLANUS
Wife, mother, child, I know not. My affairs
Are servanted to others. Though I owe   84

---

59 utmost of your having all you are going to get   **62 companion** fellow.   **say an errand** deliver a message   **63 in estimation** well regarded   **64 Jack guardant** knave on guard duty.   **office** officiously
keep   **65–66 entertainment with** reception by   **66 stand'st ... state** i.e.,
are not at risk   **67 spectatorship** watching   **68 presently** immediately
70 synod council, assembly   **74 hardly moved** with difficulty persuaded   **76 your gates** i.e., the gates of your native Rome   **77 petitionary** suppliant, petitioning   **79 block** (1) impediment (2) blockhead
84 servanted subjected.   **owe** own, possess

My revenge properly, my remission lies   85
In Volscian breasts. That we have been familiar,   86
Ingrate forgetfulness shall poison rather   87
Than pity note how much. Therefore, begone.   88
Mine ears against your suits are stronger than
Your gates against my force. Yet, for I loved thee,   90
Take this along; I writ it for thy sake, [*Giving a letter*]
And would have sent it. Another word, Menenius,
I will not hear thee speak.—This man, Aufidius,
Was my beloved in Rome; yet thou behold'st!
AUFIDIUS   You keep a constant temper.   95
        Exeunt. Manent the Guard and Menenius.
FIRST WATCH   Now, sir, is your name Menenius?
SECOND WATCH   'Tis a spell, you see, of much power.
You know the way home again.
FIRST WATCH   Do you hear how we are shent for keep-   99
ing your greatness back?
SECOND WATCH   What cause, do you think, I have to
swoon?
MENENIUS   I neither care for the world nor your general.
For such things as you, I can scarce think there's any,   104
you're so slight. He that hath a will to die by himself   105
fears it not from another. Let your general do his
worst. For you, be that you are, long; and your misery   107
increase with your age! I say to you, as I was said to,
Away!   *Exit.*
FIRST WATCH   A noble fellow, I warrant him.
SECOND WATCH   The worthy fellow is our general. He's
the rock, the oak not to be wind-shaken.   *Exit Watch.*

♣

85 properly as my own.   **remission** power to forgive   **86–88 That . . .
much** i.e., though we have been close, I will allow ungrateful forgetfulness (i.e., prompted by Rome's ingratitude) to poison the memory of our
friendship rather than allowing my pity to recall how much we meant
to each other   **90 for** because   **95 constant temper** firm mind   **s.d.
Manent** they remain onstage   **99 shent** blamed   **104 For** as for (also at
l. 107)   **105 slight** insignificant.   **by himself** by his own hand   **107 that**
what.   **long** through a long (and tedious) lifetime

5.3   *Enter Coriolanus and Aufidius [with Volscian
soldiers. Coriolanus and Aufidius sit.]*

CORIOLANUS
  We will before the walls of Rome tomorrow
  Set down our host. My partner in this action,   2
  You must report to the Volscian lords how plainly   3
  I have borne this business.

AUFIDIUS   Only their ends   4
  You have respected, stopped your ears against
  The general suit of Rome, never admitted
  A private whisper, no, not with such friends
  That thought them sure of you.

CORIOLANUS   This last old man,
  Whom with a cracked heart I have sent to Rome,
  Loved me above the measure of a father,
  Nay, godded me indeed. Their latest refuge   11
  Was to send him, for whose old love I have—
  Though I showed sourly to him—once more offered   13
  The first conditions, which they did refuse
  And cannot now accept. To grace him only   15
  That thought he could do more, a very little   16
  I have yielded to. Fresh embassies and suits,   17
  Nor from the state nor private friends, hereafter   18
  Will I lend ear to. (*Shout within.*) Ha? What shout is
    this?
  Shall I be tempted to infringe my vow
  In the same time 'tis made? I will not.

    *Enter Virgilia, Volumnia, Valeria, young Marcius,
    with attendants.*

  My wife comes foremost; then the honored mold   22
  Wherein this trunk was framed, and in her hand   23
  The grandchild to her blood. But out, affection!
  All bond and privilege of nature, break!   25

5.3. **Location: The Volscian camp, as in scene 2. The tent of Coriolanus.**
2 **Set down our host** lay siege with our army   3 **plainly** openly   4 **their
ends** i.e., the Volscians' purposes   11 **godded** deified.   **latest refuge** last
resource   13 **showed** acted   15 **grace** gratify   16–17 **a very ... yielded
to** I have conceded a little, but almost nothing   18 **Nor** neither
22 **mold** form, body (of my mother)   23 **this trunk** my body   25 **bond
... nature** natural ties and claims of love

Let it be virtuous to be obstinate. [*The women bow.*]   26
What is that curtsy worth? Or those doves' eyes,   27
Which can make gods forsworn? I melt, and am not
Of stronger earth than others. My mother bows,
As if Olympus to a molehill should
In supplication nod, and my young boy
Hath an aspect of intercession which   32
Great Nature cries "Deny not." Let the Volsces   33
Plow Rome and harrow Italy, I'll never
Be such a gosling to obey instinct, but stand   35
As if a man were author of himself
And knew no other kin.

VIRGILIA   My lord and husband!

CORIOLANUS
These eyes are not the same I wore in Rome.   38

VIRGILIA
The sorrow that delivers us thus changed   39
Makes you think so.

CORIOLANUS   Like a dull actor now,   40
I have forgot my part, and I am out,   41
Even to a full disgrace. Best of my flesh,
Forgive my tyranny, but do not say   43
For that, "Forgive our Romans." O, a kiss
Long as my exile, sweet as my revenge!   [*They kiss.*]
Now, by the jealous queen of heaven, that kiss   46
I carried from thee, dear, and my true lip
Hath virgined it e'er since. You gods! I prate,   48
And the most noble mother of the world
Leave unsaluted. Sink, my knee, i' the earth;   *Kneels*
Of thy deep duty more impression show   51
Than that of common sons.

VOLUMNIA   O, stand up blest!
                               [*He rises.*]

---

26 obstinate hard-hearted   **27 curtsy** (1) bow (2) courtesy.   **doves' eyes**
i.e., beautiful and seductive eyes. (See Song of Solomon 1:15.)
32 aspect of intercession pleading look   **33 Let** even should   **35 gosling**
baby goose (i.e., foolish inexperienced person).   **to** as to   **38–40 These**
. . . so (Coriolanus says, "I see differently now that I am not in Rome."
Virgilia replies, taking his words literally, "Our sorrow has changed us
past recognition.")   **delivers** presents   **41 I am out** I am at a loss for
words   **43 tyranny** cruelty   **46 jealous . . . heaven** i.e., Juno, patroness
of marriage   **48 virgined it** remained untouched.   **prate** talk idly
51 more impression a deeper mark

Whilst with no softer cushion than the flint
I kneel before thee, and unproperly   54
Show duty, as mistaken all this while
Between the child and parent.   [*She kneels.*]
CORIOLANUS   What's this?
Your knees to me? To your corrected son?   57
                              [*He raises her.*]
Then let the pebbles on the hungry beach   58
Fillip the stars! Then let the mutinous winds   59
Strike the proud cedars 'gainst the fiery sun,
Murdering impossibility, to make   61
What cannot be slight work.
VOLUMNIA   Thou art my warrior;   62
I holp to frame thee. Do you know this lady?   63
CORIOLANUS
The noble sister of Publicola,
The moon of Rome, chaste as the icicle   65
That's curded by the frost from purest snow   66
And hangs on Dian's temple—dear Valeria!
VOLUMNIA [*Indicating young Marcius*]
This is a poor epitome of yours,   68
Which by th' interpretation of full time   69
May show like all yourself.
CORIOLANUS [*To his son*]   The god of soldiers, 70
With the consent of supreme Jove, inform   71
Thy thoughts with nobleness, that thou mayst prove
To shame unvulnerable, and stick i' the wars   73
Like a great seamark, standing every flaw   74
And saving those that eye thee!
VOLUMNIA [*To young Marcius*]   Your knee, sirrah. 75
                              [*Young Marcius kneels.*]

54 unproperly unfittingly, violating due propriety   **57 corrected** chas-
tised   **58 hungry** unfertile, barren   **59 Fillip** strike   **61 Murdering** i.e.,
removing   **62 What . . . slight work** an easy task of what cannot be, is
impossible   **63 holp** helped   **65 moon of Rome** (Allusion to Diana,
goddess of chastity and associated with the moon.)   **66 curded** congealed   **68 epitome** abridgement. (Refers to the son of Coriolanus.)
69 by . . . time when time shall have revealed and fulfilled all. (Time will
expand the *epitome*, giving *interpretation* to its full meaning.)   **70 show**
look.   **The god of soldiers** i.e., Mars   **71 inform** inspire   **73 To shame
unvulnerable** incapable of shameful deeds.   **stick** stand out
74 seamark reference object used by mariners in navigating.   **standing**
withstanding.   **flaw** gust of wind   **75 eye thee** i.e., guide themselves by
you, use you as a *seamark*

CORIOLANUS   That's my brave boy!

VOLUMNIA
Even he, your wife, this lady, and myself
Are suitors to you.

CORIOLANUS   I beseech you, peace.
Or, if you'd ask, remember this before:
The thing I have forsworn to grant may never   80
Be held by you denials. Do not bid me   81
Dismiss my soldiers or capitulate   82
Again with Rome's mechanics. Tell me not   83
Wherein I seem unnatural; desire not
T' allay my rages and revenges with
Your colder reasons.

VOLUMNIA   O, no more, no more!
You have said you will not grant us anything;
For we have nothing else to ask but that
Which you deny already. Yet we will ask,
That, if you fail in our request, the blame   90
May hang upon your hardness. Therefore hear us.

CORIOLANUS
Aufidius, and you Volsces, mark; for we'll
Hear naught from Rome in private. [*He sits.*] Your
   request?

VOLUMNIA
Should we be silent and not speak, our raiment   94
And state of bodies would bewray what life   95
We have led since thy exile. Think with thyself   96
How more unfortunate than all living women
Are we come hither; since that thy sight, which should
Make our eyes flow with joy, hearts dance with
   comforts,
Constrains them weep and shake with fear and sorrow,
Making the mother, wife, and child to see
The son, the husband, and the father tearing
His country's bowels out. And to poor we
Thine enmity's most capital. Thou barr'st us   104

80–81 The thing . . . denials i.e., it would be unjust to regard me as
refusing to grant what I have sworn not to grant and hence no
longer have the power of granting   **82 capitulate** come to terms
83 mechanics tradesmen   **90 fail in** do not grant   **94 Should we** even if
we should.   **raiment** clothes   **95 state of** the condition of our.   **bewray**
reveal   **96 Think with thyself** reflect   **104 capital** fatal

Our prayers to the gods, which is a comfort
That all but we enjoy; for how can we,
Alas, how can we for our country pray,
Whereto we are bound, together with thy victory,
Whereto we are bound? Alack, or we must lose   109
The country, our dear nurse, or else thy person,
Our comfort in the country. We must find
An evident calamity, though we had   112
Our wish, which side should win; for either thou   113
Must as a foreign recreant be led   114
With manacles through our streets, or else
Triumphantly tread on thy country's ruin,
And bear the palm for having bravely shed   117
Thy wife and children's blood. For myself, son,
I purpose not to wait on fortune till   119
These wars determine. If I cannot persuade thee   120
Rather to show a noble grace to both parts   121
Than seek the end of one, thou shalt no sooner
March to assault thy country than to tread—
Trust to 't, thou shalt not—on thy mother's womb   124
That brought thee to this world.

VIRGILIA   Ay, and mine,
That brought you forth this boy to keep your name
Living to time.

YOUNG MARCIUS   'A shall not tread on me;   127
I'll run away till I am bigger, but then I'll fight.

CORIOLANUS
Not of a woman's tenderness to be   129
Requires nor child nor woman's face to see.   130
I have sat too long.   [*He rises.*]

VOLUMNIA   Nay, go not from us thus.   131
If it were so that our request did tend
To save the Romans, thereby to destroy
The Volsces whom you serve, you might condemn us
As poisonous of your honor. No, our suit

109 or either **112 evident** certain **113 which** whichever **114 recreant**
traitor **117 palm** i.e., emblem of victory **119 purpose** propose
120 determine come to an end, settle matters **121 grace** favor, mercy.
parts sides **124 Trust . . . not** (Read this parenthetical phrase after
sooner in l. 122.) **127 'A** he **129–130 Not . . . see** if a man is not to
yield to a womanly tenderness, he must not look upon any child's or
woman's face **131 sat** i.e., stayed here listening

Is that you reconcile them, while the Volsces   136
May say, "This mercy we have showed," the Romans,
"This we received," and each in either side   138
Give the all-hail to thee and cry, "Be blest   139
For making up this peace!" Thou know'st, great son,
The end of war's uncertain, but this certain,
That, if thou conquer Rome, the benefit
Which thou shalt thereby reap is such a name
Whose repetition will be dogged with curses,
Whose chronicle thus writ: "The man was noble,
But with his last attempt he wiped it out,   146
Destroyed his country, and his name remains
To th' ensuing age abhorred." Speak to me, son.
Thou hast affected the fine strains of honor,   149
To imitate the graces of the gods;
To tear with thunder the wide cheeks o' the air,   151
And yet to charge thy sulfur with a bolt   152
That should but rive an oak. Why dost not speak?   153
Think'st thou it honorable for a nobleman
Still to remember wrongs? Daughter, speak you;   155
He cares not for your weeping. Speak thou, boy;   156
Perhaps thy childishness will move him more
Than can our reasons. There's no man in the world
More bound to 's mother, yet here he lets me prate   159
Like one i' the stocks.—Thou hast never in thy life   160
Showed thy dear mother any courtesy,
When she, poor hen, fond of no second brood,   162
Has clucked thee to the wars and safely home,   163
Loaden with honor. Say my request's unjust,
And spurn me back; but if it be not so,
Thou art not honest, and the gods will plague thee   166

136 while so that at the same time 138 each everyone. in on 139 all-
hail general acclaim 146 attempt undertaking. it i.e., his nobility
149 affected sought, cherished 151 cheeks (On Renaissance maps the
winds were often portrayed as issuing from the cheeks of Aeolus, Greek
god of the winds.) 152 charge load. sulfur lightning. bolt thunder-
bolt 153 but rive an oak i.e., do no undeserved harm to men; Coriolanus wishes to be, like Jupiter, mighty but wise in his use of power
155 Still always 156 cares not for is unmoved by 159–160 prate . . .
stocks i.e., talk uselessly like a prisoner who has been publicly humili-
ated 162 When whereas. fond desirous 163 clucked marshaled as a
hen her brood 166 honest honorable, just

That thou restrain'st from me the duty which   167
To a mother's part belongs.—He turns away.
Down, ladies! Let us shame him with our knees.
To his surname Coriolanus 'longs more pride   170
Than pity to our prayers. Down! [*They kneel.*] An end;
This is the last. So we will home to Rome   172
And die among our neighbors.—Nay, behold 's!
This boy, that cannot tell what he would have,   174
But kneels and holds up hands for fellowship,   175
Does reason our petition with more strength   176
Than thou hast to deny 't.—Come, let us go. [*They rise.*]
This fellow had a Volscian to his mother;   178
His wife is in Corioles, and his child   179
Like him by chance.—Yet give us our dispatch.   180
I am hushed until our city be afire,
And then I'll speak a little.
                    [*He*] *holds her by the hand, silent.*
CORIOLANUS   O Mother, Mother!
What have you done? Behold, the heavens do ope,
The gods look down, and this unnatural scene
They laugh at. O my Mother, Mother! O!
You have won a happy victory to Rome;
But for your son—believe it, O, believe it!—
Most dangerously you have with him prevailed,
If not most mortal to him. But, let it come.—   189
Aufidius, though I cannot make true wars,   190
I'll frame convenient peace. Now, good Aufidius,   191
Were you in my stead, would you have heard
A mother less? Or granted less, Aufidius?
AUFIDIUS
I was moved withal.
CORIOLANUS   I dare be sworn you were.   194
And, sir, it is no little thing to make
Mine eyes to sweat compassion. But, good sir,   196

167 thou restrain'st you withhold   **170 'longs** belongs   **172 will home**
will go home   **174 This boy** i.e., Coriolanus' son.   **cannot . . . have** does
not understand what he is asking for   **175 for fellowship** merely to
keep us company   **176 reason** argue for   **178 to** for   **179 his child** this
boy, supposed his son   **180 dispatch** dismissal, leave to go   **189 mortal**
fatally   **190 true** i.e., as I vowed to do   **191 convenient** fitting, proper
194 withal by it   **196 sweat compassion** i.e., weep with pity

What peace you'll make, advise me. For my part,
I'll not to Rome; I'll back with you, and pray you, 198
Stand to me in this cause. O Mother! Wife! 199

AUFIDIUS [*Aside*]
I am glad thou hast set thy mercy and thy honor
At difference in thee. Out of that I'll work
Myself a former fortune.

　　　　　　　[*The ladies make signs to Coriolanus.*]

CORIOLANUS [*To the ladies*]　Ay, by and by; 202
But we will drink together; and you shall bear
A better witness back than words, which we, 204
On like conditions, will have countersealed. 205
Come, enter with us. Ladies, you deserve
To have a temple built you. All the swords
In Italy, and her confederate arms, 208
Could not have made this peace. 　　　　　*Exeunt.*

❖

5.4　*Enter Menenius and Sicinius.*

MENENIUS　See you yond coign o' the Capitol, yond cor- 1
nerstone?

SICINIUS　Why, what of that?

MENENIUS　If it be possible for you to displace it with
your little finger, there is some hope the ladies of
Rome, especially his mother, may prevail with him.
But I say there is no hope in 't; our throats are
sentenced, and stay upon execution. 8

SICINIUS　Is 't possible that so short a time can alter the
condition of a man? 10

MENENIUS　There is difference between a grub and a
butterfly, yet your butterfly was a grub. This Marcius
is grown from man to dragon. He has wings; he's
more than a creeping thing.

---

198 back go back　**199 Stand to** stand by　**202 former fortune** fortune
great as formerly　**204 better witness** i.e., formal document of peace
205 On . . . countersealed having agreed to the same conditions, will
both have sealed and guaranteed　**208 her confederate arms** the weapons of her allies

5.4. Location: Rome. A public place.
1 coign corner　**8 stay upon** await　**10 condition** nature

SICINIUS   He loved his mother dearly.

MENENIUS   So did he me; and he no more remembers
his mother now than an eight-year-old horse. The tart-
ness of his face sours ripe grapes. When he walks, he
moves like an engine, and the ground shrinks before   19
his treading. He is able to pierce a corslet with his eye,   20
talks like a knell, and his hum is a battery. He sits in   21
his state as a thing made for Alexander. What he bids   22
be done is finished with his bidding. He wants noth-   23
ing of a god but eternity and a heaven to throne in.   24

SICINIUS   Yes, mercy, if you report him truly.   25

MENENIUS   I paint him in the character. Mark what   26
mercy his mother shall bring from him. There is no
more mercy in him than there is milk in a male tiger;
that shall our poor city find. And all this is long of you.   29

SICINIUS   The gods be good unto us!

MENENIUS   No, in such a case the gods will not be good
unto us. When we banished him, we respected not
them; and, he returning to break out necks, they respect not us.

Enter a Messenger.

MESSENGER
Sir, if you'd save your life, fly to your house!
The plebeians have got your fellow tribune
And hale him up and down, all swearing, if   37
The Roman ladies bring not comfort home,
They'll give him death by inches.

Enter another Messenger.

SICINIUS   What's the news?   39

SECOND MESSENGER
Good news, good news! The ladies have prevailed,

---

19 engine heavy instrument of war such as a battering ram   **20 corslet**
body armor   **21 a knell** the tolling of a bell announcing a death.   **hum**
(An expression of anger.)   **battery** assault by artillery   **22 state** chair of
state.   **as . . . Alexander** as though he were a statue of Alexander the
Great (who lived after Coriolanus)   **23 finished . . . bidding** i.e., as good
as done once he orders it   **23–24 wants nothing** lacks no attribute
24 throne be enthroned   **25 mercy** i.e., he lacks mercy   **26 in the
character** to the life   **29 long of** owing to   **37 hale** drag   **39 death by
inches** slow and lingering death

The Volscians are dislodged, and Marcius gone.   41
A merrier day did never yet greet Rome,
No, not th' expulsion of the Tarquins.   43

SICINIUS
Friend, art thou certain this is true?
Is 't most certain?

SECOND MESSENGER
As certain as I know the sun is fire.
Where have you lurked, that you make doubt of it?
Ne'er through an arch so hurried the blown tide   48
As the recomforted through the gates. Why, hark you!   49
     Trumpets, hautboys, drums beat, all together.
The trumpets, sackbuts, psalteries, and fifes,   50
Tabors and cymbals, and the shouting Romans,   51
Make the sun dance. (*A shout within.*) Hark you!

MENENIUS   This is good news.
I will go meet the ladies. This Volumnia
Is worth of consuls, senators, patricians,
A city full; of tribunes, such as you,
A sea and land full. You have prayed well today.
This morning for ten thousand of your throats
I'd not have given a doit. Hark, how they joy!   58
         Sound still, with the shouts.

SICINIUS
First, the gods bless you for your tidings!
Next, accept my thankfulness.

SECOND MESSENGER
Sir, we have all great cause to give great thanks.

SICINIUS   They are near the city?

SECOND MESSENGER   Almost at point to enter.   63

SICINIUS   We'll meet them, and help the joy.

                  Exeunt.

---

41 dislodged gone from their camp   **43 th' expulsion of the Tarquins**
i.e., the expulsion of Rome's last kings and beginning of the Republic
48 arch i.e., arch of a bridge, such as London Bridge.   **blown** swollen,
driven by the wind   **49 s.d., hautboys** oboelike instruments   **50 sackbuts**
early trombones.   **psalteries** stringed instruments played by plucking
the strings   **51 Tabors** small drums   **58 doit** very small coin   **63 at
point** ready

5.5   *Enter two Senators with ladies [Volumnia,*
       Virgilia, Valeria] passing over the stage, with
       other lords.

FIRST SENATOR
   Behold our patroness, the life of Rome!
   Call all your tribes together, praise the gods,
   And make triumphant fires! Strew flowers before them!
   Unshout the noise that banished Marcius;   4
   Repeal him with the welcome of his mother.   5
   Cry, "Welcome, ladies, welcome!"
ALL   Welcome, ladies, welcome!
       A flourish with drums and trumpets. [Exeunt.]

❖

5.6   *Enter Tullus Aufidius, with attendants.*

AUFIDIUS
   Go tell the lords o' the city I am here.
   Deliver them this paper. [*He gives a paper.*] Having read
     it,
   Bid them repair to the marketplace, where I,   3
   Even in theirs and in the commons' ears,
   Will vouch the truth of it. Him I accuse   5
   The city ports by this hath entered and   6
   Intends t' appear before the people, hoping
   To purge himself with words. Dispatch.
                          [*Exeunt attendants.*]

     Enter three or four Conspirators of Aufidius'
     faction.

                         Most welcome!

5.5. Location: Rome. A street near the gate, seemingly continuous from
the previous scene; the time is virtually continuous.
4 Unshout recall, or cancel by more shouting   **5 Repeal** recall

5.6. Location: Corioles. A Volscian city. (Plutarch sets this action in
Antium, Aufidius' "native town" [l. 49], but at l. 94 and following the
place is Corioles.)
3 repair go   **5 vouch** affirm.   **Him** he whom   **6 ports** gates.   **by this** by
this time

FIRST CONSPIRATOR
  How is it with our general?
AUFIDIUS   Even so
  As with a man by his own alms empoisoned
  And with his charity slain.
SECOND CONSPIRATOR   Most noble sir,   11
  If you do hold the same intent wherein
  You wished us parties, we'll deliver you   13
  Of your great danger.
AUFIDIUS   Sir, I cannot tell.   14
  We must proceed as we do find the people.
THIRD CONSPIRATOR
  The people will remain uncertain whilst
  Twixt you there's difference, but the fall of either   17
  Makes the survivor heir of all.
AUFIDIUS   I know it,
  And my pretext to strike at him admits   19
  A good construction. I raised him, and I pawned   20
  Mine honor for his truth; who, being so heightened,   21
  He watered his new plants with dews of flattery,
  Seducing so my friends; and to this end
  He bowed his nature, never known before
  But to be rough, unswayable, and free.   25
THIRD CONSPIRATOR   Sir, his stoutness   26
  When he did stand for consul, which he lost
  By lack of stooping—
AUFIDIUS   That I would have spoke of.   28
  Being banished for 't, he came unto my hearth,
  Presented to my knife his throat. I took him,
  Made him joint servant with me, gave him way   31
  In all his own desires; nay, let him choose
  Out of my files, his projects to accomplish,   33
  My best and freshest men; served his designments   34
  In mine own person; holp to reap the fame
  Which he did end all his; and took some pride   36

11 **with his** by his own   13 **parties** as allies, partners   14 **Of** from
17 **difference** disagreement   19 **pretext** intention, motive   20 **construction**
interpretation.   **pawned** pledged   21 **truth** loyalty   25 **free** plainspoken
26 **stoutness** obstinacy   28 **That . . . of** I was about to mention that
31 **joint servant** partner   33 **files** ranks, troops   34 **designments** designs,
enterprises   36 **end all his** gather in as all his own

To do myself this wrong—till at the last
I seemed his follower, not partner, and
He waged me with his countenance, as if   39
I had been mercenary.

FIRST CONSPIRATOR   So he did, my lord.   40
The army marveled at it, and, in the last,   41
When he had carried Rome and that we looked   42
For no less spoil than glory—

AUFIDIUS   There was it
For which my sinews shall be stretched upon him.   44
At a few drops of women's rheum, which are   45
As cheap as lies, he sold the blood and labor
Of our great action. Therefore shall he die,
And I'll renew me in his fall. But, hark!   48

              Drums and trumpets sounds, with
                    great shouts of the people.

FIRST CONSPIRATOR
Your native town you entered like a post,   49
And had no welcomes home; but he returns,
Splitting the air with noise.

SECOND CONSPIRATOR   And patient fools,
Whose children he hath slain, their base throats tear
With giving him glory.

THIRD CONSPIRATOR   Therefore, at your vantage,   53
Ere he express himself or move the people
With what he would say, let him feel your sword,
Which we will second. When he lies along,   56
After your way his tale pronounced shall bury   57
His reasons with his body.

AUFIDIUS   Say no more.   58
Here come the lords.

     Enter the Lords of the city.

ALL LORDS
You are most welcome home.

---

39 waged remunerated. **countenance** patronage, favor **40 mercenary**
a hired soldier **41 last** end **42 carried** virtually overcome, or might
have overcome **44 my . . . upon** I shall exert all my strength against
45 rheum i.e., tears **48 renew** restore my reputation **49 post** messenger **53 at your vantage** seizing your opportune moment **56 along**
prostrate **57 After . . . pronounced** your own version of the story
58 reasons justifications

AUFIDIUS   I have not deserved it.
But, worthy lords, have you with heed perused   61
What I have written to you?

ALL LORDS   We have.

FIRST LORD   And grieve to hear 't.
What faults he made before the last, I think   65
Might have found easy fines; but there to end   66
Where he was to begin, and give away
The benefit of our levies, answering us   68
With our own charge, making a treaty where   69
There was a yielding—this admits no excuse.   70

AUFIDIUS   He approaches. You shall hear him.

Enter Coriolanus, marching with drum and
colors; the commoners being with him.

CORIOLANUS
Hail, lords! I am returned your soldier,
No more infected with my country's love   73
Than when I parted hence, but still subsisting   74
Under your great command. You are to know
That prosperously I have attempted, and   76
With bloody passage led your wars even to
The gates of Rome. Our spoils we have brought home
Doth more than counterpoise a full third part   79
The charges of the action. We have made peace   80
With no less honor to the Antiates
Than shame to the Romans; and we here deliver,
Subscribed by the consuls and patricians,   83
Together with the seal o' the Senate, what
We have compounded on.   [*He offers a document.*] 85

AUFIDIUS   Read it not, noble lords,
But tell the traitor, in the highest degree
He hath abused your powers.

CORIOLANUS   "Traitor"? How now?

---

61 with heed carefully   **65 made** committed   **66 easy fines** light penalties   **68 levies** expenses incurred in raising an army   **68–69 answering . . . charge** rewarding us with our own expenses   **70 yielding** surrender   **73 infected with** influenced by (but with the suggestion of contamination)   **74 hence** i.e., from Actium.   **subsisting** continuing   **76 prosperously . . . attempted** my warlike enterprise has been prosperous   **79 Doth . . . part** outweigh by a full third   **80 charges** costs   **83 Subscribed** signed   **85 compounded** agreed

AUFIDIUS Ay, traitor, Marcius!
CORIOLANUS "Marcius"?
AUFIDIUS
  Ay, Marcius, Caius Marcius! Dost thou think
  I'll grace thee with that robbery, thy stol'n name
  Coriolanus, in Corioles?—
  You lords and heads o' the state, perfidiously
  He has betrayed your business and given up,
  For certain drops of salt, your city Rome—   97
  I say "your city"—to his wife and mother,
  Breaking his oath and resolution like
  A twist of rotten silk, never admitting   100
  Counsel o' the war, but at his nurse's tears   101
  He whined and roared away your victory,
  That pages blushed at him and men of heart   103
  Looked wondering each at other.
CORIOLANUS   Hear'st thou, Mars?
AUFIDIUS Name not the god, thou boy of tears!
CORIOLANUS Ha?
AUFIDIUS No more.   .   107
CORIOLANUS
  Measureless liar, thou hast made my heart
  Too great for what contains it. "Boy"? O slave!   109
  Pardon me, lords, 'tis the first time that ever
  I was forced to scold. Your judgments, my grave lords,
  Must give this cur the lie; and his own notion—   112
  Who wears my stripes impressed upon him, that
  Must bear my beating to his grave—shall join
  To thrust the lie unto him.
FIRST LORD Peace, both, and hear me speak.
CORIOLANUS
  Cut me to pieces, Volsces. Men and lads,
  Stain all your edges on me. "Boy"? False hound!   118
  If you have writ your annals true, 'tis there   119
  That, like an eagle in a dovecote, I

97 certain . . . salt some particular tears (i.e., those of Volumnia and
Virgilia) **100 twist** cord **100–101 admitting . . . war** taking counsel
from other officers **103 heart** courage **107 No more** i.e., no more than
a boy **109 Too . . . it** swollen with rage so that my breast cannot contain it **112 notion** understanding, sense of the truth **118 edges**
swords **119 there** recorded there

Fluttered your Volscians in Corioles.
Alone I did it. "Boy"!

AUFIDIUS   Why, noble lords,
  Will you be put in mind of his blind fortune,   123
  Which was your shame, by this unholy braggart,
  'Fore your own eyes and ears?

ALL CONSPIRATORS   Let him die for 't.

ALL PEOPLE Tear him to pieces!—Do it presently!—   126
  He killed my son!—My daughter!—He killed my cousin
  Marcus!—He killed my father!

SECOND LORD Peace, ho! No outrage! Peace!
  The man is noble, and his fame folds in   130
  This orb o' the earth. His last offenses to us
  Shall have judicious hearing. Stand, Aufidius,   132
  And trouble not the peace.

CORIOLANUS   O that I had him,
  With six Aufidiuses, or more, his tribe,
  To use my lawful sword!

AUFIDIUS   Insolent villain!

ALL CONSPIRATORS Kill, kill, kill, kill, kill him!

Draw the Conspirators, and kill Marcius,
who falls. Aufidius stands on him.

LORDS Hold, hold, hold, hold!

AUFIDIUS
  My noble masters, hear me speak.

FIRST LORD   O Tullus!

SECOND LORD
  Thou hast done a deed whereat valor will weep.   139

THIRD LORD
  Tread not upon him, masters. All be quiet;
  Put up your swords.

AUFIDIUS
  My lords, when you shall know—as in this rage,
  Provoked by him, you cannot—the great danger
  Which this man's life did owe you, you'll rejoice   144
  That he is thus cut off. Please it your honors

---

123 blind fortune gift of Fortune, the blind goddess; mere good luck
126 presently immediately   **130 folds in** overspreads, enwraps
132 judicious judicial.   **Stand** stop   **139 whereat** at which   **144 Which
. . . owe you** which while this man lived was owing to you, would sooner
or later have befallen you

To call me to your Senate, I'll deliver   146
Myself your loyal servant, or endure
Your heaviest censure.

FIRST LORD   Bear from hence his body,
And mourn you for him. Let him be regarded
As the most noble corpse that ever herald
Did follow to his urn.

SECOND LORD   His own impatience   151
Takes from Aufidius a great part of blame.
Let's make the best of it.

AUFIDIUS   My rage is gone,
And I am struck with sorrow. Take him up.
Help, three o' the chiefest soldiers; I'll be one.   155
Beat thou the drum that it speak mournfully;
Trail your steel pikes. Though in this city he   157
Hath widowed and unchilded many a one,
Which to this hour bewail the injury,
Yet he shall have a noble memory.   160
Assist.   *Exeunt, bearing the body of Marcius.*
                          A dead march sounded.

146 deliver show, demonstrate **151 impatience** rage **155 be one** i.e., be
the fourth **157 Trail . . . pikes** carry your lances reversed with the
point trailing along the ground (as a sign of mourning) **160 memory**
memorial

Date and Text

Coriolanus was first printed in the First Folio of 1623. Its text was perhaps set from a transcript of the promptbook that clarified Shakespeare's stage directions while also preserving some authorial flavor in them and some Shakespearean spellings. Although printing errors and mislineations are numerous, they are for the most part easy to correct. Dating of the play is uncertain. No early performance is on record. The late style and some possible allusions point to some time around 1608. Menenius' fable of the belly (1.1.94 ff.) is probably indebted to William Camden's *Remains*, published 1605. Echoes of the play may appear in Robert Armin's *The Italian Taylor and His Boy* and Ben Jonson's *Epicoene*, both from 1609. Thus a date in 1608 is plausible but only approximate.

Textual Notes

These textual notes are not a historical collation, either of the early folios or of more recent editions; they are simply a record of departures in this edition from the copy text. The reading adopted in this edition appears in boldface, followed by the rejected reading from the copy text, i.e., the First Folio. Only major alterations in punctuation are noted. Changes in lineation are not indicated, nor are some minor and obvious typographical errors.

Abbreviations used:
F the First Folio
s.d. stage direction
s.p. speech prefix

Copy text: the First Folio.

1.1. 7 [and throughout play] Marcius Martius **15 on** one **33 s.p. Second Citizen** All **42–43 accusations. He** Accusations he **55 s.p. First Citizen** 2 Cit [and so throughout scene] **64 you. For your wants,** you for your wants. **90 stale 't** scale't **105 you. With** you with **108 tauntingly** taintingly **123 you.** you, **125 awhile,** awhile, **171 geese. You are no** Geese you are: No **214 Shouting** Shooting **218 unroofed** vnroo'st **227 s.d. Junius** Annius **240 Lartius** Lucius **242 s.p. [and elsewhere] Lartius** Tit **245, 249 [and elsewhere] First Senator** Sen **252 s.d. Manent** Manet

1.2. s.d. Corioles Coriolus **4 on** one **16 Whither** Whether

1.3. 37 that's that **44 sword, contemning. Tell** sword. Contenning, tell **82 s.p. Virgilia** Vlug **84 yarn** yearne **85 Ithaca** Athica

1.4. 13 s.d. Corioles Coriolus **18 up. Our** vp our **20 s.d. Alarum far off** [after l. 20 in F] **43 trenches. Follow 's!** Trenches followes **46 s.d. gates** Gati **and is shut in** [in F, this is part of the s.d. at l. 43] **57 left, Marcius.** left Martius. **58 entire,** intire: **59 Were** Weare **60 Cato's** Calues

1.5. 7 them, them. **8 up.** vp, **9 him!** him

1.6. 22 flayed Flead **30 wooed, in heart** woo'd in heart; **53 Antiates** Antients **70 Lesser** Lessen **73 alone, or** alone: Or **76 s.p. All** [not in F; speech assigned to Coriolanus] **76 s.d. They . . . caps** [after l. 75 in F] **77 s.p. Marcius** [not in F] **84 I** foure

1.7. 4 lose loose [and sometimes elsewhere] **7 s.d. Exeunt** Exit

1.8. 11 masked. For maskt, for **12 Wert** Wer't

1.9. 32 good . . . all good, and good store of all, **41 May** [F provides a s.p., "Mar"] **49 shout** shoot **64, 66 [and elsewhere] Caius Marcius** Marcus Caius **66 s.p. All** Omnes **67, 78, 81, 89 s.p. Coriolanus** Martius **93 s.d. A flourish. Cornets.** [at the beginning of 1.10 in F]

1.10. 19 itself. Nor it selfe, nor

2.1. 24 how are ho ware **57 cannot** can **61 you you** you **62 faces. If** faces, if **64 bisson** beesome **85 are. When . . . purpose,** are, when . . . purpose.

106 s.p. Valeria, Virgilia 2. Ladies   **122 pocket, the** Pocket ?the   **123 brows, Menenius.** Browes: Menenius,   **160 s.d. [and elsewhere] Lartius** Latius
164 Coriolanus Martius Caius Coriolanus   **177 wear** were
179 s.p. Coriolanus Com   **185 You** Yon   **203 s.d. Brutus** Enter Brutus   **Sicinius** Scicinius [and sometimes elsewhere]   **233 napless** Naples   **254 touch** teach

2.2. 25 ascent assent   **81 one on 's** on ones   **91 chin** Shinne   **92 bristled** brizled   **108 took . . . foot** tooke from face to foote: **155 s.d. Manent** Manet   **160 here . . . marketplace** heere on th' Market place,

2.3. 28 wedged wadg'd   **38 it. I say, if** it, I say. If   **67 but not** but   **88, 91, 106 s.p. Fourth Citizen** 1   **104 s.p. Fifth Citizen** 2   **111 s.p. Both Citizens** Both   **114 hire** higher   **115 toge** tongue   **118 do 't,** doo't?   **132 s.p. Sixth Citizen** 1. Cit   **134 s.p. Seventh Citizen** 2. Cit

3.1. 33 s.p. [and elsewhere] First Senator Senat   **60 abused, set on. This** abus'd: set on, this   **94 good** God!   **129 Their** There   **137 poll** pole   **146 Where one** Whereon   **176 s.d. Enter an Aedile** [after l. 175 in F]   **181 s.p. All Patricians** All   **187 s.p. [and elsewhere] All Plebeians** All   **189 s.p. All** [at l. 191 in F]   **219 s.p. All Plebeians** All Ple   **233 s.d.** [preceded in F by "Exeunt"]   **234 your** our   **235 s.p. Coriolanus** Com   **242 s.p. Cominius** Corio   **243 s.p. Coriolanus** Mene   **245 s.p. Menenius** [not in F]   **283 comes 't** com'st   **315 s.p. Sicinius** Menen   **334 bring him** bring him in peace

3.2. 7 s.p. A Patrician Noble   **14 s.d. Enter Volumnia** [at l. 6 in F]   **23 thwartings** things   **34 herd** heart   **115 drum, into a pipe** Drumme into a Pipe,   **117 lulls** lull

3.3. 34 for th' fourth   **38 Throng** Through   **59 accents** Actions   **73 hell fold** hell. Fould   **76 clutched** clutcht: **77 numbers,** numbers.   **107 it; in** it. In   **118 for** from   **145 s.d. Cominius** Cominius, with Cumalijs   **147 Hoo! Hoo!** Hoo, oo   **147 s.d.** [at l. 145 in F]

4.1. 5 chances chances.   **24 thee** the   **34 wilt** will   **37 s.p. Virgilia** Corio

4.2. 23 words, words.   **46 s.d. Exeunt** Exit

4.3. 9 approved appear'd   **32 will** well

4.4. 23 hate haue

4.5. 75 requited requitted: **83 Whooped** Hoop'd   **152 s.d. Two** Enter two   **181, 185 s.p. First and Second Servingmen** Both   **194 him, directly** him directly,   **195 Corioles;** Corioles,   **209 sowl** sole   **211 polled** poul'd   **233 sleepy** sleepe

4.6. 10 s.d. [at l. 9 in F]   **21 s.p. [and elsewhere] All Citizens** All   **36 lamentation** Lamention   **61 come** comming   **78 s.p. Second Messenger** Mes   **127 s.p. Both Tribunes** Tri   **144 one** oue   **146 s.p. All Citizens** Omnes   **151 us. That** vs, that   **165 s.d. Exeunt** Exit

4.7. 13 had haue   **19 him. Although** him, although   **21 fairly** fairely: **34 osprey** Aspray   **37 'twas** 'was   **39 defect** detect   **49 virtues** Vertue,   **55 falter** fouler

5.2. 65 by my my   **88 pity note how much.** pitty: Note how much,   **95 s.d. Manent** Manet

5.3. 15 accept. To accept, to   **16 more, a** more: A   **48 prate** pray   **63 holp** hope   **127 s.p. Young Marcius** Boy   **149 fine** fiue   **152 charge** change   **163 clucked** clock'd   **169 with our** with him with our   **192 stead** steed

5.4. 40 s.p. [and throughout scene] Second Messenger Mess   **51 cymbals** Symboles

5.5. 4 Unshout Vnshoot

5.6. 57 way his way. His   **63 s.p. All Lords** All   **104 other** others   **117 pieces, Volsces. Men** peeces Volces men   **121 Fluttered** Flatter'd   **136 s.d. Draw** Draw both   **kill** kils

Shakespeare's Sources

Coriolanus probably represents Shakespeare's last use of the first-century Greek biographer Plutarch's *The Lives of the Noble Grecians and Romans*, as translated by Sir Thomas North (1579) from a French version of Jacques Amyot. "The Life of Caius Marcius Coriolanus" provided most of the material for Shakespeare's play, just as "The Life of Marcus Antonius" had provided most of the material for *Antony and Cleopatra*. Plutarch's Coriolanus is a man of exceeding nobility but also of excessive impatience and churlish incivility. In war he practices *virtus*, or "valiantness" as North translates it. He wins his title of Coriolanus by storming the city of Corioles (Corioli) almost single-handed. He is the son of a widow whose good opinion he cherishes; as Plutarch reports, "he thought nothing made him so happy and honorable as that his mother might hear everybody praise and commend him, that she might always see him return with a crown upon his head, and that she might still embrace him with tears running down her cheeks for joy." Coriolanus vehemently disapproves of leniency toward the populace, believing it to be an invitation to anarchy. He is, naturally, an enemy of the people's first tribunes, Junius Brutus and Sicinius Vellutus, who, in Plutarch's estimation, "had only been the causers and procurers of this sedition."

Plutarch informs us that when Coriolanus stands for consul and follows the custom of appearing in the marketplace clad only in a poor gown, the people remember his martial prowess; on the day of the election itself, however, they recall their old hate of him and refuse his candidacy. Coriolanus, in his typically choleric and intemperate fashion, makes no attempt to conceal his outrage at this insult. (Plutarch comments editorially on his behavior as "the fruits of self-will and obstinacy.") When he is banished, Coriolanus goes in disguise to Antium, to the house of Tullus Aufidius, his great rival, knowing perfectly well that "Tullus did more malice and envy him than he did all the Romans besides." Coriolanus and Tullus have long been admiring rivals: "they were ever at the encounter one against another, like lusty courageous youths striving in all emulation of honor, and had encountered many times together." Returning vengefully to Rome, Coriolanus is "determined at the first to persist in his obstinate and inflexible rancor," but finally relents through "natural affection" and receives his wife and mother. Volumnia's oration to him, reported in full by Plutarch, causes Coriolanus to cry out: "You have won a happy victory for your country, but mortal and unhappy for your son."

Shakespeare's changes simultaneously enhance the haughtiness of Coriolanus and the volatility of the commoners, thereby increasing the distance between the two sides. Shakespeare's Coriolanus is revolted by the custom of wearing a robe and displaying his wounds to the people, and shows his contempt more snarlingly than does Plutarch's. He is, unlike Plutarch's protagonist, reluctant to seek office and has to be talked into it by his mother and friends. Shakespeare minimizes the legitimate griefs of the Roman people—Plutarch makes it plain that the Senate does favor the rich, and that the people are oppressed by usurers—and accentuates their political instability. Shakespeare shows them as being manipulated against Coriolanus by the scheming tribunes, whereas in Plutarch the people make up their own minds to oppose Coriolanus for the consulship. Shakespeare also magnifies the roles of Volumnia and of Menenius. Volumnia, though she is mentioned by Plutarch, takes no active part in the story until Coriolanus attacks Rome; Menenius' chief function in Plutarch is to relate the fable of the belly. Shakespeare compresses and rearranges events as he usually does: for example, in Plutarch the people actually leave Rome to demonstrate their grievances, and agree to return only when granted the election of tribunes to represent their interests, whereas in Shakespeare the tribunes have already been elected when the play begins. In Shakespeare, Coriolanus is banished as the result of a dispute over his consulship, not (as in Plutarch) as the result of an insurrection over scarcity of grain.

Shakespeare probably also knew the story of Coriolanus in another classical source, Livy's *Roman History*, Book 2, as translated by Philemon Holland (1600). Other versions of the story were available to him, including an outline of Ro-

man history by L. Annaeus Florus (also called Publius Annius Florus) written in the second century A.D., based
chiefly on Livy. Plutarch, however, seems to have provided
Shakespeare with virtually everything he needed. Even
Shakespeare's alterations of Plutarch tend to enhance rather
than revise Plutarch's overall thesis and appraisal of the
characters in his history.

The Lives of the Noble Grecians and
Romans Compared Together by . . . Plutarch
Translated by Thomas North

FROM THE LIFE OF CAIUS MARCIUS CORIOLANUS

The house of the Marcians at Rome was of the number of
the patricians, out of the which hath sprung many noble
personages, whereof Ancus Marcius was one, King Numa's
daughter's son, who was King of Rome after Tullus Hostilius.[1] Of the same house were Publius and Quintus, who
brought to Rome their best water they had, by conducts.[2]
Censorinus[3] also came of that family, that was so surnamed
because the people had chosen him censor twice. Through
whose persuasion they made a law that no man from
thenceforth might require or enjoy the censorship twice.

Caius Marcius, whose life we intend now to write, being
left an orphan by his father, was brought up under his
mother, a widow, who taught us by experience that orphan-
age bringeth many discommodities to a child but doth not
hinder him to become an honest man and to excel in virtue
above the common sort—as they that are meanly born
wrongfully do complain that it is the occasion of their casting away,[4] for that no man in their youth taketh any care of
them to see them well brought up and taught that were

1 **Ancus Marcius, Numa, Tullus Hostilius** legendary kings of Rome.
Numa is supposed to have been successor to Romulus in this office. The
family or *house* of the Marcians was *of the number of* or included
among such ancient patrician families as these.   2 **conducts** conduits
3 **Censorinus** (A patrician who was twice chosen censor, in 294 and
265 B.C., not the Roman grammarian, third century B.C., of the same
name.) A *censor* was a Roman magistrate with responsibility for both
the census and public morality.   4 **casting away** being rejected and
ruined, as if shipwrecked

meet.[5] This man also is a good proof to confirm some men's opinions that a rare and excellent wit, untaught, doth bring forth many good and evil things together, like as a fat[6] soil bringeth forth herbs and weeds that lieth unmanured. For this Marcius' natural wit and great heart did marvelously stir up his courage to do and attempt notable acts. But on the other side, for lack of education, he was so choleric and impatient that he would yield to no living creature, which made him churlish, uncivil, and altogether unfit for any man's conversation.[7] Yet men marveling much at his constancy, that he was never overcome with pleasure nor money and how he would endure easily all manner of pains and travails, thereupon they well liked and commended his stoutness[8] and temperancy. But for all that, they could not be acquainted with him as one citizen useth[9] to be with another in the city. His behavior was so unpleasant to them by reason of a certain insolent and stern manner he had, which, because it was too lordly, was disliked. And to say truly, the greatest benefit that learning bringeth men unto is this: that it teacheth men that be rude and rough of nature, by compass and rule of reason, to be civil and courteous, and to like better the mean[10] state than the higher. Now in those days valiantness was honored in Rome above all other virtues, which they called *virtus*, by the name of virtue itself, as including in that general name all other special virtues besides. So that *virtus* in the Latin was as much as valiantness.

But Marcius, being more inclined to the wars than any other gentleman of his time, began from his childhood to give himself to handle weapons, and daily did exercise himself therein. And outward he esteemed armor to no purpose unless one were naturally armed within. Moreover, he did so exercise his body to hardness and all kind of activity that he was very swift in running, strong in wrestling, and mighty in gripping,[11] so that no man could ever cast[12] him. Insomuch as those that would try masteries with him for strength and nimbleness would say, when they were over-

---

5 that were meet what would be suitable   **6 like as a fat** just as a rich, fertile   **7 conversation** society, company   **8 travails . . . stoutness** labors . . . resolution, bravery   **9 useth** is accustomed   **10 mean** lowly   **11 gripping** i.e., strength of arm and hand   **12 cast** throw

come, that all was by reason of his natural strength and hardness of ward,[13] that never yielded to any pain or toil he took upon him.

The first time he went to the wars, being but a stripling, was when Tarquin, surnamed The Proud (that had been King of Rome and was driven out for his pride, after many attempts made by sundry battles to come in again, wherein he was ever overcome), did come to Rome with all the aid of the Latins and many other people of Italy, even as it were to set up his whole rest[14] upon a battle by them who with a great and mighty army had undertaken to put him into his kingdom again—not so much to pleasure him as to overthrow the power of the Romans, whose greatness they both feared and envied. In this battle, wherein were many hot and sharp encounters of either party, Marcius valiantly fought in the sight of the Dictator;[15] and, a Roman soldier being thrown to the ground even hard by him, Marcius straight bestrid him[16] and slew the enemy with his own hands, that had before overthrown the Roman. Hereupon, after the battle was won the Dictator did not forget so noble an act, and therefore first of all he crowned Marcius with a garland of oaken boughs. For whosoever saveth the life of a Roman, it is a manner among them to honor him with such a garland. . . .

Moreover, it is daily seen that, honor and reputation lighting on young men before their time and before they have no great courage by nature, the desire to win more dieth straight[17] in them, which easily happeneth, the same having no deep root in them before. Where contrariwise, the first honor that valiant minds do come unto doth quicken up their appetite, hasting them forward as with force of wind to enterprise things of high deserving praise. For they esteem not to receive reward for service done, but rather take it for a remembrance and encouragement to make them do better in time to come, and be ashamed also to cast their honor at their heels,[18] not seeking to increase it still by like

13 ward defense   14 set . . . rest stake everything. (A metaphor from primero, a gambling game.)   15 Dictator Roman magistrate with supreme military and judicial authority   16 straight bestrid him immediately stood over the fallen man in order to defend him   17 straight immediately   18 cast . . . heels cast their honor under foot, reject it with contempt

desert[19] of worthy valiant deeds. This desire being bred in
Marcius, he strained still to pass[20] himself in manliness;
and, being desirous to show a daily increase of his valiantness, his noble service did still advance his fame, bringing
in spoils[21] upon spoils from the enemy. Whereupon, the captains that came afterwards (for envy of them that went before)[22] did contend who should most honor him and who
should bear most honorable testimony of his valiantness.
Insomuch the Romans, having many wars and battles in
those days, Coriolanus was at them all; and there was not a
battle fought from whence he returned not without some
reward of honor.

And as for other,[23] the only respect that made them valiant was they hoped to have honor; but touching Marcius,
the only thing that made him to love honor was the joy he
saw his mother did take of him.[24] For he thought nothing
made him so happy and honorable as that his mother might
hear everybody praise and commend him, that she might
always see him return with a crown upon his head, and that
she might still embrace him with tears running down her
cheeks for joy. Which desire they say Epaminondas[25] did
avow and confess to have been in him, as to think himself a
most happy and blessed man that his father and mother in
their lifetime had seen the victory he wan in the plain of
Leuctres. Now as for Epaminondas, he had this good hap to
have his father and mother living to be partakers of his joy
and prosperity. But Marcius, thinking all due to his mother
that had been also due to his father if he had lived, did not
only content himself to rejoice and honor her, but at her
desire took a wife also, by whom he had two children, and
yet never left his mother's house therefore.

Now he being grown to great credit and authority in
Rome for his valiantness, it fortuned there grew sedition in
the city because the Senate did favor the rich against the
people, who did complain of the sore oppression of usurers
of whom they borrowed money. For those that had little

---

19 not seeking . . . desert i.e., such men are ashamed not to seek to
increase their honor continually by similar deserving   **20 still to pass**
continually to surpass   **21 spoils** plunder   **22 for . . . before** out of
emulation of those who preceded them   **23 other** the others   **24 of him**
in him   **25 Epaminondas** Theban commander and victor over Sparta at
Leuctra, 371 B.C.

were yet spoiled[26] of that little they had by their creditors
for lack of ability to pay the usury, who offered their goods
to be sold to them that would give most. And such as had
nothing left, their bodies were laid hold of and they were
made their bondmen, notwithstanding all the wounds and
cuts they showed which they had received in many battles
fighting for defense of their country and commonwealth. Of
the which, the last war they made was against the Sabines,
wherein they fought upon the promise the rich men had
made them that from thenceforth they would entreat[27] them
more gently, and also upon the word of Marcus Valerius,
chief of the Senate, who, by authority of the council and in
the behalf of the rich, said they should perform that[28] they
had promised. But after that[29] they had faithfully served in
this last battle of all, where they overcame their enemies,
seeing they were never a whit the better nor more gently
entreated and that the Senate would give no ear to them but
make[30] as though they had forgotten their former promise,
and suffered them to be made slaves and bondmen to their
creditors and besides to be turned out of all that ever they
had, they fell then even to flat rebellion and mutiny, and to
stir up dangerous tumults within the city.

The Romans' enemies, hearing of this rebellion, did
straight enter the territories of Rome with a marvelous
great power, spoiling and burning all as they came. Whereupon the Senate immediately made open proclamation by
sound of trumpet that all those which were of lawful age to
carry weapon should come and enter their names into the
muster master's book to go to the wars; but no man obeyed
their commandment. Whereupon their chief magistrates
and many of the Senate began to be of divers opinions
among themselves. For some thought it was reason they
should somewhat yield to the poor people's request and
that they should a little qualify the severity of the law.
Other[31] held hard against that opinion, and that was Marcius for one. For he alleged that the creditors' losing their
money they had lent was not the worst thing that was
thereby, but that the lenity that was favored was a beginning of disobedience, and that the proud attempt of the

---

26 spoiled plundered   27 entreat treat   28 that what   29 after that
after   30 make would make, would act   31 Other others

commonalty was to abolish law and to bring all to confusion. Therefore, he said, if the Senate were wise they should betimes prevent and quench this ill-favored and worse meant beginning. The Senate met many days in consultation about it, but in the end they concluded nothing.

The poor common people, seeing no redress, gathered themselves one day together, and, one encouraging another, they all forsook the city and encamped themselves upon a hill, called at this day the Holy Hill, alongst the river of Tiber, offering no creature any hurt or violence or making any show of actual rebellion, saving that they cried as they went up and down that the rich men had driven them out of the city and that all Italy through they should find air, water, and ground to bury them in.[32] Moreover, they said, to dwell at Rome was nothing else but to be slain or hurt with continual wars and fighting for defense of the rich men's goods.

The Senate, being afeard of their departure, did send unto them certain of the pleasantest old men and the most acceptable to the people among them. Of those, Menenius Agrippa was he who was sent for chief man of the message from the Senate. He, after many good persuasions and gentle requests made to the people on the behalf of the Senate, knit up his oration in the end with a notable tale in this manner: that on a time all the members of man's body did rebel against the belly, complaining of it that it only remained in the midst of the body without doing anything, neither did bear any labor to the maintenance of the rest, whereas all other parts and members did labor painfully and was very careful to satisfy the appetites and desires of the body. And so the belly, all this notwithstanding, laughed at their folly and said, "It is true I first receive all meats that nourish man's body, but afterwards I send it again to the nourishment of other parts of the same." "Even so," quoth he, "O you, my masters and citizens of Rome, the reason is alike between the Senate and you. For matters being well digested and their counsels throughly examined touching the benefit of the commonwealth, the senators are

---

32 all Italy . . . them in (The commoners complain that Rome affords them nothing more than what they could find anywhere in Italy: free air and water and ground in which to be buried.)

cause of the common commodity that cometh unto every one of you."

These persuasions pacified the people, conditionally[33] that the Senate would grant there should be yearly chosen five magistrates, which they now call *Tribuni plebis*,[34] whose office should be to defend the poor people from violence and oppression. So Junius Brutus and Sicinius Vellutus were the first tribunes of the people that were chosen, who had only been the[35] causers and procurers of this sedition. Hereupon, the city being grown again to good quiet and unity, the people immediately went to the wars, showing that they had a good will to do better than ever they did, and to be very willing to obey the magistrates in that[36] they would command concerning the wars.

Marcius also, though it liked him nothing[37] to see the greatness[38] of the people thus increased, considering it was to the prejudice and embasing[39] of the nobility, and also saw that other noble patricians were troubled as well as himself, he did persuade the patricians to show themselves no less forward and willing to fight for their country than the common people were, and to let them know by their deeds and acts that they did not so much pass the people in power and riches as they did exceed them in true nobility and valiantness.

In the country of the Volsces, against whom the Romans made war at that time, there was a principal city and of most fame that was called Corioles, before the which the consul Cominius did lay siege. Wherefore all the other Volsces, fearing lest that city should be taken by assault, they came from all parts of the country to save it, intending to give the Romans battle before the city and to give an onset[40] on them in two several[41] places. The consul Cominius, understanding this, divided his army also in two parts, and, taking the one part with himself, he marched towards them that were drawing to[42] the city out of the country; and the other part of his army he left in the camp with Titus Lar-

---

33 conditionally on condition   **34 Tribuni plebis** tribunes of the people, of the plebeians   **35 only been the** been the only   **36 that** what
37 liked him nothing pleased him not at all   **38 greatness** authority, power   **39 embasing** debasing, degrading   **40 give an onset** make an attack   **41 several** separate   **42 drawing to** approaching

tius, one of the valiantest men the Romans had at that time, to resist those that would make any sally out of the city upon them.

So the Coriolans, making small account of them that lay in camp before the city, made a sally out upon them, in the which at the first the Coriolans had the better and drave[43] the Romans back again into the trenches of their camp. But Marcius, being there at that time, running out of the camp with a few men with him, he slew the first enemies he met withal and made the rest of them stay upon a sudden,[44] crying out to the Romans that had turned their backs and calling them again to fight with a loud voice. For he was even such another as Cato[45] would have a soldier and a captain to be: not only terrible and fierce to lay about him, but to make the enemy afeard with the sound of his voice and grimness of his countenance. Then there flocked about him immediately a great number of Romans, whereat the enemies were so afeard that they gave back presently.[46]

But Marcius, not staying so, did chase and follow them to their own gates that fled for life. And there perceiving that the Romans retired back for the great number of darts[47] and arrows which flew about their ears from the walls of the city, and that there was not one man amongst them that durst venture himself to follow the flying enemies into the city for that it was full of men of war very well armed and appointed,[48] he did encourage his fellows with words and deeds, crying out to them that fortune had opened the gates of the city more for the followers than the fliers. But all this notwithstanding, few had the hearts to follow him. Howbeit Marcius, being in the throng among the enemies, thrust himself into the gates of the city and entered the same among them that fled, without that anyone of them durst[49] at the first turn their face upon him or else offer to stay him. But he, looking about him and seeing he was entered the city with very few men to help him, and perceiving he was environed by his enemies that gathered round about to

---

43 drave drove   **44 stay upon a sudden** quickly halt   **45 Cato** Cato the Censor, 234–149 B.C., reformer and author of a book on military discipline, the subject of one of Plutarch's *Lives*. His great-grandson Cato died in 46 B.C.   **46 gave back presently** retreated immediately   **47 darts** spears   **48 for that . . . appointed** because . . . furnished   **49 without . . . durst** without any of them daring

set upon him, did things then (as it is written) wonderful and incredible, as well for the force of his hand, as[50] also for the agility of his body. And with a wonderful courage and valiantness he made a lane through the midst of them and overthrew also those he laid at, that some he made run to the furthest part of the city, and other for fear he made yield themselves and to let fall their weapons before him. By this means Lartius, that was gotten out,[51] had some leisure to bring the Romans with more safety into the city.

The city being taken in this sort, the most part of the soldiers began incontinently to spoil,[52] to carry away, and to lock up[53]* the booty they had won. But Marcius was marvelous angry with them, and cried out on them that it was no time now to look after spoil and to run straggling here and there to enrich themselves whilst the other consul and their fellow citizens peradventure were fighting with their enemies, and how that, leaving the spoil, they should seek to wind themselves out of[54] danger and peril. Howbeit, cry and say to them what he could, very few of them would hearken to him. Wherefore taking those that willingly offered themselves to follow him, he went out of the city and took his way towards that part where he understood the rest of the army was, exhorting and entreating them by the way that followed him not to be fainthearted; and, oft holding up his hands to heaven, he besought the gods to be so gracious and favorable unto him that he might come in time to the battle, and in good hour to hazard his life in defense of his countrymen. . . .

When they saw him at his first coming, all bloody and in a sweat, and but with a few men following him, some thereupon began to be afeard. But soon after, when they saw him run with a lively cheer to the Consul and to take him by the hand, declaring how he had taken the city of Corioles, and that they saw the consul Cominius also kiss and embrace him, then there was not a man but took heart again to him[55] and began to be of a good courage, some hearing him report from point to point the happy success of this exploit and

---

50 as well . . . as both . . . and   51 that was gotten out i.e., who was outside the city   52 incontinently to spoil immediately to plunder
53 lock up collect, hoard   54 wind themselves out of extricate themselves from   55 took heart . . . him took courage once again

other also conjecturing it by seeing their gestures afar off. Then they all began to call upon the Consul to march forward and to delay no lenger,[56] but to give charge upon the enemy. Marcius asked him how the order of their enemy's battle was and on which side they had placed their best fighting men. The Consul made him answer that he thought the bands which were in the vaward of their battle[57] were those of the Antiates, whom they esteemed to be the warlikest men, and which for valiant courage would give no place to any of the host of their enemies. Then prayed Marcius to be set directly against them. The Consul granted him, greatly praising his courage.

Then Marcius, when both armies came almost to join, advanced himself a good space before his company and went so fiercely to give charge on the vaward that came right against him that they could stand no lenger in his hands, he made such a lane through them and opened a passage into the battle of the enemies. But the two wings of either side turned one to the other to compass him in between them; which the consul Cominius perceiving, he sent thither straight of the best soldiers he had about him. So the battle was marvelous bloody about Marcius, and in a very short space many were slain in the place. But in the end the Romans were so strong that they distressed[58] the enemies and brake their array,[59] and, scattering them, made them fly. Then they prayed Marcius that he would retire to the camp, because they saw he was able to do no more, he was already so wearied with the great pain he had taken and so faint with the great wounds he had upon him. But Marcius answered them that it was not for conquerors to yield nor to be fainthearted, and thereupon began afresh to chase those that fled until such time as the army of the enemies was utterly overthrown and numbers of them slain and taken prisoners.

The next morning betimes[60] Marcius went to the Consul, and the other Romans with him. There the consul Cominius, going up to his chair of state in the presence of the whole army, gave thanks to the gods for so great, glorious,

56 lenger longer   **57 bands . . . battle** troops that were in the vanguard of their army   **58 distressed** overwhelmed   **59 brake their array** broke their battle lines   **60 betimes** early

and prosperous a victory. Then he spake to Marcius, whose valiantness he commended beyond the moon, both for that he himself saw him do with his eyes as also for that[61] Marcius had reported unto him. So in the end he willed Marcius he should choose out of all the horses they had taken of their enemies and of all the goods they had won, whereof there was great store, ten of every sort which he liked best before any distribution should be made to other. Besides this great honorable offer he had made him, he gave him, in testimony that he had won that day the prize of prowess above all other, a goodly horse with a caparison and all furniture to him,[62] which the whole army beholding did marvelously praise and commend. But Marcius, stepping forth, told the Consul he most thankfully accepted the gift of his horse, and was a glad man besides that his service had deserved his general's commendation. And as for his other offer, which was rather a mercenary reward than an honorable recompense, he would none of it, but was contented to have his equal part with the other soldiers. "Only this grace," said he, "I crave and beseech you to grant me. Among the Volsces there is an old friend and host of mine, an honest wealthy man and now a prisoner, who, living before in great wealth in his own country, liveth now a poor prisoner in the hands of his enemies. And yet notwithstanding all this his misery and misfortune, it would do me great pleasure if I could save him from this one danger: to keep him from being sold as a slave."

The soldiers, hearing Marcius' words, made a marvelous great shout among them, and they were more that wondered at his great contentation[63] and abstinence, when they saw so little covetousness in him, than they were that highly praised and extolled his valiantness. For even they themselves that did somewhat malice[64] and envy his glory to see him thus honored and passingly[65] praised did think him so much the more worthy of an honorable recompense for his valiant service, as[66] the more carelessly he refused the great offer made him for his profit; and they esteemed more the

---

61 for that ... for that for what ... for what   **62 a caparison ... to him** ornamental saddle cover and all equipment appertaining
63 contentation contentedness with small reward   **64 malice** regard with malice   **65 passingly** surpassingly   **66 as** in proportion as

virtue that was in him that made him refuse such rewards
than that which made them to be offered him as unto a worthy person.[67] For it is far more commendable to use riches
well than to be valiant; and yet it is better not to desire them
than to use them well.

After this shout and noise of the assembly was somewhat
appeased,[68] the consul Cominius began to speak in this sort:
"We cannot compel Marcius to take these gifts we offer him
if he will not receive them, but we will give him such a reward for the noble service he hath done as he cannot refuse.
Therefore we do order and decree that henceforth he be
called Coriolanus, unless his valiant acts have won him that
name before our nomination." And so ever since he still
bare[69] the third name of Coriolanus. And thereby it appeareth that the first name the Romans have, as Caius, was
our Christian name now. The second, as Marcius, was the
name of the house and family they came of. The third was
some addition given, either for some act or notable service,
or for some mark on their face, or of some shape of their
body, or else for some special virtue they had. Even so did
the Grecians in old time give additions to princes by reason
of some notable act worthy memory.

[After this war at Corioles, the "seditious tribunes," Sicinius and Brutus, stir up the people without real cause of
complaint. Using "flattering words," these "busy prat-
tlers" blame a scarcity of grain on a cynical conspiracy of
the patricians to cause the dearth deliberately. They also
charge the patricians with sending citizens to repopulate
the plague-stricken city of Velitres as a stratagem designed
to get rid of unwanted Romans. The commoners, thus
stirred up, refuse to answer when their names are called.
Marcius compels them to go, and, marching into the territory of the Antiates, returns with so much confiscated grain
that his reputation steadily increases—to the considerable
vexation of those who regard him as "a great hinderer of
the people."]

67 than that which . . . person i.e., than the exploits for which these
rewards were offered to such a worthy person   **68 appeased** quieted
down   **69 still bare** continually bore

Shortly after this, Marcius stood for the consulship, and the common people favored his suit, thinking it would be a shame to them to deny and refuse the chiefest nobleman of blood and most worthy person of Rome, and specially him that had done so great service and good to the commonwealth. For the custom of Rome was at that time that such as did sue for[70] any office should for certain days before be in the marketplace, only with a poor gown on their backs and without any coat underneath, to pray the citizens to remember them at the day of election. Which was thus devised either to move the people the more by requesting them in such mean apparel or else because they might show them their wounds they had gotten in the wars in the service of the commonwealth, as manifest marks and testimony of their valiantness. . . .

Now Marcius, following this custom, showed many wounds and cuts upon his body, which he had received in seventeen years' service at the wars and in many sundry battles, being ever the foremost man that did set out feet to fight. So that there was not a man among the people but was ashamed of himself to refuse so valiant a man, and one of them said to another, "We must needs choose him consul, there is no remedy." But when the day of election was come and that Marcius came to the marketplace with great pomp, accompanied with all the Senate and the whole nobility of the city about him, who sought to make him consul with the greatest instance[71] and entreaty they could or ever attempted for any man or matter, then the love and good will of the common people turned straight to an hate and envy toward him, fearing to put this office of sovereign authority into his hands, being a man somewhat partial toward the nobility and of great credit and authority amongst the patricians, and as one they might doubt[72] would take away altogether the liberty from the people. Whereupon, for these considerations, they refused Marcius in the end and made two other that were suitors[73] consuls.

The Senate, being marvelously offended with the people, did account the shame of this refusal rather to redound to

70 sue for seek   **71 instance** urgent entreaty   **72 doubt** fear   **73 suitors** candidates

themselves than to Marcius, but Marcius took it in far
worse part than the Senate and was out of all patience. For
he was a man too full of passion and choler, and too much
given to over self-will[74] and opinion, as one of a high mind
and great courage that lacked the gravity and affability that
is gotten with judgment of learning and reason, which only
is to be looked for in a governor of state; and that[75] remembered not how willfulness is the thing of the world which a
governor of a commonwealth for pleasing[76] should shun, being that which Plato called "solitariness"; as, in the end, all
men that are willfully given to a self-opinion and obstinate
mind, and who will never yield to others' reason but to their
own, remain without company and forsaken of all men. For
a man that will live in the world must needs have patience,
which lusty bloods[77] make but a mock at. So Marcius, being
a stout man of nature[78] that never yielded in any respect, as
one thinking that to overcome always and to have the upper
hand in all matters was a token of magnanimity and of no
base and faint courage—which spitteth out anger from the
most weak and passioned part of the heart, much like the
matter of an impostume[79]—went home to his house full
freighted[80] with spite and malice against the people, being
accompanied with all the lustiest young gentlemen, whose
minds were nobly bent, as those that came of noble race,
and commonly used for[81] to follow and honor him. But then
specially they flocked about him and kept him company to
his much harm, for they did but kindle and inflame his choler more and more, being sorry with him for the injury the
people offered him, because he was their captain and
leader to the wars that taught them all martial discipline
and stirred up in them a noble emulation of honor and valiantness, and yet without envy praising them that deserved
best.

In the mean season[82] there came great plenty of corn to

---

74 to over self-will to overly great willfulness. (Or perhaps it should read
over to self-will.)   **75 that** who   **76 for pleasing** if he wishes to please
(the people)   **77 lusty bloods** i.e., vigorous and arrogant young men
78 a stout man of nature i.e., valiantly stubborn   **79 impostume** abscess,
festering corruption. (In a faint and spiritless courage, anger is spitted or
spewed out of the fear-debilitated and weakened heart as though the heart
suffers from an abscess.)   **80 full freighted** fully laden, weighted down
81 used for were accustomed   **82 mean season** meantime

Rome that had been bought, part in Italy, and part was sent out of Sicily as given by Gelon, the tyrant[83] of Syracusa; so that many stood in great hope that, the dearth of victuals being holpen,[84] the civil dissension would also cease. The Senate sat in council upon it immediately; the common people stood also about the palace where the council was kept, gaping what resolution would fall out,[85] persuading themselves that the corn they had bought should be sold good cheap, and that which was given should be divided by the poll[86] without paying any penny, and the rather[87] because certain of the senators amongst them did so wish and persuade the same.

But Marcius, standing up on his feet, did somewhat sharply take up those who went about to gratify the people therein, and called them people-pleasers and traitors to the nobility. "Moreover," he said, "they nourished against themselves the naughty[88] seed and cockle[89] of insolence and sedition, which had been sowed and scattered abroad amongst the people, whom[90] they should have cut off, if they had been wise, and have prevented their greatness, and not (to their own destruction) to have suffered the people to stablish a magistrate for themselves of so great power and authority as that man had to whom they had granted it. Who was also to be feared because he obtained what he would and did nothing but what he listed, neither passed[91] for any obedience to the consuls but lived in all liberty, acknowledging no superior to command him saving the only heads and authors of their faction, whom he called his magistrates. Therefore," said he, "they that gave counsel and persuaded that the corn should be given out to the common people gratis, as they used to do in cities of Greece where the people had more absolute power, did but only nourish their disobedience, which would break out in the end to the utter ruin and overthrow of the whole state. For they will not think it is done in recompense of their service past, sithence[92] they know well enough they have so oft refused to

83 tyrant ruler lacking constitutional claim (but not necessarily tyrannical in behavior)   84 holpen helped   85 gaping . . . out eager to learn what would be decided   86 by the poll by counting of heads   87 the rather all the sooner   88 naughty wicked   89 cockle a weed that grows especially in grainfields   90 whom i.e., which   91 listed, neither passed desired, nor did he care   92 sithence since

go to the wars when they were commanded; neither for their mutinies when they went with us, whereby they have rebelled and forsaken their country; neither for their accusations which their flatterers have preferred[93] unto them and they have received and made good against the Senate. But they will rather judge we give and grant them this as abasing ourselves and standing in fear of them and glad to flatter them every way. By this means their disobedience will still grow worse and worse, and they will never leave[94] to practice new sedition and uproars. Therefore it were a great folly for us, methinks, to do it. Yea, shall I say more? We should, if we were wise, take from them their tribuneship, which most manifestly is the embasing[95] of the consulship and the cause of the division of the city. The state whereof, as it standeth, is not now as it was wont to be, but becometh dismembered in two factions which maintains always civil dissension and discord between us and will never suffer us again to be united into one body.''

Marcius, dilating the matter with many suchlike reasons, wan[96] all the young men and almost all the rich men to his opinion, insomuch they rang* it out[97] that he was the only man and alone in the city who stood out against the people and never flattered them. There were only a few old men that spake against him, fearing lest some mischief might fall out upon it, as indeed there followed no great good afterward. For the tribunes of the people, being present at this consultation[98] of the Senate, when they saw that the opinion of Marcius was confirmed with the more voices, they left the Senate and went down to the people, crying out for help and that they would assemble to save their tribunes.

Hereupon the people ran on head[99] in tumult together, before whom the words that Marcius spake in the Senate were openly reported; which the people so stomached[100] that even in that fury they were ready to fly upon the whole Senate. But the tribunes laid all the fault and burden wholly upon Marcius and sent their sergeants forthwith to arrest

93 preferred put forward   94 leave leave off, cease   95 embasing debasing   96 wan won   97 rang it out proclaimed   98 consultation deliberation, conference   99 on head headlong   100 stomached took offense at

him, presently to appear in person before the people to answer the words he had spoken in the Senate. Marcius stoutly withstood these officers that came to arrest him. Then the tribunes in their own persons, accompanied with the aediles,[101] went to fetch him by force, and so laid violent hands upon him. Howbeit, the noble patricians, gathering together about him, made the tribunes give back and laid it sore upon[102] the aediles, so for that time the night parted them and the tumult appeased.

The next morning betimes,[103] the consuls, seeing the people in an uproar, running to the marketplace out of all parts of the city, they were afraid lest all the city would together by the ears.[104] Wherefore, assembling the Senate in all haste they declared how it stood them upon[105] to appease the fury of the people with some gentle words or grateful decrees in their favor; and moreover, like wise men, they should consider it was now no time to stand at defense and in contention, nor yet to fight for honor against the commonalty, they being fallen to so great an extremity[106] and offering such imminent danger. Wherefore they were to consider temperately of things and to deliver some present and gentle pacification. The most part of the senators that were present at this council thought this opinion best and gave their consents unto it.

Whereupon the consuls, rising out of council, went to speak unto the people as gently as they could, and they did pacify their fury and anger, purging the Senate of all the unjust accusations laid upon them, and used great modesty in persuading them and also in reproving the faults they had committed. And as for the rest, that touched the sale of corn, they promised there should be no disliking offered them[107] in the price. So the most part of the people being pacified, and appearing so plainly, by the great silence and still that was among them, as yielding to the consuls and liking well of their words, the tribunes then of the people

---

101 aediles municipal officers with police functions   **102 give back . . . sore upon** give way and severely beat   **103 betimes** early   **104 would together by the ears** would be at odds, would be set against one another   **105 stood them upon** was incumbent upon them   **106 they . . . extremity** i.e., the people (the *commonalty*) having committed such violent outrage   **107 no disliking offered them** i.e., no prejudice shown against them

rose out of their seats and said, forasmuch as the Senate yielded unto reason, the people also for their part, as became them, did likewise give place unto them. But notwithstanding, they would that Marcius should come in person to answer to the articles they had devised. First, whether he had not solicited and procured the Senate to change the present state of the commonweal and to take the sovereign authority out of the people's hands. Next, when he was sent for by authority of their officers, why he did contemptuously resist and disobey. Lastly, seeing he had driven and beaten the aediles into the marketplace before all the world, if in doing this he had not done as much as in him lay to raise civil wars and to set one citizen against another.

All this was spoken to[108] one of these two ends: either that Marcius, against his nature, should be constrained to humble himself and to abase his haughty and fierce mind, or else, if he continued still in his stoutness,[109] he should incur the people's displeasure and ill will so far that he should never possibly win them again. Which they hoped would rather fall out so than otherwise, as indeed they guessed—unhappily, considering Marcius' nature and disposition.

So Marcius came and presented himself to answer their accusations against him, and the people held their peace and gave attentive ear to hear what he would say. But where[110] they thought to have heard very humble and lowly words come from him, he began not only to use his wonted boldness of speaking (which of itself was very rough and unpleasant, and did more aggravate his accusation than purge his innocency) but also gave himself in his words to thunder, and look therewithal so grimly as though he made no reckoning of the matter. This stirred coals among the people, who were in wonderful fury at it, and their hate and malice grew so toward him that they could hold no lenger,[111] bear, nor endure his bravery and careless boldness. Whereupon Sicinius, the cruelest and stoutest[112] of the tribunes, after he had whispered a little with his companions, did openly pronounce, in the face of all the people, Marcius as condemned by the tribunes to die. Then presently he commanded the aediles to apprehend him and carry him

---

108 to to bring about   109 stoutness haughtiness   110 where whereas
111 hold no lenger endure no longer   112 stoutest haughtiest

straight to the rock Tarpeian and to cast him headlong down the same.

When the aediles came to lay hands upon Marcius to do that[113] they were commanded, divers of the people themselves thought it too cruel and violent a deed. The noblemen also, being much troubled to see such force and rigor used, began to cry aloud, "Help Marcius!" So those that laid hands of him being repulsed, they compassed him in round[114] among themselves, and some of them, holding up their hands to the people, besought them not to handle him thus cruelly. But neither their words nor crying out could aught prevail; the tumult and hurly-burly was so great, until such time as the tribunes' own friends and kinsmen, weighing with themselves the impossibleness to convey Marcius to execution without great slaughter and murder of the nobility, did persuade and advise not to proceed in so violent and extraordinary a sort as to put such a man to death without lawful process in law, but that they should refer the sentence of his death to the free voice of the people.

Then Sicinius, bethinking himself a little, did ask the patricians for what cause they took Marcius out of the officers' hands that went to do execution. The patricians asked him again[115] why they would of themselves so cruelly and wickedly put to death so noble and valiant a Roman as Marcius was, and that without law and justice. "Well, then," said Sicinius, "if that be the matter, let there be no more quarrel or dissension against the people, for they do grant your demand that his cause shall be heard according to the law. Therefore," said he to Marcius, "we do will and charge you to appear before the people the third day of our next sitting and assembly here, to make your purgation for such articles as shall be objected[116] against you, that by free voice the people may give sentence upon you as shall please them." The noblemen were glad then of the adjournment and were much pleased they had gotten Marcius out of this danger.

[The patricians hope that a new war with the Antiates will take the people's mind off Marcius, but when peace is unex-

113 that what   114 of him . . . compassed him in round on him . . . formed a circle around him   115 again in reply   116 objected charged

pectedly concluded Marcius faces the tribunes once more, this time on the charge that he aspires to be king. Unable to prove their case, the tribunes fall back on other accusations old and new. He defends himself, but the vote is for perpetual banishment. Marcius bears his fortune with outward resolution and calm, though inwardly carried away with anger and desire for revenge.]

Now that Marcius was even in that taking,[117] it appeared true soon after by his doings. For when he was come home to his house again and had taken his leave of his mother and wife, finding them weeping and shrieking out for sorrow, and had also comforted and persuaded them to be content with his chance,[118] he went immediately to the gate of the city, accompanied with a great number of patricians that brought him thither. From whence he went on his way with three or four of his friends only, taking nothing with him nor requesting anything of any man. So he remained a few days in the country at his houses, turmoiled with sundry sorts and kinds of thoughts such as the fire of his choler did stir up.

In the end, seeing he could resolve no way to take a profitable or honorable course, but only was pricked forward still to be revenged of[119] the Romans, he thought to raise up some great wars against them by their nearest neighbors. Whereupon he thought it his best way first to stir up the Volsces against them, knowing they were yet able enough in strength and riches to encounter them, notwithstanding their former losses they had received not long before, and that their power was not so much impaired as their malice and desire was increased to be revenged of the Romans.

Now, in the city of Antium there was one called Tullus Aufidius, who, for his riches, as also for his nobility and valiantness, was honored among the Volsces as a king. Marcius knew very well that Tullus did more malice and envy him than he did all the Romans besides, because that many times, in battles where they met, they were ever at the encounter one against another, like lusty courageous youths striving in all emulation of honor, and had encountered

117 **even in that taking** exactly in that plight, condition   118 **chance** misfortune   119 **of** on

many times together. Insomuch as, besides the common quarrel between them, there was bred a marvelous private hate, one against another. Yet notwithstanding, considering that Tullus Aufidius was a man of a great mind and that he above all other of the Volsces most desired revenge of the Romans for the injuries they had done unto them, he[120] did an act that confirmed the true words of an ancient poet who said:

> It is a thing full hard, man's anger to withstand,
> If it be stiffly bent to take an enterprise in hand.
> For then most men will have the thing that they
>   desire,
> Although it cost their lives therefore, such force
>   hath wicked ire.

And so did he. For he disguised himself in such array and attire as he thought no man could ever have known him for the person he was, seeing him in that apparel he had upon his back; and, as Homer said of Ulysses:

> So did he enter into the enemies' town.

It was even twilight when he entered the city of Antium, and many people met him in the streets, but no man knew him. So he went directly to Tullus Aufidius' house, and when he came thither he got him up straight to the chimney hearth and sat him down and spake not a word to any man, his face all muffled over. They of the house, spying him, wondered what he should be, and yet they durst not bid him rise. For, ill-favoredly muffled and disguised as he was, yet there appeared a certain majesty in his countenance and in his silence. Whereupon they went to Tullus, who was at supper, to tell him of the strange disguising of this man.

Tullus rose presently from the board and, coming towards him, asked him what he was and wherefore he came. Then Marcius unmuffled himself, and after he had paused awhile, making no answer, he said unto him: "If thou knowest me not yet, Tullus, and, seeing me, dost not perhaps believe me to be the man I am indeed, I must of necessity bewray[121] myself to be that I am. I am Caius Marcius, who hath done to thyself particularly, and to all the

---

120 he i.e., Marcius. (The quotation that follows is from Heraclitus; the Homer is from *Odyssey* 4.246.) **121 bewray** reveal

Volsces generally, great hurt and mischief, which I cannot deny for my surname of Coriolanus that I bear. For I never had other benefit nor recompense of all the true and painful service I have done and the extreme dangers I have been in but this only surname[122]—a good memory and witness of the malice and displeasure thou shouldst bear me. Indeed the name only remaineth with me; for the rest, the envy and cruelty of the people of Rome have taken from me, by the sufferance of the dastardly nobility and magistrates, who have forsaken me and let me be banished by the people. This extremity hath now driven me to come as a poor suitor to take thy chimney hearth, not of any hope I have to save my life thereby. For if I had feared death I would not have come hither to have put my life in hazard, but pricked forward with spite and desire I have to be revenged of them that thus have banished me, whom now I begin to be avenged on, putting my person between thy enemies.[123] Wherefore, if thou hast any heart to be wreaked of the injuries thy enemies have done thee, speed thee now and let my misery serve thy turn, and so use it as my service may be a benefit to the Volsces, promising thee that I will fight with better good will for all you than ever I did when I was against you, knowing that they fight more valiantly who know the force of their enemy than such as have never proved[124] it. And if it be so that thou dare not and that thou art weary to prove fortune any more, then am I also weary to live any lenger. And it were no wisdom in thee to save the life of him who hath been heretofore thy mortal enemy and whose service now can nothing help nor pleasure thee."

Tullus, hearing what he said, was a marvelous glad man, and taking him by the hand he said unto him: "Stand up, O Marcius, and be of good cheer, for in proffering thyself unto us thou dost us great honor, and by this means thou mayest hope also of greater things at all the Volsces' hands." So he feasted him for that time and entertained him in the honorablest manner he could, talking with him in[125] no other matters at that present. But within few days after,

122 but this only surname except for this surname   123 between thy enemies i.e., into your enemy hands   124 proved tested, experienced 125 in of, concerning

they fell to consultation together in what sort they should begin their wars.

Now on the other side, the city of Rome was in marvelous uproar and discord, the nobility against the commonalty, and chiefly for Marcius' condemnation and banishment.

[Priests and soothsayers tell of ominous portents. Marcius, joined in commission with Tullus Aufidius by consent of the Volsces, invades Roman territory and does considerable damage, though he exercises care not to harm any noblemen's lands. Because of this the Roman nobility and commoners are more at odds than ever before. When Marcius hears that the commoners of Rome cravenly hope to repeal his exile but that the Senate balks (out of a refusal to give in to the commoners' demands, or to allow Marcius' return solely by the commoners' permission), he is in a greater rage than ever and leaves the siege of Lavinium to set down before Rome.

His threatening presence brings all Rome to an agreement to send ambassadors with an offer of recall from exile. The ambassadors discover him "in his chair of state," seated "with a marvelous and unspeakable majesty," having "the chiefest men of the Volsces about him." He demands full restitution of lands and rights for the Volsces, and gives them thirty days to consider. Tullus Aufidius begins to resent Marcius' reputation and achievement. The Romans meanwhile can do little but pray, among whom, constantly at the altar of Jupiter Capitoline, is the lady Valeria, sister to Publicola, who did notable service to the Romans. Valeria conceives of a plan to help Rome in its desperate situation.]

Whereupon she rose and the other ladies with her, and they all together went straight to the house of Volumnia, Marcius' mother, and coming in to her found her and Marcius' wife, her daughter-in-law, set together and having her husband Marcius' young children in her lap. Now all the train of these ladies sitting in a ring round about her, Valeria first began to speak in this sort unto her: "We ladies are come to visit you ladies, my lady Volumnia and Virgilia, by no direction from the Senate nor commandment of other magistrate, but through the inspiration (as I take it) of some god above; who, having taken compassion and pity of our prayers, hath moved us to come unto you to entreat you in a matter as well beneficial for us as also for the whole citizens in general, but to yourselves in especial (if it please you to credit[126] me), and shall redound to your* more fame and glory than the daughters of the Sabines obtained in former age when they procured loving peace instead of hateful war between their fathers and their husbands.[127] Come on, good ladies, and let us go all together unto Marcius to entreat him to take pity upon us, and also to report the truth unto him how much you are bound unto the citizens, who, notwithstanding they have sustained great hurt and losses by him, yet they have not hitherto sought revenge upon your persons by any discourteous usage, neither ever conceived any such thought or intent against you, but do deliver ye safe into his hands, though thereby they look for no better grace or clemency from him." When Valeria had spoken this unto them, all the other ladies together, with one voice, confirmed that[128] she had said.

Then Volumnia in this sort did answer her: "My good ladies, we are partakers with you of the common misery and calamity of our country, and yet our grief exceedeth yours the more by reason of our particular misfortune, to feel the loss of my son Marcius' former valiancy and glory and to see his person environed now with our enemies in arms, rather to see him forthcoming and safe kept than of any love to defend his person.[129] But yet the greatest grief of our heaped mishaps is to see our poor country brought to such extremity that all the hope of the safety and preservation thereof is now unfortunately cast upon us simple women, because we know not what account he will make of us, since he hath cast from him all care of his natural country and commonweal which heretofore he hath holden more dear and precious than either his mother, wife, or children.

---

126 credit believe   **127 daughters of the Sabines . . . husbands** (Refers to mythological accounts of a peace made between the Romans under Romulus and the Sabines after the "rape" or forcible abduction of the Sabine women. Their *husbands* are Roman, the *fathers* Sabine.)
128 that what   **129 rather to see . . . person** i.e., motivated more by a desire to ensure a militarily strong position than by a concern for his personal safety

Notwithstanding, if ye think we can do good, we will willingly do what you will have us. Bring us to him, I pray you. For if we cannot prevail, we may yet die at his feet, as humble suitors for the safety of our country.''

Her answer ended, she took her daughter-in-law and Marcius' children with her, and being accompanied with all the other Roman ladies, they went in troop together unto the Volsces' camp; whom when they saw,[130] they of themselves did both pity and reverence her, and there was not a man among them that once durst say a word unto her. Now was Marcius set then in his chair of state, with all the honors of a general; and when he had spied the women coming afar off, he marveled what the matter meant. But afterwards knowing his wife, which came foremost, he determined at the first to persist in his obstinate and inflexible rancor. But overcomen in the end with natural affection and being altogether altered to see them, his heart would not serve him to tarry their coming to his chair, but, coming down in haste he went to meet them, and first he kissed his mother and embraced her a pretty while, then his wife and little children. And nature so wrought with him that the tears fell from his eyes, and he could not keep himself from making much of them, but yielded to the affection of his blood, as if he had been violently carried with the fury of a most swift-running stream.

After he had thus lovingly received them, and perceiving that his mother Volumnia would begin to speak to him, he called the chiefest of the council of the Volsces to hear what she would say. Then she spake in this sort: "If we held our peace, my son, and determined not to speak, the state of our poor bodies and present sight of our raiment would easily bewray[131] to thee what life we have led at home since thy exile and abode abroad. But think now with thyself how much more unfortunately than all the women living we are come hither, considering that the sight which should be most pleasant to all other to behold, spiteful fortune hath made most fearful to us, making myself to see my son, and my daughter here her husband,[132] besieging the walls of his

---

130 whom when they saw i.e., and when the Volscians saw Volumnia
131 bewray reveal   **132 and my daughter here her husband** i.e., and my daughter-in-law here to see her husband

native country. So as that which is the only comfort to all other[133] in their adversity and misery, to pray unto the gods and to call to them for aid, is the only thing which plungeth us[134] into most deep perplexity. For we cannot, alas, together pray both for victory for our country and for safety of thy life also; but a world of grievous curses, yea, more than any mortal enemy can heap upon us, are forcibly wrapped up in our prayers. For the bitter sop of most hard choice is offered thy wife and children, to forgo the one of the two: either to lose the person of thyself or the nurse of their native country.

"For myself, my son, I am determined not to tarry till fortune, in my lifetime, do make an end of this war. For if I cannot persuade thee rather to do good unto both parties than to overthrow and destroy the one, preferring love and nature before the malice and calamity of wars, thou shalt see, my son, and trust unto it, thou shalt no sooner march forward to assault thy country, but thy foot shall tread upon thy mother's womb that brought thee first into this world. And I may not defer to see the day either that my son be led prisoner in triumph by his natural countrymen or that he himself do triumph of them and of his natural country.

"For if it were so that my request tended to save thy country in destroying the Volsces, I must confess thou wouldst hardly and doubtfully resolve on that. For as to destroy thy natural country, it is altogether unmeet and unlawful, so were it not just and less honorable to betray those that put their trust in thee. But my only demand consisteth to make a jail delivery[135] of all evils, which delivereth equal benefit and safety both to the one and the other, but most honorable for the Volsces. For it shall appear that, having victory in their hands, they have of special favor granted us singular graces—peace, and amity—albeit themselves have no less part of both than we. Of which good, if so it came to pass, thyself is the only author, and so hast thou the only honor. But if it fail and fall out contrary, thyself alone deservedly shall carry the shameful reproach and burthen of either party.

"So, though the end of war be uncertain, yet this notwith-

---

133 other others   **134 only . . . plungeth us** thing that plunges us utterly
135 jail delivery release, deliverance

standing is most certain, that if it be thy chance to conquer, this benefit shalt thou reap of thy goodly conquest: to be chronicled the plague and destroyer of thy country. And if fortune also overthrow thee, then the world will say that through desire to revenge thy private injuries thou hast forever undone thy good friends who did most lovingly and courteously receive thee."

Marcius gave good ear unto his mother's words without interrupting her speech at all, and, after she had said what she would, he held his peace a pretty while and answered not a word. Hereupon she began again to speak unto him, and said: "My son, why dost thou not answer me? Dost thou think it good altogether to give place unto thy choler and desire of revenge, and thinkest thou it not honesty for thee to grant thy mother's request in so weighty a cause? Dost thou take it honorable for a nobleman to remember the wrongs and injuries done him, and dost not in like case think it an honest nobleman's part to be thankful for the goodness that parents do show to their children, acknowledging the duty and reverence they ought to bear unto them? No man living is more bound to show himself thankful in all parts and respects than thyself, who so unnaturally showeth all ingratitude. Moreover, my son, thou hast sorely taken of[136] thy country, exacting grievous payments upon them in revenge of the injuries offered thee. Besides, thou hast not hitherto showed thy poor mother any courtesy. And therefore it is not only honest, but due unto me, that without compulsion I should obtain my so just and reasonable request of thee. But since by reason I cannot persuade thee to it, to what purpose do I defer my last hope?" And with these words, herself, his wife, and children fell down upon their knees before him.

Marcius, seeing that, could refrain no lenger, but went straight and lift[137] her up, crying out, "O Mother, what have you done to me?" And holding her hard by the right hand, "O Mother," said he, "you have won a happy victory for your country, but mortal and unhappy for your son; for I see myself vanquished by you alone." These words being spoken openly, he spake a little apart with his mother and

136 taken of exacted payment from (in the form of suffering) 137 lift lifted

wife, and then let them return again to Rome, for so they did request him.

And so remaining in camp that night, the next morning he dislodged[138] and marched homewards into the Volsces' country again, who were not all of one mind nor all alike contented. For some misliked him and that[139] he had done; other,[140] being well pleased that peace should be made, said that neither the one nor the other deserved blame nor reproach. Other, though they misliked that[141] was done, did not think him an ill man for that he did, but said he was not to be blamed though he yielded to such a forcible extremity. Howbeit, no man contraried his departure,[142] but all obeyed his commandment, more for respect of his worthiness and valiancy than for fear of his authority.

[The Romans rejoice at their deliverance and honor the ladies for what they have done.]

Now when Marcius was returned again into the city of Antium from his voyage, Tullus, that hated and could no lenger abide him for the fear he had of his authority, sought divers means to make him out of the way, thinking that if he let slip that present time he should never recover the like and fit occasion again. Wherefore Tullus, having procured many other of his confederacy, required[143] Marcius might be deposed from his estate to render up account to the Volsces of his charge and government. Marcius, fearing to become a private man again under Tullus being general (whose authority was greater otherwise than any other among all the Volsces), answered he was willing to give up his charge and would resign it into the hands of the lords of the Volsces if they did all command him, as by all their commandment he received it. And moreover that he would not refuse even at that present to give up an account unto the people, if they would tarry the hearing of it.

The people hereupon called a common council, in which assembly there were certain orators appointed that stirred up the common people against him. And when they had told

138 dislodged broke camp   139 that what   140 other others   141 that what   142 contraried his departure contradicted his order to depart (from Rome)   143 required demanded that

their tales, Marcius rose up to make them answer. Now, notwithstanding the mutinous people made a marvelous great noise, yet when they saw him, for the reverence they bare unto his valiantness they quieted themselves and gave still audience[144] to allege with leisure what he could for his purgation. Moreover, the honestest men of the Antiates, and who most rejoiced in peace, showed by their countenance that they would hear him willingly and judge also according to their conscience.

Whereupon Tullus, fearing that if he did let him speak he would prove his innocency to the people—because amongst other things he had an eloquent tongue; besides that the first good service he had done to the people of the Volsces did win him more favor than these last accusations could purchase him displeasure; and furthermore, the offense they laid to his charge was a testimony of the good will they ought[145] him, for they would never have thought he had done them wrong for that[146] they took not the city of Rome if they had not been very near taking of it by means of his approach and conduction—for these causes Tullus thought he might no lenger delay his pretense and enterprise, neither to tarry for the mutining and rising of the common people against him. Wherefore those that were of the conspiracy began to cry out that he was not to be heard, nor that they would not suffer a traitor to usurp tyrannical power over the tribe of the Volsces, who would not yield up his estate and authority. And in saying these words, they all fell upon him and killed him in the marketplace, none of the people once offering to rescue him.

Howbeit, it is a clear case that this murder was not generally consented unto of the most part of the Volsces. For men came out of all parts to honor his body, and did honorably bury him, setting out his tomb with great store of armor and spoils as the tomb of a worthy person and great captain. The Romans, understanding of his death, showed no other honor or malice, saving that they granted the ladies the request they made that they might mourn ten months for him. And that was the full time they used to wear blacks for the death of their fathers, brethren, or husbands, ac-

144 **and gave still audience** and quietly gave him audience   145 **ought** owed   146 **for that** in that

cording to Numa Pompilius' order who stablished the same, as we have enlarged more amply in the description of his life.

Now Marcius being dead, the whole state of the Volsces heartily wished him alive again. For, first of all, they fell out with the Aeques (who were their friends and confederates) touching[147] preeminence and place; and this quarrel grew on so far between them that frays and murders fell out upon it, one with another. After that, the Romans overcame them in battle, in which Tullus was slain in the field, and the flower of all their force was put to the sword; so that they were compelled to accept most shameful conditions of peace, in yielding themselves subject unto the conquerors and promising to be obedient at their commandment.

Text based on *The Lives of the Noble Grecians and Romans Compared To-gether by That Grave, Learned Philosopher and Historiographer, Plutarch of Chaeronea. Translated out of Greek into French by James Amyot . . . and out of French into English by Thomas North. . . . Thomas Vautroullier . . . 1579.* Whether Shakespeare read this edition or one of the subsequent editions of 1595 and 1603 (the latter also reprinted in 1612) is not certain, but the differences are minor.

In the following, departures from the original text appear in boldface; original readings are in roman.

p. 437 *lock up looke up   p. 444 *rang range   p. 452 *your our

---

147 touching over, concerning

Further Reading

Adelman, Janet. " 'Anger's My Meat': Feeding, Dependency, and Aggression in *Coriolanus*." In *Shakespeare: Pattern of Excelling Nature*, ed. David Bevington and Jay L. Halio. Newark, Del.: Univ. of Delaware Press, 1978. Rpt. in *Representing Shakespeare: New Psychoanalytic Essays*, ed. Murray M. Schwartz and Coppélia Kahn. Baltimore and London: Johns Hopkins Univ. Press, 1980. In a suggestive psychoanalytic reading, Adelman finds in the play's language of feeding Coriolanus' revulsion at his own vulnerability and dependency. His rigid masculinity is a defense against his neediness, an assertion of self-sufficiency that cannot be maintained. Coriolanus' discovery of human limitation and need at the end of the play is empty of consolation; instead of revealing the necessity of love, it brings only the agonizing collapse of the self.

Bradley, A. C. *"Coriolanus." Proceedings of the British Academy* 5 (1913 for 1911–1912): 457–473. Rpt. in *A Miscellany*. London: Macmillan, 1929. *Coriolanus,* for Bradley, is as much a drama of reconciliation as it is a tragedy, departing also from the pattern of Shakespeare's great tragedies in the absence of an effective dimension of supernatural order. Coriolanus himself is an "impossible" man. He is "the proudest man in Shakespeare," lacking self-awareness but magnificently true to a narrow ideal of conduct.

Brecht, Bertolt. *Coriolanus,* trans. Ralph Manheim. *Bertolt Brecht: Collected Plays,* vol. 9, ed. Ralph Manheim and John Willett. New York: Random House, 1972. Brecht adapts *Coriolanus* (and Manheim's edition includes an interview with Brecht on adapting the play to the modern stage) to reveal the tragedy of Rome as well as of its titular hero. Brecht, always alert to the story's political and ideological pressures, emphasizes the citizens' suffering and nobility in their irreconcilable and tragic conflict with Coriolanus.

Brower, Reuben A. "The Deeds of Coriolanus." *Hero and Saint: Shakespeare and the Graeco-Roman Heroic Tradition.* Oxford and New York: Oxford Univ. Press, 1971.

Shakespeare's dramatic subject—the Graeco-Roman
hero exposed to the complexities and compromises of the
political world—results in a curiously ironic tragedy. In
an analysis that examines Shakespeare's handling of
classical traditions, Brower argues that Coriolanus' absolute nature is both noble and absurd.

Burke, Kenneth. "*Coriolanus*—and the Delights of Faction." *Hudson Review* 19 (1966): 185–202. Rpt. in *Language as Symbolic Action*. Berkeley and Los Angeles:
Univ. of California Press, 1966. Burke, who considers *Coriolanus* a "grotesque" tragedy because of its "cantanker-
ous" hero, analyzes the structure of the play's symbolic
action. Coriolanus is a tragic figure whose hubristic excess intensifies the play's social tensions and leads inevitably to his sacrifice, which is cathartic and curative of
social repression.

Calderwood, James L. "*Coriolanus:* Wordless Meanings and
Meaningless Words." *Studies in English Literature* 6
(1966): 211–224. Calderwood finds in the breakdown of
language in *Coriolanus* an indication of the play's more
general concerns with personal identity and worth. The
play contrasts Coriolanus' desire for a private language
of fixed, unambiguous meanings with the fluid, popular
language of Rome. Coriolanus' struggle against this "lin-
guistic chaos" mirrors his struggle to affirm his own
identity: he invests the name "Coriolanus" with private,
autonomous meaning that leads him inevitably into conflict with Rome.

Cavell, Stanley. " 'Who Does the Wolf Love?': Reading *Coriolanus*." *Representations* 3 (1983): 1–20. Rev. and rpt. in
Shakespeare and the Question of Theory, ed. Patricia
Parker and Geoffrey Hartman. New York and London:
Methuen, 1985. In a subtle consideration of the play's stylistic and emotional starkness, Cavell sees Coriolanus'
desire for independence as an indication of his inability
to imagine any terms of incorporation into a community
that are not destructive or diminishing. In considering
Coriolanus' unwillingness to acknowledge communal
bonds, the audience is led, Cavell argues, to imagine—
and to participate in—the very mutuality he resists.

Charney, Maurice. "The Imagery of *Coriolanus*." *Shakespeare's Roman Plays: The Function of Imagery in the*

Drama. Cambridge: Harvard Univ. Press, 1961. Charney examines the dominant images of the play—of food, disease, and animals—that clarify the larger themes and conflicts of *Coriolanus* and help foster the play's harsh and satiric mood. Coriolanus' own character is revealed in "the extensive imagery of acting and isolation" that articulates his alienation.

Daniell, David. *"Coriolanus" in Europe*. London: Athlone Press, 1980. Nominally a description of the 1978–1979 European tour of the Royal Shakespeare Company's production of *Coriolanus*, Daniell's book combines extracts from reviews, interviews, journal entries, photographs, and his own literary criticism to explore not only the development of this important production but also the complex relations between the text of a play and the theatrical, social, and political conditions of its performance.

Dollimore, Jonathan. "*Coriolanus* (c. 1608): The Chariot Wheel and Its Dust." *Radical Tragedy: Religion, Ideology, and Power in the Drama of Shakespeare and His Contemporaries*. Chicago: Univ. of Chicago Press, 1984. For Dollimore, *Coriolanus* challenges the very idea of innate nobility, which he sees as merely an ideological underpinning of the antagonism between patricians and plebeians. Taking Aufidius' suggestion that virtues are products of social interaction rather than innate (as Coriolanus would believe), Dollimore argues that identity, like historical and political processes, is shown to be "radically contingent" in the world of the play.

Goldberg, Jonathan. "The Roman Actor: *Julius Caesar, Sejanus, Coriolanus, Catiline*, and *The Roman Actor*." *James I and the Politics of Literature: Jonson, Shakespeare, Donne, and Their Contemporaries*. Baltimore: Johns Hopkins Univ. Press, 1983. In his study of the representations of power in seventeenth-century England, Goldberg considers the relationship of *Coriolanus* to the political assumptions of King James I. In the tension between Coriolanus' insistence on his integrity and privacy and his inability ultimately to deny the bonds of state and family, Goldberg finds the tragic implications of an absolutist conception of power that insists upon its self-sufficiency and yet must be expressed theatrically.

Goldman, Michael. "Characterizing Coriolanus." *Acting and Action in Shakespearean Tragedy*. Princeton, N.J.: Princeton Univ. Press, 1985. The character of Coriolanus, Goldman argues, is meant to be seen as problematic, for Shakespeare scrutinizes in the play the inadequacy of explaining character through narrative description alone. Only through the mediation of an actor can we understand Coriolanus' depth and become fully involved in the tragic experience of the protagonist.

Gordon, D. J. "Name and Fame in *Coriolanus*." *Papers Mainly Shakespearean: Essays and Lectures by D. J. Gordon*, ed. G. I. Duthie. Edinburgh: Oliver and Boyd, 1964. Rpt. in *The Renaissance Imagination*, ed. Stephen Orgel. Berkeley, Los Angeles, and London: Univ. of California Press, 1975. Starting from an examination of the multiple uses of the word "voice" in *Coriolanus*, Gordon explores how words function in the play to confer and confirm honor. Honor or "fame" is discovered to be something given, dependent upon the act that grants it rather than the act that merits it, and so Coriolanus tragically discovers his inability to maintain an autonomous and sustaining sense of self or of honor independent of others' voices.

Hazlitt, William. "Coriolanus." *Characters of Shakespear's Plays*, 1817. Rpt., London: Oxford Univ. Press, 1966. Hazlitt views *Coriolanus* as an informed political play, exploring questions of aristocracy and democracy, power and its abuse, peace and war. Hazlitt's Jacobin sympathies are with the populace, whom, he argues, Shakespeare seems to side against, even baiting them. The "whole dramatic moral of *Coriolanus*," he concludes, "is that those who have little shall have less, and that those who have much shall take all the others have left."

Huffman, Clifford. *"Coriolanus" in Context*. Lewisburg, Pa.: Bucknell Univ. Press, 1971. Huffman's book-length study focuses on the intellectual and political concerns underlying the structure of *Coriolanus*. He examines the play's literary sources and analogues, Jacobean political currents and conflicts, and he offers an act-by-act analysis of the play's political themes. For Huffman, the play reveals the potential tyranny of both monarchic and democratic power, as it explores the possibilities of "mixed" government.

Hunter, G. K. "The Last Tragic Heroes." In *Later Shakespeare*, ed. John Russell Brown and Bernard Harris. Stratford-upon-Avon Studies 8. London: Edward Arnold; New York: St. Martin's Press, 1966. Rpt. in *Dramatic Identities and Cultural Tradition: Studies in Shakespeare and His Contemporaries*. New York: Barnes and Noble, 1978. Hunter observes that Coriolanus, like Shakespeare's other late tragic heroes, possesses a splendid self-will that fails to recognize the ultimate powerlessness of the individual. In denying social reciprocity, he is at once both godlike and "inhuman." Exiled, searching for an elusive, absolute mode of behavior, Coriolanus can fix the image of the greatness he seeks through death alone.

Kott, Jan. "Coriolanus or Shakespearean Contradictions." *Shakespeare Our Contemporary*, trans. Boleslaw Taborski. Garden City, N.Y.: Doubleday, 1964. Kott accounts for the lack of enthusiasm for this austere but strikingly modern play by noting its moral, political, and philosophical ambiguities, which satisfy neither democrats nor patricians. The play discovers no system of value that can accommodate the needs of both the heroic individual and the citizenry. For Kott, *Coriolanus* is an ironic tragedy both of the hero and of history itself.

Miola, Robert. "Rome and the Self." *Shakespeare's Rome*. Cambridge and New York: Cambridge Univ. Press, 1983. Miola argues that Shakespeare's focus on a figure who uncompromisingly embodies the Roman ideal of honor exposes the contradictions inherent in Rome's values between private virtue and public good, between the heroic self and the city. Shakespeare transforms his literary sources in depicting Coriolanus' complex relationship with Rome to ironic and tragic effect, as Coriolanus' inability to live within Rome reveals both his strengths and weaknesses and those of the city.

Phillips, James Emerson, Jr. "Violation of Order and Degree in *Coriolanus*." *The State in Shakespeare's Greek and Roman Plays*, cf. 1940. Rpt., New York: Octagon, 1972. For Phillips, the tragedy of *Coriolanus* results from the presence of "subversive democratic forces on the one hand, and on the other an individual temperamentally unfit to function in the capacity of natural governor of the state." The play explores the "conflict between democratic and aristocratic elements" that can be resolved only if each understands and submits to the social ordering "ordained by the laws of God and nature."

Rossiter, A. P. "*Coriolanus.*" *Angel With Horns and Other Shakespeare Lectures*, ed. Graham Storey. London: Longmans, Green; New York: Theatre Arts Books, 1961. *Coriolanus* is Shakespeare's "only great political play," according to Rossiter. It is a play about power, about the unstable relationship between ruler and ruled, between all the forces of order and disorder that define the political world. Rossiter argues that Coriolanus' political convictions are right, but that his insensitivity and willfulness result in a tragic clash between his pride and the needs of Rome.

Waith, Eugene M. *The Herculean Hero in Marlowe, Chapman, Shakespeare, and Dryden*, pp. 121–143. New York: Columbia Univ. Press, 1962. Locating the heroic image of Coriolanus within the moral and literary traditions of the Herculean hero, Waith discusses his heroic valor as well as his fundamental alienation from the style and values of Rome. The former demands our admiration; the latter exposes the pride and inflexibility that ensure his failure in a world where the heroic and the human are in conflict.

Wickham, Glynne. "*Coriolanus:* Shakespeare's Tragedy in Rehearsal and Performance." In *Later Shakespeare*, ed. John Russell Brown and Bernard Harris. Stratford-upon-Avon Studies 8. London: Edward Arnold; New York: St. Martin's Press, 1966. Rpt. in *Shakespeare's Dramatic Heritage*. London: Routledge and Kegan Paul; New York: Barnes and Noble, 1969. Wickham, drawing upon his production experience of *Coriolanus* (Bath, 1952), offers guidance to those who would direct this technically demanding play. His analysis focuses on Shakespeare's own "signposts" for production, as well as on the specific challenges posed by casting, staging, language, and pace.

Memorable Lines

Titus Andronicus

Sweet mercy is nobility's true badge. (TAMORA 1.1.119)

TAMORA
  O cruel, irreligious piety!
CHIRON
  Was never Scythia half so barbarous. (1.1.130–131)

These words are razors to my wounded heart.
                                        (TITUS 1.1.315)

... these dreary dumps ... (MARCUS 1.1.392)

... what you cannot as you would achieve,
You must perforce accomplish as you may.
                              (AARON 2.1.106–107)

O, here I lift this one hand up to heaven
And bow this feeble ruin to the earth.
If any power pities wretched tears,
To that I call! (TITUS 3.1.206–209)

Alas, poor man! Grief has so wrought on him
He takes false shadows for true substances.
                              (MARCUS 3.2.79–80)

Write thou, good niece, and here display at last
What God will have discovered for revenge.
Heaven guide thy pen to print thy sorrows plain.
                              (MARCUS 4.1.75–77)

O heavens, can you hear a good man groan
And not relent, or not compassion him?
                              (MARCUS 4.1.125–126)

The eagle suffers little birds to sing
And is not careful what they mean thereby.
                              (TAMORA 4.4.83–84)

Even now I curse the day—and yet, I think,
Few come within the compass of my curse—
Wherein I did not some notorious ill.   (AARON   5.1.125–127)

But I have done a thousand dreadful things
As willingly as one would kill a fly.   (AARON   5.1.141–142)

Memorable Lines

Timon of Athens

A thousand moral paintings I can show
That shall demonstrate these quick blows of Fortune's
More pregnantly than words.   (PAINTER   1.1.95–97)

'Tis not enough to help the feeble up,
But to support him after.   (TIMON   1.1.113–114)

I wonder men dare trust themselves with men.
    (APEMANTUS   1.2.43)

Men shut their doors against a setting sun.
    (APEMANTUS   1.2.144)

Every man has his fault, and honesty is his.
    (LUCULLUS   3.1.28–29)

Nothing emboldens sin so much as mercy.
    (FIRST SENATOR   3.5.4)

You fools of fortune, trencher-friends, time's flies,
Cap-and-knee slaves, vapors, and minute-jacks!
    (TIMON   3.6.96–97)

        Son of sixteen,
Pluck the lined crutch from thy old limping sire;
With it beat out his brains!   (TIMON   4.1.13–15)

"We have seen better days."   (FLAVIUS 4.2.28)

Destruction fang mankind!   (TIMON   4.3.23)

        Thus much of this will make
Black white, foul fair, wrong right,
Base noble, old young, coward valiant.   (TIMON   4.3.28–30)

Consumptions sow
In hollow bones of man; strike their sharp shins,
And mar men's spurring.   (TIMON   4.3.153–155)

This is in thee a nature but infected,
A poor unmanly melancholy sprung
From change of fortune.   (APEMANTUS   4.3.204–206)

I am sick of this false world, and will love naught
But even the mere necessities upon 't.   (TIMON   4.3.380–381)

. . . life's uncertain voyage . . .   (TIMON   5.1.201)

Memorable Lines

Coriolanus

Though soft-conscienced men can be content to say it was for his country, he did it to please his mother and to be partly proud.　　　(FIRST CITIZEN　1.1.35–37)

What's the matter, you dissentious rogues,
That, rubbing the poor itch of your opinion,
Make yourselves scabs?　　　(MARCIUS　1.1.163–165)

　　　　　The gods sent not
Corn for the rich men only.　　　(MARCIUS　1.1.207–208)

All the yarn she spun in Ulysses' absence did but fill Ithaca full of moths.　　　(VALERIA　1.3.84–85)

Nature teaches beasts to know their friends.
　　　　　(SICINIUS　2.1.6)

To seem to affect the malice and displeasure of the people is as bad as that which he dislikes, to flatter them for their love.
　　　　　(FIRST OFFICER　2.2.21–23)

The mutable, rank-scented meiny.　　　(CORIOLANUS　3.1.69)

This is the way to kindle, not to quench.
　　　　　(MENENIUS　3.1.200)

What is the city but the people?　　　(SICINIUS　3.1.202)

The people are the city.　　　(PLEBEIANS　3.1.203)

His nature is too noble for the world.　　　(MENENIUS　3.1.261)

　　　　　for in such business
Action is eloquence.　　　(VOLUMNIA　3.2.77–78)

Like a dull actor now,
I have forgot my part, and I am out,
Even to a full disgrace.   (CORIOLANUS   5.3.40–42)

O, a kiss
Long as my exile, sweet as my revenge!
(CORIOLANUS   5.3.44–45)

Should we be silent and not speak, our raiment
And state of bodies would bewray what life
We have led since thy exile.   (VOLUMNIA   5.3.94–96)

Behold, the heavens do ope,
The gods look down, and this unnatural scene
They laugh at.   (CORIOLANUS   5.3.183–185)

Thou boy of tears!   (AUFIDIUS   5.6.105)

Thou hast done a deed whereat valor will weep.
(SECOND LORD   5.6.139)

Contributors

DAVID BEVINGTON, Phyllis Fay Horton Professor of Humanities at the University of Chicago, is editor of *The Complete Works of Shakespeare* (Scott, Foresman, 1980) and of *Medieval Drama* (Houghton Mifflin, 1975). His latest critical study is *Action Is Eloquence: Shakespeare's Language of Gesture* (Harvard University Press, 1984).

DAVID SCOTT KASTAN, Professor of English and Comparative Literature at Columbia University, is the author of *Shakespeare and the Shapes of Time* (University Press of New England, 1982).

JAMES HAMMERSMITH, Associate Professor of English at Auburn University, has published essays on various facets of Renaissance drama, including literary criticism, textual criticism, and printing history.

ROBERT KEAN TURNER, Professor of English at the University of Wisconsin–Milwaukee, is a general editor of the New Variorum Shakespeare (Modern Language Association of America) and a contributing editor to *The Dramatic Works in the Beaumont and Fletcher Canon* (Cambridge University Press, 1966–).

JAMES SHAPIRO, who coedited the bibliographies with David Scott Kastan, is Assistant Professor of English at Columbia University.

❖

JOSEPH PAPP, one of the most important forces in theater today, is the founder and producer of the New York Shakespeare Festival, America's largest and most prolific theatrical institution. Since 1954 Mr. Papp has produced or directed all but one of Shakespeare's plays—in Central Park, in schools, off and on Broadway, and at the Festival's permanent home, The Public Theater. He has also produced such award-winning plays and musical works as *Hair, A Chorus Line, Plenty,* and *The Mystery of Edwin Drood,* among many others.

Shakespeare
ALIVE! ◆

☐ 27081-8 $4.50/$5.50 in Canada

From Joseph Papp, America's foremost theater producer, and writer Elizabeth Kirkland: a captivating tour through the world of William Shakespeare.

Discover the London of Shakespeare's time, a fascinating place to be—full of mayhem and magic, exploration and exploitation, courtiers and foreigners. Stroll through narrow, winding streets crowded with merchants and minstrels, hoist a pint in a rowdy alehouse, and hurry across the river to the open-air Globe Theatre to the latest play written by a young man named Will Shakespeare.

SHAKESPEARE ALIVE! spirits you back to the very heart of that London—as everyday people might have experienced it. Find out how young people fell in love, how workers and artists made ends meet, what people found funny and what they feared most. Go on location with an Elizabethan theater company, learn how plays were produced, where Shakespeare's plots came from and how he transformed them. Hear the music of Shakespeare's language and the words we still use today that were first spoken in his time.

Open this book and elbow your way into the Globe with the groundlings. You'll be joining one of the most democratic audiences the theater has ever known—alewives, apprentices, shoemakers and nobles—in applauding the dazzling wordplay and swordplay brought to you by William Shakespeare.

Look for **SHAKESPEARE ALIVE!** at your local bookstore or use the coupon below:

Bantam Books, Dept. SH288, 414 East Golf Road, Des Plaines, IL 60016

Please send me the books I have checked above. I am enclosing $_____ (please add $1.50 to cover postage and handling; send check or money order—no cash or C.O.D.s please.)

Mr/Ms _____

Address _____

City/State _____ Zip _____

SH288—2/88

Please allow four to six weeks for delivery. This offer expires 8/88. Prices and availability subject to change without notice.